Fundamentals of International Franchising

Richard M. Asbill and Steven M. Goldman, Editors

Forum on Franchising
American Bar Association

Cover design by Lisa Empleo, Gray Cat Design.

The materials contained herein represent the opinions of the authors and editors and should not be construed to be the action of either the American Bar Association or the Forum on Franchising unless adopted pursuant to the bylaws of the Association.

Nothing contained in this book is to be considered as the rendering of legal advice for specific cases, and readers are responsible for obtaining such advice from their own legal counsel. This book and any forms and agreements herein are intended for educational and informational purposes only.

Printed in the United States of America.

05 04 03 02 01 5 4 3 2 1

Library of Congress Cataloging-in-Publication Data

Fundamentals of international franchising / Richard M. Asbill and Steven M. Goldman, editors ; Forum on Franchising, American Bar Association.
p. cm.
ISBN 1-57073-973-0
1. Franchises (Retail trade)—Law and legislation—United States. 2. International business enterprises—Law and legislation—United States. 3. Franchises (Retail trade)—Law and legislation. 4. International business enterprises—Law and legislation. 5. Investments, American—Law and legislation. I. Goldman; Steven M., 1960– II. Asbill, Richard M., 1943– III. American Bar Association. Forum on Franchising.

KF2023 .F86 2001
343.7304'8—dc21

2001046064

Discounts are available for books ordered in bulk. Special consideration is given to state bars, CLE programs, and other bar-related organizations. Inquire at Book Publishing, ABA Publishing, American Bar Association, 750 North Lake Shore Drive, Chicago, Illinois 60611.

www.ababooks.org

CONTENTS

ABOUT THE EDITORS

Richard M. Asbill is a partner in the Atlanta office of Paul, Hastings, Janofsky & Walker, LLP. He focuses his practice on business law, including franchising and licensing of goods and services, mergers and acquisitions, antitrust counseling, and intellectual property, both domestically and internationally. He is a co-author of *Franchising Law: Practice and Forms* (Specialty Technical Publishers, Inc., 2001) and frequently writes and lectures on various subjects related to franchising and distribution at legal and business seminars. He is a member of the Forum on Franchising of the American Bar Association, where he served for six years as Associate Editor of the *Franchise Law Journal*, as Chair of its Governing Committee from 1997-99, and as Immediate Past Chair from 1999—2001. He serves on the editorial board of *LJN's Franchising Business & Law Alert* and is a member of the ABA's Antitrust, Business Law and Intellectual Property Sections. Mr. Asbill also is currently Chair of the International Franchising Committee (Committee X) of the Business Law Section of the International Bar Association, 1998–2002, and is a member of the IBA's Committees L (Intellectual Property and Entertainment) and M (International Sales and Related Commercial Transactions). He received his A.B. in 1965 from Princeton University and his J.D. in 1968 from the University of North Carolina at Chapel Hill, where he was a Justice on the Holderness Moot Court Bench.

Steven M. Goldman is Vice President and Assistant General Counsel for Marriott International, which franchises seven hotel brands worldwide. Prior to joining Marriott, he was Vice President, Franchise Administration, and General Counsel of the ITT Sheraton Franchise Division and Senior Litigation Counsel for Holiday Inn Worldwide. He is a frequent speaker and author on franchise and hospitality law; coeditor of the *Franchise Law Compliance Manual* (American Bar Association, 2000); a member of the Editorial Board of *LJN's Franchising*

Business & Law Alert; a member of the Board of Directors of the National Franchise Council; and a member of the Forum's Governing Committee (Publications Committee Officer and the past Director of the Corporate Counsel Division). He received his B.A. from the University of Vermont in 1982, where he was *Phi Beta Kappa,* and his J.D. from the University of Georgia in 1985, where he was Articles Editor of the Georgia Law Review.

ABOUT THE AUTHORS

Michael G. Brennan is a partner in the Chicago office of Piper Marbury Rudnick & Wolfe. He concentrates his practice on domestic and international business, licensing, and franchising matters. Brennan is co-editor of *The International Encyclopedia of Franchising* (Kluwer Law International) and a contributor to the following publications: *Franchise Legal Digest* (International Franchise Association), *Franchise Law Journal* (American Bar Association's Forum on Franchising), *Louisiana Bar Journal, Franchise Update, The International Journal of Franchising & Distribution Law, Venture Japan, Corporate Legal Times, Franchising World, The National Law Journal, Continental Franchise Review*, and *Business Franchise Guide* (Commerce Clearing House). He is a member of the ABA Sections of Business Law, International Law and the Forum on Franchising, the French-American Chamber of Commerce, and the International Bar Association. He received his J.D. from DePaul University in 1979 and his B.A. from the University of Notre Dame in 1974. He also attended the Universite Catholique de l'Ouest, in Angers, France; the Graduate Institute of the International Institute of International Studies in Geneva, Switzerland; and the Goethe Institute in Murnau, Germany.

William A. Finkelstein is a partner at Alschuler Grossman Stein & Kahan in Los Angeles. Prior to joining the firm, he was Vice President and Intellectual Property Counsel of PepsiCo, Inc. He is the author of chapters in the *Franchise Trademark Handbook, Fundamentals of Franchising*, and the *Franchise Law Compliance Manual* (American Bar Association). He has served for six years on the Governing Committee of the ABA Forum on Franchising and has been active in the International Trademark Association, serving as President from 1985 to 1986 and on its Board of Directors for many years. He has also been active in the ABA Intellectual Property Law Section and the International Franchise Association. He helped create the CPR/INTA ADR Program, is a qualified Neutral on the Trademark Panel, and is the editor/author *of ADR in Trademark and*

Unfair Competition Disputes. Finkelstein received his J.D. from Boston University School of Law, his L.L.M. from New York University School of Law, and his undergraduate degree from the University of Virginia.

Kenneth S. Kaplan is Vice President, Assistant General Counsel, and Assistant Secretary of AFC Enterprises, Inc., operator and franchisor of the Popeyes Chicken & Biscuits®, Church's Chicken®, and Cinnabon® restaurant chains, and the Seattle Coffee Company, owner of the Seattle's Best Coffee® and Torrefazione Italia® specialty coffee concepts. Kaplan is responsible for legal matters relating to franchising, international development, and distribution. Prior to joining AFC, he served as Senior Vice President and General Counsel of Everything Yogurt, Inc., and as Special Counsel to the New York State Legislature. He is the author or co-author of a number of articles for International Franchise Association Symposia and the American Bar Association's Forum on Franchising. He is Corporate Counsel Director for the Forum and a member of the International Bar Association, as well as the New York and Georgia Bars. Kaplan received his J.D. from the Thomas M. Cooley Law School in 1980 and his undergraduate degree from Michigan State University in 1976.

Andrew P. Loewinger is a shareholder with the Washington, D.C., office of Buchanan Ingersoll. He is vice-chair of the firm's Franchise and Distribution Group in an international franchising practice that represents numerous franchisors with international operations. He regularly speaks before the American and International Bar Associations, and the International Franchise Association. He has written and presented more than thirty articles, book chapters, and speeches on franchising topics. Loewinger received his J.D. from Georgetown University in 1983, his M.I.A. from Columbia University in 1980, and his B.A, from Colorado College in 1975.

Joyce G. Mazero is a shareholder with Jenkens & Gilchrist in Dallas, Texas, where she is in charge of the firm's Franchise and Distribution Law Practice Group. She has testified on a variety of franchise, intellectual property, and trade regulation issues before the U.S.T.R., the Texas Senate and House of Representatives, and the Federal Trade Commission. She regularly speaks and writes on domestic and international franchise issues, including the "Best Practices" column in *Franchise Update*. Mazero is a member of the Dallas Bar Association (Intellectual Law Section Advisory Board member), State Bar of Texas (Intellectual Law and Intellectual Property Sections), American Bar

Association (Forum on Franchising, Antitrust Law and Business Law Sections), International Franchise Association, and International Bar Association (Section of Business Law). Mazero received her J.D. from St. Mary's University School of Law in 1979 and her B.A. from Southwest Texas State University in 1976.

Timothy J. Pronley is a manager in the Milwaukee, Wisconsin, office of Arthur Andersen, LLP. He spent a year in the firm's Washington, D.C., Office of Federal Tax Services working with the International Tax Specialty Team. He provides consulting services to multinational corporate clients, including tax planning in the areas of international mergers, acquisitions, and corporate reorganizations; foreign tax credit analysis; and cross-border financing. His clients include numerous corporations with international operations. He is a co-author of the update of the BNA Tax Management Portfolio, *Foreign Corporation Earnings and Profits*. Pronley is a member of the American and Wisconsin Bar Associations and a member of the American Institute of Certified Public Accountants. He is a graduate of the University of Minnesota Law School and the University of Wisconsin School of Business.

Catherine A. Riesterer is a partner at Cooper & Riesterer, PLC, in Brighton, Michigan, where she practices primarily in the areas of business and real estate. Previously, she worked for nine years at Domino's Pizza International, Inc., as Corporate Counsel and Assistant General Counsel, where she was responsible for the franchise documentation for Domino's international expansion. During her tenure at Domino's, she was involved with franchising activities in over sixty-two international markets. Prior to joining Domino's, she worked for Miller Canfield Paddock & Stone in their Detriot and Ann Arbor offices. Riesterer has spoken to the American Bar Association Forum on Franchising on the subject of international franchising. She received her law degree from the University of Michigan Law School in 1987 and her undergraduate degree from Michigan State University in 1984.

T. Timothy Tuerff is a partner in Arthur Andersen, LLP, and practices in the Washington, D.C., Office of Federal Tax Services. He is a member of the firm's International Tax Specialty Team, consulting with multinational corporate clients concerning the U.S. ramifications of cross-border transactions. He is involved in tax planning in the areas of international mergers and acquisitions, foreign tax-credit analysis, cross-border financing, and structuring cross-border use of intellectual property. Tuerff was appointed Special Assistant to the Chief Counsel of the Internal Revenue Service and has served as Special Assistant to their Associate Chief Counsel (International). He is a member of the American and District of Columbia Bar Associations, the International Fiscal Association, and the American Institute of Certified Public Accountants. He is a graduate of the Indiana University School of Law and the Indiana University School of Business.

Erik B. Wulff is a partner in the Washington, D.C., office of Hogan & Hartson, LLP, where he has a broad-based practice in franchising law, business law, and international business transactions. He is a former member of the Board of Directors of a New York stock exchange-listed franchise company and, as President of its International Division, was instrumental in developing its business abroad. A frequent speaker on legal and business issues relating to franchising, Wulff has made presentations at programs sponsored by the American and International Bar Associations, the International Franchise Association, the Union Internationale des Avocats, among others. He is the Editor-in-Chief of *LJN's Franchising Business & Law Alert* and is a former Associate Editor of the ABA Forum on Franchising *Franchise Law Journal*. Wulff received his J.D. from the Indiana University School of Law in 1976 and his B.S. from the Indiana University School of Business in 1973. He is a citizen of the Netherlands and was born in Calcutta, India.

FOREWORD

Franchising is now a global phenomenon. The exponential growth that this method of doing business has enjoyed in the United States during the past 50 years is now being exported on a significant scale. The mission of the ABA Forum on Franchising is to be "the preeminent forum for the study and discussion of the legal aspects of franchising." We can no longer accomplish our mission unless we expand our horizons beyond U.S. legal issues and also concern ourselves with the international legal framework for franchising.

In *Fundamentals of International Franchising,* we have a comprehensive, practical guide to the critical aspects of expanding a franchise beyond the United States. The editors of this work, Steven Goldman and Richard Asbill, as well as the other nine authors, are able, experienced international franchise law practitioners. Their book gives us the benefit of the lessons they have learned.

One of the premises of *Fundamentals of International Franchising* is unassailable: "International franchising is not the equivalent of expanding the system into adjoining states or even to other regions of the franchisor's home country. Differences in language, demographics, practices, legal systems, and culture, as well as distance from franchisees, often causes extraordinary strains on the human and financial resources of the franchisor's organization." In other words, the decision to expand to other countries is not a decision a franchise company should make lightly or without competent advice. For, as the editors of this book also point out, "[e]xpanding a franchise system internationally is often a complex, collaborative effort that may include the coordinated efforts of in-house counsel, outside counsel, tax advisors, and local counsel in the host countries."

Fundamentals of International Franchising will help its users minimize the risks and maximize the rewards as they participate in the complex and often difficult process of global expansion. The book takes us through the process in an orderly way, from the initial choice and effective use of local counsel and the business decision to "go international," through legal considerations, including specific franchise, intellectual property, and other local laws with potential impact on franchise expansion, as well as U.S. tax implications and dispute resolution issues.

The book takes a straightforward, "how-to" approach that will make it particularly useful to those who are beginning or considering international expansion, as well as more experienced practitioners who need a refresher or to fill in a gap. The book's approach is predictable. Its editors are accomplished, no-nonsense franchise lawyers who bring the perspectives of in-house counsel (Steve Goldman) and outside counsel (Rick Asbill) with many years of direct experience in international franchising to their topic. Likewise, the authors of the individual chapters of this book all are experienced in the practice, not just the theory, of their subject. All of them have "been there, done that" in the global arena.

Fundamentals of International Franchising grew out of a mini-program at the Forum's annual meeting in New Orleans in 2000. The popularity and success of that mini-program made it clear that the Forum, in furthering its mission, needs to put appropriate emphasis on international franchise law. This book is a major step in accomplishing our mission.

As chair of the Forum, I have had the pleasure of working with Rick, my immediate predecessor as chair, and Steve, who has served as director of our Corporate Counsel Division and now as a member of the Governing Committee and our Publications Committee Officer. Knowing them, and the other contributing authors, it comes as no surprise that *Fundamentals of International Franchising* is an excellent work that will become an essential tool for any franchise lawyer or company engaged in, or thinking about starting, international franchising. Steve, Rick, and their team have the Forum's gratitude and will, over time, also have the thanks of the many lawyers and others who will find this book invaluable.

John Dienelt,
ABA Forum on Franchising, Chair
1999–2001

ACKNOWLEDGMENTS

The editors would like to thank W. Andrew Scott, R. Samuel Snider, and Kristin L. Burns of Paul, Hastings, Janofsky & Walker, LLP. They provided invaluable editorial assistance and support. Steve Goldman's assistant, Janice Milstead, helped with the proofreading and attended to the details in the final drafts that kept the project on track (and Steve sane). Finally, Holly Wehmeyer, Executive Editor, Book Development and Publishing, and Denise Eichhom, Director of Marketing Planning and Promotion, are the tireless American Bar Association professionals who make a book like this possible.

EDITORS' NOTE

This book was written to assist lawyers with a wide range of experience. The chapters therefore range from relatively basic to advanced.

Chapters 1–4 are intended primarily to provide a background or framework for starting an international franchise program. Chapters 1 and 2 are intended to serve as a basic introduction to franchise business and contractual structuring issues. Chapter 3 focuses on the information necessary to develop an intellectual property registration and compliance program.

Chapter 4, although a background chapter, is a relatively sophisticated treatment of the tax issues and structures relevant to international franchising. We have not seen this subject covered fully in other resources, and the chapter is intended for both experienced transactional lawyers and those responsible for tax planning for a franchisor.

Chapters 5–7 provide more detailed "how-to" coverage of disclosure, registration, and other legal issues that the franchisor is likely to encounter. The information in these chapters is intended to be useful for lawyers of all experience levels, as is the Chapter 8 resource guide, which contains contact information that enables the reader to quickly obtain information over the Internet.

Introduction and Effective Use of Counsel

RICHARD M. ASBILL AND STEVEN M. GOLDMAN

I. Introduction

This book has been developed following the Mini Program presented at the Annual Forum in New Orleans, Louisiana, on October 18, 2000. This book and the program respond to numerous requests by attendees of prior Annual Forums for additional information about international franchising. Although the primary focus of the forum's activities since its inception has been on the United States, most franchisors at least contemplate franchising outside their home country and many have already done so. Often, opportunity provides the impetus and comes from inquiries made by visitors to domestic locations. The allure of becoming an "international" company is sometimes too great for a franchisor to resist. Other times, as franchise systems mature, international expansion is the logical next step.

Most franchisors would prefer to replicate their domestic business and contractual structures for international purposes. Sometimes this works, and sometimes it does not. Many things need to be considered as a franchisor contemplates expanding internationally, especially differences in laws, customs, language, geographic concerns, capital availability, real estate markets, and customer preferences, not to mention the practical and logistical difficulties of long-distance business dealings.

This book provides a framework for counsel advising franchisors on the domestic front as they move into the international arena. If a domestic franchisor and its counsel can be armed with some practical knowledge, plus a list of the "right" questions to enable it to perform "due diligence" before committing to a particular structure, the franchisor will be able to grow more quickly and at a lower cost than if it simply rushes in and attempts to duplicate its existing format.

In the ideal world, the franchisor should develop its international program as early as possible based on sound trademark and tax planning advice. However, this "global" planning should be coordinated with local counsel versed in franchising and business matters in the host country to provide the best chance for a smooth entry into the local marketplace. Although domestic counsel may have experience and knowledge about international franchising, play a key role in the "global" planning, and may well be aware of specific laws dealing with franchising, there are too many local issues that become important.

Consultation with the right local counsel is essential when the franchisor is developing its business plan for each country, and in no event later than the time that the franchisor is ready to negotiate a letter of intent. Working out the details of the international franchise program after the letter of intent often requires some painstaking effort and renegotiation that could have been avoided. In this context, the franchisor's choices of counsel are critical.

II. Selecting Counsel for International Franchise Projects

When choosing the legal team, among the questions a franchisor should ask itself are the following:

- What type of experience should a franchisor seek in outside counsel?
- Who should the franchisor consult for trademark, franchise, and other guidance appropriate to its business?

- Who should the franchisor consult on tax and financial issues?
- How does the franchisor identify experienced local counsel and how important is franchise experience in the business of the franchisor?
- What laws will affect the "structure" of the transaction?
- Are there any applicable "franchise" laws?
- Are there any applicable laws affecting the franchisor's ability to obtain payment of the fees or royalties it is to receive?

A number of typical issues arise when a franchisor seeks help from counsel as it navigates these often-tricky waters.

A. WORKING WITH IN-HOUSE COUNSEL, OUTSIDE COUNSEL, AND LOCAL COUNSEL

Expanding a franchise system internationally is often a complex, collaborative effort that may include the coordinated efforts of in-house counsel, outside counsel, tax advisors, and local counsel in the host countries. This section will discuss the roles of the respective legal professionals and how to find, retain, and utilize the services of competent local counsel.

A "first principle" to remember when coordinating these relationships is that someone must be "in charge." This means that someone must take responsibility for ensuring that everyone understands his or her assignment and completes that assignment and no more. Failure to do this can lead to unaddressed issues and unnecessary cost, and usually both. Issues may go unaddressed because one of the lawyers or advisors made an incorrect assumption about who was addressing the issue. Costs may escalate as the lawyers and advisors duplicate each other's work.

This last point bears emphasis. Franchising is a business—cash and earnings count. A franchisor may not be able to capitalize the costs of lawyers and advisors and therefore will have to expense those costs. An international deal may be complicated, but if the cost of the lawyers and advisors is high enough, the deal ceases to make economic sense. Good, creative advice is often advice that identifies the simple solution that prevents the deal from sinking under the weight of the initial overhead.

1. In-House Counsel

For those companies that have a full-time lawyer or legal department, the role of the in-house counsel in international franchising may be any or all of the following:

- advising the company regarding the structure of the proposed transaction;
- coordinating the efforts of outside counsel, local counsel, and, if applicable, trademark and tax counsel;
- developing standard franchise documentation;
- negotiating and drafting the international franchise documents (letters of intent, master franchise agreement, development agreements, unit franchise agreements, and joint ventures) with the prospective international franchisee and its counsel;
- coordinating compliance with local country laws, including applicable franchise disclosure or registration requirements;
- coordinating compliance with and enforcement of franchise documents and, where necessary, implementing post-termination remedies, including de-identification and noncompetition;
- coordinating litigation, arbitration or other applicable dispute resolution mechanism; and
- where applicable, researching U.S. laws that might affect the proposed transaction.

If you are outside counsel, you should always have a clear, explicit understanding of the role that in-house counsel intends to play.

On occasion, in-house counsel will also serve as the franchisor's liaison with the franchisee's lawyer, lending institution, or investment bank regarding the franchisee's efforts to raise capital for the proposed international franchise project. In this regard, in-house counsel will want to review all documentation relating to the project to ensure that representations regarding the system are accurate, use of the franchisor's trademarks and other proprietary assets carry the proper legal notices, and that adequate disclaimers appear prominently in the documents advising that the franchisor makes no representation in and is not participating in the franchisee's offering.

If the franchisor does not have full-time legal professionals, or in cases where they are not available (or sufficiently experienced), it is advisable that the franchisor retain the services of competent domestic outside counsel in addition to local counsel. International transactions are invariably more complicated than domestic transactions, require extensive negotiation, and are subject to logistical challenges. It is not unusual to hire a lawyer or law firm with adequate experience in international business transactions and franchising to perform some or all of the functions described above.

2. *Domestic Outside Counsel*

The franchisor's domestic outside counsel may be charged with the responsibility of coordinating the entire legal process for the proposed international franchise transaction. In other instances, outside counsel may be asked to provide advice on specialized legal issues such as securities law, bankruptcy, litigation, and alternative dispute resolution. Outside counsel also may be a good source for general legal advice about a particular country where that lawyer or law firm has experience or has developed an expertise (possibly having a branch or correspondent office in that host country) or as a referral to a particular foreign counsel with whom outside counsel has worked previously.

3. *Local Outside Counsel*

In international franchise transactions, the franchisor must obtain comprehensive legal advice from competent local counsel in the host country (or, alternatively, from a law firm with extensive knowledge of the law, legal system, and culture of the host country and with access to counsel qualified to practice in the host country). Local counsel will conduct research and provide advice concerning various legal issues relating to the proposed expansion and to protecting the system once franchised units are in operation in the country. The selection of local counsel is a critical decision for a franchisor, and should be done with a great degree of care and research. The legal footing upon which the franchisor enters a new international market is, in essence, the foundation for the growth of the franchise system in that country. The stronger the foundation, the more stable the structure that will be built upon it.

B. FINDING AND RETAINING LOCAL COUNSEL

1. *Sources*

There is no single source for locating competent local counsel. The most reliable source is often a referral from the franchisor's domestic counsel or from another franchisor or from a lawyer who has previously used lawyers who specialize in franchising and/or international business transactions and have developed a network of foreign counsel. Other valuable sources include the following:

- referrals from other franchisors and lawyers (perhaps through the Forum on Franchising's ListServe);

- legal directories including, for example, the International Bar Association's International Franchising Committee (Committee X, which also has a ListServe);
- professional trade organizations; and
- local country franchise associations.[1]

Keep in mind that in some countries franchising is a nascent specialty area of legal practice and not all corporate legal generalists will be familiar with the intricacies of franchising. On the other hand, the fact that a lawyer may have franchise experience does not mean that the lawyer is competent or able to give advice in related areas. Often, the franchisor's best bet is a firm with enough transactional depth to provide sophisticated advice in a number of areas. For this reason, careful screening is important.

2. *Criteria*

The following is a brief list of the criteria that should be considered in selecting local counsel in a particular country:

1. experience in general corporate and transactional matters, especially licensing, real estate, and tax;
2. experience in international franchise transactions and any currency export regulations;
3. ability to communicate in the franchisor's principal language;
4. experience in international dispute resolution;
5. experience and a relationship with local government agencies regulating franchising; and
6. familiarity with the franchisor's business or industry.

C. USING LOCAL COUNSEL

Because myriad cultural and language differences exist around the world, it is generally a good idea to give local counsel written instructions. The starting place is the hire letter, an example of which is at the end of this introduction (Indonesia was chosen for no particular reason). As a rule, the franchisor should cover the following administrative items in its hire letter:

- the franchisor's billing requirements and payment terms;
- whether the firm can undertake representation of clients with interests adverse to the franchisor's interests (remember, many jurisdictions do not have the same ethical requirements for lawyers and accountants as those in the United States); and

- whether the local counsel and his or her firm must have approval before additional lawyers or other timekeepers are assigned to work on the franchisor's matter.

Most importantly, however, be absolutely certain that local counsel clearly understands the questions asked. Language barriers often cause problems and the answer therefore may not be fully responsive to the question. It is clearly preferable to ask short, specific questions rather than broad, general ones. It is also important to ask whether the inquiry might have missed something that is important. For example, the answer to the question whether the host country has a value added tax may not address whether any other taxes are applicable, and the franchisor might miss the fact that real estate transactions require an expensive stamp tax or that there are retirement taxes for all employees. It even may be helpful to ask the same questions in two different ways to be sure the questions are accurately understood by local counsel, especially when the principal language of the local counsel is different from the franchisor.

Before local counsel provides comments to the proposed franchise agreement, the franchisor should first understand whether local laws or government policies may seriously impede the establishment or operation of the proposed franchise relationship. For this purpose, see the suggested issues raised in the sample counsel hire letter at the end of this introduction.

Finally, the franchisor should specify the form in which it wants the answers to its questions. If a franchisor is silent on this issue, it may receive an extensive, often abstract, written memorandum of the law. The cost for these works is often high and the usefulness low. Moreover, the memorandum usually does not accomplish the goals of a legal opinion because the legal analysis is too abstract. *Usually, it is best to review the advice of local counsel orally and then agree on a written format, its length, specificity, and cost.*

In most instances the franchisor should consider whether it wants local counsel to reduce its advice to a legal opinion. Many franchisors do not require local counsel opinions for a number of reasons, including cost; the difficulty of obtaining a meaningful opinion, especially if the governing law is not that of the host country; and reliability concerns. Moreover, a legal opinion may provide a road map to the problems with a transaction. Nonetheless, if a franchisor has agreed to allow the host country law to govern the agreements, an enforceability opinion is worth considering. Some countries, such as Germany, have stringent execution formalities to which a U.S. lawyer may not be attuned. Failure to obtain the focus that an opinion requires can result in nasty surprises later.

III. Conclusion

When considering the issues raised by the following chapters in this book, consider whether they will be addressed by a team approach: local counsel, in-house counsel, tax advisors, intellectual property counsel, and often domestic outside counsel. Choosing and effectively managing and leading the team is one of the keys to a successful deal.

Sample Local Counsel Hire Letter[2]

Re:

Dear :

___________., a _______ Company with its principal offices in ________("Franchisor"), is preparing a [Development Agreement and a Franchise Agreement (Other)] (the "Agreements") to govern the development and operation of [___________] in [Indonesia]. We have prepared forms of both Agreements, copies of which are enclosed with this letter.

We desire to retain your firm to represent Franchisor.[3] You have agreed that your firm will not undertake any representation of another client in a matter adverse to Franchisor or its affiliates [without our prior written consent]. Franchisor's billing procedures require that bills from outside counsel must be submitted [within thirty (30) days of the end of the month of the date of service, include a detailed description of the services provided, the date the services are provided the time spent and the hourly rate, and the attorney providing those services]. Please discuss with me the use of any attorney other than yourself prior to that attorney working on this matter.

Please initially review the Agreements with respect to [Indonesian] legal issues as well as local business custom and practice that we should consider in structuring the Agreements. We are seeking a general understanding of the requirements with which Franchisor must comply, any approvals that may be necessary, and any other issues that may be particularly important or complex. Please, however, let me know if there are other issues that are relevant prior to proceeding. We recognize that many of these issues may need to be dealt with in greater detail as Franchisor proceeds with the project.

Please call me to discuss the scope, and your best estimate of cost, for your initial review of the Agreements and the law and the cost for memorializing your analysis in a memorandum. I will want to receive your initial comments verbally and, after we have discussed your comments, in a memorandum addressing the issues. Before you begin work, please give me a call to discuss your cost estimate and schedule for preparing this memorandum.

Please identify and explain:

1. *Forms of Doing Business.* Any laws or regulations that would prevent Franchiser from issuing direct licenses to master franchisees or unit franchisees from our country to yours. Any requirements that we establish a local branch or subsidiary. Any local laws that may result in the master franchisee or franchisee being regarded as an agent or employee of franchisor.

2. *Business Climate and Government Attitudes.* Any relevant restrictions on foreign investment relating to franchising. Any unfavorable attitude to the entry of foreign franchisors in [Indonesia].

3. *Presale Disclosure and Governmental Approvals.* Any laws requiring registration of the Agreements or the delivery of disclosure documents to prospective franchisees. Any franchising code of ethics or voluntary disclosure rules. Any requirement that the Agreements be in a particular language or that they must be registered with, or approved by, any governmental entity (national, local or provincial), a central bank, a trademark office or other entity. Any restrictions on advertising franchising opportunities. Any limits on the percentage or monetary amount of variable royalties, fixed royalties and/or total royalties that can be charged or on the initial franchise fee or renewal fee that can be charged.

4. *Franchise Relationship Laws.* Any franchise, dealer, sales representative, agent or other laws that would regulate the relationship under the Agreements, including the right to terminate or renew franchise relationships, restrict transfer of the franchise or the ownership of franchisee or restrict the obligation to pay any damages or an indemnity.

5. *Competition Law.* Any competition laws that apply to franchise or development relationships generally or that either of the Agreements would trigger. Note that the Franchise Agreement provides that the franchisee must purchase certain items, such as the [reservation system and safety items], only from an affiliate of Franchisor or sources of supply approved by the Franchisor.

6. *Tax and Currency Issues.* Any taxes that will apply to the various fees to be charged under the Agreements, to reimbursement of expenses, to interest charged on past due accounts, or otherwise apply to the transaction between the franchisee and Franchisor. Please note that some of the services provided by Franchisor will be provided outside of [Indonesia] and that one of the fees the franchisee must pay under the Franchise Agreement is an [International Marketing Payment] for producing advertising and promotional materials for franchisees located worldwide. If any withholding taxes apply to payments, are there ways to recharacterize the payments or restructure the transaction to minimize or eliminate the Franchisor's tax liability? Are there favorable tax treaties that would eliminate or reduce any non-resident tax liability? Please also advise whether (i) a tax "gross-up" provision, which requires the franchisee to pay the [Indonesian] taxes on payments under the Agreements, will be enforceable, and (ii) central bank or other governmental approval or registration is required or there exist any restrictions, reporting requirements, or regulations concerning the purchase, repatriation or remittance of U.S. dollars?

7. *Trademarks and Other Intellectual Property Protections.* Any requirements for granting a valid trademark license, such as the registration of the marks, the use of a registered user's agreement, or other formalities. Should we take any added precautions to protect against a franchisee using the trademarks after termination or expiration of the Agreements? What degree of protection do [Indonesian] courts afford to trademarks, service marks, trade dress, and copyrights? Can the Franchisor obtain meaningful trade secret protection in [Indonesia]? Please advise us how best to protect the Franchisor's computer software, manuals and other know-how against use or infringement by unauthorized persons. Are there any technology transfer risks?

8. *Governing Law, Language, and Dispute Resolution.* Any problems with the enforceability of choosing U.S. law (or the law of a third country, such as England) as the law governing the Agreements. Because trademarks are governed by local law, should we add any special language to address trademarks if we do not use [Indonesian] law as the general choice of law? The contracts also provide for the Agreements to be in the English language and for [ICC] arbitration of all disputes except those related to safety or the trademarks, which the Franchisor may bring directly in [Indonesian] courts. Are such provisions enforceable and respected by the [Indonesian] courts? How are foreign judgments treated? Is [Indonesia] a signatory to the New York Convention on the Enforcement of Foreign Arbitral Awards or any other treaty or convention dealing with arbitral awards or the domestication of foreign judgments?

9. *Remedies and Liquidated Damages.* Whether injunctive relief is available to prevent termination of the Agreements or prohibited transfers of the Agreements or ownership in franchisee. Are liquidated damages enforceable against the franchisee and how will a court measure termination damages if the Agreements do not contain a liquidated damages clause?

10. *Guaranty and Indemnification.* Whether the indemnification provisions of the Agreements and the guaranties of the franchisee's payment and performance obligations under the Agreements are enforceable.

11. *Local Ownership Requirements.* Any requirements that an [Indonesian] citizen or resident maintain an equity ownership position in the franchisee.

12. *Execution.* Any particular execution formalities required for the proper execution of the Agreements, particularly the guaranty, to be valid and enforceable in [Indonesia].

13. *Religious and Restaurant Laws.* Any religious laws or customs in [Indonesia] that would affect the enforceability of the Agreements or

the operation of the contemplated [hotels]. We are particularly concerned with laws affecting [hours of operation, food service (especially dietary laws and laws associated with any religious holiday), and the service of alcoholic beverages; and restaurant or food services regulations, including construction and operating licenses and permits].

14. *Applicable Commercial Laws.* Any general commercial laws that may be applicable to international transactions, such as currency exchange control laws, technology transfer laws, requirements governing trademark licensing agreements, government authorizations required for licensing of intellectual property rights. Any unusual import quotas, tariffs, duties, licensing requirements or restrictions which should be of special concern or interest to Franchisor. Any restrictions on travel for training purposes. Any employment issues. Any import and customs issues.

15. *Other Issues and Concerns.* Any other areas not covered by the foregoing but which may impact our ability to sell our franchise program or to enforce the provisions of the Agreements.

Notes

1. Note that in some countries the franchise association is essentially a franchise trade association.

2. This letter is drafted to come from in-house counsel. If the author is outside counsel, consider stating that the franchisor is the client and responsible for paying the local counsel's bills.

3. Consider putting in writing the hourly rate and a representation that such rate is the local counsel's standard hourly rate (and is the same as their domestic hourly rate).

CHAPTER ❖ 1

Deciding to Go International: Organizational and Business Considerations

KENNETH S. KAPLAN

I. General Considerations

Although the lure of foreign shores, exotic cultures, and enormous population centers is enough to induce some to begin franchising internationally, the decision is not one to make lightly. A franchise system's success in one community, state, region, or country is not necessarily an indicator of success elsewhere. International franchising is not the equivalent of expanding the system into adjoining states or even to other regions in the franchisor's home country. Differences in language, demographics, politics, legal systems, and culture, as well as distance from franchisees, often cause extraordinary strains on the human and financial resources of the franchisor's organization. Therefore, there is as much "due diligence" and care necessary for making the initial decision whether to commence international franchising as there is in any proposed financial or strategic acquisition. The same standard of care should apply to *each* potential country into which the franchisor considers expanding, as each country will present a new set of legal and practical challenges.

At the outset, the franchisor should eview its long-term objectives, consider all of the risks and benefits that international franchising presents, and then make sure its business plan and infrastructure are in synchronization with each other. This chapter will identify some of the issues that the franchisor should consider in evaluating its readiness to begin an international franchising effort and sustain it long term.

II. The Initial Decision

In considering whether to commence an international franchising effort the franchisor should create a checklist of pros and cons, taking into consideration characteristics unique to its own franchise system and organizational resources, and apply this list to the proposed international effort. The checklist might include the following analysis:

Pros	**Cons**
1. Preempts competition	1. Diverts management from primary focus, such as domestic expansion
2. Increases value of trademark and trade name	2. Distance decreases direct control over operations and intellectual property; increases costs of registering trademarks around the world
3. Increases revenue, for example, royalties from expansion into new international markets	3. Diverts use of financial resources from domestic operations
4. Increases buying leverage	4. Increase in expenses, such as travel, communications, and entertainment

III. The Franchisor's Resources

To launch and sustain an international franchise system successfully, the franchisor must commit substantial financial and human resources over the long term. This commitment begins as soon as the decision is made to "go international," and extends through the "sales and development" process into the "operational support" period, and continues throughout the life cycle of each international franchise relationship. Resource issues unique to international franchise development are discussed below.

A. FINANCIAL RESOURCES

International franchising is not for the faint of heart or those with limited financial resources. Although the rewards from successful international expansion can be significant, an equally significant financial investment by the franchisor is also essential. When considering the launch of an international franchising effort, the franchisor is wise to budget for the efforts discussed below.

1. Legal Due Diligence

The franchisor should retain competent counsel in each country in which the franchisor intends to offer franchises (the Introduction to this book contains a sample engagement letter for host country counsel). In-house (or outside) counsel in the franchisor's home country must coordinate the efforts of local counsel to ensure that all local laws and customs applicable to the franchisor's proposed franchising are carefully researched and applicable governmental filings are processed. The franchisor may decide to engage counsel in its home country with sufficient knowledge and experience of the laws and customs related to franchising in the host country.

2. Registration and Defense of Intellectual Property Rights

Although this subject is treated in great detail in Chapter 3, it is worth noting here that obtaining local country registration of the franchisor's principal trademarks and protection of other essential elements of the franchise system's intellectual property is essential *before* the franchisor begins offering franchises in the host country, and is often very costly. In many instances, the franchisor should retain separate local intellectual property counsel, as competence in this area varies from country to country, and the lawyer handling the franchisor's general corporate matters may lack sufficient experience and/or connections to perform this essential legal task. The franchisor should budget for registering each of its principal trademarks, in "wordmark" and "logo" format by each classification of goods and services for which they will be used, such as "restaurant services," "poultry products," "paper goods," or "beverages."

3. Import/Export Matters

The franchisor may need to research local sources for generic or proprietary products necessary to operate the franchise system in the target country. This often takes time and a great deal of financial resources, such as traveling to the host country to meet potential suppliers, finding comparable products to those in the home country, and testing those products. In the event local sources are not feasible and/or desirable, the franchisor must identify cost-effective means of shipping essential inventory to the host country, possibly storing it there, and a means of distributing the products to the franchised units. In addition to the logistical issues, other costs may exist on both ends of the supply line relating to official (and occasionally, unofficial) governmental regulations concerning the exportation and importation of the essential supplies. Obtaining any applicable licenses and paying any fees to transport the supplies from one country to another is necessary. Professional assistance to navigate the complexities of local import and/or export regulations is often prudent. In view of these often unanticipated costs, the franchisor should carefully consider how best to source the essential ingredients, supplies, or other materials necessary for its system, and allocate enough time and money to research all possible supply methods.

4. Foreign Exchange Costs/Withholding Taxes

For each country in which it intends to sell franchises, the franchisor must establish (usually in its international franchise documents), the method of payment, such as whether to use local currency or the currency of the franchisor's home country, and determine the allocation of risk between the franchisor and franchisee with respect to local currency fluctuation. The franchisor must also research whether there are any restrictions on converting its fees earned in the host country into the currency of its home country or upon the removal of currency from the country. In addition, in many countries some or all revenues paid to the off-shore franchisor are subject to local "withholding" taxes, which the franchisee is required to withhold and pay to the local taxing authorities. The franchisor may consider seeking professional advice from local tax counsel and/or accountants to minimize these withholdings. This subject is covered in more detail in Chapter 4.

5. Recruiting International Franchising Professionals

Picking the right people to develop, implement, and manage an international franchise system is as important as having an efficient operating system and registered trademark. As explained in Section III.D below, the credentials and experience of the candidates for international franchise positions deserve careful attention. The franchisor considering international expansion should consider not settling for less experience to save on salaries, whether the positions are related to international franchise sales, operations, or marketing. Retaining a recruiting firm is often a necessary and unanticipated start-up expense.

Practice Tip

Use recruiting firms with experience in international employment. Also, consider recruiting alumni of international business departments at major universities in the United States, Europe, and elsewhere.

6. Postage and Phone Expenses

Communicating and transmitting documents and supplies across international lines is typically a significant expense in the start-up and management of an international franchising effort. These expenses apply to communications with prospective franchisees, lawyers, accountants, suppliers, and others. The franchisor should budget for them in the initial business plan.

7. Translation of Agreements, Operations Manuals, and Other Documents

Depending on the laws and customs of the host country and the language proficiency of the franchisee and its management team, translations of the essential documents may be necessary before the first franchised unit opens in the host country.

Practice Tip

Address the issue of who pays the costs of translating these documents in the international development agreement and the franchise agreement. Also, define the language competency requirements of all individuals who will attend training and handle the on-going communications with the franchisor.

8. Travel and Entertainment Expenses

Needless to say, international travel expenses are not inconsequential. The franchisor should factor them into the start-up costs and fees charged for on-going support. These costs will, by necessity, include airfare, lodging, ground transportation, meals, and business entertainment.

9. Maintaining Host Country Support Personnel and Offices

As discussed in detail in Section III.F below, effective management of the international franchise system requires the franchisor to perform many functions in the host country, including site selection, construction coordination, training, supply sourcing, and on-going operations support. Depending on the size of the system and the scope of the support provided, the franchisor may need to hire resident staff and maintain a business office in the host country (see Section C below). The expense and tax consequences of this in-country presence will vary from country to country, and require consideration in the business plan before commencing international franchise operations.

B. ORGANIZATIONAL STRUCTURE

Initially, the franchisor must decide how to fit the international franchising effort into its existing structure. Should it be segregated from the domestic function entirely or folded within it? Some favor the former approach, as it ensures a concentrated focus on international matters, not relegating it to "stepchild" status. It also instills an "international" culture in the group effort and may attract seasoned international professionals unwilling to subordinate themselves to domestic efforts. Others consider a segregated international effort divisive and prefer to incorporate their international efforts within the organization's domestic franchising functions. This approach has the benefit of (1) eliminating financial and personnel redundancies and (2) bringing international focus (including critical intellectual property issues) to senior management.

C. INTERNATIONAL PRESENCE

In addition to the organizational structure, the franchisor must determine whether to establish offices and/or retain personnel outside of its home country. Careful consideration of each of these issues is needed as each presents a unique set of business and legal issues, which are discussed below.

1. Permanent Establishment

Employing a foreign national and/or maintaining an office in a country may result in a determination that the franchisor has a "permanent establishment" in the country, thereby subjecting it to corporate income taxes in that country. The franchisor's lawyer or accountant should conduct a country-by-country analysis to determine the applicable tax laws and corresponding "do's and don'ts" in each country. Failure to perform careful due diligence on this issue could prove very costly for the unwary franchisor.

2. Labor Laws

Another thorny issue is the status of employees performing services for the franchisor internationally. As stated above, the presence of an employee in a country may trigger permanent establishment by the franchisor in that country. In addition, the status of local support personnel may determine what labor laws are applicable. It is essential that the franchisor clearly understand what constitutes an "employee" versus an "independent contractor" in each country in which it intends to place support personnel, and the legal and tax consequences of each status. Different consequences may result from terminating an employee compared to ending a relationship with an independent contractor. For example, labor laws applicable to an employee may not apply to an independent contractor.

D. INTERNATIONAL PROFESSIONALS

Whatever organizational and geographic structure the franchisor chooses, it is essential that experienced international franchising professionals are hired and retained. Understanding the legal and cultural landscape of international franchising is essential for success. Failure to be aware of this fact could thwart development of the international franchise system. Applying domestic knowledge and experience to the international franchise setting can seriously hinder the effort, in both the short- and long-term. In-house and outside counsel should constantly ensure that they understand all applicable domestic and international laws to mitigate risks to the franchisor and ensure the best chance of success for the international franchise system.

E. HOME OFFICE SUPPORT

Establishing an international franchising effort involves a great deal more than selling the franchises and incorporating the new units into the franchisor's domestic operations. A successful effort requires recognition of the unique nature of different cultures and legal systems and the special needs of operating a franchise system internationally.

1. Sales and Development

International franchise sales require a very different skill set than domestic sales. The investment in personnel experienced in dealing with different cultures, customs, and economic systems is a must. Extensive travel, language barriers, and varying degrees of business sophistication are some of the challenges confronting the international franchise salesperson. Negotiating styles may also differ from country to country and region to region, further complicating and often delaying the negotiating process.

2. Site Selection

Although most site selection internationally is conducted in the field, the franchisor must maintain some level of home-office oversight because field personnel often change over time, so some baseline measurement of approval standards and historical performance may be necessary for future reference. In addition, in-country field personnel are often ill-equipped to monitor potentially conflicting grants of exclusivity within a country or between different franchised brands of the franchisor within a country or region. As technology improves, franchisors are increasingly deploying geographic information systems that provide sophisticated market information concerning potential sites within a country, including industry competition, traffic patterns, human demographics, and economic trends.

3. Training

Training international franchisees often involves at least one visit by the franchisee and its management team to the franchisor's offices in its home country. This visit can range from a few days of general "orientation" to months of in-store training. In developing the international training program, the franchisor should take into consideration several issues.

- The franchisor should consider the extent of training in the franchisor's home country versus training in the country in which the franchised units are developed.
- The franchisor should consider immigration issues, such as travel limitations. Research should extend beyond the franchisee's country. For example, the United States still maintains travel bans to some countries, which could prevent travel by the franchisor's training and/or "opening" team to the planned country.
- The franchisor should consider which training "costs" it will provide and which costs the franchisee will assume. These costs may include travel expenses, salaries, food, entertainment, and lodging. The development agreement and franchise agreements should allocate such costs clearly so that there are no unnecessary surprises after the franchisee completes training.
- The franchisor should consider protection from claims brought by the franchisee or its employees from incidents that occur while attending training in the franchisor's home country. Local worker's compensation laws often do not cover such individuals, thereby exposing the franchisor to unanticipated liability. Various methods are available to mitigate this liability, including express waivers and indemnities in the international development and franchise agreements, obtaining individual waivers from those attending training, and purchasing supplemental insurance to cover such potential claims.

4. Construction and Development

Ensuring compliance by the international franchisees with the franchisor's design and construction standards is often complicated by time and distance; language differences; availability of local suppliers, contractors, and materials; and unique local real estate considerations such as smaller spaces, higher rents, and significant "key money." In view of these facts, the franchisor must tailor its construction and development procedures to ensure a healthy balance of home-office review and host country due diligence and follow-up. Neglecting to implement an adequate international construction and development process may result in a denigration of the system standards outside of the franchisor's home country and long-term devaluation of the system as inconsistencies arise from country to country. Although most franchise documents mandate compliance with the franchisor's development and construction standards, such language is of little value if the franchisor does not build an organization and develop processes to address the realities of international franchise development.

5. Advertising and Marketing

The franchisor must also implement a procedure to review and approve proposed advertising and marketing material for use in international markets. This procedure involves employing personnel or consulting firms capable of translating or verifying translations provided by international franchisees conforming materials to local language, custom, and laws.

6. Accounting, Foreign Exchange, and Taxes

The franchisor should plan, budget, and staff adequately to address the processing and tax treatment of fees flowing from franchisees in other countries. Expenses related to this function may include in-house accounting specialists experienced in foreign exchange and taxation issues, outside accounting and legal services, and special banking relationships necessary to process remittance of funds from outside the franchisor's country. See Chapter 4 for a detailed discussion of tax issues.

F. IN-COUNTRY FIELD SUPPORT

1. Site Selection

As strong as the franchisor's home-office real estate department may be, success internationally requires that the franchisor obtain in-country site evaluation expertise. Selection of an inadequate or excessively expensive site may result in an early failure, which in turn could hamper the franchisor's efforts in that country for a long time. For example, a location in Asia may require a significant nonrefundable up-front payment of "key money" (amounts exceeding $1 million are not unheard of in some markets). The franchisor must develop local expertise or obtain competent professional advice to make informed and objective assessments of proposed locations submitted by its franchisee.

2. Training

As indicated earlier, training international franchisees raises unique challenges. Similar issues will arise with respect to on-going training in each country where the franchised units are located. For example, the franchisor must either learn applicable local labor laws and customs or ensure that the franchisee obtains adequate legal counsel on these issues. In addition, the franchisor must make certain that the operations manual is either translated into the local language or insist that the franchisee employ personnel competent to translate from the manual to the employees in their native tongue. Finally, if the franchisee is permitted to self-train its employees at its franchised units, then the franchisor must employ an on-going recertification system to measure periodically the adequacy of the franchisee's training programs and update the program with the franchisor's most recent training methods.

3. Supplier Sourcing

One of the franchisor's most time consuming activities is ensuring that the franchisee has a continuing source of essential supplies from vendors that meet the franchisor's standards. The franchisor must ensure that such standards are translated and communicated to the franchisee and local suppliers, and put controls in place to ensure their continued compliance over time. If a franchise system relies on proprietary or trade secret ingredients, the franchisor must arrange for its importation into the host country or enter into a co-packing arrangement with a local manufacturer. In either event, the franchisor will need competent local counsel to deal with myriad legal issues, including (1) import-export restrictions (some laws may actually require the franchisor to disclose all ingredients of its "secret" formula); (2) trade secrets (technology transfer laws may limit or even prohibit post-termination restrictions by the franchisor on the licensed local manufacturer of trade secret ingredients); and (3) remedies available to the franchisor if the franchisee cannot obtain the required ingredients in its country (banned agricultural products or restrictions by local custom or religious practice on such ingredients) or substitution of a cheaper local ingredient for the approved or designated ingredient. The franchisor must thoroughly research such issues of product sourcing and available remedies prior to granting the franchisee the right to develop and open its first franchised unit in the host country. Such terms are essential in every international franchise agreement.

4. Operations Support and Compliance

Attempting to maintain system standards without an effective host country organization in place is very difficult, if not impossible. To meet the challenge of expanding internationally while maintaining quality standards, the franchisor must develop host country operations and compliance capabilities. This system will entail developing a team of operations experts to assist with new unit openings and to service the needs of franchisees. Some franchisors base international operations personnel in the home country and send them periodically to "assess" each franchisee's operations. This approach may be adequate to assess "compliance" with system standards, but may fall short of addressing the international franchisee's day-to-day support needs and could foster a sense of "abandonment" over time.

Another approach is for the franchisor to place international operations experts in each country or in various regions of the world where franchised units are concentrated or to establish strategic business units in such regions. For example, an "International Director of Operations" (IDO) acts as a liaison with the franchisor's corporate support staff as well as various outside services. The IDOs live in the regions they service and generally speak the local language(s). The IDOs' high level of skill and experience enable them to assist the franchisee in everything from site selection and approval to general operations troubleshooting. As new techniques or training methods are developed, the IDO can provide franchisees with materials and training pieces. The IDO also may have primary responsibility for supervising the following:

- *Site Approval/Acceptance*—learning applicable demographic characteristics of the host country, evaluating each potential site for a new franchised unit, and making an objective assessment and recommendation for or against approval of the sites;
- *Construction Oversight*—ensuring that construction plans are prepared in accordance with the franchisor's standards and specifications, and are reviewed and approved;
- *Training*—coordinating initial training of the franchisee and its management team, implementing local "self-training," and ensuring that the franchisee maintains the requisite level of franchisor "certified" managers;
- *Supply Approval*—evaluating and approving local manufacturers, distributors, and suppliers to the franchise system and coordinating the importation of essential supplies from the franchisor's home country and other regional suppliers; and
- *Marketing*—coordinating and overseeing the local marketing and advertising efforts of the franchisee, including approving local language copy and establishing local and regional advertising cooperatives.

Practice Tip

Decide early on whether to centralize international advertising review in the franchisor's home country or to handle it locally by using the franchisor's host country personnel. Nothing can ruin an international franchise relationship faster than a perceived delay by the far-off franchisor in reviewing and approving critically needed marketing materials. On the other hand, be wary of granting international franchisees a "pocket approval" of local marketing materials, such that the materials are "deemed approved" by the franchisor if not expressly disapproved within a specified number of days after receipt. Whichever approach is taken, the franchisor must carefully budget for and staff local operations support to ensure both "compliance" by the franchisee and to provide the franchisee with essential service and support. Without such service and support, the international franchisee may conclude that the value of remaining in the franchisor's system will diminish over time. The Achilles heel of many failed international franchising efforts is underestimation by the franchisor of the financial and personal resources necessary to maintain (and grow) an international franchise system.

5. System Flexibility

In administering the expansion of its franchise system internationally, the franchisor must recognize that system flexibility is essential to meeting the customs, practices, and laws of the franchisee's country, including the following:

- menu modification;
- marketing and advertising techniques and content;
- trademark and logo adaptation if the franchisor's principal trademark is rejected in a particular country; and
- trademark translation: literal and phonetic translations of trademarks are possible, but extreme care is necessary to avoid a negative connotation. For example, the Chevrolet "Nova" sounded like "no va," meaning "it does not go" in Spanish.

IV. Key Business Issues to Consider in Establishing an International Franchise Program

Once the decision is made to commence an international franchising program, and the necessary financial and human resources needed to operate the business are identified, and after the contractual structure of the international system is selected (see Chapter 2 for a detailed discussion of contractual structures), then the franchisor should define the business and legal components of the program. This process will begin with a careful review of each element of the franchisor's domestic franchise system and a determination of whether such elements are applicable in the international setting. In many instances the franchisor will have to modify its domestic program to adapt to the realities of operating a franchise system in other countries. Additionally, the franchisor may lack the financing needed for both the franchisor's up-front costs of researching the feasibility of entering into a particular country and the costs of selling and servicing franchisees in such countries. Further, new elements are necessary for international franchising that are not applicable to the domestic franchise system, such as foreign currency exchange issues, international dispute resolution, translation of operations manuals, and obtaining local governmental approvals. Many of these issues are discussed elsewhere in this chapter. The international development agreement, master franchise agreement, unit franchise agreement, and other documents developed for the international franchise system should define the issues discussed in the balance of this chapter.

A. EXCLUSIVITY AND TERRITORIAL RIGHTS AND RESTRICTIONS

The development agreement and the individual franchise agreements must define the scope of any territorial grant to the franchisee. For example, will the franchisee have territorial exclusivity while actively developing new franchised units in the territory? Are there any exclusions from the territorial exclusivity? What, if any, right to develop will the franchisor reserve for itself in the territory? What post-term development rights will the franchisor grant to the franchisee? What, if any, area of protection or exclusivity will attach to each franchise agreement for individual franchised units? Many development agreements provide that exclusivity, other than that which has been granted in a unit agreement, expires upon expiration or termination of the development agreement.

Practice Tip

Pay close attention in drafting definitions of exclusive (and/or nonexclusive) territories. If available, attach maps to the agreements, particularly where the territory does not encompass an entire country or where borders are subject to change as a result of political instability or geological idiosyncrasies. See the sample "Territorial" description attached as Exhibit A to this chapter.

B. FEES

Developing a realistic and economically competitive fee structure for the international franchise system is essential at the start-up phase. In setting the fee structure, the franchisor should consider all of the anticipated (and unanticipated) costs discussed in Section III.A above. In addition, the franchisor should consider other fees. Fees applicable to the development agreement (or master franchise agreement) may include lump-sum "territorial fees" intended to cover the franchisor's "due diligence" costs in entering a country for the first time; the up-front portion of the franchise fees; and training and other costs. Fees applicable to individual franchise agreements will include franchise fees (intended to cover the franchisor's cost related to the opening of each individual franchised unit), royalty fees, and advertising fees.

Practice Tip

As indicated in Section III.A.4 above, it is essential to engage competent legal and tax advice in each country to ensure that fees are repatriated to the franchisor's home country and to mitigate any withholding taxes applicable to payments made by the franchisee to the off-shore franchisor.

C. DEVELOPMENT OBLIGATIONS AND PROCEDURES

The development agreement (and/or master franchise agreement) should clearly spell out the minimum (and, possibly the maximum) number of franchised units that the franchisee can develop in the territory, as well as any unit format and the timetable for development. It is strongly suggested that a formal development schedule should be attached to the agreement (see the sample development schedule attached as Exhibit B to this chapter). If the development territory encompasses an entire country or more than one country, then a "regional development schedule" may help to ensure timely development of the entire territory (see the sample regional development schedule attached as Exhibit C to this chapter). Without a regional development schedule the grant of exclusivity may continue for long periods without any required regional development, as long as the franchisee develops the minimum number of units required by the development schedule, *anywhere* in the territory.

Practice Tip

In drafting the development grant provisions of an international development agreement and/or master franchise agreement (see Chapter 3 for a description of each) carefully consider the consequences to the franchisee upon its failure to meet the development schedule and/or regional development schedule. Options to consider include

- terminating the entire development agreement;
- reducing the number of franchised units that the developer may develop;
- terminating the territorial exclusivity granted to the developer;
- reducing the size of the territory granted to the developer;
- refusing, pending satisfactory cure of any such default, the opening of any franchised unit then under construction; and
- accelerating the development schedule.

D. GOVERNMENTAL APPROVALS

The agreements should deal with the possible requirement of review, registration, or approval by local governmental authorities. For example, may the franchisor or franchisee "opt out" of the development agreement if the local authorities mandate a change to the form of franchise agreement that is objectionable to either party? Is any part of the up-front fees paid by the franchisee to the franchisor refundable if this occurs? Who is responsible for applying for and paying the cost of obtaining required governmental approvals?

E. PROPRIETARY MARKS

As indicated in Chapter 3 and elsewhere in this book, protection of the franchisor's intellectual property assets, including system trademarks, trade dress, trade secrets, patents, and copyrights, are equally as important as system operation. As a consequence, the agreements must cover ownership, use, and protection of these assets in extensive detail. In view of the proliferation of trademark piracy around the world, this step is crucial to the international franchise system. Clearly defining the scope of the franchisee's license to use the marks is essential, especially considering that some system marks may lack availability in all countries. Consequently, it is important that the franchisor expressly define (1) which marks are licensed for use in the country; (2) the status of any pending applications for any marks not yet registered; and (3) any rights of the franchisor to substitute another mark if the principal mark is unavailable after the franchisee commences using it in the country.

Practice Tip

Make sure the agreements define the procedure for implementing local country translations of the principal (and/or secondary) marks. Some U.S. franchisors, for instance, will insist on English-only marks, while others will permit "phonetic" or "literal" translations of the marks. In either event, retain professional assistance for *all* such translations to avoid embarrassing or unintended translations.

F. ADVERTISING AND MARKETING FUND

The franchisor must seriously consider how much control it will exercise over the advertising and marketing activities of its international franchisees. To what extent will the international franchisee contribute to the franchisor's home country advertising fund? To what extent will the marketing materials be translated for use in other countries? Is the international franchisee required to make local expenditures? What method of review and approval of the franchisee's advertising will the franchisor implement? Will the agreement contemplate (or mandate) the establishment of a national (or multinational regional) advertising cooperative (such cooperative may be necessary if more than one franchisee operates in the same country, or to achieve media efficiency by cross-border advertising efforts)?

G. DISPUTE RESOLUTION

As discussed in Chapter 7, deciding upon the preferred method of resolving unanticipated disputes in the international franchise setting is analogous to drafting a will or a prenuptial agreement. It is fraught with anxiety, but essential nonetheless. The principal issues to address in the agreements include (1) applicable laws and language; (2) choice of venue; (3) possible indemnification by the franchisee for claims brought against the franchisor; and most importantly (4) the use of arbitration or mediation or other alternative dispute resolution procedures. See Chapter 7 for a detailed analysis of this subject.

Practice Tip

Consider whether judgments and/or arbitral awards from other countries are enforceable in the target country. In many instances, judgments are treated differently from arbitral awards, often with one enforceable and the other requiring some additional judicial intervention. Additionally, it is important to inquire whether post-term covenants are enforceable. Do such covenants violate public policy? It is also important to inquire if equitable relief is available in the country to protect the franchisor's trademarks and other intellectual property after termination of the franchise agreement.

H. CONSEQUENCES OF TERMINATION/EXPIRATION

The agreements must clearly spell out what is expected of the franchisee after termination or expiration of the development agreement, master franchise agreement, and individual unit franchise agreements. Development agreements must define the status of post-termination territorial exclusivity, if any, as well as the franchisor's right to develop and/or grant third parties the right to develop the formerly exclusive territory. The master franchise agreement should detail the status of any remaining "subfranchises" after termination. Will the terminated master franchisee continue to provide essential services to the subfranchisees? Or will the subfranchise agreements revert to the franchisor (who, in some instances, may be unable to operate legally as a franchisor in the host country)? The termination of unit franchise agreements should address issues including de-identification of the franchised unit and payment of unpaid fees. Regardless of the type of agreement terminating or expiring, the franchisor should consider post-termination "noncompetition" provisions along with their enforceability under local law.

Practice Tip

In some countries, the filing by the franchisee of the franchisor's principal trademark as its "commercial name" may preclude the franchisor from using or licensing to a third party the rights to use its trademark after termination of the first franchisee's franchise agreement. To avoid this possibility, the franchisor should consider including a provision that prohibits such filings without the franchisor's consent, grants the franchisor a power of attorney to assign the "commercial name" registration to itself or to a successor franchisee, or allows for the filing of a revocation by the franchisor of the "commercial name" registration.

Exhibit A: Sample Territorial Description

TERRITORY

The following area(s) and its(their) respective political boundaries exist as of the effective date of the Development Agreement:

1. Kingdom of Saudi Arabia, as set forth in the highlighted area of the map attached hereto as Exhibit "A-1"
2. The Republic of Lebanon, as set forth in the highlighted area of the map attached hereto as Exhibit "A-2"
3. The State of Bahrain, as set forth in the highlighted area of the map attached hereto as Exhibit "A-3"
4. The State of Qatar, as set forth in the highlighted area of the map attached hereto as Exhibit "A-4"
5. The United Arab Emirates, as set forth in the highlighted area of the map attached hereto as Exhibit "A-5"
6. The Sultanate of Oman, as set forth in the highlighted area of the map attached hereto as Exhibit "A-6"

Each of the above six (6) countries, individually, are referred to herein as "Regional Development Areas" or "RDAs.: The above six (6) countries, collectively, constitute the "Territory."

TO BE INITIALED BY BOTH PARTIES:

FRANCHISOR: ________ **DEVELOPER:** ________

Exhibit B: Sample Development Schedule

DEVELOPMENT SCHEDULE

Number of Franchised Units to be Open and in Operation	Date Opened	Cumulative Number of Franchised Units to be Open and in Operation
5 Franchised Units	by December 15, 2002	Five (5)
11 Franchised Units	by December 15, 2003	Sixteen (16)
22 Franchised Units	by December 15, 2004	Thirty-eight (38)
20 Franchised Units	by December 15, 2005	Fifty-eight (58)
7 Franchised Units	by December 15, 2006	Sixty-five (65)

TO BE INITIALED BY BOTH PARTIES:

FRANCHISOR: _______ **DEVELOPER:** _______

Exhibit C:
Sample Regional Development Schedule

Regional Development Schedule*	**2002 12/15**	**2003 12/15**	**2004 12/15**	**2005 12/15**	**2006 12/15**	**Country Totals**
Saudi Arabia	3	4	5	6	7	25
Lebanon	0	2	5	8	0	15
Bahrain	0	2	3	0	0	5
Qatar	0	0	2	3	0	5
U.A.E.	2	3	5	0	0	10
Oman	0	0	2	3	0	5
Annual Totals	5	11	22	20	7	65

*For the purpose of the Regional Development Schedule, the Regional Areas are defined as set forth in the Territorial Description.

TO BE INITIALED BY BOTH PARTIES:

FRANCHISOR: _______ **DEVELOPER:** _______

CHAPTER ❖ 2

Structuring the Contractual Relationship

CATHERINE A. RIESTERER

I. General Considerations

When a franchisor enters an international market, the relationship between the franchisor and its franchisees is critical to the success of the franchise system. As the primary means of formalizing this relationship, the contractual structure that a franchisor uses can make or break a franchisor's entry into a particular market. This chapter identifies two primary and three secondary factors that a franchisor must consider to determine the type of system to implement upon entering a particular international market, and examines several types of contractual relationships in light of these factors.

A. PRIMARY FACTORS

1. Resources

The availability of financial resources plays a critical role in determining the type of system a franchisor can implement in a target market.

In general, the greater the desired interaction at the individual unit level, the greater the resources that the franchisor must commit to the market. A franchisor with substantial resources may establish a subsidiary to operate corporate units in a given market or enter the market by developing a direct franchise system or a system in which the franchisor grants multiple area development agreements. On the other hand, if resources are limited, the franchisor may choose to enter into a licensing arrangement or a master franchise agreement that uses the resources of the local licensee or master franchisee.

2. *Control*

Along with the financial resources of the franchisor, the level of control necessary to implement a successful system is a primary factor in determining the type of contractual relationship to establish in a targeted international market. If the franchise business is highly technical, substantial control may be necessary to ensure system quality and performance. In such businesses, a franchisor may prefer a direct franchising system in which the franchisor can oversee the performance of individual franchisees. If a franchisor has the ability and resources, joint ventures with local businesses also allow substantial control. If resources are limited, or if expansion and growth are higher priorities than strict quality controls, master franchising may be a more attractive alternative.

B. SECONDARY FACTORS

The resources available to a franchisor and the control necessary for a franchise system to be effective are the primary factors that a franchisor must consider when determining the type of system to implement in a particular market. However, although resource availability and control requirements are likely to determine the ultimate structure chosen by a franchisor upon entering a new market, each of the following factors must be accounted for to determine how resources will be deployed and control will be exercised.

1. *Market-Specific Concerns*

Each market that a franchisor targets for expansion of the franchise system will have a wide range of issues specific to that market that will affect, and may dictate, the ultimate structure of the franchise system in the target market. For instance, cultural or language barriers may require a franchisor to use local assistance. A franchisor with substantial resources available to dedicate to the target market may be able to establish a local office and hire local managers to administer the system, resolving cultural and language barriers while allowing the franchisor to maintain a substantial degree of control over the system. Franchisors with more limited resources may partner with a local master franchisee to bridge the cultural and language gap, and thereby relinquish some control over the system.

2. *Training*

Franchisors offering systems with complex or technical underlying businesses often must provide substantial training to its franchisees to ensure their individual success as well as the success of the system. Because training not only assists franchisees in establishing successful businesses, but also serves as a point of control for franchisors, decisions regarding the type of training system to implement can be critical to the success of the system in a given market. One fundamental issue in far-ranging international systems is that it may not be feasible for a franchisee abroad to travel to the franchisor's headquarters for training. If strict system control and training guidelines are essential for the success of each franchisee, a franchisor may have to opt out of competing in a given market rather than implement substandard training or allow a third party to train franchisees. On the other hand, if control is less essential, it may be feasible to allow a master franchisee to perform system training or for the franchisor to provide a dedicated or periodic on-site trainer to the particular market.

3. *Distribution*

In certain franchise systems, one of the franchisor's primary functions is to establish the system's distribution network, particularly in systems that require franchisees to purchase goods directly from the franchisor or goods proprietary to the system. In such systems, or in other cases in which franchisees cannot obtain inventory or supplies on a cost-effective basis, the franchisor must bear the burden of either establishing a local distribution network itself or establishing a relationship with a third party to service franchisees in the target market. For instance, a franchisor may opt to establish a master franchisee in a market, rather than engaging in direct franchise sales to single-unit franchisees, if the master franchisee is capable of establishing a distribution network for its subfranchisees.

II. Types of Franchise Systems

This section describes several common franchise systems used by franchisors entering into international markets and examines the pros and cons of each system in light of the factors discussed above.

A. DIRECT FRANCHISING

In a direct franchise system, a franchisor grants to a franchisee the right to operate a single franchise unit. This type of system allows franchisors to maintain a franchise agreement for each franchise unit, even if several units are owned by the same owner. Further, the franchisor is not required to split system revenues with intermediate parties such as master franchisees.

1. Franchisee Profile

Direct franchisees tend to be hands-on owner-operators with a single franchise unit or a small number of units. As entreprenurial small business owners, direct franchisees also tend to have less access to capital and less business knowledge and experience than master or area franchisees. Thus, direct franchisees are likely to require more training and business assistance—particularly with regard to financial matters—from their franchisor.

2. Resources

The franchisor must provide for the needs of its local franchisees. In addition to distribution networks, training, and other concerns, a franchisor often must provide the bulk of the advertising and promotional budget during the early stage of the system. Once the system has reached a critical mass in the target market it may be possible for the franchisees to bear the burden of advertising and promotion, but in many systems it may take years to reach such a critical mass.

One of the most costly decisions that a franchisor must make is whether system needs of local concerns in the target market necessitate that the franchisor establish a local office. If the system requires substantial franchisor control, substantial training, a local distribution network, or a high level of interactivity between the franchisor and its franchisees, a local office may be necessary despite often high costs.

3. Control

Initially, direct franchising allows the franchisor to select franchisee candidates and award franchises to worthy candidates, as well as giving the franchisor the opportunity to train its selected franchisees. On an ongoing basis, the franchisor may maintain control over advertising and promotional efforts, and retain direct privity of contract with franchisees so that it may monitor the operations of each unit and enforce system compliance.

Some franchisors further increase their control of individual franchisees by leasing the real estate on which the franchise unit is located to the franchisee. Acting as a landlord as well as a franchisor allows franchisors to control the unit in the event of termination, and provides additional leverage for enforcing system compliance. However, it also significantly increases the economic resources that the franchisor must deploy in the target market.

4. Training

In a direct franchise system, the franchisor bears the sole responsibility to train franchisees. As noted above, this is both advantageous because it allows a substantial degree of up-front control over the franchisee's entry into the system, and costly because it requires a substantial investment by the franchisor. Several factors must be considered in developing a training program, including language and cultural barriers, the ability to provide training through existing programs, the expected level of growth in the target market, and whether training will occur at the franchisor's headquarters or in the target market. In general, the more complex the franchise system the greater the level of training required.

5. Market-Specific Concerns

Because a franchisor cannot rely on assistance from local intermediaries in a direct franchise system, the franchisor must address a wide range of issues specific to the target market. In addition to the impact that language and cultural barriers have on the ability to provide training to franchisees, local laws and regulations often create substantial barriers to an effective franchise system in a foreign target market. The franchisor, either directly or through outsourcing, bears sole responsibility for ensuring that the franchisee complies with local laws related to the underlying business of the franchise system. Further, and perhaps more importantly, the franchisor must ensure that its own operations comply with any local laws or regulations that govern the franchise relationship.

Enforcement of the franchise agreement and other system standards may also be difficult, particularly if a franchisor must resort to bringing suit in the target market. A foreign franchisor's actions are often closely scrutinized in a target market's courts, and the franchisor must ensure that all of its documentation and actions indicate that it has acted reasonably and in good faith. The use of highly qualified local counsel to guide a franchisor through potential legal pitfalls is critical to the success of the system if the franchisor faces the possibility of litigation.

6. *Distribution System*

Because direct franchise systems typically involve owner-operator franchisees, the franchisor is usually responsible for establishing the distribution network for its system in the target market. The nature of the distribution system and the role and resources that the franchisor must commit vary with the underlying business of the system. Standard considerations include whether inventory and equipment can be purchased locally or must be imported, whether volume discounts are available if the franchisor negotiates with suppliers for the entire system, and whether the system involves proprietary goods that must be imported from the franchisor's home country. Even when complete local procurement is possible, the franchisor may be in a better position to develop a distribution and warehousing network absent sophisticated franchisees capable of developing their own local network.

7. *Common Applications*

Direct franchise systems are most common when the target market is close to the franchisor's home country and travel and distribution expenses are minimized. However, direct franchising is also successful when greater distances separate the franchisor from the target market if the underlying business is not complex and the franchisor will not need to exercise substantial training and control. Additionally, direct franchising is common when local tax laws or business regulations prevent the franchisor from developing the target market itself.

In addition to systemic reasons for using a direct franchise system, some franchisors use direct franchising as an exploratory device to test the waters of a target market. Direct franchising can allow a franchisor to develop a viable concept for a target market while spreading the financial risk of the venture among multiple parties.

B. AREA DEVELOPMENT AGREEMENTS

Area development agreements allow franchisors to enter into direct relationships with individual franchisees to develop the franchise system in a target market by developing a series of individual franchise units. An area development agreement is similar in concept to a direct franchise system that requires franchisees to develop multiple units, typically granting the franchisee an exclusive right to develop units in a defined territory within a particular market.

1. Fundamental Concerns in Area Development Agreements

a. Territory. When using an area development agreement, the franchisor must determine the size of the area that it is willing to grant to its franchisees. Franchisees typically expect a greater degree of responsibility and control over the development of the system if they are granted large areas. Rather than granting a large area to an untested franchisee, it is common for franchisors to grant a franchisee a small portion of the desired territory with options that allow the franchisee to assume a larger territory upon meeting growth, profitability, or performance targets.

Practice Tip

One strategy that has been successful for franchisors is to grant several area development agreements in a particular market with a plan to grant a master franchise to the most successful franchisee. If this strategy is used, it is important to ensure that the documents allow the franchisor to assign the territories of the unsuccessful franchisees and to clearly address this issue with the franchisees upon implementation.

b. Relationship Structure. In an area development system, there are typically two contractual relationships between the franchisor and its area developer franchisee. The first is established in the area development agreement itself, which grants exclusive rights to the territory and governs the development of the system in that territory. The second relationship is established at the individual unit level. Typically, franchisors require franchisees to execute individual contracts for each unit because it allows the franchisor to terminate the area development agreement or individual units without terminating the franchisee's right to operate all of its units in the territory. On the other hand, some franchisors also combine area development agreements with individual unit agreements. This practice has the advantage of allowing a franchisor to completely remove a problem area developer from the system, although such a result could be accomplished through use of cross default provisions in a multicontract structure. The single document approach is most common in jurisdictions with onerous disclosure requirements because it allows franchisees to avoid the necessity of maintaining an ongoing disclosure document for the market.

c. Use of Marks. Franchisors using an area development agreement system must determine whether to license the area developer to use the franchisor's marks or limit the use of the marks to the rights granted in the franchise agreements for individual units. If a franchisor does not include a license to use its marks in the area development agreement, its area developer franchisee will not be licensed to use the marks on its headquarters building, company materials, or for other uses not directly related to the operation of its individual units.

d. System Growth Requirements. The fundamental principle of an area development agreement system is that the franchisee, rather than the franchisor, is responsible for the growth of the system in a target market. Thus, franchisors typically establish growth goals, either as targets or as requirements, that an area developer agrees to meet. In new territories, particularly in unfamiliar markets, franchisors must be sensitive to the vagaries of establishing growth targets without a complete understanding of the local market. In the international context, franchisors often grant area development agreements for a small territory to determine appropriate growth and profitability targets prior to granting an area development agreement for a larger territory or significant number of units.

Although area development agreements for a small territory may alleviate problems associated with entering a new market, franchisors must also consider the efficiency of a single or small number of area developers versus a large number of small area developers. If a franchisor grants a large area to a single area developer and the system does not grow as originally anticipated, the impact on the system may be devastating. On the other hand, if the franchisor grants small development agreements to several franchisees, the administrative costs will be substantially higher.

e. Transfer Provisions. Because area development agreement systems rely on a single or a small number of franchisees to develop the area, it is critical to restrict the transferability of individual franchise units lest the area developer sell individual units to third parties creating, in effect, a direct franchise system. Franchisors almost always prohibit transfer of individual franchise units without the franchisor's prior written consent, and often establish certain prerequisites for transfer. In the international context, however, this can be problematic because most countries prohibit total restrictions on transferability and limit a franchisor's ability to include even reasonable restrictions, some even voiding the underlying agreement if transfer restrictions are included. Thus, a franchisor must perform a careful review of local laws to ensure that transfer provisions will be enforced.

2. Franchisee Profile

Because area development agreements can produce widely divergent systems depending on the size of the exclusive areas in the system, a single franchisee profile does not exist. For systems in which small exclusive areas are granted, area development franchisees tend to be similar to direct franchisees—small owner-operators without easy access to capital that require substantial business assistance from the franchisor.

In larger area systems, particularly in systems in which a single area development agreement is granted for an entire target market, franchisees tend to be large enterprises that have already established successful businesses. Although large area developers have easy access to capital and a substantial degree of business sophistication, they are usually more effective as business managers than as operators, and will be less involved at the individual unit level.

3. Resources

Area development agreement systems generally require substantially less capital investment by the franchisor than direct franchise systems because there are fewer franchisees in the system and development costs are spread between the franchisor and the area developer. If large area developers are used, administrative costs are reduced, training and monitoring requirements are minimized, and the need for direct franchisee contact is less than in a direct franchise system. However, if the system uses small area developers, the resource allocation will be much closer to that of a direct franchise system.

4. Control

As with training, the same principles apply to area development agreement systems that apply to direct franchising systems regarding control. The primary distinctions, however, revolve around the size of the franchisee. Small owner-operator area franchisees will require substantial business training in addition to training in the operation of the underlying business, whereas large area developer franchisees are generally more sophisticated and may not require any training in business and managerial affairs. Additionally, franchisors that control their marks very tightly in direct franchise relationships may allow large franchisees to utilize the marks more broadly—particularly in developing advertising and promotional material and in developing target market business offices.

5. Training

Because the contractual relationship remains between the franchisor and a franchisee that operates individual franchise units, the same considerations regarding training apply to area development agreement systems as apply to direct franchise systems. The franchisor must consider geographic distance, cultural and language barriers, and training needs to determine the resources that must be dedicated to training. However, systems using area development agreements involve fewer franchisees, and many of these are sophisticated business entities, so training costs may be lower than those of a direct franchise system.

6. Market-Specific Concerns

Area development agreement systems are generally more effective in addressing market-specific concerns than direct franchise systems because area development systems utilize the resources of local area franchisees to a greater extent. When the local franchisee is a sophisticated business, the franchisee will be able to resolve cultural and language barrier problems and provide insight into applicable laws and local regulations. However, when a franchisor uses a small area development agreement with owner-operators similar to direct franchisees, it shoulders the burden of resolving market-specific concerns.

7. Distribution

The role of the franchisor in developing distribution networks in an area development system depends on the size of the franchisee. If the franchisor uses small area development agreements, it must take on a role similar to that in a direct franchise system in which it develops a distribution network to serve owner-operator franchisees. If franchisees are large, sophisticated businesses, they are more likely to be able to provide for their own distribution needs. Indeed, franchisors have been known to utilize very sophisticated and successful area developers to fulfill the distribution needs of the system outside the market that the franchisee serves.

8. Common Applications

Franchisors typically utilize area development agreement systems in situations in which the franchisor desires to maintain direct control over individual units and receive an undiluted royalty stream, but does not want to invest in or develop relationships with a large number of franchisees. Because many area development franchisees will require substantial training in small area development agreement systems, such systems should only be used in situations in which there are no cultural, linguistic, or geographical barriers to successful implementation, or in which such barriers can be overcome. Finally, such systems are useful in target markets in which tax laws, business regulations, or other considerations prevent the franchisor from developing the target market directly, but in which the franchisor does not wish to relinquish the control and revenue required when using a master franchisee.

C. MASTER FRANCHISE AGREEMENTS

In direct franchise and area development agreement systems, the franchisor maintains a direct contractual relationship with franchisees that own and operate system units. Master franchise systems depart from this type of contractual relationship by allowing the franchisor to shift part of the responsibility for developing the system, including selling units to subfranchisees, to a master franchisee in the target market. Although the franchisor may maintain a franchise agreement with the master franchisee for each unit owned and operated by the master franchisee, the contractual relationship between owners of subfranchised units is, typically, solely between the subfranchisee and the master franchisee.[1]

1. Fundamental Concerns In Master Franchise Systems

a. Growth. A franchisor's success in a master franchise system hinges on the ability of the master franchisee to develop a successful franchise system. Thus, it is essential that the franchisor establish minimum growth requirements so that the franchisor may replace unsuccessful master franchisees as expeditiously as possible. Like such requirements in area development agreement systems, it can be extremely difficult to establish meaningful minimum growth requirements for a new target market without first developing several units to determine the best competitive practices in the target market. To resolve the tension between the difficulty in establishing meaningful minimum growth requirements in a new market and the necessity of such requirements, many franchisors establish multitiered growth requirements that allow the franchisor to suspend certain rights, such as exclusive development rights, if the master franchisee does not meet the highest threshold, but prohibits the franchisor from terminating the agreement unless the master franchisee fails to meet some lower threshold of growth. On the flip side, many franchisors offer incentive systems that provide for lower royalty rates payable to the franchisor for higher levels of system growth attained by the master franchisee.

Because master franchisees face tremendous pressures to grow the system as quickly as possible, the master franchise agreement should set forth acceptable and unacceptable means for achieving system growth. Regardless of the underlying business of the franchise system, master franchisees should be required to maintain a certain number of system units prior to subfranchising so that the master franchisee understands the franchised business and can effectively relate to and train its subfranchisees. In successful systems, such requirements are generally uncontroversial. However, if the master franchisee is struggling to develop the market, it may want to subfranchise despite its own failure to maintain a minimum number of company stores. To avoid disputes, it is necessary to establish these minimums in the master franchise agreement.

Practice Tip

Remember to include language that requires the master franchisee to *maintain* a minimum number of units. For instance, if the development schedule states that a master franchisee cannot subfranchise until it has *opened* twenty units, the franchisor may sell its own company units to subfranchisees as soon as the twenty-unit threshold is reached.

A final growth issue that the master franchise agreement must address is the method for determining what constitutes a system unit. When crafting a growth provision, the franchisor may envision standalone units, but must consider whether "mini" or seasonal stores, such as those found in baseball parks and football fields, will constitute a unit in terms of minimum growth requirements.

b. Ownership. In addition to paying strict attention to the ownership of the master franchisee when granting a master franchise, franchisors must also monitor carefully the ownership of individual "company-owned" units. Master franchisees often wish to establish subsidiaries or affiliates to operate its internally developed units, and if the master franchise agreement is not drafted carefully the franchisor may lose cross-default rights between the master franchise agreement and the unit franchise agreements, as well as any other unit-specific rights set forth in the master franchise agreement. Further, it is not uncommon for master franchisees to establish joint venture relationships or to include outside share- or interest-holders in the ownership of the entity operating company units. The franchisor must review local business laws carefully to determine the percentage of ownership necessary for the operating entity to remain an affiliate or subsidiary of the master franchisee, and prohibit master franchisees from establishing companies in which it holds less than that percentage.

c. Property Control. As noted earlier, it is not uncommon for franchisors to control the property on which individual units are located as a means of increasing system control. In some instances, franchisors have allowed master franchisees to control the relevant property or leaseholds. If a franchisor allows its master franchisees to maintain this level of control, it is vital that the franchisor ensure that assignment provisions are in place to allow the franchisor to step into the shoes of the master franchisee if the master franchisee defaults. It is particularly important to be certain that the relevant assignment language is enforceable in the target market.

d. Termination. In a master franchise system, the success of the franchisor and the system as a whole is almost entirely determined by the success of the master franchisee. Thus, it is essential to ensure that the master franchisee comply with all system requirements, and to establish mechanisms for terminating unsuccessful master franchisees. When establishing termination procedures, the franchisor must consider whether it will allow the master franchisee to continue to operate individual franchise units, or whether it will require the ability to force the master franchisee to sell its units back to the franchisor or to a new master franchisee.

The franchisor must also be cognizant of its subfranchisees in the target market. Most franchisors include language in the master franchise agreement that requires the master franchisee to assign subfranchises back to the franchisor in the event that the master franchisee fails. In drafting assignment language, franchisors should insist that the assignment occur at the sole option of the franchisor to allow the franchisor to refuse assignment of individual units with substantial liabilities. However, in many countries assignment without the transfer of liabilities is not possible, and if the franchisor assumes a substantial portion of the master franchisee's contracts it may be deemed to assume the master franchisee's business, including its liabilities as well as the franchisees with substantial liabilities. On the other hand, business relationship laws in the target market may prevent the franchisor from terminating subfranchise agreements without some form of due compensation. In any event, it is critical to scrutinize closely the laws of the target market to assess the franchisor's ability to assume subfranchise agreements, limit its assumption of liabilities, and terminate underperforming subfranchisees.

In addition to the laws of the target market, the franchisor must monitor the master franchisee's sales process and agreements to ensure that the master franchisee includes the appropriate assignment provisions in its agreements. If the master franchisee has not been diligent in complying with the system documentation requirements, the franchisor could inherit substantial liabilities and labyrinthine contractual relationships.

2. *Franchisee Profile*

The conceptual model of a master franchise system requires a master franchisee with resources sufficient to develop fully the franchise system in the target market. The ideal master franchisee, therefore, is an experienced, sophisticated entity capable of both developing the system by selling subfranchises and maintaining successful relationships with its subfranchisees through training, enforcement of system standards and operating systems, and resolving subfranchisee disputes, all while successfully developing its own system units. Thus, because the master franchisee stands in the place of the franchisor for its target market, it must act more as a manager and less as an operator.

3. *Resources*

Franchisors often implement master franchise systems because they require much less capital investment than direct franchise or area development agreement systems. Because master franchisees bear so much responsibility and financial risk, however, master franchisees demand a large percentage of the royalty and revenue stream flowing from the subfranchisees. Thus, although the upfront capital investment necessary to establish a master franchise system may be less than that required in other systems, the franchisor also receives less revenue.

4. Control

One of the greatest disadvantages of implementing a master franchise system is that the franchisor must cede a tremendous amount of system control for the target market to the master franchisee. The master franchisee selects its own subfranchisees, provides training and distribution networks, and may control advertising and promotion for the target market. Although the franchisor can include strict requirements in the master franchise agreement, it must rely on the master franchisee to implement those requirements—particularly because the franchisor is not in direct privity of contract with the subfranchisees. Thus, while it is essential to include strict system requirements in the master franchise agreement to allow at least some remedy to the franchisor, in practice the master franchisee controls how the system is implemented in the target market.

5. Training

Typically, the master franchisee is responsible for training subfranchisees in the target market and bears the financial burden associated with training. However, the franchisor must provide at least initial training to the master franchisee, and often require that the master franchisee or its key personnel attend training courses at the franchisor's headquarters, as well as providing ongoing on-site training in the master franchisee's market. Initially, the franchisor may play a more substantial role in training subfranchisees, but as the master franchisee matures it is usually required to develop its own internal training department.

6. Market-Specific Issues

One of the primary benefits of master franchising is that it allows franchisors to enter target markets without bearing the burden of solving local market issues. Master franchisees are chosen because of their familiarity with the target market and, as sophisticated business entities, often have little difficulty negotiating the perils associated with cultural and language barriers. Further, master franchisees are usually in a much better position to ensure that the system and the operation of individual units complies with local laws and ordinances. Indeed, it is not uncommon for businesses that are not otherwise engaged in franchising to implement a master franchise system in a market in which the business has been unsuccessful with past in-house attempts to enter the market.

Practice Tip

It may be helpful to consider how other franchise systems have entered a target market, and to learn from their successes and failures. For instance, certain fast-food companies were boycotted and picketed by local groups in India upon entering that market. Subsequent entrants used prominent local businessmen as master franchisees and were able to enter the market much more successfully.

One important issue to note, however, is that in countries with stringent disclosure requirements the franchisor may be compelled to register or disclose documents each time that it grants a new unit franchise to the master franchisee. In such markets, it may be necessary to draft the master franchise agreement so that individual unit franchise agreements are not necessary each time that the master franchisee opens a new company unit to avoid the need for maintaining an ongoing disclosure document.

7. Distribution

In general, master franchisees have the resources and capital necessary to establish their own distribution networks. Regardless of the ability of its master franchisees, however, a franchisor may wish to retain responsibility for distribution of inventory and equipment, particularly when the system involves the sale of a large number of proprietary items or if the franchisor maintains or intends to establish warehousing and distribution centers in markets close to the target market. Master franchisees, however, often desire to distribute inventory and equipment to their subfranchisees to retain control of the distribution network and the accompanying revenue stream. Many systems offer a compromise, in which the master franchisee is responsible for distribution of locally procured products while the franchisor retains control over distribution of proprietary goods.

8. Common Applications

Master franchising is used most frequently when a franchisor does not have the resources or local market expertise to develop a target market itself, and must rely on a third party to ensure system success in the target market. In a franchise system requiring substantial management and training for individual unit franchisees, master franchising is also desirable as a method to spread the costs and risks of administrative and support functions. For all of these reasons, master franchising is one of the most popular and successful systems for international franchising because it allows the franchisor to enter a target market with minimal capital investment.

D. JOINT VENTURES

Unlike master franchise and area development agreement systems, in joint ventures a franchisor allows a local party to own part of the entity operating the franchise system in a target market. Because joint ventures allocate profits and losses and create incentives by sharing ownership in a business entity, the types of entities and roles of each of the parties can be structured in any number of ways. If the franchisor uses a joint venture to take advantage of a local party's knowledge and expertise regarding the target market, the franchisor typically grants a smaller ownership interest in the operating entity to the joint venturer. On the other hand, franchisors may want to use the capital or resources of a local entity while retaining some ownership in the system in the target market. In such systems, the franchisor often grants a controlling interest in the joint venture to the joint venturer, but requires the joint venture entity to operate under a master franchise or area development agreement.

1. Fundamental Concerns in Joint Venture Systems

a. Relationship. Because the franchisor maintains an ownership interest in joint venture entities, the relationship between the franchisor and the joint venture must be clearly articulated to avoid contractual disputes and legal confusion—particularly in joint ventures in which the franchisor holds a minority interest. For instance, depending on the franchisor's involvement with the operations of the joint venture, it is likely to have constructive or actual notice of events that require notice pursuant to the master franchise or area development agreement under which the venture operates. However, the franchisor should draft the joint venture agreement clearly to require notice in its capacity as franchisor in addition to any notice it receives as an owner of the joint venture entity. Additionally, it is often necessary to ensure that both joint venture partners and other franchisees understand that the joint venture must comply with the same requirements as any other entity executing a master franchise or area development agreement, and that the franchisor will not discriminate in favor of its joint venture.

Practice Tip

Some franchsors use joint ventures to test new products to ensure that the test is performed according to the franchisors' standards. Although useful, such practices can expose franchisors to allegations of differential treatment if the tests are not well-documented and performed according to a predefined plan.

b. Exit Strategies. In addition to drafting clear relationship structures, the franchisor must consider its exit strategies when drafting the joint venture agreement and retain flexibility to exit or remain in the venture depending on the success of the venture. In some instances, such as if a franchisor establishes a joint venture with a franchisee to assist in the early development of a franchise unit or territory, the franchisor may know at the outset how long it intends to participate in the joint venture and may need an exit strategy to free its capital to assist other franchisees. The joint venture agreement, however, must remain flexible to accommodate unanticipated system needs. In the above scenario, for instance, it may become clear that the franchisee cannot operate the unit successfully, and the franchisor may desire to either take over the entire joint venture, continue as a co-venturer until the unit is successful, or sell the unit entirely. Thus, it is necessary both to articulate a clear exit strategy upon entering into a joint venture agreement and to remain flexible to adjust to changing economic, legal, or practical conditions.

2. *Joint Venturer Profile*

The type of entity that a franchisor chooses as a joint venturer varies depending on what role the franchisor must fill to implement the system successfully in the target market. If the joint venturer is used to fulfill local ownership requirements that exist in many target markets or to raise local capital, the joint venturer is usually a sophisticated, successful business entity that will act as an investor capable of ensuring compliance with local business and financial laws and regulations, rather than as an operator running individual units. On the other hand, franchisors often use local joint venturers to supply local market knowledge, in which case the joint venturer will play a heightened role in the daily operations of the joint venture entity.

3. Resources

The resources necessary to establish a successful joint venture franchise system in a target market vary with the franchisor's role in the joint venture. Generally, however, a substantial financial investment is necessary because franchisors typically provide capital while the local joint venturer provides target market expertise. Further, because the franchisor has an ownership interest in the joint venture, it has an even greater incentive to make additional capital contributions to the joint venture to ensure its success.

4. Control

Again, the franchisor's control of the franchise system depends on the nature of the joint venture. Joint ventures typically allow the franchisor to exert a greater degree of control than master franchise systems because the franchisor is a participant in the development of the system in the target market through its ownership in the joint venture entity. Franchisors must be careful, however, to ensure that the actual control they exert is consistent with their perceived control to prevent other franchisees from perceiving unfair or discriminatory treatment.

5. Training

In joint ventures in which the franchisor actively participates in the operations of the franchise system, it is likely to provide the primary training services to the joint venture. Indeed, even in markets in which there are substantial cultural or linguistic barriers to application of the franchisor's training system, local joint venturers often act as interpreters, allowing the franchisor to implement its system without substantial modification. Again, however, the degree to which the franchisor is responsible for providing training to franchisees varies with the degree of control and participation that the franchisor has in the joint venture.

6. Market-Specific Issues

Joint ventures require franchisors to scrutinize local business and financial laws much more closely than other types of franchise systems because the franchisor is a part owner in a business generally established under the laws of the target market. The franchisor must consider local income tax issues, problems associated with repatriating capital invested in overseas joint ventures, the ability of courts to pierce the corporate veil in target markets, and the liability of shareholders and directors under local law.

7. Distribution

Because the franchisor typically takes an active role in the joint venture, it will retain the responsibility and the consequent cost burden of developing distribution networks to some extent regardless of whether distribution remains in the province of the franchisor or is established at the joint venture level. It is unusual, however, for development of the distribution network to fall to franchisees because the joint venture typically acts as a direct franchise system franchisor or grants small area development agreements. Thus, other than allowing substantial assistance from joint venturers in fulfilling target market distribution needs, the joint venture approach does not offer significant savings to the franchisor in terms of distribution requirements.

8. Common Applications

Joint venture systems are typically used in markets in which a franchisor desires to retain an equity stake in the primary developer of the franchise system in the target market, but needs to minimize its exposure to financial risk or use a local partner with target market expertise. Joint venture systems are also common in target markets that give substantial tax or business advantages to businesses that raise capital locally or include a substantial percentage of local ownership. In practice, however, the joint venture system does not alter substantially the development of the franchise system—the target market is still developed through a master franchisee or an area developer. The primary difference between these systems is that in a joint venture the master franchisee or area developer happens to be owned, to a greater or lesser extent, by the franchisor.

III. Conclusion

A franchisor contemplating entry into an international target market faces a number of decisions that may have a substantial effect on the success of the system, the first of which is the determination of which type of franchise system will be most effective in the target market. As this analysis shows, there is no "best" system structure that a franchisor should use in all markets. Rather, the franchisor must examine the resources available to commit to the market, the level of control necessary to establish a successful system, the training and distribution requirements of the system, and any local market issues that may deter the franchisor from operating without local assistance.

Please refer to Chapter 6 for a discussion of specific clauses and contractual language used in international franchising. Finally, please note the recommendations regarding effective use of local counsel in the Introduction to this book.

Notes

Thanks to R. Samuel Snider of Paul, Hastings, Janofsky & Walker LLP for his help in preparing this chapter.

1. Please note the reference materials in Chapter 8 for additional information regarding master franchise systems. Specifically, please note INTERNATIONAL FRANCHISING (Alex S. Konigsberg, Q.C. ed, 2d ed., Juris Publishing 2000, www.jurispub.com); and INTERNATIONAL INSTITUTE FOR THE UNIFICATION OF PRIVATE LAW (UNIDROIT), GUIDE TO INTERNATIONAL MASTER FRANCHISE ARRANGEMENTS (International Institue for the Unification of Private Law 1998, www.unidroit.org).

CHAPTER ❖ 3

Protecting Trademarks and Related Intellectual Property Rights

WILLIAM A. FINKELSTEIN

I. Introduction

The value and success of most franchising concepts are often substantially based on intellectual property—primarily trademarks, trade names, copyrights, trade secrets, and patents. This property often includes names, symbols, designs, trade dress, advertising and other artistic creations, domain names, software, inventions, formulas, and special methods of doing business. If a franchisor is to capitalize on the exclusivity of its unique intellectual property to provide it and its franchisees a competitive advantage, legal protection of these valuable assets is essential in all countries of present and contemplated business.

Two crucial aspects of such protection must be understood. First, there are very fundamental differences between the various types of intellectual property, both in the scope of protection and the means to achieve it. Second, territoriality is the guiding principle of international intellectual property law. While there continue to be positive developments in the areas of multicountry harmonization and means to assist filing (especially in the trademark arena), the fact remains that legal protection for intellectual property is on a national basis and varies greatly from country to country, including laws, regulations, systems, and enforcement. Thus, with some exceptions, rights must be acquired and protected on a piecemeal basis: there are no blanket or automatic global intellectual property rights.

Franchisors seeking to expand their businesses outside their home country must be aware of the obstacles as well as the opportunities, and need to develop a proactive yet flexible legal strategy for protecting their intellectual property assets internationally. The results from improperly anticipating business needs, waiting too long, or failing to commit adequate resources, could be disastrous to a franchise business that most likely is dependent on uniformity and distinctive proprietary attributes.

In a typical franchise business, trademark rights are often of paramount importance, followed by trade secret rights, which might cover methods of doing business and technical know-how. There usually are some copyright-related aspects to the business, such as advertising, promotional, and marketing materials, as well as software and an operations manual. Occasionally, patents will be important, either utility patents that might cover a proprietary piece of machinery, design patents that might cover a building design, or business method patents. The focus of this chapter will be on trademarks.

II. Trademarks and Franchising

A. THE FUNCTION OF TRADEMARKS

Trademarks are, in most franchised businesses, the single most dominant element from a consumer perspective and the focal point of the franchise package. Trademarks are virtually any distinctive characteristics that identify the goods or services of a particular business, be it a manufacturer, merchant, or provider of services, and distinguish these from the goods and services offered by others. They include designs, words, pictures, slogans, colors, labels, sounds, product shapes, package configurations, or three-dimensional manifestations of the site where the business is located, or any combination of these, which sometimes is termed "trade dress." By identifying the source of goods or services, trademarks convey valuable data to consumers while reducing the costs of acquiring information about the particular products or services since consumers can come to rely upon a trademark and the brand image it conveys.

B. TRADEMARK GOODWILL AND FRANCHISING

As a result of favorable consumer acceptance, trademarks develop value for their owners. A well-recognized, respected trademark can become a business asset of incalculable value, usually referred to as business goodwill. Franchisors can exploit this goodwill by attracting investment from shareholders and new franchisees. Trademarks bind a franchise system together by providing a common identity, allowing for effective and efficient use of advertising, marketing, and supply.

C. TRADEMARK PROTECTION

The goal of trademark legal protection is two-fold: protecting the value of the goodwill of a business while at the same time protecting consumers from confusion between the goods or services of different businesses. Confusingly similar marks not only dilute the value of the goodwill of the legitimate mark but also increase inefficiencies and consumer costs in the marketplace. Accordingly almost every legal jurisdiction in the world recognizes the need for trademark protection.

Realistically, however, the standards and effectiveness of such protection vary from country to country.

D. TRADEMARKS AND SERVICE MARKS

Traditionally, "trademarks" was the term used for identifiers of goods and "trade name" was used for corporate or other business names. Since most service businesses used their trade names or an abbreviation as the name of their establishment, service mark protection was relatively late in acceptance. In fact, it was not until quite recently that marks for services were granted equal protection in many countries. While some refer to these as "service marks," in fact they are merely a species of trademarks, which is the inclusive term used by the laws and practitioners in almost all countries. This is especially appropriate in view of the common practice in many franchise businesses to simultaneously use the same marks for both goods and services.

E. THE BRAND CONCEPT

For many years, "brand" was commonly used as an alternative term for a word trademark, but increasingly it has taken on a much more expansive role. It is often based of a bundle of several marks, including words, slogans, designs, and trade dress, which, as a result of advertising or other marketing activity, come to represent a particular brand image or identity. This identity transcends mere labels or signs; it signals to consumers not only a source of goods or services but also conveys attributes such as a feeling, attitude, or promise. For example, a particular franchise concept successful in the United States because consumers like the taste of the products and value of the services may be attractive to consumers in other countries because the brand connotes a romanticized Americana feeling. The increasing utilization of successful brands on an international scale as part of multicountry marketing strategies by franchisors is a growing phenomenon with significant impact.

F. TRADEMARKS AS A MARKETING STRATEGY

Many international companies have discovered that particular market segments show considerable similarities from one country to another, despite supposed linguistic and cultural barriers. Moreover, they have recognized that by communicating a consistent and precise message, well-chosen trademarks reduce the complexity of the purchase analysis, rendering global marketing cost-effective, efficient, and less risky. The uniformity that is integral to the franchising concept renders franchising businesses well positioned to take advantage of this situation. Furthermore, the recognition that opportunities exist for introducing goods or services with established brand image and recognition increases the likelihood of finding a local business partner willing to invest and pay fees or royalties for a franchise opportunity.

III. Trademark Licensing as a Key to Franchising

A. DEFINITION

One of the best ways to implement multicountry marketing strategies and take advantage of brand goodwill on an international basis is through trademark licensing and its more sophisticated version, franchising. Properly executed, trademark licensing provides an excellent opportunity to take advantage of established brand identity for all parties concerned: the trademark owner, the local country licensee, and the consumers in the local country. Trademark licensing is, in almost all cases, the cornerstone of a franchise system. It is a legally sanctioned business agreement between the owner of a trademark and the associated valuable goodwill, information, formulas, processes. and ways of doing business, and another party that desires to use the trademark as the identifying element in its business under the control of the licensor/franchisor.

B. ADVANTAGES OF LICENSING

In the international setting, a trademark owner's decision about whether to conduct business directly itself in another country or to license the right to do so to another party, that is, the franchisee, involves a complex mix of economic, practical, cultural, and legal considerations. The most salient business factors include the availability of investment capital and the level of risk, as well as various marketing considerations, including acceptability of the mark and the services offered, distance, and unfamiliarity with local conditions.

From the perspective of a local licensee, it is quite advantageous to license a previously successful mark since it enables the local business to obtain the benefits of the mark's image and reputation. This is a shortcut to commercial success because it saves time and money in creating and developing a new trademark and earning consumer acceptance. Moreover, in the franchise framework, local businesses can rapidly obtain know-how, techniques, and other proven methods of conducting a successful business without much experimentation and risk. On the other side of the equation, in addition to the infusion of local capital, a prime benefit to the franchisor is the ability to draw on the particular knowledge, contacts, and skills of the local franchisee to assist in overcoming any obstacles to doing business and in planning the local marketing strategy.

C. FRANCHISING

Franchising, in its simplest terms, is a more complex program or system of licensing. Franchising most often involves a system of marketing and distribution for the provision of services and/or the supply of goods in accordance with established standards and practices of the trademark owner, which furnishes a well-established trademark and brand image, expertise, training, stability, and marketing know-how. In return, the trademark owner/franchisor obtains new sources of expansion capital, new distribution markets, and self-motivated vendors of its products or services. It can therefore penetrate new markets more quickly.

The franchise agreement is wrapped around the trademark license within it, and both are supported by the validity and legal enforceability of the franchisor's trademark rights. The key to success is the proper implementation of the franchisor's marketing plan and business format coupled with the recognition that protection of the trademark is essential. This includes both registration and enforcement of trademark rights in every country where business is conducted or contemplated. It also requires compliance with trademark licensing laws and regulations in many countries.

IV. Overview of International Trademark Strategy

A. STRATEGIC GUIDELINES

For the franchisor desiring to expand outside its home country, developing and protecting rights in the marks that it has taken for granted up to that point can be expensive, time-consuming, and often frustrating. The franchisor must deal with different ways of doing business, different cultures, different languages, and most importantly, different legal systems. Moreover, a franchisor should be prepared for the fact that it may have to use different marks in other countries.

1. *Foresight*

It is imperative that planning, long lead times, and the territoriality concept of trademark protection be integrated into the development of a global franchising strategy to select, clear, and register trademarks successfully in countries of commercial importance. Even a franchisor with no immediate expansion plans beyond its home country should consider defensive or preemptive filings. Otherwise, successful and valuable trademark assets in one's home country may be useless for franchising in international markets.

2. *Verify Suitability And Usability*

It is entirely possible that a trademark, whether word or design, used in one's home country will not be suitable for use in other countries. Local market research will be necessary and a coordinated, cohesive approach between marketing personnel and lawyers is recommended in choosing the solution (for example, translations, transliterations, logos, and designs) that will work well across cultural and linguistic boundaries, as discussed in Section V.A.2. of this chapter.

3. *Perform Clearance Searches to Determine Availability*

Clearance searches in each country prior to entering into franchise discussions, let alone final agreements, are essential: to avoid inadvertent infringement of another's coincidental prior right or to discover piracy of one's own mark, perhaps even by a prospective franchisee. Such searches can also uncover suitability issues.

4. *File Early and Widely*

Trademark rights are strictly territorial. Registration in one's home country confers no rights elsewhere. Rights must be perfected on a country-by-country basis (with some limited exceptions) and the sooner the better since trademark piracy is widespread internationally. In most jurisdictions, the first party to file places itself in a superior position. It is extremely difficult to overcome a prior registration of one's own mark by another party based merely upon proof of one's prior use or reputation (assuming such proof exists). Domain names do have worldwide coverage but early filing is crucial to preempt pirates from registering domain names containing one's mark. Mechanisms exist to attempt recovery of such domain names but are by no means automatically successful.

5. Portfolio Maintenance and Enforcement

Maintaining and protecting international trademark portfolios are a continual responsibility (and expense) for the life of the franchise business. This is true before, during, and after a particular country has been franchised. This involves registration and regular renewal, defense of the marks from challenge, pursuit of infringing uses, and filing oppositions to attempts to register confusingly similar marks by third parties. Not only are these activities good business practices but the franchise agreement will usually require a certain level of trademark protection by the franchisor and indemnification.

B. ADMINISTRATIVE AND STRATEGIC GUIDELINES

1. International Counsel

It is necessary to employ local counsel in every jurisdiction where protection is sought. Often the local firm handling the general commercial aspects of a franchise business may not have intellectual property expertise. It is highly recommended that specialized firms or counsel be used for this work. Often they may not be lawyers but "agents" qualified in this practice area, which is quite acceptable. On the other hand, if appropriate, try to ascertain that a firm has specific trademark as opposed to patent expertise. Many firms combine these practices and do both quite well but they are different specialties requiring different backgrounds and training. One source of local trademark counsel is the International Trademark Association based in New York. While it does not police the standards of its members, its members usually have a certain level of trademark law expertise.

Multicountry trademark portfolio management can be a time-consuming and voluminous administrative task requiring software, filing systems, and extra personnel. If the franchisor does not have in-house counsel or the additional resources needed to handle this, there are firms in the home country that can assume this role. It is essential that there be centralized coordination of such a program to maximize efficiencies and effectiveness.

2. Budget

There are no easy or inexpensive ways to achieve pervasive international trademark rights. Government filing fees and local counsel fees will make up the largest portion of the filing costs. These fees vary widely and in some instances are extremely steep, bearing no relationship to the economic importance of a country. The European Community (EC) trademark system is a key exception: its filing fee is a veritable bargain considering that it covers fifteen commercially important countries. The Madrid Protocol, which is discussed in Section VI.F.3. of this chapter, has promise (the United States is expected to join), enabling one to quickly preserve a priority date (with cost savings at all stages but especially at the "back end") but it is merely a filing mechanism subject to variable national laws and standards. Ultimately all international trademark filing programs become a difficult balancing exercise between costs and protection.

3. *Protection Strategy*

There are three primary components to consider in an international trademark filing program. The first is identification of how many countries in which to file. A helpful tool is to set up categories: those of present business or current interest, those of likely future interest, and those with more remote or possible future interest. These must be overlaid with one more consideration: those countries where piracy or counterfeiting is likely and there is a need to preempt such activity whether or not the jurisdiction is of immediate interest. In other words, where would it be damaging to one's business or reputation if another party owned the mark? For example, while a business might never set up a franchise in country A it is a frequent tourist destination. Or, is country B a likely location for the exportation of infringing merchandise bearing the mark into other countries of interest?

Second, how many marks need to be protected? Again, a business needs to categorize its portfolio. Some marks are obviously essential while others are only secondary in usage and importance, such as advertising slogans or menu item names in a restaurant franchise. Determine the likely duration of use of some of these latter marks. Similarly, a difficult decision involves choosing which and how many formats of each mark should be registered. Registering in ordinary letters usually gives the broadest protection and allows for the constant evolution of logos and design marks over time without the need to re-register. On the other hand, most franchise business's most valuable trade identities are logos and trade dress and thus are the most likely to be infringed. Clever infringers will often mimic the style of a logo or design layout using different words; the absence of specific registrations for these renditions could make it quite difficult to stop these uses.

Third, what are the goods and services of interest? As noted in the section below on classification, franchise businesses often overlap several classes of goods or services. Yet additional classes add incremental cost. There is a need to determine how many classes are needed for a minimal, adequate, or best level of protection. Moreover, possible future growth into new categories cannot be ignored, lest another party preclude such expansion.

V. Selection of Trademarks

A. COMMERCIAL ACCEPTABILITY

1. Going International

Unfortunately, it is the exception rather than the norm that a franchisor chooses a name for a new business venture with sufficient foresight to encompass potential international expansion. In most cases, only after a franchise concept has shown itself to be successful in the home country is international franchising contemplated. The problem, however, is that the already successful and valuable trademark may not be suitable for international use, either commercially or legally.

Franchisors seeking to develop a global brand marketing strategy by having uniformity throughout their system are often torn between the options of keeping the mark in their native language, translating it into myriad local languages, or transliterating it into an equally large number of local language sound-alike words. Arriving at the appropriate linguistic solution on a global scale, or even sometimes within a region or even a country, can often be quite difficult.

Practice Tip

Never assume that an extensively used and successful trademark in one country will be suitable for use in other countries.

2. Linguistic Issues

The mark may simply not sound good in other languages or, worse yet, may translate poorly or not at all. Seemingly inoffensive trademarks in the home-country language may have negative cultural, nationalistic, or religious connotations in other countries. For example, China banned the Yves Saint Laurent fragrance brand Opium on the basis that it recalled a humiliating period in Chinese history and could cause "spiritual pollution" among Chinese youth.

Some marks, such as Nestle, seem to work well across most linguistic and cultural differences, but others need adaptation or interpretation. Some, luckily, translate well: for example, Pillsbury's Green Giant brand from the United States is successfully marketed in Italy under the trademark Gigante Verde Italia.

On the other hand, translations can be minefields. For example, in Japanese there is no adequate word to translate the Mexican/American cuisine "taco," yet Taco Bell, the largest American franchisor of this type of fast food, encountered a problem with the Japanese word that transliterates, or sounds like, "taco" because that word means octopus. Pizza Hut, another American-based international franchisor, has had a different problem, namely the proper connotative translation of the word "hut." While this word may be cute and suggestive in English, an improper translation of "hut" could come out as "shanty," "shack," or other word, creating a negative impression of the franchise business.

Some classic examples of the misadventures of translation include the ill-fated attempt by Chevrolet to market its Nova automobile in several Latin American countries a few years ago, only to discover that this mark sounds like "no va," meaning "doesn't go" in Spanish. Exxon encountered nearly the same situation in Japan when searching for one worldwide mark to replace Esso. One of the reasons Exxon was chosen over Enco was that the latter means "stalled car" in Japanese. Finally, the Perdue slogan "It takes a strong man to make a tender chicken" was originally translated into Spanish as: "It takes an aroused man to make a chicken affectionate."

Taking famous marks and creating pleasant-sounding, marketable transliterations isn't easy. When The Coca-Cola Company first entered China, it wanted to use Chinese characters that would be pronounced in a manner as close to the rest of the world as possible. Unfortunately, the Chinese characters chosen also represented the words "bite the wax tadpole." After researching over 40,000 characters to find a phonetic equivalent, Coca-Cola changed the characters to ones that may not have sounded as close to what it wanted, but its new meaning, "happiness in the mouth," was an obvious improvement.

3. Designs

One often-used solution to the international word mark problem is the uniform and consistent use of the same design or logo, perhaps coupled with a similarly uniform trade dress and site presentation format from which the franchising services are provided. In this way, multi-country consistency can be achieved even when different translations or transliterations are used. The Shell and Pepsi logos, Colonel Sanders's likeness, and the McDonald's Golden Arches are examples of successful global marketing tied together across language and cultural barriers by pictorial and three-dimensional symbols.

On the other hand, even logos may encounter unexpected obstacles to use in other countries. Signal Graphics Printing used a British "bobby" and a stoplight design for many years to identify its printing business in the United States only to discover in its first international franchising foray into Argentina how much the British were hated over the Falklands episode. Gerber learned that it could not use its famous label with the happy baby picture in parts of Africa since, with the high rate of illiteracy, pictures on packaging commonly denoted what was inside the bottles.

B. REGISTRABILITY

Practice Tip

Trademark rights are strictly territorial. Trademark registrability standards vary from country to country. Just because a mark is registrable in one's home country or other countries does not mean it is necessarily registrable anywhere else.

Trademark rights are purely and solely territorial in scope. Each of the over 200 countries or jurisdictions throughout the world has its own law, regulations, and registration systems. Registrability refers to those criteria in a local law (or in the case of the EC, the Community regulations) governing what is considered to be a trademark capable of registration. These would include factors such as genericness, descriptiveness, geographic terms, surnames, and issues such as whether a descriptive term in one language can be a registrable trademark in a country where the language is unknown. Despite attempts at harmonization that have been targeted to benchmark levels, standards of registrability can vary greatly.

A mark registrable in one's home country may not necessarily be registrable in other countries. For example, many trademarks first created in the United States, especially in the franchising context, use surnames, geographic names, and groups of initials. While these are not optimum trademark choices, they can be protected in the United States once sufficient use and reputation are established. In many countries, however, surnames, geographic names, and initials will not be protected. Moreover, many countries will not recognize acquired distinctiveness by virtue of extensive use.

For example, the American applicant for registration of the mark THE CHICAGO PIZZA PIE FACTORY in Switzerland was refused registration because the geographical implication of "Chicago" would cause the mark to be deceptive if used on goods that did not come from there. The applicant argued that "Chicago" was a generic term for a particular type of pizza and thus not geographically meaningful for those goods. The decision held that notoriety of Chicago-style pizza in the United States was of no consequence for the purposes of determining registrability of the mark in Switzerland. The mark must first become generic there—a status generally recognized only after several decades of generic use by many different businesses—before the generic implication would supplant the geographical one and render the mark eligible for protection.

At the other end of the spectrum, there are countries where it is much easier to register trademarks that consist of extremely descriptive, if not generic, terms, especially in a different language. In some countries, no inquiry at all is made as to what a foreign language mark means.

C. AVAILABILITY

Practice Tip

There is no worldwide trademark registration system. Separate trademark clearance searches are essential. Trademark rights must be obtained on a country-by-country basis (with the exception of the EC) and priority in time of filing is a significant advantage.

It is very important to conduct a proper trademark clearance search in each country contemplated for franchising. This is necessary to avoid the possibility of inadvertent trademark infringement of another's prior right, to discover possible trademark piracy of one's own mark, and to make sure that the mark is available for licensing as part of a franchising relationship. Even in a multicountry arrangement such as the European Community, the grant of its unitary registration can be blocked by the prior rights of another party in merely one of the member countries.

In virtually every jurisdiction throughout the world, the first to file an application for trademark registration usually places itself in a very advantageous position to obtain trademark rights. Often, by the time a franchisor decides to embark upon an international trademark registration filing program, the franchisor discovers that others, either coincidentally or intentionally, have established a presumptively valid claim to trademark rights in certain jurisdictions. The speed and scope of the information flow on the Internet and satellite television, for example, clearly accelerates the risk. Various sections of this chapter will discuss more precisely how trademark rights are acquired and how trademark owners may be able to recapture their trademark rights in other countries under certain circumstances.

VI. Acquisition of Trademark Rights

A. REGISTRATION

Practice Tip

Registration is imperative to protect the ability to do business in a country. Registration should be sought, as quickly as feasible, for every mark contemplated, for as broad a range of goods and services as possible, in every jurisdiction considered for possible expansion.

In almost every legal jurisdiction in the world, there are very significant benefits that flow from trademark registration. With some limited exceptions for prior users in a number of countries, trademark registration will usually provide the franchisor with the exclusive right to use the mark in a particular jurisdiction for the goods or services covered by the registration.

The benefits of registration may (on a country-by-country basis) include:

- crucial presumptions as to the validity of the trademark and the franchisor's ownership;

- important substantive, procedural, and tactical benefits to franchisors in litigation against infringers;
- the mark's presence in a searchable database, putting other parties on public notice of the franchisor's trademark rights (with a possible deterrent effect on the adoption of the same or similar mark by others);
- a basis for a trademark office, when examining applications of others, to block such applications without the necessity or expense of action by the franchisor;
- a basis to oppose subsequent applications (or cancel subsequent registrations) by others for confusingly similar marks;
- prevention of unauthorized importation of infringing products by recording with local customs officials;
- the key foundation for licensing within the franchise relationship; and
- satisfaction of the franchisor's contractual obligations under the franchise agreement.

Registration is essential in those countries with required license recordal and approval as well as in those countries regulating repatriation of licensing fees and royalties.

B. USE AS A BASIS

In a minority of countries, trademark rights can be acquired by priority of use and enforced without the necessity of an actual trademark registration. Most of these countries are usually categorized as "common law" jurisdictions, primarily those with a legal system derived from British law. Also, in many countries owners of famous marks have the capability of trying to block others from using or registering their marks upon a sufficient showing of prior use or reputation, but success is far from assured. However, in none of these situations will most of the rights enumerated in the last section be available.

Therefore, relying on rights derived from use rather than registration is a poor basis for trademark protection for a franchising business and is not recommended. Prospective franchisees will be quite reluctant to enter into a franchise arrangement requiring substantial investment and the payment of continuing fees and royalties absent the far greater certainty of a trademark registration. Franchisors that have failed to avail themselves of the maximum trademark protection available could easily expose themselves to litigation for breach of contract, rescission, indemnification, and damages.

Most countries do not require use as a condition for filing an application. The U.S. system provides applicants with an alternative filing basis: either actual use or a sworn declaration of a *bona fide* intent to use. In the latter instance, however, proof of actual use is required prior to a registration being granted.

C. CLASSIFICATION ISSUES

Practice Tip

A registration filing strategy involving classification must be developed, taking into account varying standards in particular countries. Expense factors must be balanced against the necessity of full coverage for a franchise business that does not neatly fall into one particular class as well the need to preempt certain other categories for future use and/or to block potential infringers.

1. *Classes of Goods and Services*

Nearly all countries (with the pertinent exception of Canada) have a classification system segmenting the various goods and services that registrations may cover. Almost all countries now use the "International Classification" system, but care should be taken not to mistakenly instruct filings by number alone in case there is a special local classification system. In view of the fact that many franchising businesses have fairly unique approaches to service-oriented enterprises that also include the sale of goods, great care must be given to filing in the appropriate classes.

It should be noted that many countries take a rigid approach to classification. In these jurisdictions, when the marks of the junior party do not strictly fall under the coverage of the class category of the otherwise senior registration, the senior marks may not be provided enforcement against infringing uses or subsequent applications of others or be cited as blocking references by a trademark registrar. For example, a registration for a food product may not be useful against the use or a later application by another for the exact same mark in connection with restaurants serving those products, or vice versa. Accordingly, it is important to register in as many classes as may be directly or peripherally involved in the franchise business. In many countries (but not the United States), applications will be allowed for an entire class coverage, irrespective of the actual intended use, thereby granting broader coverage.

Registering in multiple classes can substantially increase filing expense but in many countries (not the United States) adding additional classes usually results in a cost break, especially for the local attorney's fees. Therefore, if possible, it is recommended that such extra classes be instructed at the same time as the initial application. Class coverage should be an integral part of a thoughtful filing strategy.

D. TRADEMARK PIRACY

Practice Tip

Trademark piracy is an international fact of life. Priority of rights flows from priority of filing in most instances, so it is imperative to file for registration as early as possible.

In many, if not most, countries, all rights derive from registration, despite the legitimate creation and use of the same mark elsewhere. In the majority of countries, the first party to file an application for trademark registration is typically the one to achieve presumptively superior rights in that trademark.

A party whose mark has been pirated has several avenues of approach if it does not wish to pay an exorbitant sum to acquire the registration. In some countries, the registration may be open to challenge where an applicant was required to allege a bona fide intent to use the mark or a business connection between its commercial enterprise and the mark applied for. In others, it may be able to attack an old registration on the grounds of nonuse abandonment. As previously noted, if it can prove its mark is famous in that country it may have a chance to prevail.

The trademark offices in many countries do not perform an examination for prior registrations, and in those that do, the process is not always accurate. Furthermore, no country will search for or cite the rights of prior users. Accordingly, constant surveillance is necessary. Moreover, one's own business associates, prospective franchisees included, will often seek to protect "your interests" by filing in their name. This should be covered by contractual provision in the franchise documentation but sometimes it is too late. In South Africa, Toys "R" Us had little choice but to sign up as its franchisee a local party that had registered the mark there first. And, adding insult to injury, it paid an upfront fee and a royalty to this party, its own franchisee.

E. DOMAIN NAMES

Practice Tip

A prudent franchisor should promptly register as many domain names as practical that include all its significant trademarks. Domain names need to be acquired in addition to trademark registrations but not as substitutes. Piracy of domain names containing trademarks is widespread, so franchisors should also register preemptively any likely misspellings, abbreviations, or intuitive variations of their marks. Constant surveillance is essential.

Domain names are quite different from trademarks and are not considered intellectual property *per se.* Registration of domain name addresses on the Internet is an international system transcending jurisdictional boundaries that exists completely separately from trademark registration. There are overlapping domain name registration systems, including the most common top levels such as ".com," ".net," and ".org." There are also country-specific domains such as ".uk" and ".fr." Not all domain names consist of or contain trademarks.

Registrars of these systems will register to the first applicant any domain name not already taken without any screening or examination for trademark issues (except that some country-level registrars do restrict ownership in different ways). Thus, the same second-level domain (the prefix) could be registered to different parties in the different top levels and in different countries. Moreover, domain names will be issued to different parties if there is merely one letter, character, or punctuation difference. Thus, it is virtually impossible to preempt every domain name variation including trademarks of a franchisor from imaginative interlopers. As a result, piracy of domain names containing trademarks is widespread, and constant surveillance is highly recommended.

It is unclear in many jurisdictions whether prior trademark rights or registrations can be used to block the use of domain names identical or similar to, or containing a mark, by proceeding under traditional trademark infringement statutes when no actual use as a Web site has been made. Therefore, for example, in the United States action has been taken under the dilution law and special legislation passed in 1999—the Anticybersquatting Act. Other countries have used other statutes such as China's Anti-Unfair Competition Law ("ikea.com.cn"); Taiwan's Fair Trade Law ("carrefour.com.tw"); Japan's Unfair Competition Law ("jacs.co.jp"), and Russia's Law on Competition ("kodak.com.ru").

All top-level domain name registrars must now subscribe to the Uniform Dispute Resolution Policy promulgated by The Internet Corporation for Assigned Names and Numbers (ICANN), the nonprofit body charged with administering the Internet. (See www.icann.org.) Under this procedure, owners of trademark rights can initiate an administrative complaint proceeding directed at having the allegedly pirated domain name canceled or transferred to the trademark owner. It is in the nature of an arbitration, conducted completely on-line and limited to one filing by each party. Therefore, this procedure is quick, relatively inexpensive, and the success rate for trademark owners is high. It is especially effective in the international setting since it eliminates the necessity of attempting court action in another country. Unfortunately, the results are only binding on the registrars; thus, it is not a final disposition since both parties have parallel recourse to a court.

One technique that can be used against country-specific domain name piracy of new trademarks is to use the Paris Convention's six-month priority provision. If, after filing a trademark application in one's home country for a new mark, the attendant publicity of launching the new mark precipitates a domain name rip-off containing the mark in a country-specific registry, within the first six months after the first filing the owner can file a trademark application in the target country claiming a filing date that reverts back to home-country filing date, thereby acquiring priority over the domain name filing.

Owning a domain name registration does not necessarily generate trademark rights, and thus mere ownership of a domain name registration is undoubtedly not sufficient to fully protect any trademark rights in the domain name or words within it. Therefore, it is recommended that overlapping trademark and domain name registrations be obtained, even if the business is not a e-commerce business, so as to preempt others from domain name piracy. Franchisors should also amend their agreements to provide for approval and control of franchisee domain names using trademarks of the system.

F. TREATIES

1. Paris Convention

Virtually all commercially significant countries belong to the International Convention for the Protection of Industrial Property (1883), better known as the Paris Convention. This treaty (which has been revised many times) contains many general provisions regarding protection of patents, trademarks, and other forms of proprietary property, and provides some very minimum standards for member countries. The key provision is that each member pledges that it will grant the nationals of other member countries the same protection, subject to the same conditions, as nationals of its own country. Therefore, it neither purports to harmonize national laws nor does it set up the granting of a worldwide trademark right. Moreover, in some countries the convention is not self-executing and national courts have chosen to ignore or interpret certain provisions.

One specific provision that affects trademark registration in member countries (and that is followed by all members) is a priority scheme whereby an applicant that files a first application in a member country is entitled, for six months, to file corresponding applications in other member countries and effectively backdate the application date to the date of first filing. Moreover, for those member countries (except for Canada) that require use as a prerequisite to either filing or obtaining registration, those requirements are superseded by a filing under the Paris Convention.

2. Madrid Agreement

The oldest and most established multinational registration procedure is the Madrid Agreement Concerning the International Registration of Marks (1891), known as the Madrid Agreement. It is operated by the World Intellectual International Property Organization (WIPO). (See www.wipo.org.) The Madrid Agreement has 52 members, primarily European countries, but does not include many major economic powers such as the United States, Japan, or the United Kingdom. It facilitates filing in member countries (as an alternative to direct filing) by providing for one application to WIPO resulting in a so-called "International Registration." This is simultaneously considered the equivalent of an application in each country designated (and paid for) by the applicant. The filing with WIPO must be based upon a home registration in a member country.

All the derivative applications are examined under the individual law and registrability standards of each country, however, and can be rejected by individual countries as they see fit. Moreover, any subsequently obtained derivative registrations in countries based upon the agreement filing are vulnerable to being canceled if the home country registration is lost within the first five years after the date of deposit with WIPO. This vulnerability (referred to as "central attack") and certain other perceived shortcomings of the agreement have resulted in a limited membership and limited prospects for growth.

3. Madrid Protocol

Practice Tip

The European Community trademark system has established the first effective multicountry registration. The Madrid Protocol promises to be a swift, cost-effective, and efficient means to acquire and manage international trademark protection.

Due to the recognized deficiencies of the Madrid Agreement, WIPO initiated the development of a parallel system (and potentially an eventual replacement) that came into force on December 1, 1995, and became operational on April 1, 1996. It is the Protocol Relating to the Madrid Agreement concerning the International Registration of Marks (1989), or simply the Madrid Protocol. Presently there are 46 members of the protocol, including significant countries such as Japan, Germany, Spain, and the United Kingdom. Following a long delay involving a technical political dispute, the United States is expected to join the Madrid Protocol, most probably effective in 2002.

The Madrid Protocol, like the Madrid Agreement, does not abrogate the territoriality principle nor establish minimum standards for protection for trademarks but merely provides a procedural filing system. It establishes requirements for obtaining trademark registrations on a multicountry basis as a result of only one filing procedure. This can result in substantial cost savings, both at the time of application and renewal, modification, or transfer of any registrations that are granted. (The national government fees will still be paid, but fees for local lawyers and agents will be sharply reduced.) But as with the Madrid Agreement, each member country will still examine (and can reject) a trademark application according to its national law.

The Madrid Protocol significantly improves upon the Madrid Agreement in at least three key areas. First, one need not wait for a home country registration to be issued; under the Madrid Protocol, a protocol application can be based upon an application or a registration. This means that not only will there be no delays that could allow pirates to intervene, but applicants will be able to use the Paris Convention's six-month priority backdate provision to even further solidify early protection. Second, under the Madrid Protocol both English and French are designated official languages rather than just French as under the Madrid Agreement. Third, and perhaps most importantly, the serious defect of central attack under the Madrid Agreement is tempered by allowing a transformation of any Madrid Protocol registration that has been successfully attacked into national registrations in any countries where the attacking party does not have rights.

Therefore, once the United States joins the Madrid Protocol, U.S. franchisors embarking on international expansion will be able to quickly, efficiently, and inexpensively launch an international trademark filing program, at least to the extent of those countries that join. It is expected that U.S. adherence will generate a membership groundswell and increased filing activity.

4. European Community

This relatively small in number (fifteen countries, thirteen jurisdictions due to the Benelux Confederation) but obviously extremely economically important group has seen two parallel important developments in recent years. First, a 1988 EC directive mandated that by 1995 all the jurisdictions would harmonize their trademark laws in many important substantive and procedural aspects. As might be expected, "harmony" turned out to be more like thirteen different tunes along the same theme rather than unanimity but, nonetheless, significant improvements were made to the laws and procedures of many of the jurisdictions that had been lagging behind certain benchmark standards

Second, as of April 1, 1996, the European Community trademark system came into existence, accepting applications for Community Trademark Registrations (CTMs). (See www.oami.eu.int.) The Office for Harmonization in the Internal Market (OHIM) is the EC's trademark office located in Alicante, Spain. The CTM registration conveys multicountry protection through the filing of a single application under one set of rules, laws, and enforcement procedures. Thus, the CTM system goes far beyond either Madrid system.

The principal advantages of the CTM system include the following:

- a unitary registration with exclusive rights to use a mark in fifteen countries;
- the cost effectiveness of one filing (the fees are equal to national filings in three or four separate jurisdictions);
- one opposition proceeding, one renewal, and one filing for administrative matters such as assignments, change of address, change of name, and so forth;
- use of the CTM mark in just one country is sufficient to protect against cancellation of the CTM registration on the grounds of nonuse; and
- a single infringement action may be enforceable throughout the entire EC.

It is important to note that the thirteen individual national trademark laws and registration procedures continue to exist in tandem with the CTM for all those parties that don't want or need one. If another party owns superior trademark rights in just one of those thirteen jurisdictions, it can block the entire EC application. In that event, the application is transformed into national applications in the remaining countries where it has not been blocked. Therefore, it is crucial to conduct trademark searches throughout all the jurisdictions as well as in the OHIM to determine if there are any parties who may have superior rights. Thus, it sometimes is difficult to obtain CTM registrations since the number of jurisdictions multiplies the possibility of objection.

A CTM registration can only be assigned as a whole and cannot be partially transferred for particular countries. Franchisors should take special note that a CTM mark can be partially licensed, however, for just some of the territory within the EC.

The CTM system provides an excellent way to obtain blanket coverage throughout the European Community at substantially reduced cost both for application and maintenance. A very significant advantage is the fact that use need only be proven in any one of the member countries to maintain a CTM registration. This is quite beneficial to a developing franchise system that wishes to evaluate its success in one or two countries before committing to further investment and expansion.

VII. Maintenance of Rights

Practice Tip

Trademark rights can last indefinitely but registrations must be renewed periodically and are subject to attack for abandonment for lack of continuing use of the mark. The definition of use, the extent of use needed to maintain rights, the time periods constituting nonuse, and the standards and procedures for cancellation vary widely. Administrative procedures must be put in place to manage an international trademark portfolio to avoid the adverse consequences of loss of registrations.

A. USE REQUIREMENTS

Trademark rights are of potentially infinite duration. Registrations, when obtained, are indefinitely renewable in all countries, subject to varying conditions, with the typical term of registration being ten years. In most commercially significant countries, however, a trademark registration can be canceled if use has not been made in a particular period of time. The procedural specifics and standards defining "use" vary greatly among the countries and must be carefully studied.

The definition and extent of use needed to allege use to maintain a registration may be different from that needed to prove use in a cancellation proceeding brought by another party. Most countries provide for the cancellation of registrations on the basis of nonuse but the standards and procedures for achieving such cancellation vary widely.

Unfortunately, many statutes are silent about what actually constitutes use. This is usually left to judicial interpretation and shifting administrative policies and regulations that can be the source of many technical traps. Most countries requiring use have specific time periods that constitute nonuse, usually three to five years. It can be difficult to overcome or excuse an allegation of nonuse. If a registration is vulnerable to attack, consideration should be given to filing a new application for registration to take its place to restart the time period. In addition to the expense, an older priority date will be lost but this must be balanced against saving a valuable mark.

In some countries, actual *bona fide* use is required. In other countries, sporadic token use would probably be sufficient to at least make an allegation of use. Moreover, the nature of the business will dictate the determination of whether the extent of the use is consistent in that industry. Use on products that are only exported from the country will qualify as use in some jurisdictions but not in others, where the law finds that the mark has not been exposed to the consumers of the source country. Sometimes, imported products solely for sale in embassies or military bases may be sufficient.

Of particular assistance in proving use in the franchising context are those countries that will allow advertisements as evidence of use. The content, frequency, and type of publication necessary and appropriate to act as an alternative to actual use will depend on local requirements.

In some jurisdictions, use for goods or services falling in one category of classification will suffice to comply with the use requirements for the mark in other classes. This approach is particularly helpful in those countries that permit so-called defensive registrations in other classes for the identical mark. It is especially beneficial in franchising where trademark owners often obtain several registrations in addition to the basic service mark class to erect a preemptive registration posture in related classes. Most countries, on the other hand, will usually require use in each class to sustain the registration's validity in that class.

Foreign language marks are a potential technical problem. In many countries, use in a language (even if a direct translation or transliteration) different than registered may not be sufficient to prove use of the registered mark. Since it is difficult to anticipate all future modes of use of a mark, all important marks should be registered in translations and transliterations to preempt pirates and to ensure that at least one registration will not be lost for failure to prove use.

Some countries will accept certain justifications for nonuse. Business reasons, such as failure to find a franchisee or adverse economic conditions, are generally not acceptable. On the other hand, those falling into a *force majeure* category might be. Some of the more difficult situations have involved political sanctions by the franchisor's home country preventing expansion into certain countries and prohibitions on foreign investment by the host country.

B. EFFECTS OF NONUSE

1. *Loss of Registration*

In those countries requiring use, failure to use may result in the inability to renew a registration, keep a registration alive by filing the appropriate affidavit, or defend a nonuse cancellation petition by a third party. Rarely will a trademark office attempt to cancel a registration *ex officio.* In some instances, a registration may only be partially canceled or limited in some respect by deleting those goods or services for which use could not be proven, while retaining that part of the registration related to actual proven use.

Maintaining a registration can be a hyper-technical adventure, especially when use is through a franchisee. Franchise agreements should require cooperation by the franchisee in furnishing documentation and other assistance. Registrations can easily be inadvertently lost even when the mark is in use, and care should be taken in drafting the franchise agreement so that the agreement does not automatically lapse if a registration is temporarily lost.

2. Inability to Enforce Rights

Failure to have or to be able to prove use of the mark in those countries requiring it will severely impair, if not impede, the enforcement of one's rights against third-party applicants or infringers. In filing oppositions against applications for registration by third parties based upon a prior registration, an allegation of use is not normally required. If this takes place in a country requiring use to maintain registrations, however, it is likely that the applicant will either request proof of use (in Germany, for example) or will simply counterattack by filing a cancellation petition (if warranted by the facts) against the opposer's own registration.

Practice Tip

Attempting to enforce rights in a mark that is not in use can expose a registration to attack and, therefore, such action should be subject to a thoughtful analysis balancing the benefit against the risk.

In infringement cases, the situation is a little more variable. In some countries, evidence of use, advertising, or sales, will be introduced by the plaintiff to buttress the infringement claim, especially if coupled with a claim of unfair competition. In most civil law countries, a trademark registration is treated as an exclusive property right and the plaintiff need not address its own use. If the plaintiff is not using a mark, however, it is taking a risk since a prime defensive strategy for the infringer would be to counterattack with a cancellation petition for nonuse if warranted by the facts.

C. USE OF REGISTRATION NOTICES AND SYMBOLS

Practice Tip

Displaying a registration notice with a registered trademark is required in some countries, including a precise format and language. Even in those countries where it is optional, it is highly recommended to use a notice, such as the ® symbol, since there can be specific benefits. Local counsel should be consulted to ensure compliance with local law and care should be taken when using the same materials in more than one country.

Many countries provide for the use of a symbol or words designating a trademark as registered when the mark is displayed on packaging, advertising, signs, and other materials. In some countries, it is mandatory that a registered trademark always be accompanied by a designated registration symbol. In other countries, such usage is optional, but often use of a notice will result in enhanced benefits for the trademark owner. For example, in the United States, failure to use a registration notice will not bar obtaining injunctive relief against an infringer. However, only U.S. trademark owners who have displayed either a ® or the words "Registered in U.S. Patent and Trademark Office" or "Reg. U.S. Pat. & Tm. Off." can recover damages and profits from an infringer, unless the defendant had actual notice of the registration.

In many of the countries that have provisions on registration notices, the required or suggested notice will be in the local language, for example, *Marca Registrada.* The ®, originally American, has gained increasing acceptance internationally, especially for trademark owners looking for a "one world" look and cost efficiencies. However, it must be emphasized that materials generated in one country may not be usable in another without changing the language of the registration notice or using a multi-language display of notices. It is imperative that local counsel be consulted to make sure the materials are in compliance with national laws and regulations.

In those countries that do not require notices, it is nonetheless a recommended practice to use notices to indicate registration. Use of a notice or symbol provides an aura of legitimacy to consumers and, moreover, puts competitors and potential infringers on actual notice of legal rights that could be very helpful in an infringement action. It is important to note, however, that serious penalties could accrue if a party uses a symbol or notice signifying that a mark is registered when it is not. Thus, prior to using any materials from one country in another, a careful review must be undertaken to make sure that the mark (and in some cases, in the exact same format) is registered in the destination country.

It is also generally recommended to give public notice of a claim to trademark rights when a mark is new and just in the application stage. In the United States and some other countries, an informal practice has developed of using the symbols "TM" (for trademark) and "SM" (for service mark) to denote a claim to trademark rights prior to registration. These have no codified legal effect but can be effective in putting the world on notice of a claim to trademark rights, especially in countries that recognize use-based trademark rights. Such notice could also buttress an allegation of bad faith against a defendant second-comer.

VIII. Protection of Rights

A. RIGHTS BASED ON REGISTRATION

1. Criminal Proceedings

Practice Tip

Criminal remedies may be effective in those jurisdictions where civil proceedings are very slow but the decision to request criminal remedies should be made with caution.

In most countries, registrations are afforded protection as a property right granted from the government. Therefore, the government can be used to enforce these exclusive rights in the courts under criminal statutes. Clearly, the latter can be extremely effective, if not draconian, in instances of grievous infringement or counterfeiting. In Iran, for example, trademark infringement is theoretically punishable by up to 74 lashes. Under the Mexican statute, use of confusingly similar trademarks is considered an "administrative offense" punishable by fines up to a certain amount, closing of facilities, and administrative arrest up to 36 hours. Use of an exact infringing or counterfeit trademark is considered a "felony" punishable by higher fines, seizure of goods, closing of facilities, and imprisonment from two to six years.

In Mexico, as in most other jurisdictions providing for criminal remedies for this type of activity, such criminal prosecution is at the discretion of the authorities. Often the trademark owner must instigate the criminal prosecution by its own investigation, persuade the authorities to act after supplying the evidence, and even sometimes provide the legal briefing. It should be noted, however, once such criminal proceedings are initiated, it is often difficult to have them terminated, even when the defendant is willing to arrive at an equitable settlement.

2. *Civil Action*

Oppositions against applications (or cancellation against registrations in those countries that do not allow oppositions) are routinely available. If they are based on a prior application or registration, these are generally relatively simple and inexpensive proceedings (as compared to the practice in just a few countries, for example, the United States, where these can become a mini-litigation). They usually consist of the submission of papers only and generally reflect a very narrow, strict approach to categories of goods and services. Depriving a trademark pirate of a registration can be helpful in parallel litigation since it takes the evidentiary presumptions away from the pirate.

In most jurisdictions, remedies available in civil infringement litigation include injunctive relief and monetary compensation based upon actual damages and/or the infringer's profits. In many countries, attorney's fees will automatically be recovered by the successful party, plaintiff, or defendant, pursuant to a policy designed to discourage frivolous litigation. Civil litigation for trademark infringement matters in most jurisdictions will vary in complexity but, generally, extensive discovery procedures are virtually unknown and elaborate trials are rare.

Practice Tip

It can be difficult to enforce a registration against similar or identical marks for different goods or services.

The most common difficulties encountered by trademark owners relate to the restrictive interpretation of the scope of registrations owing to differences in classes, goods, or services. For example, in Pakistan the respective owners of the 7-UP and SONY marks filed oppositions against several applications for registrations of the same marks for a diverse range of goods. The Supreme Court of Pakistan sustained the oppositions where there was some relation between the respective goods, for example, 7-UP for confectionery, but rejected the oppositions where there were greater differences between the goods, for example, SONY for sporting goods and 7-UP for wool, thread, and soap. On the other hand, McDonald's was victorious in the Philippines against the use by a company called L.C. Big Mak of BIG MAK BURGER as the name of a restaurant, despite the fact that McDonald's only had its BIG MAC mark registered as a trademark for food products. The Philippines court gave weight to the extensive use and advertising of the plaintiff's mark in denying the defendant's attempt to technically distinguish between the goods of McDonald's registration and its offending use. (Note, however, that the Philippines is a common law country.)

Some jurisdictions have unfair competition statutes that supplement trademark infringement. For example, DC Comics, Inc., was able to stop the use of the BATMAN logo on sneakers in Korea based upon a fairly broad Korean law that allows for either a civil action, a complaint to the Korean Intellectual Property Office to issue a cease and desist order, or a criminal complaint, which could result in fines or imprisonment. Apparently DC Comics used several of these options to force a quick settlement and cessation of the infringing use.

Practice Tip

Generally speaking, swift and broad civil relief for trademark infringement is difficult to obtain in many international jurisdictions. It is often quicker to get relief in counterfeiting situations.

Generally speaking, it can be very difficult to get expeditious *ex parte* or other interim civil relief internationally in routine trademark infringement situations, with the exception of the United States, many British law-based countries, including Hong Kong, and other jurisdictions primarily in Europe. In grievous counterfeiting situations, it is somewhat easier. In some jurisdictions, notably China, swift and extremely effective administrative relief on a local level is available against both infringement and counterfeiting if the authorities can be convinced of the complainant's standing and case.

B. RIGHTS BASED ON FAME OR USE

Due to the significant expense, administrative burdens, and delays in registering trademarks on a global basis, it is unreasonable to expect a trademark owner to register all of its marks in all classes in all countries. Therefore, international treaties and laws have developed certain doctrines to provide special protection for trademarks without complete registration coverage that are considered "well-known."

In theory, the Paris Convention provides protection for the owner of an established trademark that is misappropriated in another country, either by registration or use or both, by an unauthorized third-party when the "true" owner has not yet registered there. Article 6*bis* provides that a registration can be canceled, or use prohibited, of a mark "considered by the competent authority of the country of registration or use to be well known in that country as being already the mark of a person entitled to the benefits of this Convention and used for identical or similar goods."

In practice, however, the protection offered is far from certain and complete, due to the varying interpretations of this language and other relevant national laws as well as the difficulties of proof in such reputation cases. Overcoming the prior registration of one's mark by another party based upon proof of prior use or reputation in the jurisdiction will be based upon an extremely fact-driven and equity influenced analysis, thereby leading to an uncertain outcome. The uneven results and unpredictability of the local treatment of this treaty provision confirm how important it is to register one's mark as early as possible in as many jurisdictions as possible.

IX. Licensing Issues

A. LOCAL LICENSE REQUIREMENTS

Franchisors seeking to expand to various international markets should obtain advance advice about the applicability of any local laws or regulations controlling the licensing of trademarks, and especially those requiring the recordal of the license with a governmental entity. In such countries, government approval is deemed necessary to either validate the license and/or the underlying trademark rights. The varied reasons for these requirements include a concern that multiple-party usage of a trademark is somehow confusing to consumers; the legal approach in civil law that any encumbrance affecting a government grant of rights should be subject to governmental review; the desire to regulate the transfer of technology; the need to impose currency and export controls; and various economic objectives focused on protecting nationals with unequal bargaining positions and supporting local businesses.

Practice Tip

Franchisors should obtain advance advice about the applicability of any local laws or regulations controlling the licensing of trademarks, and especially those requiring government recordal and/or approval of the license. Recordal requirements are most often merely routine, burdensome, and costly, but they can be a technical trap if not properly complied with and, occasionally, a difficult hurdle to overcome.

B. REGISTERED USER

In a thankfully dwindling number of jurisdictions that use the former British trademark law as a model, licensed users of a registrant's trademarks are to be recorded with the trademark office. "Registered users" usually refers to those separate legal entities (even those that may have a corporate affiliation, for example, a subsidiary) that have some public role in producing a product or conducting a service under a license of the mark. This excludes suppliers and subcontractors (which have no interaction with the public) as well as distributors or retail outlets (which merely take title and pass it on). Most countries have either abolished or made registered user recordal optional to the point that it is being ignored.

Registered user and other types of license recordal requirements are most often merely routine, burdensome, and costly, but they can be a technical trap if not properly complied with and, occasionally, a difficult hurdle to overcome. In some countries, for example, the registered user system has been used as a tool to implement state policies on foreign investment. In this approach, recordal is seen as a way to protect the development of indigenous industry by regulating the use of foreign brand names.

C. LICENSE RECORDAL

In the jurisdictions requiring license recordal, the actual procedures and practice cover the spectrum. At one end are those countries where recordal is basically permissive and often ignored. Then there are those for which required recordal is a perfunctory act, with no substantive review. The countries of most concern to franchisors are those, usually lesser economically developed ones, that take an active role in analyzing the entire transaction to see if it complies with governmental policies on royalty rates, export restrictions, and technology transfer, for example. These more active countries will seek to impose conditions of use, royalty ceilings, and the like. The number of active countries has substantially declined due to multinational pressure.

D. CONSEQUENCES OF A FAILURE TO RECORD

The failure to properly comply with registered user or other license recordal requirements could have the following ramifications:

- the license may be found to be void and not enforceable against the licensee or third parties;
- the licensor may be unable to collect royalties and fees and/or to remit them out of the local country; and
- the use by the licensee will not inure to the benefit of the licensor, meaning that trademark rights will be considered lost or abandoned because the licensor may be unable to prove use to maintain its registration, defend against a nonuse cancellation action, or enforce its trademark rights against third-party infringers or applicants.

Moreover, if the trademark rights are lost, it probably means the franchisor will have breached its franchise agreement, thereby subjecting it to a lawsuit for rescission and damages. Therefore, actively enforced license recordal requirements cannot be ignored due to the potential negative consequences to trademark ownership as well as to the validity of the license supporting the franchising structure in a particular country.

X. Other Intellectual Property

Practice Tip

There are no blanket international rights for trade secrets, patents, or copyrights. Protection of trade secrets is primarily dependent on contractual rights. Patents are territorially registered but can be obtained in many countries through a filing convention that enables extensions of home-country patent applications. Copyright rights for some types of works can get varying cross-border protection without filing formalities but must be territorially enforced.

A. TRADE SECRETS

1. Definition and Coverage

Trade secret law protects the owner's right to control and protect certain proprietary information under very limited conditions. A trade secret can include a formula, pattern, compilation, program, device, method, technique, or process that is valuable because it is not generally known to the public and is maintained in secrecy, giving the owner the opportunity to obtain an advantage over competitors who do not know or use it. The types of material subject to trade secret protection are often found in the franchise business context. These include technological know-how, such as a cooking process; a method of doing business, such as teaching speed-reading, instruction of ballroom dancing, or a program for quitting smoking; or such items as customer lists, marketing and research information, and accounting and inventory management techniques.

2. Election of Protection

Trade secret protection is often viewed as an alternative to patent protection. There are two primary reasons why a franchisor would opt for trade secret status over patent protection. First, trade secret protection potentially can last indefinitely and second, the material might not rise to the level of patentability—trade secret standards of inventiveness and nonobviousness are not as high. However, there are great risks in the decision not to seek patent protection. If a strict compliance program covering the franchisor and franchisees is not in effect and properly executed, a trade secret could easily be lost without legal recourse since by definition a trade secret only exists until it is no longer a "secret." While this could happen by independent discovery or reverse engineering by others, a franchisor needs to prevent accidental or intentional disclosure by its own employees, franchisees, outside suppliers, and the like. Accordingly, while there can be an excellent competitive advantage to maintaining a trade secret, it is a perilous course that needs extensive legal input and control.

3. International

Trade secrets are much more difficult to protect internationally than any other form of intellectual property. There are no international conventions and many countries have no or, at best, ineffective laws covering this subject. In some of the jurisdictions with relevant laws, a finite term of years for protection is imposed. In others, preemptive injunctive relief is not available. A franchisor's primary recourse is to set up strict security measures with its suppliers and franchisees and to rely on contractual remedies if a breach occurs. However, once the secret is revealed, breach of contract damages will often be inadequate. Franchisors will often add substantial liquidated damages clauses to franchise agreements and other contracts to try to anticipate the potential loss while sensitizing the other party to the secrecy obligation. Chapter 6 provides a more in-depth look at this subject.

B. PATENTS

1. Definition

A patent gives the owner an exclusive right to exclude others from making, using, selling, and offering for sale the patented invention. Utility patents cover new and useful processes and machines. Design patents cover new and original ornamental designs for articles of manufacture. Patents can be granted in the United States for software, especially that which embodies a business method or model. Business method patents can be important in the franchise context, although often others can effectively design around them by making minor changes. Accordingly, their scope and validity are often questionable.

While generally patent protection is not a major factor in many franchise businesses, occasionally it can provide a real advantage, especially over the short term. There are very precise procedures and technical requirements for obtaining patents. For example, publicly using an invention for more than a year eliminates the ability to obtain a patent.

In the franchise context, it is important to regularly review decisions to treat certain material as patentable versus retaining it as a trade secret. Once the patent route is chosen, the invention will be disclosed to the public and the owner's protection will expire after a certain number of years. Trade secret protection, on the other hand, can result in indefinite protection and often is a vital long-term element of a successful franchise business.

2. International

The principal of territoriality governs international patent protection. The Paris Convention mandates the same reciprocal treatment for nationals regarding patents as it does for trademarks. It gives patent applicants a year to file in other countries and obtain the earlier filing date. Protectible subject matter will vary from country to country. For example, patents for business methods and software are not available in many countries.

The United States is a member of the Patent Cooperation Treaty in which patents filed in a member country obtain a single priority date for all designated countries. The applicant can delay expenditures for prosecuting the patent application in the other countries for thirty months, giving it time to test the technology. Once the decision is made to proceed, separate prosecution must be made on a country-by-country basis. Finally, there is a European Patent Convention that grants a single patent for fourteen countries. However, it has been beset with criticism and reform efforts are being pursued.

C. COPYRIGHTS

1. *Definition and Coverage*

Copyright law protects original works of authorship that can be tangibly expressed, as opposed to a mere idea or concept. A copyright owner has the exclusive right to reproduce the work, distribute copies to the public, and to publicly perform and display it. In the franchise context, this includes materials such as operations manuals, computer software programs, advertising (print, TV, radio, music), architectural blueprints, building designs, and any other such materials that are independently created.

Creation and authorship are key concepts in copyright law to which special attention must be paid. For example, many materials subject to copyright are created by outside parties hired by the franchisor (or the franchisees) and careful scrutiny must be exercised to make sure that these parties assign their copyright rights to the franchisor or, under certain circumstances, acknowledge that their work is a "work made for hire" if it fits into specific guidelines under the law. Otherwise, valuable copyright rights could be lost.

2. *International*

Internationally, copyright is primarily governed by two multinational treaties: the Berne Convention for the Protection of Literary and Artistic Works (1886) and the Universal Copyright Convention (1955). Almost all commercially important countries belong to Berne. The United States belongs to both conventions. Berne has stronger and more effective substantive standards that must be met by its members. All works of American authors must "automatically" be protected in Berne member nations but since Berne, like the Paris Convention for trademarks and patents, is based on national treatment, such works will only obtain whatever level of protection in afforded in the host country. Moreover, enforcement is also based on territoriality since copyright laws rarely have extraterritorial effect.

3. Registration

The Berne Convention prohibits formalities such as notice and registration from being a precondition to copyright rights. However, it does permit member countries to confer benefits for compliance with some local formalities. So, for example, copyright registration is still highly recommended in the United States for many reasons, including the ability to recover statutory damages and attorney's fees, and as a prerequisite to an infringement suit. There are several other countries where registration is possible and recommended by local counsel but, generally, protection without registration is the norm.

4. Notice

Use of a copyright notice is permissible under Berne. Effective March 1, 1989, in the United States a notice is no longer required for works published after that date. However, under U.S. law use of a notice can overcome an innocent infringer defense. Moreover, the Universal Copyright Convention prescribes the use of a notice to gain automatic protection, and there are countries belonging to it but not Berne. Therefore, it is highly recommended that a copyright notice be used in a "reasonable" location so that it can be seen, as follows: ©, the year of first publication, and the name of the copyright owner. Note the notice should reflect the current owner's name if the actual author has assigned the rights.

Therefore, once a copyrightable work is created in the United States, the potential for copyright protection exists in other countries without doing more, subject to the advice to use a notice and to register in the United States and elsewhere where recommended by local counsel.

CHAPTER ❖ 4

U.S. Tax Considerations Related to Cross-Border Franchise Transactions

T. TIMOTHY TUERFF AND TIMOTHY J. PRONLEY

I. Overview

This chapter summarizes tax issues that must be addressed by corporations engaged in cross-border franchising activities. The primary focus of this analysis is the U.S. income taxation of franchise revenue; however, some discussion concerning foreign withholding taxes and foreign transaction taxes is also included. An exhaustive discussion of the U.S. income tax issues resulting from cross-border franchise operations is beyond the scope of this chapter. Thus, the following material summarizes the primary issues that must be addressed by corporations engaged in these transactions.[1]

The financial return derived from international franchise operations may be greatly altered by the tax liability imposed on these operations. To maximize the return derived from these operations, certain tax issues must be addressed at the onset of negotiations with prospective franchisees or licensees. A U.S. corporation is taxable on its worldwide income; thus, income earned from international operations is immediately included in its taxable income if the operations are conducted directly by the U.S. corporation. It is possible, if not likely, that franchise income derived from foreign franchisees earned by the U.S. corporation will also be subject to tax in the country in which the franchisee is located. The U.S. corporation must obtain a foreign tax credit against its U.S. income tax on the foreign franchise income to avoid double taxation of the same income—once in the country of the franchisee and again in the United States.

Double taxation of cross-border franchise income must be avoided, if at all possible, as it will greatly reduce the return on international operations and create havoc with the financial results of the company. Thus, advisors to a U.S. corporate franchisor must review the impact of the foreign tax credit on their international transactions. This review requires an analysis of the type of income earned (often referred to as the "character" of the income), the source of the income, the type of foreign taxes imposed on the franchising income, and the limitation on the amount of foreign tax credit that may be claimed against the U.S. tax on that income.

If the U.S. corporate franchisor conducts its non-U.S. franchise operations through a foreign subsidiary, the income is not automatically included in the taxable income of the U.S. parent company.[2] Generally, income of a foreign subsidiary is deferred from taxation until it is distributed as a dividend to the U.S. parent corporation. Certain income earned by a controlled subsidiary that is passive in nature or from related party transactions is not deferred and is included in income of the U.S. parent corporation as a deemed dividend from the foreign subsidiary. In addition, to maintain deferral, earnings of the foreign subsidiary must be reinvested outside of the United States. Thus, the franchise income derived by foreign subsidiaries of the U.S. parent corporation must also be examined for possible current taxation in the United States.

A foreign corporation earning income from U.S. franchisees must determine if it will be subject to U.S. income tax on that income. It must review the character and source of the income derived from its U.S. operations and determine if it is deriving income from the conduct of business activities in the United States. Alternatively, if the foreign corporation does not have sufficient operations in the United States to cause the U.S. taxation of such income, it may still be subject to U.S. withholding tax on the payment of a franchise fee from a U.S. franchisee.

This chapter first addresses the character and source of the income derived in a franchise transaction. The same character and source rules are applicable to U.S. corporations and their foreign subsidiaries with offshore operations and to foreign corporations earning franchise income from U.S. franchisees. The character of income must be analyzed to determine the source rule applicable to the income. Different source rules apply depending on whether the income is characterized as sales, services, royalties, rent, interest, or dividends. The source rules are particularly relevant to the foreign tax credit calculation for income earned by U.S. taxpayers. For foreign franchisors, the source of the income is a critical factor in determining whether the U.S. taxing jurisdiction extends to the income derived from a U.S. franchisee. Following this background, the chapter will discuss the tax considerations related to the operation of a franchise business directly by a U.S. corporation and then the tax considerations related to a franchise business conducted through a controlled foreign subsidiary of a U.S. parent corporation. Next, the chapter addresses the U.S. income tax issues that a foreign corporation must address when it earns franchising income from a U.S. franchisee. Finally, the chapter summarizes certain tax issues that may apply to franchising revenue.

II. Characterization and Source of Cross-Border Franchise Revenue

A. OPERATION OF CHARACTER AND SOURCE RULES

The Internal Revenue Code (the Code) prescribes rules for the taxation of various categories of income, such as sales, service fees, rents, royalties, dividends, and interest.[3] Most importantly, the rules that classify income as U.S. or foreign source income are dependent on the type of income. For example, sales income is subject to a different source rule than the source rule applicable to services or royalties. Thus, franchise income must first be characterized as sales, services, royalties, and so forth, to determine the appropriate source rule. As noted above, the source of the income (U.S. or foreign source income) will determine the extent to which a foreign tax credit is allowed, in the case of a U.S. company, and the scope of the taxing jurisdiction, in the case of a foreign corporation.

The Code and applicable case law do not place franchise income in a particular income category. Franchise income is characterized by reviewing the facts surrounding the franchise arrangement to determine what the franchisor provides to the franchisee in exchange for the franchise income. Generally, franchise income is a payment for the right to use (or own) intangible and tangible property and for providing personal services.[4] Thus, it may be necessary to allocate a lump-sum franchise fee into various categories of income depending on the amount properly attributable on an arm's-length basis to the different property or services provided by the franchisor.

B. INTANGIBLE PROPERTY

A significant portion of franchise fees are often characterized as consideration for the use of intangible property, such as trademarks, trade names, designs, marketing programs and related information, know-how, training materials, and operating systems. Payments for the use of intangibles will represent sales or royalty income depending on the rights transferred.

The transfer of substantially all of the rights to an intangible asset represents a sale of the asset, which typically would result in the taxable transfer of the asset. If less than substantially all of the rights are transferred, then the payments received are taxable as royalty income.[5] The manner of payment (periodic vs. lump sum) is not a controlling factor; rather, the cases characterizing the income as sales or royalty turn on the rights transferred, not the form of the consideration tendered in the exchange.[6]

The following factors are often considered in analyzing whether substantially all of the rights have been transferred: (1) the term of the contract; (2) whether or not the franchisee obtains exclusive or nonexclusive rights to use the intangibles within a given jurisdiction; (3) whether the franchisee has an unrestricted right to sublicense or dispose of the intangible; and (4) whether or not the franchisee is subject to additional restrictions on the use of the intangible. To characterize the transfer as a sale, the franchisor must be giving up substantially all of the rights to use the intangible over the entire useful life of the intangible. Thus, if the franchisor retains a right to license the intangible to another franchisee within the franchisee's country or if the franchisor restricts the franchisee's ability to transfer the intangible to another party, it is likely that the income derived would be taxable as a royalty and not a sale. In such a case, the source rules for royalty income apply to the franchise fee received.[7]

Income from the sale of intangible property is generally treated as U.S. or foreign source income according to the residence of the seller.[8] The source of royalty income is dependent on where the property is used by the buyer/payor. A payment of a royalty for the right to use an intangible, such as a trademark or trade name, in the United States is treated as U.S. source income, and a payment to use the intangible outside the United States is treated as foreign source income.[9] If a royalty is paid for the use of worldwide rights, the royalty payment is allocated between U.S. and foreign source income based on actual use of the intangible asset.[10]

Source of income is particularly relevant in the case of royalty payments because the royalty income may be subject to a withholding tax in the payor's jurisdiction. Withholding taxes are generally a creditable tax under Section 903; however, the ability to claim a foreign tax credit is dependent on the U.S. franchisor earning sufficient foreign source taxable income.[11] It is important to note that other jurisdictions may treat income as a royalty payment and subject the income to withholding tax, even if it represents a payment for substantially all of the rights to use the intangible and is thus taxable as sales income for U.S. tax purposes. The character of income, as a result, particularly franchise fees, may not be symmetrical in the United States and in the payor's jurisdiction. In these cases, if the income is treated as U.S. source income, but subject to withholding tax, it is possible that the income will be subject to double taxation. Relief from such double taxation may be allowed under income tax treaties between the country of the payor and the United States.

C. PERSONAL PROPERTY

Income derived from the disposition of all substantial rights to personal property is taxable as sales income. The source of the sale of inventory property is determined according to the location at which title and risk of loss is transferred to the buyer (often referred to as the "title passage" rule).[12] Income from the sale of noninventory property is generally sourced according to the residence of the seller, subject to various exceptions.[13] Income derived from the use of personal property for a period that is less than the useful life of the property is taxable as rental income. The source of rental income is the location where the property is used.[14]

The different source rules for sales income compared to royalty and rental income require analysis of whether or not the income is derived from the sale of substantially all of the rights to the property or if it is derived from the right to use the property in a more limited way.

D. PERSONAL SERVICES

Income derived from the performance of personal services is taxed as services income and is sourced according to the location where the services are performed.[15]

E. FRANCHISE INCOME

Characterization of franchising income may be difficult because the consideration for the use of intangibles, services, and the sale or lease of personal property is not always clearly delineated in the franchise agreement. It may be necessary to allocate a lump-sum consideration into separate components that reflect the amounts paid for use of intangible property, for sale or use of personal property, and for the performance of services. This is a purely factual analysis. If a license is accompanied by a *de minimis* amount of services, then the income may be characterized entirely as royalty income.[16] If substantial services or personal property are provided in exchange for a franchise payment, then the amount allocable to each category of income must be determined on an arm's-length basis.[17]

These character and source rules are a starting point for any analysis of the taxation of international operations. The same character and source rules apply to U.S. corporations and their foreign subsidiaries and to foreign corporations engaging in U.S. based franchise operations.

III. Franchise Revenue Earned by a U.S. Parent Corporation

A. STRUCTURE EXAMPLE

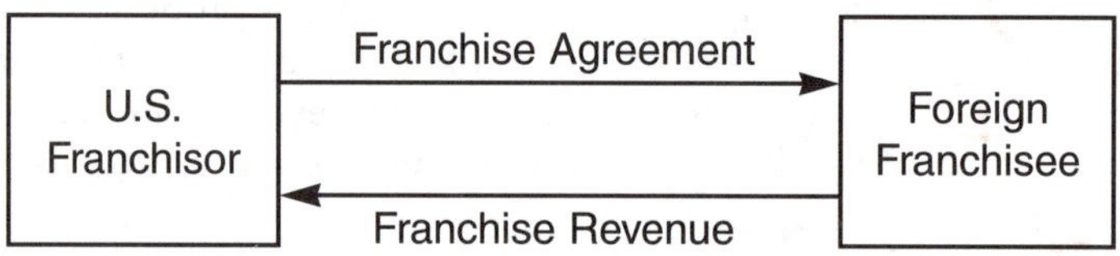

1. Facts

For purposes of analyzing the taxation of a U.S. corporation engaged in international franchising operations, assume that U.S. Franchisor, a U.S. corporation, executes a franchise agreement with Foreign Franchisee, an unrelated corporation organized under the laws of another country.

2. Issues

This fact pattern raises the following issues:

a. *Non-U.S. Taxation:* Is U.S. Franchisor subject to foreign tax on the franchise revenue? Withholding tax? Net income tax?
b. *Character of Income:* What is the character of the income received by U.S. Franchisor? Royalties? Sales? Services?

c. *Source of Income:* Is the income treated as U.S. source or foreign source income for U.S. tax purposes?
d. *Foreign Tax Credit:* Will U.S. Franchisor qualify for a foreign tax credit for the foreign tax paid with respect to the franchise revenue?

B. TAXATION OF A U.S. CORPORATION

As noted above U.S. Franchisor is taxed in the United States on its worldwide income, including the franchise fee paid from Foreign Franchisee. If U.S. Franchisor engages in direct business activities in another country, that country may also impose a direct income tax on U.S. Franchisor. Even if all operations are conducted in the United States, the country in which Foreign Franchisee operates may impose a withholding tax on all or a portion of the payment made by the franchisee. In this case, Foreign Franchisee may operate as a withholding agent for the tax that is legally imposed on U.S. Franchisor. In this role, Foreign Franchisee generally will withhold the tax from the franchise fee and remit the balance unless the payment is "grossed up" as discussed in Section III.D.6. of this chapter and in Chapter 6.

To avoid double taxation, U.S. Franchisor may claim a direct foreign tax credit under Sections 901 or 903 for the taxes imposed directly on the franchise income. Indirect foreign tax credits are allowable with respect to dividends paid from certain foreign subsidiaries, subject to various ownership and income restrictions. It is important to note, however, that a foreign tax credit may only be claimed with respect to the category of foreign source income to which the foreign taxes are allocated: for example, general limitation, passive, 10/50 basket, or other. Absent relief under an income tax treaty, no foreign tax credit may be claimed to reduce U.S. source income even though in some cases this income may be subject to foreign tax. To be entitled to claim a foreign tax credit, the foreign tax must be a creditable income tax, as defined under U.S. rules, and the U.S. corporation must earn sufficient foreign source taxable income in the appropriate category of income.

C. INCOME TAX TREATIES

In determining whether a U.S. corporation engaged in international franchise transactions will be subject to tax in another jurisdiction, it is necessary to determine whether U.S. Franchisor's activities are exempt from tax under the terms of a U.S. income tax treaty. In addition, a treaty may reduce the level of withholding tax imposed on the franchise fee, to the extent the royalty income is not attributable to a fixed place of business operated by the franchisor in the payor's country of residence. The following treaty analysis emphasizes the provisions of the U.S., Organization for Economic Cooperation and Development (OECD), and United Nations Model Treaties. The principles of these model treaties are reflected in the actual treaties between the United States and a number of other countries, but the specific language of the applicable treaty must be reviewed.

1. Resident

Treaty benefits generally apply to persons resident in the respective contracting states. The term "person," as defined in the U.S. and OECD Model Treaties, includes "an individual, a company and any other body of persons."[18] The term "resident" under the OECD and United Nations Model Treaties is defined as "any person who, under the laws of that state, is liable to tax therein by reason of his domicile, residence, place of management, or any other criterion of a similar nature."[19]

The U.S. Model Treaty is broader in that it also includes citizenship and place of incorporation as a determination of residence.[20] This is due to the U.S. system of taxing its citizens, residents, and corporations on their worldwide income. With regard to the system of taxing on a worldwide basis, the United States includes in each of its tax treaties a "saving clause."[21] With certain exceptions, this clause provides that a U.S. citizen, resident, or corporation will be subject to U.S. tax without regard to the provisions of the tax treaty.

2. Business Profits and Permanent Establishment

Tax treaties encourage trade or business contacts between countries by providing benefits dealing with business profits. The model tax treaties include a business profits article that provides business profits of an enterprise of one country will be exempt from tax in the other treaty country, unless the enterprise carries on a business in the latter country through a permanent establishment situated there.[22]

The U.S. Model Treaty defines the term "business profits" to mean "income derived from any trade or business, including income derived by an enterprise from the performance of personal services, and from the rental of tangible personal property."[23] The United Nations Model Treaty expands the taxing jurisdiction of the host country to include not only income attributable to the permanent establishment, but also sales in the host country of goods or merchandise of the same or similar kind as sold through the permanent establishment and other business activities carried on in the host country of the same or similar kind as those effected through the permanent establishment.[24]

The OECD Model Treaty provides that in determining profits of a permanent establi.shment, expenses may be deducted, "including executive and general administrative expenses so incurred, whether in the country in which the permanent establishment is situated or elsewhere."[25] The U.S. Model Treaty expands the examples of deductible expenses to include "reasonable allocations of . . . research and development expenses, interest, and other expenses incurred for the purpose of the enterprise as a whole (or the part thereof which includes the permanent establishment) whether incurred in the state in which the permanent establishment is situated or elsewhere."[26]

The model treaties provide the following examples of situations that do not constitute a permanent establishment:

- the use of facilities solely for the purpose of storage, display, or delivery of goods or merchandise belonging to the enterprise;
- the maintenance of a stock of goods or merchandise belonging to the enterprise solely for the purpose of storage, display, or delivery;
- the maintenance of a stock of goods or merchandise belonging to the enterprise solely for the purpose of processing by another enterprise;
- the maintenance of a fixed place of business solely for the purpose of purchasing goods or merchandise, or collecting information for the enterprise; and
- the maintenance of a fixed place of business solely for the purpose of carrying on, for the enterprise, any other activity of a preparatory or auxiliary character.[27]

Depending on the structuring of its operations, a franchisor may be able to store inventory in a jurisdiction without being subject to local country taxation. The U.S. and OECD Model Treaties provide that the maintenance of a fixed place of business solely for a combination of the above activities will also not constitute a permanent establishment.

When an employee or dependent agent habitually exercises the authority to conclude contracts in the name of the enterprise, such agency relationship will be deemed to be a permanent establishment in the host country with respect to any activities that the person undertakes for the enterprise. Generally, a subsidiary (not acting as a general agent) located in the host country will not have the actual or apparent authority to conclude contracts and, thus, will not constitute a permanent establishment of the parent in the host country.

The model tax treaties also provide that an enterprise shall not be deemed to have a permanent establishment merely because it carries on business in the host country through a broker, general commission agent, or any other agent of independent status, provided that such persons are acting in the ordinary course of their business. A partner is deemed to have a permanent establishment if the partnership satisfies the treaty requirements.[28]

To the extent it is possible to avoid creating a permanent establishment within the host country, business profits that would otherwise be subject to tax in the host country will generally be exempt from tax under a tax treaty. Depending on how operations are structured, it is possible for the franchisor to maintain storage of inventory without being subject to net income taxation. However, many times it is not possible to work through independent agents, or due to the nature of the business activities, it is necessary to place a permanent establishment in the host country. To this extent, a tax treaty will generally limit taxation in the host country to business profits attributable to the permanent establishment. Income not attributable to the permanent establishment will be taxed as otherwise provided by the tax treaty.

If there is no permanent establishment, the franchisee country may impose a withholding tax on the franchise fee. To the extent the franchise fee is characterized as a payment for the right to use intangible property in the franchisee's country of residence (a royalty), the franchise fee may be subject to withholding tax. The amount of the withholding tax, however, is often reduced or even eliminated under the terms of the income tax treaty between the franchisor's country of residence and the franchisee's country of residence.

3. *Planning*

The business profits exemption can be a significant benefit to the extent that U.S. Franchisor has diverse business activities taking place in or through the host country and not all of its activities are required to be operated through a permanent establishment. Also, to the extent that unrelated income, such as interest, dividends, and royalties are derived from the host country, such income generally will not be grouped with the trade or business income attributable to the permanent establishment but rather taxed in accordance with other provisions of the tax treaty.

Additional planning opportunities exist where a business activity can be divided into a number of independent segments. Business activities should be analyzed to determine whether the activities, in reality, constitute a number of activities that can be separated from the permanent establishment in the host country. For example, a franchise agreement may include items such as exchange of know-how, training, financial systems and support, and other items that need not be done through the permanent establishment. These bundled activities could be separated to ensure that not all are deemed to be attributable to the permanent establishment in the host country and subject to taxation in that country. Certain income, such as royalties, may be paid by the Foreign Franchisee without being subject to taxation in the Foreign Franchisee's country of incorporation depending upon the applicable income tax treaty, if any.

Consideration should also be given to the various types of income included in the franchise fee. Accurately characterizing income as sales, royalties, commissions, interest, or service fees will alter the treatment of such income in the host country. Separate identification of the different types of income contained in the franchise arrangement will impact the drafting of franchise agreements. For example, it may be necessary to execute a separate license agreement reflecting the license of intangible assets to the franchisee in exchange for a separately enumerated royalty payment. In addition, a separate management and sales agreement may address the sale of products or supplies and the provision of services, including management, marketing, and training. The tax result is more certain if the amount paid as sales, royalties, and services are separately stated in the agreements.

To minimize international tax exposure, it is important to consider potential tax treaty benefits in conjunction with the internal laws of the country from which the treaty benefits are to be derived.[29] The United States, however, has relatively few tax treaties with developing countries, and a franchisor may wish to consider establishing a holding company in a country with which the United States has a tax treaty and which has an extensive treaty network with other countries. Such factors as low international tax rates, the ability to make payments (for example, dividends, interest, or royalty payments) free from withholding tax, and financial and bank secrecy laws have made a number of treaty countries desirable places to establish operations. U.S. tax treaties with the Netherlands, Switzerland, and Luxembourg are favorable, and thus make these jurisdictions preferable candidates for holding companies.

4. Anti-Treaty Shopping Provisions

Since the early 1980s, anti-treaty shopping provisions have been incorporated in each new U.S. income tax treaty or protocol in an effort to prevent use of the treaty by residents of third countries that are not otherwise entitled to treaty benefits. Although the specifics of these so-called "limitation of benefits" articles vary from treaty to treaty, they generally contain similar provisions. The article usually indicates that individuals who are residents of the treaty country and the treaty country itself or subdivisions thereof are entitled to treaty benefits. However, a corporation or other entity that is a resident of the treaty country will only be entitled to the benefits of the treaty if the entity meets one of several tests to determine if the entity claiming the treaty has sufficient nexus with the country to justify awarding the benefit of the treaty. These provisions may look to ultimate ownership by bona fide residents of the treaty country, the existence of an active trade or business in the treaty country, whether a corporation is publicly traded in the treaty country (as defined in the treaty), or whether the entity has a principal purpose of avoiding U.S. taxation.

In addition to these treaty restrictions, U.S. tax authorities may assert anti-treaty shopping case law to nullify the protection of a treaty. These cases generally deny treaty benefits if the entity claiming the treaty benefits has minimal substance or the transaction executed by the entity does not have an independent business purpose, absent the tax benefits.[30]

Finally, U.S. Treasury Department regulations also limit potential tax treaty benefits. Treasury has issued regulations under Section 7701(l) of the IRS Code addressing "conduit" transactions that utilize an intermediary entity to reduce U.S. withholding taxes. If applicable, the regulations recast the form of the transaction, resulting in increased U.S. withholding taxes. The regulations apply to loans, advances, deposits, leases, and licenses, and must be reviewed closely when U.S. withholding tax is reduced as a result of related party or financing transactions.[31] In addition, Section 894(c), and the regulations thereunder (final and proposed) provide new limits on the availability of reduced rates of withholding under an income tax treaty when payments are made to and by a partnership or other flow-through entity.[32] Generally, the reduced treaty rates apply only to the extent that the U.S. source income is treated for purposes of the foreign country's tax laws as an item of income either to the partnership or a partner.[33]

D. FOREIGN TAX CREDIT

As noted above, U.S. Franchisor may be subject to a foreign tax on net income if under local country law, as modified by income tax treaties, its operations constitute a taxable presence in Foreign Franchisee's country of operation. Alternatively, if U.S. Franchisor does not maintain sufficient nexus, the payment of the franchise fee from Foreign Franchisee may be characterized as a royalty or some other type of income that is subject to withholding tax imposed by the foreign country. Because U.S. corporations and citizens are taxed by the United States on all income regardless of geographical source, double taxation arises when income from foreign sources is taxed by foreign tax authorities and also by the United States under its worldwide jurisdictional concept. The foreign tax credit is designed to mitigate double taxation.

U.S. Franchisor is entitled to reduce its U.S. income tax on foreign source income by the amount of foreign income taxes imposed on foreign source income that is classified in a similar category.[34] By claiming a credit, as opposed to a deduction for foreign taxes, the U.S. tax on foreign source taxable income is reduced dollar for dollar to the extent that the income has already been subject to a foreign income tax. This regime requires that there be a computation of foreign source taxable income within various categories and an allocation of foreign taxes imposed on income within that category.

There are principally two types of foreign tax credits available to U.S. Franchisor: tax credits allowed on a direct income tax or tax credits allowed on an indirect income tax that is attributed to the earnings that are distributed from a 10 percent or greater owned (by vote) foreign subsidiary. Direct tax credits are provided under Sections 901 and 903 of the IRS Code and arise when an income tax is imposed directly on a U.S. taxpayer. A typical example of a Section 901 direct tax is a foreign tax on net income imposed on a branch operation of U.S. Franchisor operating in the Foreign Franchisee's country of operation. Another form of a direct foreign tax credit is a withholding tax imposed on dividends, interest, rents, or royalties received by U.S. Franchisor from Foreign Franchisee.[35]

Indirect foreign tax credits are allowed for income and withholding taxes that are imposed on the income of lower-tier subsidiaries. These taxes may be claimed as a credit under Section 902, as discussed in Section IV.F. of this chapter, when U.S. Franchisor receives a dividend from lower-tier subsidiaries. To obtain the credit, however, U.S. Franchisor must own 10 percent or more of the voting stock of the subsidiary.[36]

1. Choice of Credit or Deduction

The choice of claiming a foreign income tax credit or deducting the foreign income taxes is made annually and can be changed each year without IRS permission.[37] Normally, it is more advantageous to claim a credit for foreign income taxes. However, in a loss year when no U.S. tax liability exists and it is projected that the credits will not be utilized in "carryover years," it may be desirable to deduct foreign taxes to create or increase a net operating loss, which then can be carried back or forward to other tax years over a longer period.[38] An indirect or deemed paid credit cannot be deducted. A taxpayer cannot claim a credit for some eligible foreign taxes and a deduction for other eligible foreign taxes in the same taxable year.[39]

2. *Allowable Foreign Tax Credits*

The local country tax law imposing the tax must be examined to determine if the foreign tax will qualify as a creditable tax. Specifically, the foreign levy must satisfy the definition of a tax and the predominant character of the tax must be an income tax.[40] To qualify as a creditable tax, the foreign levy must meet the following criteria: (1) the levy is not compensation to the foreign government for a specific economic benefit;[41] (2) the levy is likely to reach net gain;[42] and (3) the levy requires a compulsory payment pursuant to the authority of a foreign jurisdiction to levy taxes.[43]

If a foreign levy includes a compulsory payment in exchange for a specific economic benefit, the levy is considered to be comprised of two elements: a tax and a payment in exchange for specific economic benefits.[44] Taxpayers making such payments are considered "dual-capacity" taxpayers. Only the amount of the levy that is considered a tax is creditable.[45]

The foreign tax also must be considered likely to reach net gain. Generally, this test is met if the tax is based on an event that constitutes the realization of income and is imposed on the basis of gross receipts reduced by expenses.[46] A foreign tax is not creditable if the tax liability is dependent on the ability of the taxpayer to obtain a foreign tax credit in the United States.[47] In addition, an amount of tax paid is not a creditable tax to the extent it is used, directly or indirectly, to provide a subsidy to the taxpayer, to a related person, to any party to the transaction, or to any party to a related transaction.[48]

If a tax does not qualify as a tax on net income, the tax may still represent a creditable income tax if it is a tax imposed in lieu of an income tax.[49] In such a case, the tax must be imposed in substitution for and not in addition to an income tax or series of income taxes otherwise generally imposed. The most common example of an "in lieu of" tax is a withholding tax imposed on gross income, such as royalties, rents, interest, and dividends. These taxes will often be imposed on cross-border royalty payments if the licensor does not conduct business operations in the payor's country. Absent imposing such a tax, the payor's country would lose its tax base because the licensee generally receives a tax deduction for the royalty payment to the cross-border licensor. Thus, a withholding tax is imposed on the licensee on the royalty income. The franchisee operates as the withholding agent for the tax, withholds the applicable tax from the franchise fee, and remits the withholding tax to the local government.

3. Limitation on Foreign Tax Credit: Section 904

As noted above, a foreign tax credit is allowed only to the extent of the U.S. tax imposed on foreign source income. This restriction on the use of foreign tax credits is generally referred to as the "Section 904 limitation." This limitation is best expressed by the following fraction:

$$\frac{\text{Foreign Source Taxable Income}}{\text{Worldwide Taxable Income}} \quad X \quad \begin{array}{c}\text{U.S. Tax}\\ \text{Liability}\\ \text{Before Credits}\end{array}$$

The Section 904 limitation is applied separately to various categories of foreign source income to limit the averaging of high-taxed foreign source income with low-taxed foreign source income. Creditable foreign taxes that cannot be used in a current year, due to the operation of Section 904(a), can be carried back two years and forward five years.[50] In the year of application, the creditable foreign taxes arising in that year are applied first, and the credit carryover is then applied to the extent it is allowable under the Section 904 limitation.[51]

Section 904(d)(1) states that separate foreign tax credit limitations must be computed for the following categories of foreign source income:

- passive income;
- high withholding tax interest;
- financial services income;
- shipping income;
- dividends from 10 to 50 percent owned foreign subsidiaries;
- Domestic International Sales Corporation (DISC) dividends;
- Foreign Sales Corporation (FSC) income attributable to foreign trade income;
- FSC dividends; and
- general limitation income.[52]

These separate categories are sometimes referred to as "baskets." For franchising purposes, general limitation is the most important category of income because it includes all foreign source income that is not included in any of the other separately enumerated Section 904(d) limitation categories discussed below.[53] In most cases, this category will include most of the operating income derived by U.S. Franchisor from its franchise operations with foreign franchisees. This category of income generally includes income subject to relatively high foreign taxes. Tax advisors look to generate lower-taxed foreign source income to include in this category to "cross-credit" the high-taxed foreign source income with low-taxed foreign source income. Cross-crediting is merely the averaging of high-taxed income with low-taxed income in the same foreign tax credit limitation category. This averaging allows foreign taxes imposed at rates in excess of the U.S. tax rate to offset the U.S. tax on foreign source income that is subject to foreign tax at a rate below the U.S. tax rate. The impact of cross-crediting is the reduction of the overall effective rate of tax reported by U.S. Franchisor.

Passive income is generally defined as any income included in the definition of foreign personal holding company income under Section 954(c).[54] Passive income includes dividends, interest, rents, royalties, gains from the sale of stock and certain capital assets, net currency gains, net commodity gains, and income equivalent to interest.[55] Although royalties from third parties would normally be characterized as passive income, U.S. Franchisor may rely on an important exception. Generally, if the income is derived from third parties and is from the active conduct of a licensing business in which U.S. Franchisor develops or markets the intangible property, the income is treated as general limitation income. This exception, however, requires that sufficient activities be performed by the taxpayer with respect to the development or marketing of the intangible.[56] By including the income in the general limitation category, it may be averaged with other types of franchising income, thereby increasing the opportunity for cross-crediting.

Other categories of income that may be earned by U.S. Franchisor include high withholding tax interest[57] and dividend income from noncontrolled subsidiaries. For this purpose, a noncontrolled subsidiary is a foreign subsidiary in which all 10 percent or greater (by vote) U.S. shareholders own less that 50 percent of the vote and value of the stock, either directly, indirectly through a chain of companies, or through attribution from related parties ("10/50 companies").[58] The dividends received from each 10/50 company are subject to a separate Section 904 limitation on a company-by-company basis.[59] Thus, the dividend income and corresponding foreign tax credits from one 10/50 company cannot be combined with dividend income from another 10/50 company. Thus, there is no cross crediting for dividends from 10/50 companies.

Note that effective for taxable years of U.S. Franchisor beginning after December 31, 1997, a dividend from a controlled foreign corporation that is paid from earnings derived when the corporation qualified as a controlled foreign corporation but before the U.S. shareholder owned the stock will receive look-through treatment, rather than 10/50 company treatment.[60] For taxable years beginning in 2003, the pre-2003 earnings for all separate 10/50 category earnings will be combined into a single category of income and look-through rules will apply.[61]

4. Allocation of Deductions

The Section 904 limitation on the foreign tax credit restricts the amount of the credit to the U.S. tax imposed on the foreign source taxable income within a given category of income listed above. After gross income is allocated according to these categories, deductions must be allocated or apportioned to the various categories of income in order to calculate the taxable income in each category. The following discussion is a summary of the rules for allocating deductions to the various categories of foreign source income and to U.S. source income. As a general rule, a U.S. corporation seeks to claim the greatest amount of foreign source taxable income to avoid restricting its ability to claim foreign tax credits. The IRS Code requires that for purposes of computing taxable income from U.S. or foreign sources there shall be deducted the expenses, losses, or other deductions properly apportioned or allocated thereto and a ratable part of any expenses, losses, or other deductions that cannot definitely be allocated to some item or class of gross income.[62]

In general, all expenses, losses, and other deductions must be allocated and apportioned among the various classes of gross income, and between the statutory and residual groupings.[63] Expenses are charged against gross income in a two-step process: first, expenses are allocated to the classes of gross income to which the expenses are definitely related; then, the expenses are apportioned within each class among statutory and residual groupings of gross income as determined by the relevant operative sections of the IRS Code.[64] Other expenses that are allocated under the consolidated method include stewardship or supportive expenses, research and experimentation expenses, and legal and accounting expenses.[65]

a. Interest Expense Allocation. One of the most challenging areas of expense allocation is the treatment of interest expense incurred by U.S. Franchisor. Under the fungibility concept, interest expense is considered related to all income producing activities and assets of the taxpayer. The method of allocation and apportionment of interest expense is based on the approach that money is fungible and that interest expense is attributable to all activities and property regardless of any specific purpose for incurring an obligation on which interest is paid. This approach recognizes that all activities require funds and that management has flexibility as to the source and use of funds. Generally, when money is borrowed for a specific purpose, such borrowing will free other funds for other purposes.[66]

The concept that capital is fungible, as adopted by the regulations, implies that interest normally relates more closely to the amount of capital utilized or invested in an activity or property than to the gross income generated from it. Therefore, interest expense is generally apportioned on the basis of asset values and not gross income.[67] After assets have been separated between domestic and foreign assets (as well as among the separate Section 904(d) categories), interest is apportioned between the various Section 904(d) categories and U.S. source income according to the percentage of assets in each category compared to total assets.

The regulations divert from the asset-based apportionment concept in three areas: certain nonrecourse indebtedness transactions; certain integrated financial transactions; and, subject to various limitations, transactions where U.S. Franchisor borrows from third parties and loans to its controlled foreign corporations.[68] The nonrecourse financing and the integrated financial transaction exceptions are generally helpful, but they are narrowly applicable.[69] The third exception for loans to controlled foreign corporations is harmful to the foreign tax credit position if certain thresholds are exceeded because, if U.S. Franchisor borrows in the United States and lends to its controlled foreign corporations, a portion of the interest expense incurred by the U.S. corporation may be specifically allocated against the interest income paid by the controlled foreign corporation. This specific allocation of U.S. interest expense to interest income from controlled foreign corporation loans will only occur if there is an increase in indebtedness to controlled foreign corporations (related group indebtedness) and an increase in indebtedness of the U.S. corporation (U.S. shareholder indebtedness) over such amounts computed for a five-year base period.[70] The value of the related U.S. shareholder's total assets within each separate limitation category is then reduced by the principal amount of the shareholder's third-party indebtedness that is allocated to assets in that particular category.[71] The regulations, however, do provide an exception to this rule allowing loans to controlled foreign corporations up to 10 percent of the total asset values of all controlled foreign corporations.[72]

b. Allocation of Research and Experimentation Expenditures. Treasury Regulation Section 1.861-17 requires allocation of research and experimentation (R&E) expenses in accordance with income earned in three-digit SIC code categories. R&E expenses are allocated as though all members of an affiliated group are a single corporation.[73] U.S. Franchisor may elect either the sales method or the gross income method for the first taxable year beginning in 1996.[74] Under the sales method, 50 percent of R&E expense is apportioned to the geographic location (U.S. or foreign) where more than 50 percent of the R&E is performed. The remainder is allocated based on sales. If there is no location where more than 50 percent of total R&E is performed, then all R&E expense is allocated based on sales. Special rules are provided for including related and unrelated party sales.[75]

Under the gross income method, 25 percent of U.S. Franchisor's R&E expense is allocated to the place where more than 50 percent of the R&E is performed. The remainder is allocated based on gross income. The R&E allocated to foreign source income under this method must be at least 50 percent of the amount allocated to foreign source income under the sales method.[76] Specific allocation of expenses to particular classes of income is possible where the R&E is mandated to meet legal requirements imposed by a political entity and the results of the R&E cannot reasonably be anticipated to generate income outside of the geographic location imposing the requirement.[77]

c. Charitable Contributions. Current regulations provide that charitable contributions shall be treated as deductions that are not definitely related to any gross income and, therefore, are to be ratably apportioned on the basis of gross income.[78] Under proposed regulations, a deduction for charitable contributions is allocated solely to U.S. source income or solely to foreign source gross income in certain circumstances. If U.S. Franchisor, at the time of the contribution, designates the contribution for use solely in the United States and U.S. Franchisor reasonably believes the contribution will be so used, the proposed regulations allow the deduction to be allocated to U.S. source income.[79] When, at the time of the contribution, U.S. Franchisor knows or has reason to know the contribution will be used solely outside the United States, or the contribution may necessarily be used outside the United States, the proposed regulations require the deduction to be allocated to foreign source gross income.[80]

d. Stewardship Expenses. Stewardship expenses represent expenses incurred by a parent company in the oversight of its subsidiary. These expenses are not operating expenses of the parent company or the subsidiary. Rather, stewardship expenses are generally duplicative from a business perspective, as they represent expenses reviewing and protecting the investment in a subsidiary and not related to its operations. As with the other expenses, stewardship expenses are apportioned as if all members of the affiliated group were a single taxpayer. If members of the group, other than the member that incurred the stewardship expense, receive or may receive dividends, all such members (even though fewer than all the members of the group) are treated as a single corporation.[81]

e. Supportive Expenses. Supportive expenses (that is, overhead, general and administrative, and supervisory expenses) may relate to other deductions and may be allocated and apportioned along with those deductions.[82] Alternatively, supportive expenses may be allocated to all or a broad class of gross income of the member that incurred the expense. However, to the extent such expenses are not directly allocable to a specific activity or property of the member incurring the expense, the expenses must be allocated and apportioned as if all members of the affiliated group to whom the expenses relate were a single corporation.[83]

f. State Income Taxes. The expense allocation regulations further specify that expenses related to state, local, and foreign income, war profits, and excess profits taxes are considered definitely related and allocable to the gross income with respect to which the taxes are imposed.[84]

g. Allocation of Losses from the Disposition of Personal Property. Regulations issues under Section 865 prescribe rules for allocating losses from the disposition of stock and other personal property. As a general rule, this regulation provides that losses with respect to stock are allocated to the same class of income to which gain on the stock (other than gain treated as a dividend under Section 1248) would give rise in the hands of the seller. This rule generally provides for sourcing a loss according to the residence of the seller.[85] If the stock loss is attributed to a foreign office, however, the loss is allocated to foreign source income if a gain on the sale of the stock would be taxed by the foreign country and the highest marginal tax rate is at least 10 percent.[86]

Anti-abuse rules were included in the final and temporary regulations that are designed to prevent the tax-free movement of stock or other personal property prior to recognition of a loss to obtain a change in allocation of the loss; or the recognition of a domestic source loss that is offset by a corresponding foreign source income transaction.[87]

h. Expense Allocation Planning Opportunities. In analyzing its foreign tax credit position, U.S. Franchisor must regularly monitor its allocation of expenses. In particular, the company should consider making loans to its controlled foreign corporations up to the amount of the 10 percent safe harbor under Treasury Regulation Section 1.861-10. In addition, a loss incurred from the disposition of stock or other personal property as well as operating losses should be analyzed to determine if they can be characterized as a U.S. source loss.

It may be possible to mitigate the impact of the interest allocation rules by leasing assets rather than borrowing and purchasing assets. Economically, a lease expense clearly represents, in part, a payment attributable to the time value of money. The interest allocation regulations, however, do not require an asset-based apportionment of lease expense.[88]

If a taxpayer does not have sufficient foreign source income to fully utilize its foreign tax credits and for interest allocation purposes it is using the tax book value method for valuing assets, it should consider electing the fair market value method of interest allocation. While this method of valuation does require appraisal of a taxpayer's worldwide assets, it should be considered because it often provides a substantially better interest allocation result.

5. Section 904(f) Loss Recapture

Expenses are allocated to categories of income even if there is no income in a particular category.[89] Therefore, interest allocation and other expenses allocated to a category of income may result in a loss in a particular category. A loss in one category of foreign source income offsets foreign source income in another category before it reduces U.S. source income. If foreign losses reduce U.S. income, an overall foreign loss (OFL) is created and subsequent foreign source income is recharacterized ("recaptured") as U.S. source income. Additionally, loss recapture also occurs between categories of income.[90]

6. Other Pitfalls and Planning Under Section 904

Section 904(d)(3) allows look-through treatment with respect to certain payments received from a controlled foreign corporation. Interest, rents, and royalties paid either between controlled foreign corporations or from a controlled foreign corporation to a U.S. shareholder will be characterized according to the category of income the expense reduced at the controlled foreign corporation level. Dividend distributions are allocated according to the proportionate amount of earnings of the distributing controlled foreign corporation in each category of income under Section 904(d).[91] These look-through rules are important in tracking the different category of income paid in transactions involving related controlled foreign corporations and are often used to generate sufficient foreign source income to utilize foreign tax credits.

As noted above, foreign source income may be recharacterized as U.S. source income if prior foreign losses have been utilized to reduce U.S. source taxable income. This recharacterization is usually detrimental because the U.S. tax on the recharacterized U.S. source income can not be reduced by foreign tax credits. Recapture may be beneficial, however, in a year in which there is U.S. loss and foreign source income.[92] Foreign source income may also be characterized as U.S. source income where a controlled foreign corporation conducts U.S. operations and generates U.S. source income. This structure, however, is not optimal in most circumstances from an income tax perspective.

7. Gross-Up Clauses

The impact of these complex foreign tax credit rules often causes a franchisor to request a gross-up fee attributable to withholding taxes imposed on a franchise fee. A gross-up is generally computed as an amount of additional franchise fee sufficient to compensate ("gross-up") the franchisor for the cost of withholding tax imposed on the franchise fee. Assuming the Foreign Franchisee's country of residence imposes a 10 percent withholding tax on a franchise fee of $500,000, the total amount of the franchise fee sufficient to provide the franchisor with $500,000 after imposition of the withholding tax is $555,556. This grossed-up franchise fee is calculated by multiplying the base amount of the franchise fee ($500,000) by the fraction 1/(1 – the withholding tax rate). Under this example, the grossed-up franchise fee is calculated as follows: $555,556 = $500,000 / .90. The $55,556 gross-up is often a sticking point in negotiations between the parties.

Some franchisees request that the franchise agreement provide that the gross-up adjustment be reduced (or reimbursed) to the extent U.S. Franchisor obtains a foreign tax credit for the withholding tax. The foreign tax credit is determined according to the aggregate categories of income described above. As illustrated in the complex foreign tax credit provisions described above, it is often difficult, if not impossible, to determine on a per item basis whether or not U.S. Franchisor obtains a foreign tax credit for an amount of withholding tax imposed on a particular franchise fee. In addition, U.S. Franchisor may not wish to disclose to its franchisees the operational results necessary to verify the amount of the foreign tax credit claimed. Given these considerations, U.S. Franchisor and Foreign Franchisee may negotiate a reduced amount of gross-up to generally account for the impact of the foreign tax credit.

IV. Franchise Revenue Earned by a Foreign Subsidiary of a U.S. Corporation

A. STRUCTURE EXAMPLE

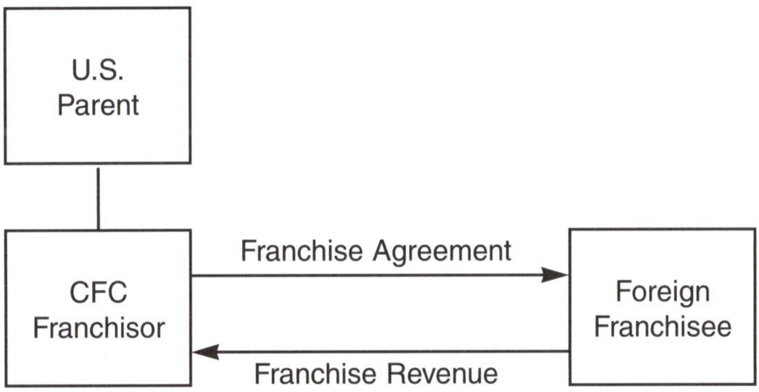

1. Facts

Assume U.S. Parent, a corporation organized in the United States, owns 100 percent of the stock of CFC Franchisor, a corporation organized outside the United States. CFC Franchisor executes a franchise agreement with Foreign Franchisee, an unrelated corporation organized and operating outside the United States.

2. Issues

a. *Organization:* Is the transfer of assets by U.S. Parent to the foreign subsidiary a taxable event?
b. *Deferral:* Is the income earned by the foreign subsidiary currently taxable to U.S. Parent as a deemed dividend?
c. Will the foreign income tax imposed on the earnings of the foreign subsidiary qualify as a creditable foreign tax to reduce the U.S. tax liability of U.S. Parent when the earnings are distributed (or deemed distributed) to U.S. Parent?

B. ORGANIZING A FOREIGN SUBSIDIARY

In making the decision to engage in franchising activities through a foreign corporation, the U.S. Parent establishes a CFC Franchisor, which will likely be taxable in one or more foreign countries. The formation of the company may result in a taxable transaction for U.S. tax purposes because assets are being transferred to a foreign corporation. Secondly, certain income of CFC Franchisor may be subject to current U.S. taxation as a deemed dividend if the income qualifies as "Subpart F" income under the Code.

If a U.S. person transfers assets to a foreign corporation in a transaction that would not otherwise result in gain recognition, Section 367(a)(1) states that, unless otherwise provided in regulations, taxable gain is triggered on the outbound transfer. Exceptions are provided for transfers of certain assets used in an active trade or business conducted outside the United States.[93] Certain property is treated as "tainted" property, however, and is not eligible for tax-free treatment, even if it meets the active trade or business exception. Tainted property includes inventory, trademarks, copyrights or similar property, installment obligations, accounts receivable or other similar property, foreign currency, intangible property, and certain leased property.[94] In the case of business assets that have been depreciated or amortized in the United States, the depreciation and amortization deductions attributable to the U.S. usage of those assets is recaptured at the time the assets are transferred to the foreign subsidiary.[95]

Significant tax may therefore result from contributing intangible assets, such as trademarks, to a foreign subsidiary.[96] In addition, allowing a subsidiary the right to use intangibles without compensation may be treated as a deemed capital contribution of the intangible asset to the foreign subsidiary. Section 367(d) acts as a penalty imposed on a U.S. taxpayer that transfers intangibles to a foreign corporation in a transaction that would otherwise be a nontaxable contribution or reorganization. Generally, a transfer of an intangible asset is treated as a deemed sale of the intangible in exchange for installment payments that are contingent upon the future use of the intangible.[97]

The foreign subsidiary's resident country is unlikely to allow a deduction for the deemed income required to be recognized for U.S. income tax purposes. Absent this deduction, the deemed annual inclusion under Section 367(d) may result in double taxation of the inclusion if the U.S. tax on this income is not offset by excess foreign tax credits. From a practical perspective, Section 367(d) requires U.S. Parent to license its intangibles to a foreign corporation rather than contribute the intangible to the capital of the subsidiary. If the license is not a sham transaction it should be respected, and Section 367(d) would not apply.[98]

C. TAX CONSEQUENCES TO SHAREHOLDERS OF A CONTROLLED FOREIGN CORPORATION

This section (Section C) provides a summary of the tax consequences to the U.S. shareholder of CFC Franchisor with respect to deemed and actual dividends from CFC Franchisor. Sections D, E, and F of this chapter provide an expanded discussion of these issues.

If CFC Franchisor satisfies the definition of a controlled foreign corporation and U.S. Parent owns CFC Franchisor stock for at least thirty days during its taxable year, then U.S. Parent must include in gross income its pro rata share of the corporation's tainted (Subpart F) income for the year.[99] Thus, income earned by CFC Franchisor from offshore franchise transactions may be currently taxed as a deemed dividend to U.S. Parent. The tax may be imposed even though no actual dividend is paid to U.S. Parent.

A controlled foreign corporation is a foreign corporation that has more than 50 percent of the voting power or value of its stock owned by U.S. shareholders. In determining this more than 50 percent threshold, only U.S. shareholders owning 10 percent or greater voting stock are taken into account.[100] Constructive ownership rules apply to attribute ownership of stock held by related parties.[101]

1. Deemed Dividends Under Subpart F

If U.S. Parent owns the stock of CFC Franchisor on the last day of its taxable year and CFC Franchisor qualified as a controlled foreign corporation for at least thirty consecutive days during the taxable year, then U.S. Parent must include in its gross income as a deemed dividend the Subpart F income earned by CFC Franchisor as well as any increase in earnings invested in U.S. property.[102] The amount of an inclusion of Subpart F income is limited to the controlled foreign corporation's current year earnings and profits.[103] The excess of Subpart F income over current year earnings and profits is carried forward and causes non-Subpart F income in subsequent years to be recharacterized as Subpart F income.[104]

If CFC Franchisor earns Subpart F income that is taxable as a deemed dividend to U.S. Parent, then a distribution of those earnings in a later year should not be subject to U.S. taxation again.[105] A distribution of previously taxed income from CFC Franchisor to U.S. Parent, however, will likely result in currency gain or loss recognized equal to the difference between the dollar amount of the Subpart F income compared to the dollar value of the earnings distributed as previously taxed income. This currency gain or loss is included as ordinary income or loss in U.S. Parent's gross income for the taxable year of the distribution.[106]

2. *Dividend Planning*

Dividends received from a lower-tier subsidiary are included in the receiving corporation's earnings and profits. As described in Section F below, a corporate shareholder may claim a deemed paid foreign tax credit with respect to foreign income taxes on earnings distributed from certain lower-tier subsidiaries. The effective tax rate on a dividend received by a U.S. shareholder through tiers of lower-tier controlled foreign corporations reflects an average effective tax rate for the chain of corporations. This average effective tax rate will impact the foreign tax credit claimed by the U.S. shareholder with respect to the dividend income received.[107] Taxpayers can take advantage of this averaging of earnings and foreign taxes by paying a distribution through a chain of corporations. By distributing through the chain, the averaging of the effective tax rate may either dilute a high tax rate (for example, decrease the effective tax rate of a high-tax foreign corporation [HTFC] by paying a dividend from a low-taxed subsidiary of HTFC to HTFC) or increase the effective tax rate of a foreign corporation's earnings.

Alternatively, taxpayers could avoid the averaging of effective tax rates by making a loan from a lower-tier controlled foreign corporation (that is, not a first-tier controlled foreign corporation) directly to its indirect U.S. shareholder. Such a loan would be treated as an indirect distribution of the earnings of the controlled foreign corporation making the loan to the indirect U.S. shareholder. The loan would be taxable as a deemed dividend directly from the controlled foreign corporation and no averaging of effective tax rates with upper-tier subsidiaries would occur.[108] The importance of these two alternatives is to provide U.S. Parent with options as to the manner in which it effectuates the repatriation of certain foreign earnings. An actual distribution up the chain of controlled foreign corporations would likely have a different foreign tax credit result than if a lower-tier controlled foreign corporation made a loan directly to U.S. Franchisor, which would be taxable as a deemed dividend directly from the lending subsidiary.

D. CATEGORIES OF SUBPART F INCOME

Subpart F income, which is currently taxed as a deemed dividend, is defined in Section 952(a) as the sum of the following:

- foreign base company income under Section 954;
- insurance income under Section 953;
- international boycott income under Section 952(a)(3);
- bribes and other illegal payments under Section 952(a)(4); and
- Section 901(j) country income under Section 952(a)(5).

The most common form of Subpart F income derived in regular business operations is foreign base company income, which is further divided into the following categories under Section 954(a): foreign personal holding company income, foreign base company sales income, foreign base company services income, foreign base company shipping income, and foreign base company oil-related income.

1. Foreign Personal Holding Company Income

CFC Franchisor must review its franchise income to determine if it earns foreign personal holding company income (FPHCI) that will be currently taxed as a deemed dividend to U.S. Parent. FPHCI consists of income that is considered more passive in nature or easily transported to a low-taxed jurisdiction. FPHCI is defined to include dividends, interest, rents, royalties and annuities, net gain from certain property transactions, net gain from commodities transactions, net foreign currency gains, income equivalent to interest, net income from notional principal contracts and payments in lieu of dividends under Section 1058 securities transactions.[109]

Dividends and interest from related persons may be excluded from the definition of FPHCI if the dividends satisfy the "same country" dividend exception. Under this exception, dividends and interest from "related" persons[110] are excluded if the payor is organized under the laws of the same foreign country as the controlled foreign corporation recipient and more than 50 percent of the payor's assets is used in a trade or business in that foreign country. Further, the earnings and profits to which a dividend is attributable must have been earned when the above requirements were met.[111]

The restrictions placed on the same country dividend exception are also a reason why the Section 338 election, which generally provides a step-up in the basis of the assets acquired for U.S. tax purposes, is generally beneficial when acquiring a foreign corporation. For example, assume a U.S. company anticipates the acquisition of a foreign corporation by acquiring the stock and making a Section 338 election. The election eliminates the earnings and profits of the company and gives a fair market value basis in its assets, including its goodwill, an amortizable asset for U.S. tax purposes. Converting the foreign corporation to a branch or a partnership for U.S. tax purposes would give additional benefits. Upon conversion of the entity to a branch or partnership, this stepped-up basis in these assets, including goodwill, is brought into the U.S. tax return and amortization of the goodwill is possible against the current U.S. tax liability. Alternatively, if the entity is left as a foreign corporation, the goodwill amortization is deductible for earnings and profits purposes but may not be a deduction for local tax purposes. This Section 338 election will increase the effective tax rate of these earnings and the taxpayer must be able to utilize the excess foreign tax foreign tax credits resulting from the increased foreign effective rate of taxation.

FPHCI does not include rents or royalties from a payor that is a related person if the rents or royalties are for the use of, or the privilege of using, property within the country in which the controlled foreign corporation recipient of the payments is created or organized.[112] Rents and royalties are not excluded from foreign personal holding company income to the extent that the related party payor claimed deductions for the payments and allocated the deductions in a manner that reduced the foreign base company income or other Subpart F income of the payor.[113] Rents and royalties are also excluded from foreign personal holding company income if the income is derived by the controlled foreign corporation in the active conduct of a trade or business and is received from an unrelated person (a person other than a related person as defined in Section 954(d)(3)).

Franchise income is often predominantly characterized as royalty income. If a portion of the franchise fees paid by Foreign Franchisee to CFC Franchisor is characterized as royalty income, the income will be treated as active trade or business income only to the extent CFC Franchisor engages in the active conduct of either the production of the intangible assets being licensed or the marketing of the intangible assets to third parties.[114]

FPHCI also includes the excess of gains over losses from the sale or exchange of property that gives rise to dividends, interest, rents, royalties, annuities, or passive investment assets that produce no current income and are held for resale. This category is often important if CFC Franchisor disposes of stock of a lower-tier foreign subsidiary. Gain on the sale of the stock of a controlled foreign corporation is first characterized as a dividend to CFC Franchisor, to the extent of the subsidiary's earnings.[115] If the gain on the sale of the subsidiary exceeds the amount of the earnings of the subsidiary, then the gain is taxable as Subpart F income. In general, all capital gain transactions executed by CFC Franchisor must be examined to determine if they constitute foreign personal holding company income. There is a broad exception for capital gains from the sale of assets used in CFC Franchisor's active trade or business.

Except for certain currency gains derived in conjunction with active business transactions or hedging transactions, income related to currency gains and losses and income from financial derivative transactions are included in the definition of FPHCI. In general, the excess of foreign currency gains over losses attributable to any Section 988 transactions (that is, certain transactions in a nonfunctional currency of CFC Franchisor) is included in the definition of FPHCI.[116] Income equivalent to interest is also included in FPHCI. This income is derived from investment transactions in which the payment, cash flow, or return on investment predominantly reflects the time value of money and transactions in which payments are for the use of money but are not generally treated as interest.[117] Notional principal contract income is generally included in Subpart F income; however, transactions executed as hedges for active trade or business transactions are excluded from FPHCI. In addition, a hedge of another category of FPHCI is not included in the notional principal contract income category; rather, the income, gain, deduction, or loss from such hedges is included in that other category of FPHCI.

2. Foreign Base Company Sales Income

If CFC Franchisor executes sales transactions involving related parties, the income derived in connection with the sale may constitute Subpart F income. Foreign base company sales income is the category of Subpart F income that includes income, such as profits, commissions, or fees, derived from (1) the purchase of personal property from a related person and its sale to anyone; (2) the sale of personal property to anyone on behalf of a related person; (3) the purchase of personal property from anyone and its sale to a related person; and (4) the purchase of personal property from anyone on behalf of a related person.

Certain important exceptions apply to exclude income from this category. Specifically, income derived in connection with property that is manufactured by CFC Franchisor; property that is manufactured, produced, or grown in the same country as CFC Franchisor is organized; or property that is sold for use, consumption, or final disposition in the same country as Foreign Franchisor.[118]

If CFC Franchisor invests in a partnership interest, the income derived by the partnership must be analyzed for Subpart F purposes. Partnerships owned by controlled foreign corporations raise issues as to whether the Subpart F rules are applied at the partnership level (the entity theory of partnership taxation) or at the partner level (the aggregate theory of partnership taxation). In Revenue Ruling 89-72,[119] the IRS held that a controlled foreign corporation's distributive share of partnership sales income will be treated as foreign base company sales income. In the ruling, the IRS stated that for purposes of Subpart F, the character of an item of income includes the attributes of such income, including whether the person from whom the goods are purchased is a related person with respect to the controlled foreign corporation partner and whether the sale occurs outside the controlled foreign corporation partner's country of incorporation.[120] While similar rulings have been issued in other areas, this is an uncertain area of Subpart F income. The uncertainty of the area was increased by proposed regulations applying different aggregate and entity theories of taxation for various categories of Subpart F income and exceptions to Subpart F income.[121]

3. Foreign Base Company Services Income

Foreign base company services income is income in the form of compensation, commissions, and fees derived from the performance of services on behalf of a related person and performed outside CFC Franchisor's country of organization. Services are performed on behalf of a related person if the CFC Franchisor is paid or reimbursed by a related person for performing services, if the CFC Franchisor performs services the related person was obligated to perform, or if CFC Franchisor performs services with substantial assistance from a related person.[122] A fee for the guaranty of performance paid to CFC Franchisor from a related person does not generate foreign base company services income if: (1) the related person's sole obligation is to guarantee performance; (2) CFC Franchisor is fully obligated to perform the services; and (3) the related person does not in fact perform any of the services or pay another person to perform the services or provide any substantial assistance to CFC Franchisor for performing the services.[123]

4. Insurance Income

Insurance income is defined as any income that is attributable to the issuing or reissuing of any insurance or contracts related to risks outside the controlled foreign corporation's country of incorporation, which would be taxed under Subchapter L if the company were a domestic corporation.[124] Insurance income derived by CFC Franchisor with respect to insuring the risks of a shareholder or a person related to a shareholder may be taxable as related-person insurance income. The U.S. shareholder ownership test for related-person insurance income is dropped to 25 percent or more rather than more than 50 percent otherwise used to determine controlled foreign corporation status. Additionally, there is no minimum 10 percent ownership threshold to be considered a U.S. shareholder. An exception is available, however, if less than 20 percent of the stock is held by persons insured by the company or by related parties. Elections are also available to tax the corporation similar to a U.S. corporation or to treat the insurance as effectively connected with a U.S. trade or business.[125]

5. *International Boycott Income and Illegal Payments*

Subpart F income includes income derived in connection with an international boycott income and income derived in connection with illegal bribes, kickbacks, or other payments made to government officials.[126]

6. De Minimis *and Full Inclusion Tests*

If the sum of gross foreign base company income and gross insurance income of CFC Franchisor is less than the lesser of 5 percent of its gross income or $1 million, then adjusted gross foreign base company income and insurance income are generally zero.[127] The *de minimis* exception does not apply to income from related-party factoring of trade and service receivables.[128] If the sum of gross foreign base company income and gross insurance income for the tax year exceeds 70 percent of CFC Franchisor's gross income, all of its gross income will be included in adjusted gross foreign base company income and insurance income.[129] Items of gross income included in adjusted gross income because of the full inclusion test are treated as "full inclusion foreign base company income" and are treated as a separate category of adjusted gross FBCI for purposes of allocating and apportioning deductions.[130]

7. *High Tax Exception*

An item of income is excluded from net foreign base company income if it meets the high taxed exception. Foreign base company oil-related income, however, is not eligible for the high tax exception. The high taxed exception applies if the item of income was subject to creditable foreign income taxes at an effective foreign tax rate that is greater than 90 percent of the maximum U.S. tax rate (31.5 percent under current corporate income tax rates) and if an election is made to exclude the income from Subpart F income.[131]

8. Effectively Connected U.S. Income Exception

Subpart F income does not include U.S. source income effectively connected with a U.S. trade or business, unless the item of income is exempt from tax or subject to a reduced rate of tax due to a tax treaty.[132]

9. Earnings and Profits: Limitation of Subpart F Income

The Subpart F income reported by CFC Franchisor and included in income of U.S. Parent as a deemed dividend is limited by the earnings and profits of CFC Franchisor.[133] CFC Franchisor may reduce its Subpart F income by certain prior year deficits in earnings and profits; however, the reductions are subject to limitations and conditions.[134] Post–1986 deficits may be applied in limited circumstances to reduce Subpart F income generated from the same "qualifying activities."[135] CFC Franchisor may elect to reduce the amount of its Subpart F income that is attributable to a qualified activity by the amount of any deficit of a "qualified chain member" for a taxable year ending with (or within) the taxable year of CFC Franchisor to the extent such deficit is attributable to the qualified activity. If a deficit is applied to another controlled foreign corporation under the chain deficit rule, it will not be available to shelter future Subpart F income of the qualified chain member as a qualified deficit.[136]

10. Recharacterization Provisions

In cases where CFC Franchisor's Subpart F income is limited due to the application of the earnings and profits limitation, non-Subpart F earnings earned by CFC Franchisor in any subsequent year of that corporation is recharacterized as Subpart F income and currently included in U.S. Parent's taxable income as a Subpart F deemed dividend.[137]

E. PLANNING TO AVOID CONTROLLED FOREIGN CORPORATION STATUS: DECONTROL

The application of the Subpart F rules only applies to controlled foreign corporations. Controlled foreign corporation status can be avoided if the U.S. shareholders do not have more than 50 percent voting power and do not own more than 50 percent of the total value of the corporation. This standard may be satisfied if the stock is widely held such that the 10 percent ownership requirement for U.S. shareholders status is not satisfied. Effective control of the foreign corporation can be maintained even if the literal terms of the statute are not met. Suppose, for example, ten U.S. investors want to set up and control a foreign corporation. If the corporation issues 1,000 shares of voting stock, each U.S. investor may be issued 99 shares and the remaining 10 voting shares may be issued to an unrelated investor. This keeps effective control of the foreign corporation in the ten U.S. persons. The ten U.S. persons do not meet the statutory requirements of being U.S. shareholders and, thus, the foreign corporation is not a controlled foreign corporation. If, however, artificial devices, such as informal agreements for voting stock, are used to transfer voting power away from U.S. shareholders, the IRS will look-through that arrangement to determine true control.[138] One caution: Additional anti-deferral provisions of the IRS Code apply to widely held foreign corporations.[139]

F. INVESTMENT OF EARNINGS IN U.S. PROPERTY

CFC Franchisor obtains the benefit of deferring its non-Subpart F income from current U.S. income taxation, provided that it reinvests its earnings outside the United States. This restriction on investing earnings outside the United States stems from the operation of the Section 956 investment in U.S. property rules.[140]

In general, an investment in U.S. property by a controlled foreign corporation is treated as a deemed dividend—similar to Subpart F income. The use of an investment in U.S. property, such as a loan to the domestic parent rather than the payment of a dividend, can avoid foreign withholding taxes in certain countries and allow the use of excess foreign tax credits. Taxpayers that affirmatively use Section 956 to repatriate earnings and foreign tax credits must consider the quarterly averaging in computing the amount of their deemed dividend for taxable years ending prior to the effective date of this change.

For Section 956 purposes, U.S. property is any property that is acquired by a foreign corporation during any tax year[141] that is (1) tangible property located in the United States; (2) stock of a domestic corporation; (3) an obligation of a U.S. person; or (4) certain intangible assets used in the United States.[142] The pledge or a guarantee of an obligation of a U.S. person by a foreign corporation is treated as if the foreign corporation held the obligation.[143] A trade or service receivable acquired from a related U.S. person, the obligor of which is a U.S. person, is U.S.

property notwithstanding the exceptions below.[144] Any right to the use, in the United States, of a patent, copyright, secret formula, a process, or any similar intellectual property is also treated as U.S. property for this purpose.[145]

A controlled foreign corporation is considered to hold indirectly the investments in U.S. property held on its behalf by a trustee or a nominee. This rule also applies at the discretion of the IRS district director to U.S. assets held by any other foreign corporation that is created or organized or funded, through capital contributions or debt, by a controlled foreign corporation if the other foreign corporation is controlled by the controlled foreign corporation and if one of the principal purposes of using the other foreign corporation is to avoid application of Section 956 with respect to the controlled foreign corporation. This rule effectively prevents a foreign corporation with significant earnings from establishing a new subsidiary with no earnings and profits to make an investment in U.S. property that is funded through a loan or capital contribution from its parent.[146]

In general, if CFC Franchisor loans to U.S. Parent, the loan must be outstanding on the quarter-end to be an investment in U.S. property. Accordingly, an obligation could be paid off just prior to quarter-end and a new obligation created after the start of the new quarter. In Rev. Rul. 89-73, 1989-1 C.B. 258, the IRS ruled that in certain situations it would look at the substance of the transaction rather than the form and treat roll over loans as one continuous loan, even if it is interrupted for relatively brief periods of time. Increases in the payable balances owed by U.S. Parent to CFC Franchisor represent earnings of a controlled foreign corporation invested in U.S. property and dividend income to the taxpayer.[147] The quarterly test for Section 956 purposes requires that intercompany accounts be reviewed at the end of each quarter.

G. DEEMED PAID FOREIGN TAX CREDITS: SECTION 902

The foreign tax credit analysis contained in the first example addressed the case where U.S. Parent operated a foreign branch or received foreign franchise payments directly. In the case of the foreign subsidiary, the franchise income is not earned directly by U.S. Parent. Rather, the income is recognized only when U.S. Parent receives a dividend from CFC Franchisor or when U.S. Parent recognizes a deemed dividend under Subpart F or Section 956. In the case of an actual or deemed dividend, the income will likely be taxed in the local country. If U.S. Parent does not receive the benefit of a foreign tax credit with respect to foreign income taxes paid by CFC Franchisor on the distributed earnings, then double taxation will occur. Section 902 prevents double taxation by allowing U.S. Parent to claim a deemed paid credit for foreign income taxes paid by CFC Franchisor.

In general, the deemed paid credit applies to foreign income taxes that are imposed on certain first through sixth-tier foreign corporations and that are passed up to U.S. corporate shareholders through dividend distributions from a first-tier foreign corporation in which the domestic corporation owns 10 percent or more of the voting stock and an indirect ownership test is satisfied with respect to lower-tier subsidiaries.[148]

The amount of the deemed paid foreign tax credit is equal to the proportionate amount of creditable income taxes imposed on the amount of the dividend. The amount of the deemed paid foreign tax credit is computed using the following formula:

$$\frac{\text{Dividends Received}}{\text{After-Tax Earnings and Profits}} \times \text{Creditable Foreign Taxes Paid} = \text{Deemed Paid Credit}$$

If U.S. Parent claims a deemed paid foreign tax credit for taxes paid by CFC Franchisor, it must include in gross income a gross-up amount equal to the amount of the deemed paid foreign tax credit. This amount is characterized as additional dividend income.[149]

For taxable years beginning after 1986, the computation of the deemed paid credit is made on a pooling basis. The earnings and profits within each separate foreign tax credit category of income and the foreign taxes attributable to such income are placed into a separate pool. Distributions are generally taken proportionately from each pool of income resulting in an averaging of credits over the different years' earnings in each pool. A separate deemed paid credit calculation is made for a distribution from each foreign tax credit category of income. For distributions from pre-1987 taxable years, the deemed paid foreign tax credit is computed on a year-by-year basis. There is no pooling of earnings for pre-1987 tax years. A pooling of earnings occurs for a foreign corporation in the first year beginning after 1986 in which there is a 10 percent or greater U.S. shareholder of the foreign corporation.[150]

H. SALE OF CFC FRANCHISOR: SECTION 1248

The gain realized by U.S. Parent on the sale of CFC Franchisor stock is recharacterized as a dividend to the extent of CFC Franchisor's post-1962 earnings and profits.[151] The dividend income is subject to the look-through rules that are particularly beneficial for foreign tax credit purposes.[152] Gain from the sale of a lower-tier controlled foreign corporation is treated in the same manner as if the stock was directly owned by a U.S. person, thereby allowing deemed dividend treatment on the sale of lower-tier shares. By recognizing a deemed dividend up to the amount of the earnings of the subsidiary, the selling corporation may be able to claim a deemed paid foreign tax credit for the taxes paid by the subsidiary being sold. This foreign tax credit relief greatly reduces the incidence of double taxation on the sale of lower-tier controlled foreign corporations. The same country exception from Subpart F income, however, does not apply to the deemed dividend recognized by a controlled foreign corporation.[153]

V. U.S. Taxation of Foreign Franchisor

A. STRUCTURE EXAMPLE

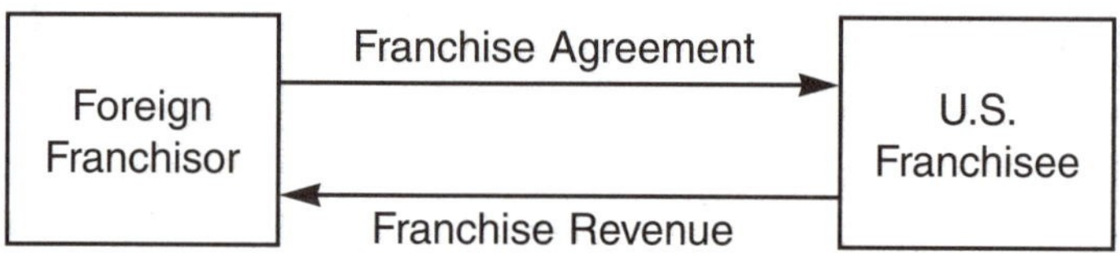

1. *Facts*

Foreign Franchisor, a corporation organized outside the United States, executes a franchise agreement with U.S. Franchisee, an unrelated corporation organized and doing business in the United States. U.S. Franchisee pays an annual franchise payment to Foreign Franchisor.

2. *Issues*

a. *Character of Income:* What is the character of the income derived under the franchise agreement?
b. Is the income effectively connected with the operation of a trade or business by Foreign Franchisor in the United States?
c. Is the income subject to 30 percent withholding tax?
d. Is the amount of the U.S. income tax reduced under an income tax treaty?

B. INTRODUCTION

Foreign Franchisor may be taxed in the United States under one of two separate tax regimes. If Foreign Franchisor is engaged in a U.S. trade or business, it is taxable on its net income that is treated as effectively connected with its U.S. trade or business. Only certain types of foreign source income are treated as effectively connected income. U.S. source income earned by Foreign Franchisor, on the other hand, is more likely to be treated as effectively connected with a U.S. trade or business. The second taxing regime only applies to U.S. source income derived by Foreign Franchisor that is not effectively connected with the conduct of a U.S. trade or business. This second taxing regime is a withholding tax imposed on certain types of U.S. source income.

Both taxing regimes are dependent on the character and source of the income derived by Foreign Franchisor. Thus, the first step in determining the U.S. tax imposed on Foreign Franchisor is to characterize and source the franchising revenue. The character and source rules discussed in Section I of this chapter are applied to determine the type and source of income derived from franchise fees paid by U.S. Franchisee.

The determination of whether Foreign Franchisor is engaged in a trade or business in the United States is crucial to determine the extent and manner in which the company will be taxed in the United States. If Foreign Franchisor is not treated as engaged in a U.S. trade or business it is nevertheless subject to 30 percent withholding tax on U.S. source fixed or determinable annual or periodical gains, profits, and income.[154] A foreign corporation engaged in a trade or business in the United States is subject to the ordinary U.S. corporate income tax on its net taxable income. If a U.S. tax return is filed in a timely manner, the corporation is entitled to offset its gross income by effectively connected deductions.[155]

C. CONDUCT OF A U.S. TRADE OR BUSINESS

Neither the Code nor its regulations define the term "trade or business."[156] The rules for determining whether other activities constitute a U.S. trade or business have been developed over the years through revenue rulings and judicial decisions. Consequently, the determination of whether the franchising activities of Foreign Franchisor constitute a U.S. trade or business is based on the facts and circumstances surrounding the U.S. activities.

The determination of whether a trade or business exists is measured by relatively objective standards. Engaging in "considerable, continuous, and regular" activity constitutes a trade or business. The passive collection of income does not constitute a U.S. trade or business. This standard was developed by the Second Circuit Court of Appeals in *Pinchot v. Comm'r*.[157] The court distinguished between real estate investment and a trade or business of managing real estate, noting that a trade or business required considerable, regular, and continuous activity. Most cases addressing the presence of a U.S. trade or business have continued to apply this standard. To constitute a U.S. trade or business, such activity must be conducted in the United States. In contrast, a single transaction generally does not amount to engaging in a U.S. trade or business.[158]

The amount of income earned, or loss incurred, is generally held to have no substantial bearing on the question of whether a foreign taxpayer is engaged in a U.S. trade or business. A foreign person may be engaged in a U.S. trade or business whether or not its activities show a profit. Two general factual trends emerge in the cases: a trade or business involves the active pursuit of business activity and the activity is continuous or regular.

U.S. trade or business status is determined for each taxable year. A foreign person is engaged in a U.S. trade or business if such person is so engaged at any time during the taxable year. Income or gain attributable to a sale or exchange of property or the performance of services in a particular year that is received in another year, however, will be treated as effectively connected income in the year of receipt if it would have been effectively connected income in the year to which it is attributable.[159] Gain from the disposition of any property that has been used or held for use in a U.S. trade or business within ten years of the trade or business ceasing its activities will be treated as effectively connected income if it would have been effectively connected income if the disposition had occurred immediately before the cessation of business.[160]

The following activities have been held to constitute a U.S. trade or business in IRS rulings:

- sales of goods in the United States;[161]
- sales in the United States by salesmen;[162]
- sales in the United States through an agent;[163]
- technical services in connection with sales of goods;[164]
- active management of leased U.S. real estate;[165]
- management of rental real estate through an agent;[166] and
- frequent purchases and sales of real estate.[167]

There are specific statutory rules imputing a trade or business for partnerships. A trade or business is imputed from a partnership to each partner and from a trust to its beneficiaries. It is noteworthy that in the case of a partnership this imputation would apply not only to a general partner but also to a limited partner.[168]

Although a foreign individual or corporation may not be present in the United States, a U.S. agent's business activity will be attributable to the foreign person or corporation for purposes of determining whether the foreign individual or corporation is engaged in a U.S. trade or business.[169] The amount of the agent's business undertaken for a foreign individual or corporation necessary to create a U.S. trade or business depends upon the facts and circumstances. However, in one case where over 90 percent of the agent's business was for a foreign corporation, the agent was held to be an exclusive agent and the foreign corporation was deemed to be conducting a U.S. trade or business through the agent.[170] Thus, the question may be both one of the authority of such agents or employees as well as their U.S. activities. Some measure of affirmative corporate activity is necessary to constitute engaging in or conducting a U.S. trade or business.

Certain personal services and securities transactions are excluded from the U.S. trade or business category are excluded. A nonresident alien who performs personal services within the United Sates is not considered to be engaged in a U.S. trade or business for a particular taxable year if: (1) the nonresident alien is not present in the United States for more than 90 days during such year; (2) the compensation does not exceed $3,000 for such year; and (3) the services are performed for a foreign person not engaged in a trade or business in the United States or for a foreign branch of a U.S. person's business.[171] Most U.S. tax treaties extend a broader exemption for temporary services than the exemption that is provided by the Code. These treaties also provide exemptions for income resulting from performance of "independent personal services" such as the practice of a profession.

Based on the specific facts considered, the following activities have been held not to constitute a U.S. trade or business in cases or IRS rulings:

- investigation of business opportunities in the United States;[172]
- mere ownership of rental real estate;[173]
- ownership of real estate subject to a net lease;[174]
- isolated sales of real estate;[175]
- holding securities for investment;[176]
- occasional sales of securities;[177] and
- fractional working interest in an oil and gas lease held via trust.[178]

D. U.S. SOURCE EFFECTIVELY CONNECTED INCOME

If the taxpayer is engaged in a U.S. trade or business, all U.S. source income other than certain fixed and determinable income and gains is automatically treated as effectively connected income whether or not it is related to a U.S. trade or business.[179] If a taxpayer is engaged in a U.S. trade or business, fixed or determinable income and capital gains from U.S. sources are effectively connected if they are deemed to be related to U.S. business activity.

1. Special Rules for Fixed or Determinable Income and Capital Gains

Two classes of income are subject to U.S. tax as effectively connected income only if they are related to U.S. business activity: (1) gain or loss from the sale or exchange of capital assets; and (2) fixed or determinable annual and periodical income, including interest, dividends, rents, and royalties.[180] Two factors are used to determine whether such income is effectively connected with a U.S. trade or business: (1) whether the income or loss is derived from assets used in the conduct of the trade or business, or (2) whether the activities of the trade or business were a material factor in the realization of the income, gain, or loss. These "asset-use" and "business activities" tests must be used to determine whether this income is effectively connected with a U.S. trade or business.[181]

a. Asset-Use Test. Assets held for use in a business are divided into three categories: (1) assets held for the principal purpose of promoting the present conduct of a trade or business; (2) assets acquired and held in the ordinary course of a trade or business; and (3) assets otherwise held in a direct relationship to a trade or business.[182] The income generated by working capital of a business is generally treated as effectively connected income. For example, the interest on bank deposits held for current operations or on accounts receivable is effectively connected income under this test. The third category includes assets held to meet operating expenses. However, assets held for future diversification, expansion, future plant replacement, or contingent events (that is, investment capital) do not give rise to effectively connected income. There is a presumption of a direct relationship to a business if assets are acquired with funds generated by the business. When dividends or interests are derived from U.S. sources by a U.S. manufacturing or selling branch, the asset-use test should be applied to determine the character of the income.[183]

b. Business Activities Test. Income is effectively connected under the business activities test if the activities of the business were a "material factor in its realization."[184] The performance of services in the United States is usually a "trade or business," therefore compensation for services is effectively connected income under this test. The business activities test has primary significance in testing the effectively connected income status of U.S. source fixed or determinable income that "arises directly from the active conduct of the taxpayer's trade or business."[185]

In this regard, if Foreign Franchisor conducts an active licensing business in the United States, it may be treated as operating a U.S. trade or business. Royalty income will be treated as income effectively connected with that trade or business if the business activities were a material factor in the realization of the royalty income.

2. *All Other U.S. Income*

Other U.S. source income that is not treated as effectively connected under the above two categories will nevertheless be treated as effectively connected with a U.S. trade or business.[186] This "force of attraction" rule includes U.S. source business profits, including all gains from the sales of goods, and various other types of income.

Once it is determined that Foreign Franchisor is engaged in a U.S. trade or business, all U.S. source income earned by Foreign Franchisor must be carefully reviewed. Any U.S. source income that is not subject to gross withholding tax or taxable as capital gain income will be treated as effectively connected with Foreign Franchisor's U.S. trade or business and will be subject to net income tax. Thus, if Foreign Franchisor sells products from its inventory to U.S. Franchisee with U.S. title passage, this income will also be treated as effectively connected to Foreign Franchisor's U.S. trade or business.[187]

E. *INVERWORLD* DECISION

In *InverWorld v. Comm'r*,[188] the Tax Court interpreted the regulations that apply to a foreign corporation with business activity in the United States. The case is significant because of its detailed analysis of whether the foreign corporation was conducting a U.S. trade or business through the activities of its U.S. subsidiary. The taxpayer in *InverWorld* was a Cayman Islands company, InverWorld, Ltd. (LTD), owned by principals of a Mexican investment firm. LTD owned indirectly 100 percent of InverWorld, Inc. (INC), a Delaware corporation with an office in San Antonio, Texas. LTD was formed to provide a vehicle for Mexicans to make various non-Mexican investments, such as investments in U.S. CDs, bank deposits, and other stocks and securities.

Services provided by LTD to its clients included, among other things, giving investment advice, executing and managing accounts, record keeping, and other currency transactions. Of the activities conducted by LTD, only soliciting clients and entering into investment contracts took place in Mexico. These activities were performed by InverMexico, a Mexican company owned by the same principals that owned LTD. The remaining activities took place in the United States and were performed by INC as an "independent contractor" under a consulting agreement with LTD. Under an agreement giving it the authority to act for LTD, INC purchased and sold securities and dealt in the name of LTD. All records of LTD were maintained by INC in the United States. A separate article of the consulting agreement provided that INC, for all purposes, was an independent contractor and not an agent or employee of LTD and that it had no authority to act for, represent, bind, or obligate LTD or any of its affiliates or any account managed or advised by LTD.[189]

The Tax Court determined that LTD was engaged in the active conduct of a banking or financing business in the United States and therefore was engaged in a U.S. trade or business.[190] The court concluded that INC was not independent because it was the exclusive agent of LTD and over 90 percent of its business was for services performed for LTD. The court held that the office of INC could be imputed to LTD.[191] Reviewing the agreement as a whole, the court determined that the authority given to INC in other parts of the agreement overrode the paragraph stating that INC did not have the power to act on behalf of or bind LTD. Thus, LTD did not qualify for the first exception from a U.S. trade or business because it was not trading through an independent agent and because it had a U.S. office.

The court determined that the activities conducted by LTD through INC in the United States were sufficiently regular, continuous, and extensive to constitute a U.S. trade or business under the applicable case law.[192] The court then determined that LTD's U.S. source income was effectively connected with a U.S. trade or business. Under the business activity test, the U.S. source income from the management fees, U.S. CDs and bank deposits, non-U.S. CDs and term loans, currency exchange transactions, and other commissions and fees was effectively connected income because LTD's activities, including activities conducted by its dependent agent, INC, were a material factor in the realization of income.[193]

In 1997, the court denied a motion to reconsider its original holdings, thereby strengthening the validity of this case. This case must be considered when analyzing the activities performed in the United States by agents acting on behalf of Foreign Franchisor.

F. FOREIGN SOURCE EFFECTIVELY CONNECTED INCOME

Three classes of foreign source income can be treated as effectively connected with a U.S. trade or business of the taxpayer, but only if the taxpayer has an office or other fixed place of business in the United States to which the income is attributable.[194]

1. Classes of Foreign Source Income That May be Effectively Connected

Rents or royalties for the use of intangible property, developed in the United States and derived in the active conduct of a U.S. trade or business, are characterized as effectively connected with a U.S. trade or business.[195] This rule only affects rents or royalties derived from intangible property used or located outside the United States and, thus, this rule only applies to foreign source income. With respect to gains realized on the sale of such property, the general rule treats the gain recognized by a nonresident as foreign source income. However, if the intangible property is inventory property, the title passage rule would apply.

The second type of foreign source income that may be treated as effectively connected income is dividend income or gain from the sale or exchange of stock or notes, bonds, or other evidences of indebtedness, either derived in the active conduct of the banking, financing, or similar business within the United States or received by a corporation, the principal business of which is trading in stocks or securities for its own account.[196] There are two elements to this standard: the type of income and the nature of the taxpayer's business generating the income. However, once again, only foreign source income is characterized as effectively connected income under this provision.

Foreign source income from sales of inventory property through the U.S. office can be taxed as effectively connected income.[197] However, if the property is sold for use outside the United States and a foreign office materially participates in the sale, the income would not be treated as effectively connected to a U.S. trade or business.

2. Office or Other Fixed Place of Business

No foreign source income earned by Foreign Franchisor would be treated as effectively connected income unless it maintains an office or fixed place of business in the United States and the income is attributable to the office. Similar to a permanent establishment, whether a taxpayer has a fixed place of business in the United States is a facts and circumstances determination.[198] The law of a foreign country is not controlling in determining whether a foreign person has a fixed place of business in the United States.[199]

A fixed place of business is a fixed facility, a place, site, structure, or similar facility through which a foreign person engages in a trade or business; or a factory, store, workshop, mine, quarry, or other place of extraction of natural resources.[200] Use of another person's office to transact a trade or business on a relatively sporadic or infrequent basis, taking into account the overall needs of the trade or business, will not cause the other person's office to be deemed to be the office of a foreign person.[201] Foreign Franchisor will not be considered to have a fixed place of business merely because a person controlling that corporation has a fixed place of business from which general supervision is exercised. Provided that Foreign Franchisor has officers that conduct the corporation's day-to-day activity, the fact that management decisions affecting Foreign Franchisor are made in the United States does not by itself mean that it has an office in the United States.[202]

In determining whether Foreign Franchisor has a fixed place of business in the United States, a dependent agent is disregarded unless the agent has the authority to negotiate and conclude contracts in the name of the foreign person and regularly exercises that authority or has a stock of merchandise belonging to the foreign person from which orders are regularly filled on behalf of the foreign person. An agent is considered to regularly exercise authority to negotiate and conclude contracts or to fill orders on behalf of a foreign principal only if the authority is exercised with some frequency over a continuous period of time. A dependent agent is any agent other than an independent agent.[203]

An independent agent is a commissioned agent, broker, or other agent of independent status, acting in the ordinary course of his or her business. The determination of whether an agent is an independent agent is made without regard to whether either the agent or the principal owns or controls, or is owned or controlled by, the other. The facts and circumstances determine whether an agent is acting in the course of his or her usual trade or business and in a manner to constitute an independent agent. An independent agent is not treated as a fixed place of business of his or her principal irrespective of whether the agent has the authority to negotiate and conclude contracts or maintains a stock of goods from which he or she regularly fills orders.[204]

The fact that a foreign person is related to another person who has a fixed place of business in the United States does not in itself mean that the fixed place of business is attributable to the foreign person.[205]

Note that in the *InverWorld* decision discussed in detail in Section V.E above, a 100 percent owned U.S. subsidiary was determined to be a dependent agent of its foreign parent when the subsidiary conducted greater than 90 percent of its business on behalf of the parent.

G. ALLOCATION AND APPORTIONMENT OF NONINTEREST DEDUCTIONS

If Foreign Franchisors engaged in a U.S. trade or business, the income treated as effectively connected with the trade or business is reduced by deductions allocated and apportioned to that income.[206] Specifically, deductible expenses are allocated and apportioned to effectively connected gross income except for interest expense deductions, which are allocated and apportioned under special rules.[207] The properly allocable deductions are only allowed if the taxpayer claims the deductions on a timely filed tax return.[208] The Tax Court dealt with this issue in two recent cases, one of which involved an individual[209] and the other a corporation.[210] In both cases, the IRS argued, and the court agreed, that no deductions were allowed because the taxpayers had not filed "true and accurate" returns as required by the statute. Neither taxpayer had filed tax returns before the IRS completed and filed substitute returns on their behalf.[211]

In *InverWorld*, the IRS also evaluated the fees the parent paid to its U.S. subsidiary pursuant to their consulting agreement.[212] The court determined that the income earned by the U.S. subsidiary was less than the amount the parent quoted to the public, which should represent a fair measure of an arm's-length charge. The difference between the service fee originally recognized by the subsidiary and the court's redetermined fee was added to the subsidiary's taxable income as a transfer pricing adjustment. The court disallowed the parent's deduction for the correlative adjustment arising from the reallocated service fee to the subsidiary because the parent did not file a U.S. tax return for the years in question.

H. IMPACT OF INCOME TAX TREATIES ON EFFECTIVELY CONNECTED INCOME TAX

If Foreign Franchisor is a resident of a country that has executed an income tax treaty with the United States, it may be protected from taxation in the United States on income effectively connected with a U.S. trade or business if it does not operate through a permanent establishment in the United States. The rules for determining when

Foreign Franchisor is engaged in a U.S. trade or business and what income is attributed to that trade or business are superseded by treaty provisions.[213] The rules discussed concerning permanent establishment in Section III of this chapter may also be relied on by Foreign Franchisor to limit the taxing jurisdiction of the United States. In general, treaties limit net income taxation to cases where Foreign Franchisor operates in the United States through a permanent establishment. A treaty may also limit the amount of income attributed to the U.S. trade or business and may reduce the rate of gross withholding tax imposed on fixed or determinable annual or periodic income (that is, certain U.S. source income that is not effectively connected with a U.S. trade or business).[214]

I. INCOME SUBJECT TO GROSS BASIS TAX

The U.S. source, fixed or determinable income of Foreign Franchisor is subject to a flat 30 percent U.S. tax unless it is effectively connected with a U.S. trade or business.[215] This tax regime reaches a broad class of U.S. source income and a wide range of foreign investors making passive investments in the United States. The tax is collected at the source by the person making a payment to the foreign person.[216] The payor is required to withhold at the statutory rate or the applicable treaty rate and to pay over all withheld taxes to the IRS.[217] As marginal tax rates in the United States have fallen, the impact of the 30 percent withholding tax has substantially changed. When graduated rates were higher than 50 percent, the 30 percent gross withholding tax was a much less significant burden than it is now with a maximum corporate rate of 35 percent imposed on net taxable income.

There are four types of U.S. source income subject to 30 percent tax for a nonresident alien individual.[218] The first category is fixed or determinable annual or periodic income.[219] This income includes interest (other than original issue discount (OID)), dividends, rents, salaries, wages, premiums, annuities, compensations, remunerations, emoluments, and other fixed or determinable annual or periodical gains, profits, and income. This list sets out many items of income that are easily identified, some of which are not, and the general phrase "other fixed or determinable annual or periodical gains, profits and income" covers a very broad range of income categories.

The second category of income includes income from contingent sales of intangibles. The gains from contingent sales of patents, copyrights, secret processes and formulae, goodwill, trademarks, trade brands, franchises, and other like property or any interest in such property are subject to 30 percent tax to the extent the gains are contingent on the productivity, use, or disposition of the property or interest sold or exchanged.[220] The net effect of this provision is to recast as a royalty the proceeds from a contingent sale of an intangible asset.

The other categories of income include certain gains from pension plan distributions, gains from sales of certain depletable products, and original issue discount. These types of income are not usually found in franchise operations.[221]

J. CAPITAL GAINS

One category of income that is not "fixed or determinable" is gain from the sale or exchange of property.[222] This income is significant for foreign investors in the United States since the statutory exemption ensures that foreign taxpayers' gains from the sale of personal property held for investment are not subject to tax in the United States.[223]

K. IMPACT OF INCOME TAX TREATIES ON WITHHOLDING TAX

The withholding tax rate applicable on fixed or determinable annual or periodical income may be reduced under an income tax treaty between the United States and the country of residence of the foreign payee. If Foreign Franchisee is a resident of a country that has executed an income tax treaty with the United States, the withholding tax may be reduced for specific types of income to the extent enumerated in the applicable treaty. Because franchise revenue is often characterized, in part, as royalty income, the use of tax treaties may significantly reduce or eliminate U.S. withholding tax on franchise fees.

L. CONDUIT PAYMENTS

The IRS has discretion to disregard the participation of any intermediate entities in a multiparty financing arrangement for the purposes of imposing the U.S. gross-basis tax on interest, rents, royalties, and certain other transactions where the entities meet the "standard for conduit treatment."[224] If the IRS exercises this discretion, liability for the U.S. gross-basis tax is effectively shifted from the intermediary entity to the ultimate lender. This recast of the transaction may change the economics of the franchise operations.

The regulations do not focus on tracing the type and amount of payments in and out of the intermediary entity or whether the intermediary entity has "dominion and control" over the funds received.

Instead, they inquire whether "a financing arrangement" exists and, if so, whether it meets the "standard of conduit treatment." This is a facts-and-circumstances test, with little guidance given as to how the IRS will evaluate the given criteria.

The regulations affect all multiparty financing transactions involving financing, licensing, or leasing transactions of a U.S. individual or entity, or a foreign entity engaged in a U.S. business (collectively referred to here as the "financed entity"), executed with an intermediary that are entered into to avoid U.S. gross-basis tax. They also affect multiparty business-motivated transactions where reducing U.S. withholding tax is one objective but not the principal purpose.

From a franchising perspective, the most important aspect of the anti-conduit regulations is the application of the regulations to royalties and rental income because these types of income are often included in franchising revenue. If Foreign Franchisee derives franchise fees through intermediary entities resulting in a reduction of U.S. withholding tax, the anti-conduit regulations should be reviewed to determine if the reduction of tax under a treaty will be respected upon examination.[225]

VI. Other Issues to Address

A. TRANSFER PRICING

Local country entities are often established when operating a cross-border franchising business. These structures result in cross-border sales, services, and licensing between related parties. Related-party transactions are subject to transfer pricing adjustments both within the United States and in other countries.[226] Many countries, including the United States, require the existence of contemporaneous documentation of transfer pricing policies to avoid penalties related to transfer pricing adjustments resulting in increased tax liability.[227]

B. FOREIGN CURRENCY TRANSACTIONS

Cross-border transactions pose treasury and tax issues related to currency management. Under Section 988, currency gain or loss is recognized with respect to transactions conducted in a currency other than the currency in which the subsidiary or branch normally operates (nonfunctional currency). In addition, currency gains and losses are recognized with respect to hedging transactions.[228]

Currency gain or loss is recognized as ordinary income or loss equal to the difference between an amount accrued with respect to nonfunctional currency indebtedness (including accounts payable and receivable) and the amount ultimately paid, when converted into the taxpayer's functional currency.[229] Hedging transactions such as currency swaps and forwards may also result in taxable gain or loss, to the extent the hedging transactions are not integrated with the transaction being hedged resulting in a conversion of the nonfunctional currency transaction into a functional currency transaction.[230]

C. INDIRECT TAXES

Transactional taxes, such as value added tax (VAT), customs duties, registration taxes, and stamp taxes are often overlooked in setting up an international structure. These tax regimes require not only the proper amount of taxes be collected but proper registration of the entity for purposes of processing transactions is also necessary. This registration may lead to broader tax inquiries by local authorities. VAT may apply to the cross-border franchising transactions, depending on the products and services being transferred between countries. Although the initial transfer of intangibles to an offshore holding company will generally not require the transferor to charge VAT to the recipient entity, it is important to consider the VAT liability of the entity receiving such a transfer. Most countries with a VAT regime will require the recipient to "reverse charge" (self-assess the VAT similar to that of a U.S. use tax) for the supply. Although this does not require the recipient to actually pay VAT to the tax authorities, there are associated compliance obligations. The holding company must also consider the VAT liability derived from supplying these intangibles domestically and internationally as well as other intercompany charges.

VII. Conclusion

To maximize the return from international franchise operations, analysis of the tax consequences of those operations must be a part of structuring the business enterprise and negotiating franchise agreements. Reviewing the impact of tax on the business in the initial planning stage will allow the franchise income to be earned in the most favorably taxed manner. With proper planning, income from international operations may receive very favorable tax treatment. Absent such planning, the tax consequences can be punitive. If the revenue derived from foreign franchisees is significant, proper planning is merited.

Notes

1. The authors would like to acknowledge Steven M. Goldman of Marriott International, Inc., who initiated the preparation of this chapter to promote a better understanding of the tax consequences of cross-border franchising transactions and the practical business application of such consequences that must be addressed by franchise lawyers and executives.

2. The term "foreign corporation" in this chapter means a corporation organized outside of the United States. The term "foreign" is used throughout this chapter in place of the term "non-U.S." This terminology is a bit archaic, given the global nature of international business and the overall theme of this book. However, the term is used because it is consistent with terminology used in the Internal Revenue Code of 1986, as amended.

3. Unless otherwise provided, all section references in this chapter refer to the Internal Revenue Code of 1986, as amended, and the regulations issued thereunder.

4. Ingram v. Bowers, 47 F.2d 925 (2d Cir. 1931); Pierre Boulez v. Comm'r, 83 T.C. 584 (1984).

5. Waterman v. Macenzie, 138 U.S. 252, 256 (1891); Glen O'Brien Movable Partition Company v. Comm'r, 20 T.C. 492, 500 (1978); and Rev. Rul. 55-540, 1955-2 C.B. 39.

6. *See, e.g.,* Comm'r v. Wodehouse, 337 U.S. 369 (1949); Pickren v. United States, 378 F.2d 595 (5th Cir. 1967).

7. It should be noted that very detailed regulations concerning the characterization of software income are provided in Treasury Regulations Section 1.861-18. These rules will define when a payment for software constitutes a royalty payment or a sale.

8. However, in the case of intangible property held as inventory, the source of the income is based on the location in which title passes to the buyer. This rule may be altered in the case of software that is manufactured in the United States and sold with foreign title passage. Such income is partially allocated as U.S. source income and partially allocated as foreign source income under Section 863(b).

9. I.R.C. §§ 861(a)(4) and 862(a)(4).

10. The source of a sale of intangible property may differ, however, if the consideration paid is contingent on the use of the intangible. If the payments are tied to the productivity or use of the asset, the source of the sales income is dependent on where the intangible is used. *See* I.R.C. §§ 861(a)(4) and 862(a)(4). Even sales transactions with payments contingent upon the use of the intangible will be sourced in this manner. *See* I.R.C. § 865(d)(1).

11. It may be possible to reduce the foreign withholding tax under the terms of an income tax treaty between the United States and the payor's jurisdiction.

12. Treas. Reg. § 1.861-7.

13. Treas. Reg. § 1.861-7(c) and I.R.C. § 865.

14. I.R.C. §§ 861(a)(4) and 862(a)(4).

15. I.R.C. §§ 861(a)(3) and 862(a)(3).

16. Rev. Rul. 64-56, 1964-1 C.B. 133, amplified by Rev. Rul. 71-564, 1971-2 C.B. 179 (transfer of intangibles accompanied by mere ancillary and subsidiary services may be accorded tax-free treatment under I.R.C. § 351); Cloward Instrument Corp. v. Comm'r, T.C. Memo 1986-345, *aff'd without op.*, 842 F.2d 1294 (9th Cir. 1988) (where compensation for services represents a mere de minimis portion of a royalty payment, the entire payment may be characterized as a royalty).

17. Sierra Club, Inc. v. Comm'r, 86 F.3d 1526 (9th Cir. 1996) (remanding, in part, to determine whether payments were for services); *See also* U.S. Universal Joints Company v. Comm'r, 46 B.T.A. 111 (1942).

18. *See* U.S. Model Treaty and OECD Model Treaty, Article 3(1).

19. *See* OECD Model Treaty and United Nations Model Treaty, Article 4.

20. U.S. Model Treaty, Article 4(1).

21. *See* U.S. Model Treaty, Article 1(4).

22. *See, e.g.*, U.S. Model Treaty, Article 7(7).

23. U.S. Model Treaty, Article 7(7).

24. United Nations Model Treaty, Article 7(1).

25. OECD Model Treaty, Article 7(3).

26. U.S. Model Treaty, Article 7(3).

27. *See, e.g.*, U.S. Model Treaty, Article 5.

28. Donroy Ltd. v. Comm'r, 301 F.2d 200 (9th Cir. 1962).

29. The ability to form a company in developed or developing countries will also have a bearing on potential international tax planning.

30. Perry R. Bass v. Comm'r, 50 T.C. 595 (1968); Aiken Industries, Inc. v. Comm'r, 56 T.C. 925 (1977).

31. The regulations also impose reporting requirements. Treas. Reg. §§ 1.881-3 and -4.

32. Section 894 was enacted in the Tax Reform Act of 1997; final regulations under Treas. Reg. § 1.894-1(d) were published on June 30, 2000 (T.D. 8889); Prop. Treas. Reg. § 1.894-1(d)(2)(ii) was published on February 27, 2001.

33. I.R.C. § 894(c); Treas. Reg. § 1.894-1(d); and Prop. Treas. Reg. § 1.894-1(d)(2)(ii).

34. I.R.C. §§ 901 and 903.

35. Withholding taxes qualify as a foreign tax "in lieu of" an income tax under Section 903. These taxes are distinguished from income taxes under Section 901 that are imposed on net income.

36. Note that certain additional ownership limitations apply to distributions from lower-tier subsidiaries. If U.S. Franchisor claims an indirect foreign tax credit attributable to a dividend of its subsidiary's earnings, U.S. Franchisor must "gross-up" its income by including in taxable income an amount equal to the foreign taxes and then will claim a foreign tax credit for the indirect taxes. I.R.C. § 78.

37. The method of handling such taxes (credit or deduction) may be

changed at any time up to the expiration of the statute of limitations period under Section 6511(d)(3)(A). Treas. Reg. § 1.901-1(d) and Hart v. U.S., 585 F.2d 1025 (Ct. Cl. 1978).

38. *See* Section D, 3, *infra,* for a discussion of the foreign tax credit carryover/carryback rules.

39. I.R.C. § 275(a)(4).

40. Treas. Reg. § 1.901-2(a)(1).

41. Treas. Reg. § 1.901-2(a)(2)(i).

42. Treas. Reg. §§ 1.901-2(a)(3)(i) and (3).

43. Treas. Reg. § 1.901-2(a)(1)(i).

44. Treas. Reg. § 1.901-2(a)(2)(i).

45. Treas. Reg. § 1.901-2(a)(2)(ii).

46. Treas. Reg. §§ 1.901-2(b)(2) through (4).

47. Treas. Reg. § 1.901-2(a).

48. Treas. Reg. §§ 1.901-2(e)(3)(i)(A) and (B). The subsidy must be determined directly or indirectly by reference to the amount of the tax or the base used to compute the tax. If the subsidy is not targeted to or tied to transactions that give rise to a foreign tax credit, and the benefit applies to a broad range of transactions, the tax may be a creditable tax, notwithstanding the fact that a coincidental subsidy is provided to the taxpayer.

49. Treas. Reg. § 1.903-1(b)(1).

50. I.R.C. § 904(c).

51. I.R.C. § 904(c) and Treas. Reg. § 1.904-2.

52. I.R.C. § 904(d)(1).

53. I.R.C. § 904(d)(1)(1).

54. I.R.C. § 904(d)(2)(A)(i) and Treas. Reg. § 1.904-4(b).

55. Treas. Reg. § 1.954-2(a)(1).

56. Treas. Reg. §§ 1.954-2(b)(6) and (d).

57. The high withholding tax interest category includes any interest subject to a foreign withholding tax of 5 percent or more. I.R.C. § 904(d)(2)(B) and Treas. Reg. § 1.904-4(d).

58. The direct and indirect ownership rules under Sections 902(a) and (b) must be satisfied to qualify as a noncontrolled company for this purpose. These ownership rules include direct or indirect ownership thresholds that must be satisfied by lower-tier subsidiaries.

59. In the case of a partnership owning a foreign corporation, the determination of whether a taxpayer meets the requisite ownership requirements of Section 902 will be made with respect to the partner's indirect ownership and not the partnership's direct ownership in the foreign corporation.

60. I.R.C. § 904(d)(3). Under the look-through rules, a dividend is prorated over the various Section 904 limitation categories of income earned by the controlled foreign corporation.

61. I.R.C. § 904(d)(4)(B)(ii).

62. I.R.C. §§ 861(b), 862(b) and 863(a).

63. Treas. Reg. § 1.861-8.

64. Treas. Reg. § 1.861-8(a). Under Section 864(e), certain expenses, including interest, that are not directly allocable to a class of gross income, must be allocated and apportioned as if all members of an affiliated group (whether or not a consolidated return is filed) were a single corporation. I.R.C. §§ 864(e)(1) and (e)(6); and Temp. Treas. Reg. §§ 1.861-1T and -14T. An affiliated group generally consists of all 80 percent or greater commonly controlled U.S. corporations. Specific rules for determining the affiliated group are prescribed under Section 1502, as modified by Section 864(e) for this purpose. Temp. Treas. Reg. §1.8§ 61-14T(d)(1) and (2).

65. Temp. Treas. Reg. § 1.861-14T.

66. Temp. Treas. Reg. § 1.861-9T(a).

67. Temp. Treas. Reg. § 1.861-9T(a). Taxpayers may use either the fair market value method or the tax book method to value assets. Permission is not required to adopt the fair market value method; however, to change from the fair market value method is treated like a change in an accounting method and requires IRS consent. Temp. Treas. Reg. § 1.861-8T(c)(2). An average of asset values determined on the basis of beginning and ending values is used unless such averaging results in a substantial distortion of asset values. Temp. Reg. § 1.861-9T(g)(2)(i). If the fair market value method is elected, the taxpayer must establish the fair market value to the satisfaction of the IRS Commissioner. Temp. Reg. § 1.861-9T(g)(1)(iii).

68. Temp. Treas. Reg. § 1.861-10(e).

69. The nonrecourse debt exception allows the interest expense on nonrecourse acquisition financing to be directly allocated to the income derived from the financed property. This exception is helpful if the interest expense is allocated to a domestic asset financed by the nonrecourse loan and the asset produces only U.S. source income. This exception, however, is very narrowly drafted and is generally limited to real estate financing. Temp. Reg. § 1.861-10T(b)(2). According to the temporary regulations, interest may be allocated to income from an integrated financial transaction if the taxpayer incurs the indebtedness for the purpose of making an identified term investment; identifies the indebtedness as incurred for such purpose at the time the indebtedness is incurred; and makes the identified term investment within 10 business days after incurring the indebtedness, and the term of the investment coincides with the term of the loan. Temp. Reg. § 1.861-10T(c)(2)(i).

70. *See* Treas. Reg. § 1.861-10(e)(2), describing a step-by-step approach to this calculation.

71. Treas. Reg. § 1.861-10(e)(7).

72. Treas. Reg. § 1.861-10(e)(2)(iv).

73. Treas. Reg. § 1.861-14T.

74. Once elected, the method must be applied for the year of election and the four subsequent years.

75. Treas. Reg. § 1.861-17(c).

76. Treas. Reg. § 1.861-17(d).

77. Treas. Reg. § 1.861-17(b)(4).

78. Treas. Reg. §1.861-8(e)(9)(iv).

79. Prop. Treas. Reg. § 1.861-8(e)(2)(i).

80. Prop. Treas. Reg. § 1.861-8(e)(2). When a deduction is not allocated directly to U.S. source income or foreign source income as outlined above, the deduction shall be ratably apportioned as required under existing regulations. However, the proposed regulations clarify that the ratable allocation of an affiliated group is done by treating the entire group as a single taxpayer.

81. Temp. Treas. Reg. § 1.861-14T(e)(4).

82. Temp. Treas. Reg. § 1.861-8T(b)(3).

83. Temp. Treas. Reg. § 1.861-14T(e)(3). The distinction between stewardship and supportive expenses is often difficult and contentious. Stewardship expenses are allocable to dividend income as they represent expenses of a parent company overseeing its investment in a subsidiary. These expenses are not directly related to current operations but represent oversight expenses. Supportive expenses are not directly allocable to a particular category of income, but they do relate to the current operations of the corporation, rather than the oversight of the activities of a subsidiary.

84. Temp. Treas. Reg. § 1.861-1T(e)(6)(i).

85. Treas. Reg. § 1.865-2(a)(1).

86. Treas. Reg. § 1.865-1(a)(2). Separate rules are also provided for sales by U.S. citizens or residents with foreign tax homes. These rules do not apply to stock held as inventory under Section 1221. The regulations require allocation of the loss to the category of dividend income recognized with respect to the stock, to the extent of dividends paid within 24 months prior to the disposition of the stock. Treas. Reg. § 1.865-2(b). Temporary regulations also provide rules for losses on personal property other than stock that follow the same general principles of residence-based sourcing. Temp. Treas. Reg. § 1.865-1T.

87. Temp. Treas. Reg. § 1.865-1T(c)(6); Treas. Reg. § 1.865-2(b)(4); and Temp. Treas. Reg. § 1.865-2T(b)(4)(iii). The temporary and final Section 865 regulations are generally applicable for losses recognized on or after January 11, 1999; however, an election is possible to retroactively apply these rules. Temp. Treas. Reg. § 1.865-1T(f); Treas. Reg. § 1.865-2(e); and Temp. Treas. Reg. § 1.865-2T(e). The allocation of a loss from the disposition of stock was the issue addressed in *International Multifoods v. Comm'r*, 108 T.C. 579 (1997), which addressed the issue in a tax year prior to the issuance of the Section 865 regulations. In this case, the taxpayer was allowed to allocate losses on the basis of residence under the statutory authority of Section 865, even though regulations prescribing additional restrictions under Section 865 had not been issued. Given the favorable result in *International Multifoods*, it is unlikely that taxpayers will elect to apply the more restrictive provisions related to the retroactive application of the Section 865 rules.

88. The IRS has stated in Notice 89-91, 1989-2 C.B. 408, that this matter is under review and future regulations may prescribe asset-based apportionment for lease expenses.

89. Treas. Reg. § 1.861-8(a).

90. I.R.C. § 904(f) and Notice 88-71, 1988-2 C.B. 374.

91. Treas. Reg. § 1.904-5.

92. I.R.C. § 904(f).

93. Temp. Treas. Reg. § 1.367(a)-2T. Reporting requirements are imposed under Section 6038B with respect to such a transfer. *See* Temp. Treas. Reg. §§ 1.367(a)-2T(a)(2) and 1.6038B-1T.

94. Temp. Treas. Reg. § 1.367(a)-4T(c)(1).

95. Temp. Treas. Reg. § 1.367(a)-4T(b).

96. Intangible property is defined by a cross-reference to Section 936(h) and includes: patents, inventions, know-how, trademarks, trade names, franchise rights, licenses, contracts, and similar property with substantial value that is independent of the services of any individual. Exceptions to the general definition of intangibles are provided for foreign goodwill and going concern value. Temp. Treas. Reg. § 1.367(a)-1T(d)(5).

97. The installment payments must be commensurate with the income attributable to the intangible and these payments are recognized annually over the useful life of the intangible. Although under prior law the annual installments were treated as U.S. source income, Section 367(d) was amended in 1997 to provide that the source of the royalty payments is based on where the intangible is used. Accordingly, intangibles transferred to foreign corporations and used outside the United States will generate foreign source income. In certain cases, a taxpayer may elect to recognize all of the gain attributable to the transferred intangibles and avoid the annual deemed installment payments. Temp. Treas. Reg. § 1.367(d)-1T(g)(2).

98. Temp. Treas. Reg. § 1.367(d)-1T(g)(4).

99. I.R.C. § 951(a)(1).

100. I.R.C. §§ 954 and 957. For this purpose, a U.S. shareholder is a U.S. person (a U.S. citizen, U.S. resident, or domestic corporation) who owns 10 percent or more of the total voting power of the foreign corporation. I.R.C. § 951(b). *See* I.R.C. § 953(c)(1)(A) for a special rule regarding insurance companies.

101. I.R.C. §§ 958(a) and (b). These ownership rules apply for determining U.S. shareholder status under Section 951(b), related party status under Section 954(d)(3), attribution of ownership of a domestic corporation's stock to a U.S. shareholder of a foreign corporation under Section 956(b)(2)(F), and controlled foreign corporation status under Section 957.

102. I.R.C. §§ 951(a).

103. Rules for calculating earnings and profits are provided in Treas. Reg. § 1.964-1 and Temp. Treas. Reg. § 1.964-1T(g)(2). The amount of the Subpart F income included in the CFC Franchisor's income is translated into U.S. dollars using the weighted average exchange rate for the taxable year of the controlled foreign corporation. I.R.C. § 989(b)(3).

104. I.R.C. § 952(c).

105. I.R.C. § 959. It is important to carefully analyze earnings and profits before making dividends to assure that the previously taxed earnings will be distributed in the manner anticipated.

106. I.R.C. § 986(c).

107. A deemed foreign tax credit with respect to dividends from CFC Franchisor is allowed under Section 902, provided certain ownership tests are satisfied. The operation of the deemed foreign tax credit regime under Section 902 is described in Section E, below.

108. I.R.C. § 956. A discussion of Section 956 is provided in Section E, below.

109. I.R.C. § 954(c) and Treas. Reg. § 1.954-2(a)(1). This is the same definition of passive income used for the foreign tax credit limitation under Section 904. FPHCI includes amounts treated as ordinary income or interest income under Sections 482, 483, 864(d), 1273, 1274, 1276, 1281, 1286, 1288, and 7872, including interest on tax-exempt obligations and amounts treated as original issue discount (OID) and interest under any other provisions of the law. Treas. Reg. § 1.954-2(b)(1).

110. As defined in Section 954(d)(3).

111. Treas. Reg. § 1.954-2(b)(4). Actual ownership of the distributing corporation in the same vertical chain of ownership during the period the earnings were accumulated is required. Treas. Reg. § 1.954-2(b)(4)(ii). Any multinational company that relies on this exception must review their structure and their earnings and profits to determine the extent to which the same country dividend exception will be available in future taxable years.

112. Treas. Reg. § 1.954-2(b)(5).

113. I.R.C. § 954(c)(3)(B) and Treas. Reg. § 1.954-2(b)(5)(ii).

114. Treas. Reg. §§ 1.954-2(c) and (d).

115. I.R.C. § 964(e).

116. Treas. Reg. § 1.954-2(g)(2).

117. Treas. Reg. §§ 1.954-2(h)(l)–(6).

118. Treas. Reg. §§ 1.954-3(a)(2)–(4). Agricultural commodities that are not grown in the United States in commercially marketable quantities are also excluded from Subpart F income. Treas. Reg. § 1.954-3(a)(1)(ii)(b).

119. 1989-1 C.B. 257.

120. *Id. See also* Prop. Treas. Reg. §§ 1.952-1(g) and 1.954-1(g).

121. The proposed "Brown Group" regulations under Sections 702, 952, and 954 were issued on March 26, 1998, in conjunction with the hybrid branch proposed regulations under Notice 98-11, 1998-1 C.B. 433. Treasury formally withdrew the proposed regulations on July 13, 1999, in REG-113909-98, 64 FR 37727. However, on September 20, 2000, the "Brown Group" regulations were reproposed in similar form. *See* Prop. Treas. Reg. § 1.954-1(g).

122. Treas. Reg. § 1.954-4(b)(1).

123. Treas. Reg. § 1.954-4(b)(2)(i).

124. I.R.C. § 953(a).

125. I.R.C. §§ 953(c) and (d).

126. International boycott income is defined in Section 999 and income derived in connection with illegal bribes is defined in Section 952(a)(4).

127. I.R.C. § 954(b)(3)(A) and Treas. Reg. § 1.954-1(b)(1)(i). *See* Treas. Reg. § 1.954-l(b)(4) for an anti-abuse rule.

128. As described in I.R.C. § 864(d)(1) or (6), and Treas. Reg. § 1.954-l(b)(1)(i)(C).

129. Treas. Reg. § 1.954-1(b)(1)(ii).

130. Treas. Reg. § 1.954-1(b)(2).

131. I.R.C. § 954(b)(4) and Treas. Reg. § 1.954-1(d)(1) and (5). The regulations provide grouping rules that are designed to combine items of income with substantially similar effective tax rates.

132. I.R.C. § 952(b).

133. I.R.C. § 952(c)(1)(A); Prop. Treas. Reg. § 1.952-1(e)(1).

134. I.R.C. §§ 952(c)(1)(B) and (2).

135. I.R.C. § 952(c)(1)(B) and (c)(1)(C)(i).

136. I.R.C. § 952(c)(1)(C).

137. I.R.C. § 952(c)(2); Prop. Treas. Reg. §§ 1.952-1(e)(3) and (f). To the extent that the full inclusion rule of Section 954(b)(3)(B) requires income in excess of foreign base company income and insurance income to be included as Subpart F income, such excess does not reduce the amounts subject to recharacterization under Section 952(c)(2). Treas. Reg. § 1.954-l(b)(3).

138. Treas. Reg. § 1.957-1(b)(2).

139. *See, e.g.*, I.R.C. §§ 1291–1297.

140. Under this provision, U.S. Parent is required to include in its taxable income a deemed dividend in the amount of CFC Franchisor's average amount invested in U.S. property held as of the close of each quarter, less amounts previously taxed under Section 956. I.R.C. §§ 951(a)(1)(B) and 956(a)(1). The amount of the Section 956 inclusion is limited to the applicable earnings of CFC Franchisor. For this purpose, applicable earnings is defined under Section 956A with the exception that earnings accumulated in taxable years beginning before October 1, 1993, are included in calculating the Section 956 deemed dividend. Certain pre-controlled foreign corporation earnings are not included in this definition.

141. Beginning after December 31, 1962.

142. I.R.C. § 956(c)(1).

143. I.R.C. § 956(d).

144. I.R.C. § 956(c)(3).

145. I.R.C. § 956(c)(1)(D). A very limited exception is available for loans of less than 30 days that are outstanding for a total of less than 60 days during the taxable year. Notice 88-108, 1988-2 C.B. 105. This exception is designed to allow the repayment of loans on a quarterly basis to improve quarterly balance sheets. Section 956(b)(2) provides a list of exceptions from U.S. property, including certain investments in stocks and bonds of unaffiliated companies, certain U.S. bank deposits, and certain loans from CFC Franchisor to U.S. Parent that represent trade account balances related to the sale of goods and the performance of services that are outstanding for a commercially reasonable period of time. Treas. Reg. § 1.956-2(b)(1)(v) and Temp. Treas. Reg. § 1.956-2T(d)(2).

146. Temp. Treas. Reg. § 1.956-1T(b)(4). *See also* Rev. Rul. 87-89, 1987-2 C.B. 195, and Rev. Rul. 74-436, 1974-2 C.B. 214.

147. I.R.C. § 956(b)(1)(B). Gulf Oil Corp. v. Comm'r, 78 T.C. 548 (1986) (payable balance was a single obligation, even though it reflected the results of many intercompany transactions).

148. Indirect ownership of at least 5 percent is required for all lower-tier subsidiaries. Unlike the Section 902 foreign tax credits from certain first- through third-tier foreign subsidiaries, the extension of the indirect credit to fourth- through sixth-tier subsidiaries only extends to U.S. shareholders of controlled foreign corporations and applies with respect to foreign taxes accrued during taxable years beginning after August 5, 1997. The deemed paid credit for foreign taxes imposed on second- through sixth-tier foreign corporations is only available where such corporations distribute dividends through a first-tier foreign corporation at least 10 percent owned (by vote) by the U.S. corporate shareholder and where such U.S. corporation's indirect stock ownership in the second- through sixth-tier foreign corporation is at least 5 percent. Affiliates filing a consolidated return may not aggregate their shareholdings in a foreign corporation to meet the 10 percent shareholding requirement. I.R.C. § 902(b); First Chicago Corp. v. Comm'r, 96 T.C. 14 (1991); Rev. Rul. 79-74, 1979-1 C.B. 241; and PLR 7904095. Section 960(a) allows deemed paid foreign tax credits with respect to earnings that are included in a U.S. shareholder's income under the provisions of Subpart F.

149. I.R.C. § 78 and Treas. Reg. § 1.902-1(c)(2).

150. Notices 88-70 and 88-71, 1988-2 C.B. 369 and 374, respectively, and Treas. Reg. § 1.902-1. Taxes are allocated to different foreign tax credit baskets of income under Treasury Regulations Section 1.904-6.

151. I.R.C. § 1248.

152. I.R.C. § 904(d)(3).

153. I.R.C. § 964(e).

154. I.R.C. §§ 881(a) and 1442.

155. I.R.C. § 882.

156. Section 864(b) merely states that a trade or business includes the performance of services.

157. 113 F.2d 718 (2nd Cir. 1940).

158. In *Linen Thread Co. v. Comm'r*, 14 T.C. 725, isolated and relatively unplanned sales were held not to constitute a U.S. trade or business. Similarly, in *Continental Trading v. Comm'r*, 265 F.2d 40 (9th Cir. 1959), the court stated that "in light of the whole enterprise," the U.S. sales were "casual or incidental transactions" not rising to the stature of a trade or business.

159. I.R.C. § 864(c)(6).

160. I.R.C. § 864(c)(7).

161. GCM 21219, 1939-1 C.B. 849.

162. Rev. Rul. 56-165, 1956-1 C.B. 849.

163. Handfield v. Comm'r, 23 T.C. 633 (1955).

164. PLR 7739023 (September 29, 1977).

165. GCM 18835, 1937-2 C.B. 141.

166. de Amodio v. Comm'r, 34 T.C. 894 (1960), and Lewenhaupt v. Comm'r, 20 T.C. 151 (1953).

167. Investor's Mortgage Security Co. v. Comm'r, 4 T.C.M. 45 (1945).

168. I.R.C. § 875, Unger v. Comm'r, 91-2 USTC ¶ 50,328 (D.C. Cir. 1991), and Donroy, Ltd. v. U.S., 301 F.2d 200 (9th Cir. 1962).

169. Rev. Rul. 70-424, 1970-2 C.B. 150.

170. InverWorld, Inc. et. al., v. Comm'r, T.C. Memo 1996-301.

171. I.R.C. § 864(b)(1).

172. Abegg v. Comm'r, 50 T.C. 145 (1968).

173. Neill v. Comm'r, 46 BTA 197 (1942), and Herbert v. Comm'r, 30 T.C. 26 (1958).

174. Rev. Rul. 73-522, 1973-2 C.B. 226.

175. Pinchot v. Comm'r, 113 F.2d 178 (2d Cir. 1940).

176. Higgins v. Comm'r, 312 U.S. 212 (1940).

177. Continental Trading Inc. v. Comm'r, 16 T.C.M. 724 (1957), *aff'd.*, 265 F.2d 40 (9th Cir. 1959).

178. DiPorta Nova v. U.S., 690 F.2d 169 (Ct. Cls. 1982).

179. The treatment of U.S. source income is governed under Sections 864(c)(2) and 864(c)(3).

180. I.R.C. § 864(c)(2). The first category refers to capital gain arising from disposition of capital assets as defined in Section 1221 and the second category includes income "of the types described in Sections 871(a)(1), 881(a), or 881(c)."

181. *Id.*

182. Treas. Reg. § 1.864-4(c)(2)(ii).

183. Treas. Reg. § 1.864-4(c)(2)(i).

184. Treas. Reg. §§ 1.864-4(c)(1) and 1.864-4(c)(3)(i).

185. Treas. Reg. § 1.864-4(c)(3)(i).

186. I.R.C. § 864(c)(3).

187. Treas. Reg. § 1.864-4(b), Example 3.

188. T.C. Memo 1996-301 (1997).

189. LTD did not file a Form 1120-F, relying on the exclusion from a U.S. trade or business for trading activities conducted through a resident broker, commission agent, custodian, or other independent agent under Section 864(b)(2)(A)(i) and on the trading on your own account exception under Section 864(b)(2)(A)(ii).

190. The court determined that the first exception from a U.S. trade or business contained in Section 864(b)(2)(A)(i) required trading through an independent agent and that INC was not an independent agent as that term is defined in Treasury Regulations Section 1.864-7(d)(3)(i).

191. Specifically, it held that LTD had a fixed facility because it used the San Antonio office of INC to engage in its business activities, it used the office as its address, it kept all client files in the office, and its use of the office was so extensive that it could not be considered sporadic or infrequent. LTD also had a fixed facility in San Antonio because the day-to-day management decisions of LTD's business were conducted in the San Antonio office. The court also determined that the office of INC could be attributed to LTD because INC had the power to contract on LTD's behalf.

192. LTD argued that its real business was rendering business advice in Mexico; that all of the activities relating to its business occurred in Mexico including solicitation, opening accounts, and making changes to the accounts

with the help of Mexican advisors; and that its activities in the U.S. were merely ministerial. The court determined LTD was engaged in a trade or business and that LTD's real business was not merely to render investment advice to clients in Mexico because its income came from management fees, interest, currency transactions, other fees, and commission income from affecting financial transactions in the United States.

193. The portfolio management exception did not apply because LTD's primary business was the maintenance of investments. The foreign source interest income from nonresident clients and Mexican companies was also effectively connected income because it was attributable to a U.S. office or other fixed place of business based on the tests in Section 864(c)(5). Under these tests, INC regularly exercised the authority to negotiate and conclude contracts for LTD, and the activities associated with the U.S. office were a material factor in the production of the interest income.

194. I.R.C. § 864(c)(4)(B).

195. I.R.C. § 864(c)(4)(B)(i).

196. I.R.C. § 864(c)(4)(B)(ii).

197. I.R.C. § 864(c)(4)(B)(iii).

198. Treas. Reg. § 1.864-7(a)(2).

199. Treas. Reg. § 1.864-7(a)(3). For an extensive discussion of these rules, see *InverWorld,* discussed above.

200. Treas. Reg. § 1.864-7(b)(1).

201. Treas. Reg. § 1.864-7(b)(2).

202. Treas. Reg. § 1.864-7(c).

203. Treas. Reg. § 1.864-7(d)(1).

204. Treas. Reg. § 1.864-7(d)(2).

205. Treas. Reg. § 1.864-7(f).

206. I.R.C. § 882(c)(1)(A).

207. Treas. Reg. §§ 1.861-8, 1.882-5, and 1.882-4(b).

208. This requirement is contained in Treasury Regulations Section 1.874-1(b) for nonresident individuals claiming deductions and Treasury Regulations Section 1.882-4(a)(3) for foreign corporations.

209. Espinosa v. Comm'r, 107 T.C. 146 (1996).

210. *InverWorld, supra.*

211. It is interesting to note that no deductions were allowed even though both cases involved tax years before the issuance of the regulations with the "timely filed" language.

212. *InverWorld, supra.* The IRS proposed adjustments under Section 482.

213. I.R.C. § 894(a).

214. This gross withholding tax is addressed in Section I, below.

215. I.R.C. §§ 871(a), 881, 1441, and 1442

216. I.R.C. §§ 1441, 1442 and 1461.

217. It is important to note that under Sections 71(a) and 881, tax is imposed on gross income and no tax deductions are allowed in computing this income.

218. I.R.C. § 871(a).
219. I.R.C. § 871(a)(1)(A).
220. I.R.C. § 871(a)(1)(D).
221. I.R.C. §§ 871(a)(1)(B), (C), and 871(g).
222. Treas. Reg. § 1.1441-2(b)(2).
223. Note, however, gain from the disposition of stock in a U.S. real property holding corporation or an interest in U.S. real estate, although not fixed or determinable, annual or periodic income, is subject to tax under Section 897.
224. I.R.C. § 7701(L). In general, affected payments include payments under Sections 871, 881, and 884(f)(1)(A). Treas. Reg. § 1.881-3(a)(1).
225. *See* Treas. Reg. § 1.881-3.
226. I.R.C. § 482.
227. Treas. Reg. § 1.6662-6.
228. I.R.C. § 988.
229. *See* Treas. Reg. § 1.988-2.
230. Detailed rules under Treasury Regulations Section §1.988-5 prescribe the circumstances in which a hedging transaction will be integrated with the transaction being hedged.

CHAPTER ❖ 5

Disclosure and Registration

MICHAEL G. BRENNAN

I. Overview of Franchise Disclosure Laws in the United States

Depending on the specific circumstances of an international transaction, the parties to the transaction may be subject to either U.S. franchise laws or foreign franchise laws, or both. Sections II and III of this chapter will discuss the application of U.S. franchise laws to international transactions, both outbound (that is, sales made by U.S. franchisors for units to be located in foreign countries) and inbound (that is, sales of franchises made by foreign franchisors for units to be located in the U.S.). As this discussion will show, trying to use a disclosure document that complies with U.S. franchise laws for international transactions is akin to fitting a square peg in a round hole because international transactions were not contemplated when the U.S. franchise laws were written. Sections IV through VIII of this chapter will focus on foreign laws that may affect franchise sales by a U.S. franchisor in a given foreign country.

The Federal Trade Commission's Trade Regulation Rule, entitled "Disclosure Requirements and Prohibitions Concerning Franchising and Business Opportunity Ventures"[1] (the FTC Rule), became effective in 1979, and requires disclosure, but not registration, in connection with the offer and sale of franchises throughout the United States. The FTC Rule preempts state law only to the extent that state laws are less restrictive. In states having registration and disclosure statutes, franchisors are required to comply with both the state and federal requirements. Fifteen states[2] have enacted franchise registration or disclosure laws that seek to protect prospective franchisees by ensuring that they receive pertinent information about a franchisor and the franchised business before they execute an agreement. The information in this chapter concerning the FTC Rule and the state franchise laws is current as of August 2001. Of course, they are subject to amendment and one should always check the latest version before proceeding.

II. Federal Trade Commission Rule

A. DEFINITION OF FRANCHISE

The FTC Rule applies to all commercial relationships that meet the definition of a franchise, unless an enumerated exclusion or exemption from coverage is available. A commercial relationship is deemed a franchise under the FTC Rule if it has the following three elements: (1) distribution of goods and services associated with the franchisor's trademark; (2) significant control of, or significant assistance to, the franchisee's method of operation; and (3) required payment by the franchisee to the franchisor of at least $500 at any time before, to within six months after, the business relationship begins. If a commercial relationship is covered by the FTC Rule, the franchisor must satisfy certain presale disclosure requirements. However, *there is no registration or filing requirement under the FTC Rule.*

B. JURISDICTIONAL SCOPE

The FTC Rule applies to "advertising, offering, licensing, contracting, sale, or other promotion" of franchises affecting "commerce" as defined in the FTC Act. The FTC Rule does not address the geographic scope of its application. It makes no distinction based upon the location of the franchise or the residence of the prospective franchisee, although there is no question that it was intended to require presale disclosure to domestic franchisees. Therefore, the applicability of the FTC Rule to international transactions depends on the jurisdiction of the FTC Act to regulate such transactions. (See the discussion in Section I.F, below.)

C. OVERVIEW OF REQUIRED DISCLOSURES

To facilitate the preparation of disclosure documents, the Federal Trade Commission (FTC) has determined that compliance with the FTC Rule may be accomplished by following the Uniform Franchise Offering Circular Guidelines (UFOC Guidelines), as amended by the North American Securities Administrators Association (NASAA) on April 25, 1993.[3] Most franchisors use a UFOC to satisfy FTC Rule disclosure obligations because the UFOC allows the franchisor to meet state disclosure requirements as discussed in Section III of this chapter. The UFOC Guidelines prescribe the format for disclosure that must be contained in the UFOC and are not, standing alone, the law or regulations of any jurisdiction.

Generally, the UFOC Guidelines are intended to provide a prospective franchisee with sufficient information about the franchisor and the franchise to make an informed investment decision. An offering circular prepared pursuant to the UFOC Guidelines consists of separate substantive categories, each referred to as an "Item," as follows:

- Item 1: general information regarding the franchisor, its predecessors and affiliates, and a description of the franchise being offered;
- Item 2: employment history for the past five years of certain key principals and executives;
- Item 3: certain litigation, administrative, criminal, and other actions;
- Item 4: bankruptcy history;
- Item 5: initial franchise fee;
- Item 6: payments by the franchisee during the term;
- Item 7: pre-opening payments and costs;
- Item 8: franchisor restrictions on franchisees' sources of products and services;
- Item 9: principal in-term obligations of the franchisee;
- Item 10: financing arrangements offered by the franchisor, its agents, or affiliates;
- Item 11: obligations of the franchisor to the franchisee;
- Item 12: any exclusive territory granted to the franchisee;
- Item 13: principal trademarks to be licensed to the franchisee;
- Item 14: patents, copyrights, and proprietary information;
- Item 15: franchisee's obligation to participate personally in the direct operation of the franchised business;
- Item 16: restrictions or conditions on the goods or services that the franchisee may sell or the customers to whom the franchisee may sell goods or services;

- Item 17: provisions dealing with termination, renewal, transfer, dispute resolution, and other important aspects of the franchise relationship;
- Item 18: public figures used in promoting the franchise;
- Item 19: "earning claims," which are any statements of sales, costs, income, or profit from franchised or nonfranchised units or costs (not required if the franchisor does not make such statements to prospective franchisees);
- Item 20: number and location of franchised and company-owned outlets;
- Item 21: franchisor's financial statements for the last three fiscal years;
- Item 22: copies of all agreements the franchisor proposes for use in connection with the offering of a franchise; and
- Item 23: receipt of the offering circular by the prospective franchisee.

D. DISCLOSURE PROCEDURES

Under the FTC Rule, the disclosure document must be delivered at the earlier of either the "first personal meeting" or the "time for making of disclosures." While each state statute has its own delivery requirements, complying with the FTC Rule delivery requirements will constitute compliance with delivery requirements in every state.

The first personal meeting is defined as a face-to-face meeting between a prospective franchisee and a franchisor, franchise broker, or any agent, representative, or employee of either, at which time a serious discussion occurs about a franchise purchase. A first personal meeting does not include communication by telephone, e-mail, fax, or regular mail. If there is no first personal meeting, the delivery of disclosure documents must be made at the time for making disclosures. This term is defined as ten business days prior to the earlier of (1) the execution by the prospective franchisee of any franchise agreement or any other agreement imposing a binding legal obligation on the prospective franchisee in connection with the sale or proposed sale of a franchise; or (2) the payment of any consideration by the prospective franchisee.

In addition to the delivery of disclosure documents within the required time frame, a franchisor must also deliver to the prospective franchisee a copy of the franchisor's franchise agreement and related agreements intended to be executed by the parties at least five business days prior to the date the agreements are to be executed.

E. APPLICATION OF FTC RULE TO INBOUND TRANSACTIONS: DIFFICULTIES IN COMPLYING

Compliance with the FTC Rule with respect to purely domestic transactions is easy to understand and implement. Offers and sales of franchises by foreign franchisors for franchises that will be located within the United States, however, raise a number of issues for foreign franchisors.

1. Financial Statements

The FTC Rule provides that the franchisor's audited financial statements for the past three fiscal years must be attached as an exhibit to the offering circular and must be prepared in accordance with generally accepted accounting principles (GAAP).[4] Neither the FTC Rule nor the UFOC Guidelines specifically state that the franchisor's financial statements need to be prepared in accordance with U.S. GAAP. However, it has been generally assumed that U.S. GAAP is required. This is because it would be difficult for most prospective franchisees to obtain advice from their local advisors concerning financial statements prepared under foreign accounting principles. State franchise examiners also share this view and generally will not allow the use of such statements in UFOCs. This requirement often poses a serious problem for foreign franchisors who must comply with the FTC Rule. Moreover, compliance by a foreign public company with the laws of its home country may require use of that country's GAAP. A foreign company generally prepares its financial statements in accordance with the generally accepted accounting principles of its home country. For a foreign company to have an accounting firm in the United States prepare financial statements in accordance with U.S. GAAP represents a significant financial burden and is often impractical. Therefore, some franchisors have tried to comply with this requirement by having a summary of the material differences between U.S. GAAP and the accounting principles of their home countries attached to the financial statements. Although some registration states have accepted this method, it would not technically comply with U.S. GAAP. Other foreign franchisors have set up a U.S. subsidiary to be the franchisor so only the subsidiary would need financial statements prepared in accordance with U.S. GAAP. The U.S. franchisor company would have to include in its initial offering circular an audited opening balance sheet. The company would then have its financial statements audited after the end of its first fiscal year and each fiscal year thereafter.

Practice Tip

To ease the burden of franchise law compliance, foreign franchisors should consider creating a newly established subsidiary to act as the franchisor in the United States, but should be aware of potential tax complications caused by such structure.

2. Franchisee's Estimated Initial Investment

A foreign franchisor without any outlets in the United States will most likely have difficulties preparing an estimate of the franchisee's initial investment due to lack of experience in the United States and differences in the price of goods and services between the United States and the franchisor's home country. One way to resolve this problem is for the foreign franchisor to operate one or more outlets in the United States before it begins to franchise in the United States. However, this is probably not an acceptable solution for most franchisors due to the time and cost involved. Therefore, a foreign franchisor will usually want to deal with this disclosure in some other way. For example, it could interview real estate brokers, building contractors, equipment suppliers, and other suppliers regarding the costs involved for each required item. Even after such an investigation, the franchisor would be well advised to disclose clearly in the offering circular that the franchisor has no experience in the United States and, therefore, its estimate is not based on firsthand experience.

A foreign franchisor may also consider engaging in a collaborative review of Item 7, the franchisee's estimated initial investment, with a prospective franchisee after providing the prospective franchisee with an offering circular. If a prospective U.S. franchisee has differences in opinion regarding the amount of initial investment required for the franchise, the franchisor may want to take the prospective franchisee's opinion into consideration and amend the offering circular. The franchisor can then provide the prospective franchisee with the updated offering circular prior to the franchisee's execution of the franchise agreement. Of course, this may delay the completion of the transaction.

3. Cost of Compliance

Preparation of the disclosure document required under the FTC Rule usually involves significant cost in attorneys' and accountants' fees.

Therefore, it may not be financially practical for a foreign franchisor to sell franchises in the United States unless a large transaction or a number of transactions are being contemplated. The granting of a franchise for a small number of units would normally not justify the costs necessary for legal compliance.

4. Other Difficulties

The UFOC Guidelines require that the franchisor disclose franchisees' obligations to purchase or lease goods, services, supplies, fixtures, equipment, inventory, and computer hardware and software from the franchisor, its designee, or from suppliers approved by the franchisor. If a foreign franchisor has certain suppliers in its home country that it designates for its franchisees to use, it may not be cost effective for U.S. franchisees to use the same suppliers. On the other hand, it may be difficult for a foreign franchisor to find suppliers that meet its criteria without having any experience with them. Therefore, a franchisor may want to start by utilizing suppliers in its home country while testing suppliers in the United States. The franchisor can then slowly phase out the foreign suppliers as qualified suppliers are identified in the United States. Of course, this raises issues of importing goods into the United States and may have a significant impact on time and costs.

The UFOC Guidelines do not address whether a franchisor must include information on units located outside of the United States. It would be very cumbersome for a franchisor with franchises worldwide to list all of its franchise locations in Item 20 (List of Outlets) of the offering circular, and the authorities in the various franchise registration states do not require information on foreign franchisees. One could argue that information regarding foreign units is not relevant to a prospective U.S. franchisee and might be misleading. One reason for providing a list of all franchise outlets is that it enables a prospective franchisee to contact other franchisees about their experiences with the franchisor. Ten years ago, it was not likely that a prospective franchisee in the United States would contact a franchisee in Japan for information (assuming the franchisor had any franchisees in Japan at all!). However, in the 21st century, it is more likely that information regarding foreign units could be of some relevance in the absence of better information. Not only is there an increase in the number of people who speak English, but also with recent technological advances, it is much easier to communicate with people across the world. Thus, it may be that more franchisors will elect to include this information in the future.

Under the FTC Rule, a franchisor is not required to provide an earnings claim in its offering circular. However, a franchisor may not make earnings claims in connection with an offer or sale of a franchise unless the earnings claims information is included in Item 19 of the offering circular. It would be very difficult for a foreign franchisor with no experience in the United States to have a reasonable basis for making an earnings claim in connection with an offer or sale of a franchise in the United States. Any earnings information for outlets in foreign countries may not have any geographical relevance.

Practice Tip

Beware of including earnings claims information based on performance in foreign markets in a UFOC to be used by a foreign franchisor in the United States.

F. APPLICATION OF FTC RULE TO OUTBOUND TRANSACTIONS

1. Jurisdictional Issues

The FTC Rule was promulgated to protect prospective franchisees from unfair and deceptive acts. The FTC Rule makes no distinction based upon the residence of the franchisees or the location of the franchised business. Whether the FTC Rule applies to cross-border sales of franchises by U.S. franchisors depends upon the jurisdiction of the FTC to regulate such sales under the Federal Trade Commission Act[5] pursuant to which the FTC Rule was adopted, and on the interpretation of the FTC Rule itself.

a. Nieman v. Dry Clean U.S.A. Franchise Company, Inc. Authority on the applicability of the FTC Rule in the international franchising context did not exist until recently. In June 1999, the franchise community received a long-awaited appellate judicial decision involving international franchise sales. In *Nieman v. Dry Clean U.S.A. Franchise Company, Inc.,*[6] Nieman had successfully sued for return of a $50,000, nonrefundable deposit paid with the execution of an option agreement for a master franchise to sell franchises throughout Argentina. Nieman failed to raise the necessary capital and requested the return of his $50,000 deposit. DryClean U.S.A. refused to return the deposit and Nieman sued under the Florida Deceptive and Unfair Trade Practices

Act[7] claiming that DryClean U.S.A. failed to disclose as required by the FTC Rule.

The court of appeals first examined whether Congress intended for the FTC Rule to apply extraterritorially. The court found that there is a presumption against applying U.S. law extraterritorially absent a clear expression of Congress's intent to extend the reach of the relevant statute beyond places where the United States has sovereignty or has some measure of legislative control. Thus, for the FTC Act to apply extraterritorially, the FTC Act itself must clearly indicate Congress's intent to apply it extraterritorially. The court could find no such expression of intent.[8]

Furthermore, the court noted that even if Congress intended the unfair trade provisions of the FTC Act to give the FTC the authority to apply regulations extraterritorially, there are three independent reasons not to do so. First, the FTC Rule was not intended to protect franchisees in foreign countries. When the FTC Rule was promulgated, it was accompanied by a Statement of Basis and Purpose that reviewed the history of franchising in the United States. The FTC Rule was silent regarding the history of franchising in other countries. Second, the provisions of the FTC Rule itself reveal a purely domestic focus. For example, the FTC Rule addresses potential conflicts with state law, but not foreign law. Finally, the FTC has never indicated that the FTC Rule was intended to apply to foreign franchisees.

b. Proposed Amendment to the FTC Rule. Shortly following the court's ruling in *Nieman*, the Federal Trade Commission issued the Notice of Proposed Rulemaking, which includes a new addition to Section 436.2 of the FTC Rule that reduces the FTC Rule's scope to exclude the sale of franchises to be located outside the United States and its territories and possessions. The adoption of this new section would finally clarify the jurisdictional scope of the FTC Rule in this respect.

c. Why Franchisors May Still Decide to Disclose. The court's decision in *Nieman* is not binding in the other federal circuits. Furthermore, the case was based on very straightforward facts. It dealt with a transaction between a U.S. company and a foreign franchisee for a location in a foreign country. It is not clear whether the court would have reached the same result had the facts been more complicated (for example, if the franchisee was a U.S. resident).

If the proposed amendment to the FTC Rule is adopted, a franchisor would clearly not have to comply with the FTC Rule with respect to franchisees located outside the United States. However, the proposed amendments have not been adopted. Until that time, a franchisor would be able to rely on *Nieman* for a transaction with the same fact pattern that is subject to the law of the Eleventh Circuit. Franchisors nationwide may choose to rely on *Nieman* as well in similar circumstances (that is, foreign franchisee for a location in a foreign country). The way the FTC has structured the exemption for foreign franchises under the proposed amendments, it would appear to apply to all outbound transactions, whereas *Nieman* would not necessarily apply so broadly. Therefore, until the proposed amendments to the FTC Rule are finally effective, there may not be any clear safe harbor for all U.S. franchisors selling abroad. As a practical matter, though, the FTC would not likely institute an enforcement action if the transaction would be exempt under the proposed amendments to the FTC Rule.

Due to a lack of a clear safe harbor under the current FTC Rule for outbound transactions, a U.S. franchisor with a potential outbound transaction that does not have the same fact pattern as *Nieman* (for example, where the prospective franchisee is located in the United States) may still want to comply with the FTC Rule until the proposed amendments to the FTC Rule are adopted. Moreover, some franchisors find that some form of disclosure actually simplifies negotiations and therefore wish to comply with the FTC Rule for practical reasons.

2. Difficulties in Complying

In complying with the FTC Rule for an outbound transaction, a U.S. franchisor may come across a number of difficulties. Because many of the disclosures required under the FTC Rule are based on a franchisor's experience in the United States, they are extremely difficult to address when applied to an outbound transaction. Further, to comply with the "first personal meeting" disclosure requirement, a U.S. franchisor would have to adapt its U.S. offering circular for use in offering franchises in a foreign country before it knows whether a prospective franchisee is seriously considering a franchise. The lack of reliable information for so many countries and the costs involved to comply with this requirement alone may make such an approach impossible. Unlike the United States, many countries do not have franchise laws, and even those countries that have disclosure laws seem to allow negotiations prior to providing a formal disclosure document so that the disclosure document will reflect the negotiated deal between the parties.

a. Franchisee's Estimated Initial Investment. A U.S. franchisor offering franchises overseas would have the same problem with preparing initial investment estimations for Item 7 as would a foreign franchisor offering franchises in the United States. Because many U.S. franchisors do not operate units in foreign countries, it would be difficult to estimate the amount of initial investment required to open an outlet abroad. Especially if a franchisor offers franchises in many countries, it would be very time-consuming to investigate costs in the markets where the franchisor wishes to franchise. Even where two countries are fairly close in geographic proximity (for example, Japan and China), the amount of initial investment can vary greatly. As a practical matter, the foreign franchisee will often have a better idea of the initial investment necessary in its home country. Therefore, some franchisors include the estimated initial investment for a unit in the United States and provide a disclaimer that the amount of estimated initial investment is for a U.S. location and the amount required for other markets will most likely vary.

Practice Tip

Be sure a foreign franchisee's estimated initial investment in Item 7 of the UFOC is based on actual costs in the foreign franchisee's home country.

b. Negotiated Transactions. U.S. franchisors often grant master franchises and area development rights overseas, rather than individual franchises. Due to the size of the territory and the substantial investment involved for a typical international transaction, these transactions are usually highly negotiated. Therefore, it would be very difficult to prepare an offering circular containing "standard" terms of a franchise because there may be no standard terms with respect to international transactions. Negotiated changes in such agreements potentially give rise to disclosure issues. The FTC Rule does not address whether a franchise offering circular must be amended to incorporate disclosures for negotiated changes. The FTC Rule does state, however, that if only minor changes are made at the franchisee's request, and these benefit the franchisee and provide minimal benefit to the franchisor, a revised franchise offering circular need not be delivered and the parties do not need to wait an additional five business days prior to signing the franchise agreement. Therefore, the FTC Rule implies that if more than minor changes are made, a revised franchise offering circular needs to be delivered and the parties must wait another five business days before signing the agreements (see Section II.D, above).

3. Other Difficulties

Franchisors will encounter various other difficulties when trying to comply with the disclosure obligations for outbound transactions. Item 1 requires franchisors to provide a general description of the competition. This will obviously be difficult to do if a franchisor is not familiar with the particular market abroad. Furthermore, a franchisor who wants to use one offering circular to offer and sell in various regions around the world cannot provide a generic description of the competition around the world. For example, the competition for a pizza store could be significantly different in Italy than the competition in China.

The UFOC Guidelines require franchisors to disclose U.S. trademark, patent, and copyright registrations in Items 13 and 14. Obviously, U.S. trademark, copyright, and copyright registrations would be largely irrelevant to a franchise located outside of the United States. It would appear that franchisors need to adapt the UFOC Guidelines for outbound transactions by either omitting those items or providing trademark, copyright, and patent registration information in the relevant countries.

Practice Tip

Do not mechanically use a domestic UFOC for sale of franchises abroad. Adapt it for international transactions.

G. PENALTIES FOR NONCOMPLIANCE

There is no private right of action under the FTC Rule. The FTC may enforce the FTC Rule either in an administrative proceeding leading to the issuance of a cease and desist order to stop an unfair or deceptive trade practice, with civil penalties of up to $12,000 per violation for any violation of such order, or by a lawsuit for injunction and damages. There is also the possibility that a franchisee who did not receive an offering circular as required under the FTC Rule could bring an action under an applicable state unfair trade practices statute.

H. POSSIBLE EXEMPTIONS

1. Fractional Franchise

Even if a cross-border transaction, inbound or outbound, falls under the jurisdictional scope of the FTC Rule, it may be exempt from coverage by the FTC Rule if it qualifies under one of the exemptions. One such exemption is the "fractional franchise exemption." This exemption typically applies to a relationship where an existing business adds a franchised product line or service to its existing line of goods and services. The fractional franchise exemption is available if the franchisee or any of its current directors or officers has more than two years of experience in the same or similar business as the franchise being offered and the parties in good faith anticipate, at the time of entering into the arrangement, that the sales arising from the proposed relationship would represent no more than 20 percent of the dollar volume of the franchisee's projected gross sales. With respect to the first element, the Interpretive Guides to the FTC Rule state that the franchisee's business experience may be in the same business selling competitive goods or services or in a business that would ordinarily be expected to sell the type of goods to be distributed under the franchise. For example, the experience requirement would be met in a franchise for tires, batteries, and accessories granted to a service station dealer, but not a truck rental franchise granted to a service station dealer. With respect to the 20 percent requirement, the Interpretive Guides state that the FTC expects parties invoking this exemption to take into account in good faith the franchisee's anticipated sales for a period of one year after the franchisee begins selling the franchise's goods or products.

Occasionally a company that wants to acquire franchise rights, and that has the relevant experience required for the fractional exemption, may prefer to form an affiliated company to actually acquire and operate the franchise. Two questions then arise in relation to the fractional franchise exemption: (1) Can the experience of the existing company be attributed to the new affiliate?; and (2) Can the revenue of the existing company be aggregated with the new affiliate for purposes of the "20 percent" test? The FTC addressed these issues in Informal Staff Advisory Opinion 99-5 (AO 99-5), July 2, 1999.[9] Turning to the first question, while AO 99-5 does not provide for attribution of the parent company's experience to the new subsidialy, the FTC staff noted that the experience of the new entity's directors or officers could be used to satisfy the first prong of the fractional franchise test. As to the second question, AO 99-5 provides that the income of a parent company may be aggregated with the income of a wholly-owned subsidiary franchisee for the purposes of the "20 percent" test.

2. *No Fee in First Six Months*

One of the elements in the definition of a franchise is the required payment to the franchisor of at least $500 either before or within the first six months after commencement of the franchised business as a condition of obtaining or commencing the business. A franchisor may want to structure its international transaction so that it does not include this element by deferring all payments until after the first six months of operation. It is important to note, however, that the FTC has stated that this fee element will be met in a variety of different types of payments, including fees for advertising assistance, training, promotional literature, purchases of equipment, signs and supplies, and continuing services and royalty payments. Payments that are not made pursuant to the franchise agreement but under another related contract (such as a software license agreement) may also meet this element. The FTC has also indicated that the payment may be required either by contract or by practical necessity. Therefore, while a franchisor may give a franchisee the option to make a purchase from the franchisor or third parties, if the only practical alternative is to purchase from the franchisor (or its affiliate), the required payment element will be met.

It is interesting to note that the fee element will not be present even if the franchisee promises at the time of purchasing the franchise to pay a sum greater than $500, so long as the payment does not become due until after the first six months of operation. Furthermore, the franchisor need not give the franchisee the option to terminate the relationship as a prerequisite to collecting the payment.

However, the FTC has excluded from the definition of required payment any payments made by a franchisee for "reasonable amounts" of merchandise to be used for resale on the condition that the merchandise be sold to the dealer at a "bona fide wholesale price." Reasonable amounts of merchandise is construed to mean amounts not in excess of those that a reasonable business person normally would purchase by way of starting inventory or supply or to maintain an ongoing inventory or supply. If an excess price is charged for merchandise or if the franchisee must carry excessive or unnecessary inventory, the exclusion would not apply.

3. *Single Franchise*

The FTC Rule specifically excludes from the definition of a franchise, an agreement between a licensor and a single licensee where the license granted by the licensor of a trademark, service mark, trade name, or other commercial symbol is the only one of its general nature and type to be granted by the licensor with respect to such trademark, service mark, trade name, or other commercial symbol. Therefore, if a foreign franchisor intends to grant only one license in the United States, the foreign franchisor would not have to comply with the FTC Rule with respect to the grant of such a license.

III. State Franchise Disclosure Laws

A. DEFINITION OF A FRANCHISE

In addition to federal law, the states of California, Hawaii, Illinois, Indiana, Maryland, Michigan, Minnesota, New York, North Dakota, Oregon, Rhode Island, South Dakota, Virginia, Washington, and Wisconsin have enacted legislation that regulates the offer and sale of franchises. All of these states, with the exception of Oregon, require a franchisor to register under the state law before a franchisor may make an offer or sale of a franchise in the state.

With some variation, each of these state franchise statutes define a franchise in a manner similar to the FTC Rule. Although these definitions differ from state to state, the three elements of a franchise are generally described as (1) the franchisee is granted the right to offer, sell, or distribute goods and services under a marketing plan or system prescribed in substantial part by the franchisor; (2) the business is substantially associated with the franchisor's marks; and (3) the franchisee is required to pay, directly or indirectly, a fee. Rather than the marketing plan component, the laws in a minority of states (Hawaii, Minnesota, South Dakota, and Washington) include instead as an element of the definition of a franchise a "community of interest" between the franchisor and the franchisee in the subject business. In New York, a franchise exists if a fee is charged and there is either a marketing plan or trademark association.

B. JURISDICTIONAL SCOPE

1. General

For the most part, state franchise laws follow a similar jurisdictional approach for determining whether an offer or sale of a franchise is subject to the state's regulation. The state franchise laws typically apply when an offer or sale of a franchise is made "in this state." An offer of a franchise is usually broadly defined to include all methods of solicitation of an offer to buy a franchise. Therefore, a franchisor may not even advertise in a state prior to registration if an offer is deemed to be made "in this state." An offer or sale may be deemed to take place in the state

- where the prospective franchisee is domiciled;
- from which the offer to sell a franchise originates;
- to which the offer to sell a franchise is directed;
- to which the acceptance of a franchise is directed;
- where meetings between the franchisor and the prospective franchisee take place;
- where the proposed franchise business will be located; or
- where the sales territory granted to the franchisee is located.

Any given state franchise statute may contain some or all of these tests.

2. Multijurisdiction Transactions

Under this jurisdictional approach, for example, it is possible for the New York franchise law to apply even if an Indonesian franchisor sells a franchise to be located in Canada to a resident of New York. It is also possible for New York law to apply to a transaction where a New York franchisor sells a franchise to an Indonesian franchisee for a franchise to be located in Indonesia. Furthermore, if a New York franchisor offers a franchise to an Indiana resident for a franchise to be located in Montreal, both the New York and Indiana registration laws will apply. Because of the broad jurisdictional scope of state franchise registration laws, sales activities can subject a franchisor to a registration law in a state where the franchisor is not registered.

Practice Tip

Be sure to consider all the countries whose laws could apply to an international transaction. The analysis does not necessarily begin and end with federal and state laws of the United States.

C. OVERVIEW OF STATE REGISTRATION/DISCLOSURE REQUIREMENTS

Of the fifteen states that have enacted disclosure laws, eleven states have a formal registration process that requires registration of the information in connection with the offer and sale of franchises. On the other hand, Oregon does not have any notification or registration requirements, and Indiana, Michigan, and Wisconsin only require the filing of a notice of intent to offer franchises in the state (with a copy of the standard franchise offering circular in Wisconsin's case).

State franchise laws arguably do not apply to international transactions. However, there has been no judicial authority supporting the proposition that a franchisor does not have to comply with state law. If a franchisor is negotiating in, or if either party is from one of the fifteen states with registration or disclosure laws, the franchisor needs to look at the state statutes carefully and keep an eye on which entities it negotiates with and which entity will ultimately be the franchisee. The states requiring formal registration and disclosure provide by statute and regulation for the contents of the application for registration and of the offering circular. Generally, a registration application will require the submission of the offering circular along with certain other related documents and a filing fee.

As with the FTC Rule, the state franchise laws are ill-suited for international transactions. Under the current state of these franchise laws, however, unless and until the franchisor has complied with the registration or notification requirements, it may not offer or sell franchises in those states. This means that any contact, whether in person or by letter, telephone, or e-mail, made with prospective franchisees in these states in an attempt to further the possible sale of a franchise should be handled with extreme caution. In addition, no contact should be made outside these states with any of their residents or with prospects who are contemplating buying franchises to be located or operated in those states without first analyzing the applicable statute.

D. APPLICATION OF STATE FRANCHISE LAWS TO INBOUND TRANSACTIONS: DIFFICULTIES IN COMPLYING

1. Cost of Registration

In each of the eleven states that require a formal registration process, the franchisor must submit the offering circular for review and approval prior to offering or selling franchises in the state. Although the filing fees are not very high (ranging from $250 to $675 for initial registration), the total cost to a franchisor can be rather significant by the time the registrations are approved. Not only will the franchisor incur legal fees to prepare the offering circular, it will incur additional legal fees during the registration process. To reduce costs, foreign franchisors should carefully consider in which states it is interested in selling franchises and only register in those states.

2. *Timing of Registration*

Upon submission of all required information to the designated office in the state administration, a franchise examiner will review a registration application and return a comment letter noting deficiencies, if any. After these deficiencies are corrected and returned to the franchise examiner, an order of registration is issued. The entire registration process, from the submission of registration materials to the issuance of an order of registration, may take from a few weeks to several months, and it is not unusual for more than one comment letter to be forthcoming if an examiner believes that a franchisor's response to a prior comment letter is not satisfactory. This often poses a problem for franchisors contemplating inbound transactions because a foreign franchisor would certainly not want to go through the registration process unless someone was interested in purchasing a franchise in the state in question. If a franchisor does not start the registration process until a prospective franchisee expresses interest in a franchise, however, the prospective franchisee could lose interest by the time the franchisor is registered in a state.

NASAA has developed and is currently testing a coordinated review registration process to make it easier and faster for franchisors who want to register with all states that require franchise registration. Under this procedure, the various registration states send all their comments to an examiner of one designated state (currently Maryland), and this examiner reviews and consolidates all of the comments and sends the franchisor a single comment letter. The program is in its infancy and is not yet available to all franchisors.

3. *Negotiated Transactions*

Most international transactions are highly negotiated, and it is almost impossible to prepare an offering circular in advance that contains the pertinent terms of the franchise that is eventually sold. As with the FTC Rule, state franchise statutes also are either unclear or inconsistent on the issue of disclosing negotiated changes to an offering circular, and state policies toward negotiations range from requiring negotiations to prohibiting them unless the negotiated changes are filed with the state. For instance, Virginia requires franchisors to negotiate agreements with prospective franchisees and does not require them to report any negotiated changes. The Illinois, Wisconsin, and Washington franchise laws state that negotiated changes do not require a presale amendment to the registered franchise offering circular. In Maryland, it is an unwritten policy that negotiated changes do not require a presale amendment to the registered franchise offering circular. In contrast, California takes the position that, after closing a negotiated transaction, a franchisor must comply with a number of filing requirements. These requirements impose obstacles to negotiations when the California franchise law is implicated. The statutes in the remaining franchise registration states do not address negotiated changes, and their regulatory agencies have not announced policies on this issue.

Another issue concerning negotiated changes relates to disclosing the negotiability of agreements. If the franchisor has negotiated, or is willing to negotiate, certain provisions of the franchise agreement routinely, its willingness to do so may be itself a material fact that should be disclosed in the franchise offering circular.

Finally, franchisors should be aware that California and North Dakota prohibit franchisors from soliciting material modifications to existing franchise agreements unless the franchisor has filed an application (in California only) to register the material modification and delivers a disclosure document (in both states) a certain number of days before the franchisee's execution of the modification.

E. APPLICABILITY OF STATE FRANCHISE LAWS TO OUTBOUND TRANSACTIONS: DIFFICULTIES IN COMPLYING

Outbound transactions are less likely to trigger the various state franchise laws because the franchised unit will not be located in a franchise registration state. Further, the prospective franchisee is usually not a resident of a franchise registration state. This is not always the case, however, and compliance will likely be required if the prospective franchisee is a resident of a registration state. If any of the state franchise laws do apply, a franchisor located in the United States and selling franchises abroad will have many of the same difficulties in complying with state franchise laws as foreign franchisors selling franchises in the United States

As discussed above, a foreign franchisor trying to comply with state franchise laws for inbound transactions has to determine whether the size of the transaction is significant enough to justify the registration costs. A U.S. franchisor desiring to sell franchises abroad would encounter the same problem. The time necessary to register could also pose a problem for franchisors engaging in outbound transactions. As with an inbound transaction, momentum of a transaction is very important. In fact, the effect of delay could be even more detrimental for an outbound transaction, depending on the culture of the country involved. Most countries do not have laws that are akin to the U.S. state franchise registration laws and, therefore, prospective franchisees located abroad may not be very understanding about why a franchisor could not proceed with a transaction at a faster pace. In addition, outbound transactions, like inbound transactions, may be highly negotiated. Therefore, U.S. franchisors will have to overcome the same obstacles as discussed above concerning foreign franchisors in negotiating international transactions. Finally, because compliance with state franchise disclosure laws means that a franchisor would have to prepare an offering circular, a franchisor will also encounter the issues that arise when preparing an offering circular for compliance with the FTC Rule. (See Section II, above, for a discussion of these issues.)

F. PENALTIES FOR NONCOMPLIANCE

The franchise registration/disclosure laws provide that the seller or offeror of a franchise who does not comply with these laws or who employs fraudulent or misleading acts in connection with the sale or offer of a franchise may be liable to the purchaser in a civil proceeding. The action may be brought against the franchisor, subfranchisor, franchise broker, or anyone else who participated or aided in making the franchise sale. There is considerable variation among the statutes, however, regarding how much the franchisee can recover. For example, Hawaii and Washington allow awards as high as three times the actual damages sustained. Minnesota, South Dakota, and North Dakota do not specifically provide for treble damages, but the courts may award "such relief as the court deems appropriate." On the other hand, some states (Maryland, Michigan, New York, and Virginia) limit awards to actual damages sustained, plus interest, reasonable attorneys' fees, and costs and disbursements.

In addition to the franchisee's right of action, the franchise registration and disclosure laws also provide that the state can punish violators with fines and criminal sanctions.

G. POSSIBLE EXEMPTIONS

All state franchise registration and disclosure laws provide certain exemptions from a franchisor's registration obligations. An exemption from registration, however, does not necessarily relieve the franchisor from its disclosure obligations. Some states require disclosure to qualify for a particular exemption from registration.

1. Large Franchisor Exemption

The registration exemption a franchisor in an international transaction will most frequently rely upon is the "large franchisor" exemption. This exemption is available to franchisors that meet minimum net worth or franchise experience standards. The criteria and procedure for qualifying for the large franchisor exemption varies from state to state. Many states set a minimum net worth at $5 million (or $10 million) and require that the franchisor have five years of experience (or that its parent company have such experience) in the business to be franchised or that the franchisor has had at least twenty-five franchisees conducting business at all times during the five years immediately preceding the offer or sale in that state. Does a foreign franchisor's experience in its home country or with its franchisees there qualify for this exemption for an inbound transaction? Although the state statutes do not specify that a franchisor must have experience in the United States, a state examiner or a franchisee/plaintiff in a civil action may argue that the purpose of the exemption would be frustrated if franchisors with no experience in the United States can rely on this exemption.

Franchisors who qualify for the exemption under a state franchise law are exempt from registration under such state law, but they are not typically exempt from providing disclosure to prospective franchisees or from filing an exemption notice with such state. While claiming the exemption does not relieve the franchisor from having to prepare an offering circular, there are many reasons why a franchisor may wish to use it. Most of the state laws that contain the large franchisor exemption do not require franchisors who qualify for the exemption to submit the franchisor's offering circular to the state for review. Not only will this save the franchisor some time, the decreased state involvement with the offering circular should translate into less expense as well.

2. Sophisticated or Experienced Franchisee Exemption

In certain states, a franchisor can qualify for an exemption from the state's registration requirement if its prospective franchisee meets the definition of a sophisticated or experienced investor. Each of the six states with a sophisticated or experienced franchisee exemption (California, Illinois, Maryland, Rhode Island, Washington, and Wisconsin) defines the exemption criteria in a different way. While Maryland equates sophistication with the amount of initial investment required (at least $750,000), Rhode Island and Wisconsin provide minimum net worth and income requirements and require that the investor have knowledge and experience to evaluate the merits and risks of the franchise. Care should be taken to consider the applicability of this exemption when the franchisee is not an individual.

3. State Fractional Franchise Exemption

The fact that a franchise program qualifies for the federal fractional franchise exemption does not mean that it will qualify for the form of state fractional franchise exemption available under state law. This exemption or some form thereof is available in eight of the fifteen states with franchise laws.[10] Like the federal fractional franchise exemption, these state exemptions are intended for situations where an existing business adds additional product lines or services offered by the franchisor. Unlike federal law, however, there are no published opinions by state agencies or case law that interprets the application of these exemptions.[11]

4. Out-of-State Sale Exemption

Of the fifteen states with franchise laws, nine states provide for an out-of-state sales exemption that applies to registration and disclosure requirements. In addition, one state provides for an exemption that only applies to registration. These out-of-state exemptions generally apply if the franchisee is not domiciled in the state. However, there may be other conditions placed upon the exemption. Exhibit A at the end of this chapter provides a summary of the out-of-state exemptions under state franchise laws.

IV. Overview of Foreign Disclosure Laws

Because U.S. franchise regulation is extremely comprehensive, franchisors who have a U.S. UFOC should be able to comply with most foreign disclosure requirements without the need to compile vast amounts of additional information, with the notable exception of Malaysia. (See the discussion in Section VII, below.) However, the required format may vary, and translation into the local language may be necessary. There is no substitute for experienced local counsel in a particular country, but this summary should provide a useful overview.

V. Scope and Governing Authority Under Foreign Disclosure Laws

For each country, this section provides the official name of the franchise law, the government agency that administers it, and the jurisdictional scope of the franchise legislation. Each statute has a different definition of what constitutes a franchise and each must be examined carefully to determine whether it applies to a given transaction. The information about foreign laws in the remainder of this chapter is current as of August 2001. However, the laws and regulations summarized are subject to amendment, and one should update the information provided here before proceeding in any of the countries.

A. AUSTRALIA

Australia adopted a mandatory Franchise Code of Conduct on July 1, 1998. On June 28, 2001, the Australian government amended the Code of Conduct through regulations that come into force on October 1, 2001. The information about the Code of Conduct in this chapter reflects these amendments. This Code of Conduct takes the form of a regulation prescribed under the Australian Trade Practices Act and has the force of law. The Australian Competition and Consumer Commission (ACCC) is charged with monitoring and enforcing the Code of Conduct, which means that the ACCC may take action at any time against a franchisor for noncompliance with the Code of Conduct. The Code of Conduct applies to all businesses that are bound by the Trade Practices Act and applies to a franchisor that renews, extends, transfers, or enters into a franchise agreement with a franchisee on or after October 1, 1998. It should be noted that, in addition to registration and disclosure requirements, the Australian law contains some relationship provisions that franchisor counsel should consider before closing a regulated transaction. However, those provisions are outside the scope of this chapter. Parties to existing franchise agreements as of October 1, 1998, are under no obligation to rewrite those agreements to meet the requirements of the Code of Conduct. Those parties must, however, be aware that conditions in those agreements that would infringe the Code of Conduct are unenforceable. Clause 5(3) of the Code of Conduct states that the it applies to foreign franchisors franchising in Australia, except where the franchisor grants only one franchise or master franchise to be operated there.

B. BRAZIL

In 1995, Brazil enacted its Franchising Law, Law Number 8.955/94, which requires franchisors to provide a disclosure document to prospective franchisees. Article 8 of the Franchising Law provides that the law applies to franchising systems established and operated in the national territory of Brazil. The Franchising Law does not identify a governmental agency responsible for administration and enforcement of the disclosure requirements but, in practice, the National Institute of Industrial Property (known by its Portuguese initials as INPI) administers the statute.

C. CANADA (PROVINCE OF ALBERTA)

In Canada, until very recently, only the Province of Alberta had legislation expressly regulating franchising. In 1995, Alberta enacted the Franchises Act, Chapter F-17.1. Section 3 of the act limits the jurisdictional scope of the act to the sale of a franchise where (1) the franchised business is to be operated either wholly or partly in Alberta, *and* (2) where the franchisee is an Alberta resident or has a permanent establishment in Alberta for purposes of the Alberta Corporate Tax Act. The Director, Franchises and Registrar appointed by the Alberta Securities Commission Agency handles the day-to-day administration of the Franchises Act.

D. CANADA (PROVINCE OF ONTARIO)

On May 17, 2000, the Ontario legislature passed Bill 33, known as the Arthur Wishart Act (Franchise Disclosure) 2000. The bill received Royal Assent on June 8, 2000. The act generally applies to any franchised business if (1) the franchise agreement was entered into, extended, or renewed on or after the effective date of the act, and (2) if the franchised business is to be operated partly or wholly in Ontario. The act imposes a statutory duty of fair dealing upon the parties to franchise agreements, gives franchisees the right to associate and organize, and creates new disclosure obligations for franchisors. On July 1, 2000, the portions of the act not dealing with disclosure, including definitions, application of the statute, relationship provisions, and various administrative provisions, were proclaimed in force. On October 31, 2000, the Minister of Consumer and Commercial Relations for the Province of Ontario promulgated regulations that implement the disclosure requirements of the act. The disclosure requirements came into force on January 31, 2001.

E. CHINA

In November 1997, China became the third Asian country to regulate franchising when the Chinese Ministry of Internal Trade issued the Measures for Administration of Franchise Operations (for Trial Implementation), Domestic Trade Xing-Zi (1997) No. 124, dated November 14, 1997 (the Measures). The Measures require written disclosure of franchise information to prospective franchisees and the recordal of disclosures with the China Chain Enterprises Association. Article III of the Measures states that the Measures apply to entities that engage in franchise operations within the territory of the People's Republic of China.

F. FRANCE

In 1989, France enacted its franchise disclosure law, Law No. 89-1008 of December 31, 1989, Relative to the Development of Commercial and Trade Enterprises and the Improvement of Their Economic, Legal and Social Environment (known as the Doubin Law). The Finance Section of the Council of State issued implementing regulations. The Minister of Justice, the Minister of Industry and Development, and the Minister Delegate for Commerce and Trades are charged with the execution of the Doubin Law. The Doubin Law applies, according to Article 1 thereof, to "any person who puts at the disposal of another person, a trade name, trademark or commercial symbol, while requiring from such other person a commitment of exclusivity or quasi-exclusivity with respect to the conduct of such other person's business."

G. INDONESIA

In July 1997, the government of the Republic of Indonesia issued Government Regulation No. 16/1997 on Franchising (Regulation 16). This regulation, together with the Decree of the Minister of Industry and Trade No. 259/MPP/Kep/7/1997 on the Provisions and Procedure for the Implementation of Franchise Business Registration (Decree 259), now form the basis of Indonesia's Franchise Law. These regulations are administered by the Minister of Industry and Trade. Neither Regulation 16 nor the more comprehensive Decree 259 contains a limitation on jurisdictional scope. The Indonesian statute also contains some relationship restrictions that merit review. However, they are beyond the scope of this chapter.

H. JAPAN

The Medium-Small Retail Business Promotion Act (the "Retailers Law") was adopted in Japan in 1973. It allows small retailers (companies having capitalization of less than 10 million yen and companies having less than fifty employees) to take advantage of certain government incentives intended to help small businesses to compete with large businesses. These incentives include government assistance in obtaining financing and favorable depreciation allowances. This statute is administered by the Ministry of International Trade and Industry (MITI). Franchisors of retailing chains may apply to MITI to qualify for the incentives provided by the statute. There is no definition of "franchise" in the legislation.

I. MALAYSIA

In December 1998, Malaysia enacted the Malaysia Franchise Act 1998, Act 590. However, the law did not come into force until accompanying regulations were finalized and published in the *Gazette* in October 1999. According to Section 3 thereof, the act applies throughout Malaysia to the sale of a franchise in Malaysia. The sale of a franchise is deemed to be in Malaysia where (1) a franchise business is operated in Malaysia, or (2) where an offer to sell or buy a franchise is either (a) made in Malaysia and accepted within or outside Malaysia or (b) is made outside Malaysia and accepted within Malaysia (Section 3). Note that the Malaysia Franchise Act, like American state franchise laws, requires a franchisor to be registered before it may *offer or sell* a franchise in Malaysia. The Malaysia Franchise Act is administered by the Registrar of Franchises, an appointee of the Minister of Entrepreneur Development. The Malaysian franchise statute contains what may be the most draconian relationship provisions. Franchisors would be well advised to understand them fully before committing to a transaction in Malaysia.

J. MEXICO

In 1991, Mexico enacted its Law on Industrial Property. This federal legislation regulates franchising as well as other forms of intellectual property and generally requires presale disclosure to prospective purchasers and registration of the transmission of trademark rights to a franchisee. The statute itself is quite vague in its requirements. However, implementing regulations were issued in 1994 clarifying many issues. The law is administered by the Ministry of Commerce and Industrial Development. The statute does not contain a limit on its jurisdictional scope. Although the law does not contain a jurisdictional scope provision, one point worth noting is that under the law the definition of a franchise does not include as an element the payment of any fee by the franchisee to the franchisor. Thus, the definition of a franchise under Mexican law is broader than under U.S. law.

K. ROMANIA

In 1997, the government of Romania issued an Ordinance Regarding the Legal Status of Franchises (Government Ordinance 52/1997) that requires franchisors to provide certain presale disclosures to franchisees. The ordinance does not provide the name of the government agency that will be charged with enforcing it, nor does it provide any limitations on its jurisdictional scope. However, as in the Mexico statute, it should be noted that the definition of a franchise does not require a fee element. Franchise is defined in Article 1(a) as a marketing system based on continuous operation between persons each of whom is financially independent, whereby a franchisor grants to a franchisee the right to operate a business.

L. RUSSIA

In 1996, Russia enacted franchise legislation requiring registration of franchise agreements with a government agency (Chapter 54 of Part II of the Russian Civil Code). The law does not provide for a specific agency that is charged with its enforcement, nor does it contain any specific limits on its jurisdictional scope.

M. SOUTH KOREA

In 1997, Korea's Fair Trade Commission issued criteria for what constitutes an unfair trade practice in a franchised business. These franchise-specific regulations were issued pursuant to more general licensing laws already in effect in Korea. Although the licensing laws do not specifically mention franchising, they had been interpreted to govern franchise agreements. The regulations essentially restate general licensing law concepts in the franchise context. The regulations are set forth in Notice Number 1997-4 of the Fair Trade Commission. These regulations do not contain a jurisdictional scope provision that describes their applicability to transactions occurring partially in Korea or partially outside of Korea.

N. SPAIN

In 1996, Spain enacted its disclosure/registration law, Article 62 of Act 7/1996 on the Regulation of Retail Trading. It was enacted January 15, 1996. Article 62 establishes a registry of franchisors operating in Spain and a disclosure process for prospective franchisees. Article 62 states that it applies to all persons who intend to carry out a franchise operation in Spain. In addition, Royal Decree 2485/1998 provides the details of the requirements outlined in the statute. The Directorate General for Domestic Trade of the Ministry of Economy and Finance is charged with maintaining the franchise register.

VI. Requirements of Foreign Laws

A. OVERVIEW

The descriptions that follow are based upon the English versions of these franchise laws that are contained in the *Business Franchise Guide* published by CCH Incorporated. Many of these statutes were not originally drafted in English. In certain instances, these English translations contain ambiguities. Where such ambiguities exist, we have merely quoted from the English translation. It is difficult to determine whether the original language was unclear, whether the passage lost something in the translation, or both.

Practice Tip

The franchise laws around the world are relatively new and many have a number of ambiguities. Proceed with caution and consult local counsel.

B. REGISTRATION

Registration requirements vary widely among the laws discussed below. Some statutes require presale registration of the required disclosure document (as exists in the United States), while other statutes require registration of the signed franchise agreement within a certain number of days after its execution. For each country, this section addresses (1) what, how, and with whom to register; (2) anything peculiar about the registration process in that country; (3) duration, amendment, and renewal of registration; and (5) level of review and type of scrutiny given to registered documents.

1. China

Article 17 of the Measures requires a franchisor to submit its disclosure document to the China Chain Enterprises Association for the record. In exercising its charge of reviewing disclosure documents, the China Chain Enterprises Association is to formulate some time in the future rules and codes of conduct for franchise operations, help franchise enterprises to practice "self-discipline," and provide services to both the franchisor and the franchisee.

2. Indonesia

The Indonesian Franchise Law requires the franchisee to obtain a franchised business registration certificate, or STPUW. To obtain its STPUW, the franchisee must register the franchise agreement along with the disclosure document it received at the Ministry of Industry and Trade (Article 11). Additionally, Article 10 of the Indonesian law provides that the minister or other official may suggest improvements to a franchise agreement to protect the interest of a franchisee and protect the participation of small- and medium-scale enterprises as franchisees or as suppliers of goods and services. Article 11 provides that the franchisee must register for its STPUW within thirty working days from the date the Franchise Agreement takes effect. The application form for an STPUW may be obtained from the Directorate General of Domestic Trade or at a local regional office of the Ministry of Industry and Trade. If the minister "considers" that the STPUW application is "complete and in correct order," he shall issue an STPUW within a maximum period of five working days. If the minister "considers" that the STPUW application and its accompanying documents are not "complete and in correct order," he shall, within a maximum period of five working days, reject the application and provide a list of reasons for the rejection. Although it is not clear, presumably the minister has broad discretion in determining when an application is in "complete and in correct order." An applicant whose application is rejected may resubmit an STPUW application after fulfilling the requirements stipulated in the rejection order. Article 13 of the law provides that an STPUW shall remain valid as long as the franchise agreement is valid. Article 14 provides that if a franchise agreement is terminated prior to the end of its term, and a new franchisee is appointed for the territory, the new franchisee will not be issued an STPUW unless the franchisor has settled all problems arising from the original franchise and has signed a "Clean Break Joint Statement" with the former franchisee. Although the STPUW lasts for as long as the franchise agreement is in effect, Article 21 of the law provides that a franchisee must submit a report and amend its STPUW if certain changes in its relationship with the franchisor occur such as: expansion or reduction of the franchised business activities, transfer of the ownership of the business, change in the address of the franchised business, change in management of the franchisee or franchisor, and a change in the term of the franchise agreement.

3. *Malaysia*

Section 6 of the Malaysia Franchise Act provides that a franchisor must register the franchise with the registrar before it may make an offer to sell a franchise to any person. A person who fails to comply with the registration requirements commits an offense unless he or she has been exempted pursuant to Section 58 of the act. To register a franchise, the franchisor must submit a disclosure document, the franchise agreement, the operations manual, the training manual, its latest audited financial statements and auditor's report, and any additional information required by the registrar. However, we have been advised by the Ministry of Entrepreneur Development that it announced at a conference on August 2, 2000, that in practice the Registrar of Franchises does not require copies of the manuals to be retained at the registry. The operations manual of a foreign franchisor need not be filed with the registrar but must be available at the franchisor's office. This policy was a response to franchisors' concerns that their trade secrets would be disclosed if their manuals were filed with a government agency. Section 11 of the Franchise Act requires the franchisor to amend its registration and submit updated versions of the required materials if there is any material change in the documents described above. Section 14 of the Franchise Act requires registration of franchise brokers. Section 16 provides that the franchisor must update its registered materials within thirty days from the anniversary date of the registration each year. Sections 53 through 55 provide that the registrar may refuse a registration application without giving any reason for the refusal if the franchisor is a foreign person. Section 57 also requires filing of advertisements with the registrar.

Form 2 of the implementing regulations contains the application for registration of a foreign franchisor. This application requires much more detail than its counterpart under U.S. state registration laws. A franchisor must include on the application its business activities, addresses of all company-owned outlets, capital structure, bank accounts, identity of directors and shareholders, and its present employment structure (including numbers of employees in each type of position and whether such employees are Malaysian nationals).

4. Mexico

Any "transmission" of rights in a trademark, including a franchise, must be registered with the Ministry of Commerce and Industrial Development in accordance with the regulations issued pursuant to the Law on Industrial Property, Article 143. Neither the statute nor the regulations require registration of the disclosure document. Registration requirements apply only to the franchise agreement, and registration occurs after the agreement is signed. Either the franchisor or the franchisee may register the agreement, but it is in the franchisor's best interest to ensure that the registration is properly filed. Article 10 of the regulations issued pursuant to the statute require that the application to register a franchise must include (1) the name, nationality and domicile of the franchisor and the franchisee; (2) the effective period of the agreement; (3) whether the agreement reserves to the franchisor the authority to exercise legal action to protect the trademarks; (4) the products or services that the licensee may offer under the marks; and (5) all other data requested on the official form. Article 5 of the regulations requires all documents comprising a registration application to be in Spanish. The regulations allow for the omission from the filed copy of the economic terms of the agreement, technical information and confidential information regarding channels of distribution. In practice, few franchisors seem to register their franchise agreements. Instead, most franchisors register a short-form summary of the trademark licensing provisions of the franchise agreement. This not only reduces the cost of translation, it also prevents the entire agreement from becoming a public document.

5. Russia

Article 1028 of the franchise law provides that franchise agreements must be in writing and must be registered by "the agency [that registered] the legal entity or individual entrepreneur acting under the contract as [the franchisor]." If the franchisor is registered as a legal entity or an individual in a foreign state, the registration of the franchise agreement shall be effectuated by "the agency to have registered the legal entity or individual entrepreneur [who is the franchisee]." The franchisor and franchisee may not refer to the franchise agreement in their relationships with third parties until the agreement has been registered. If the franchise agreement involves a patent, it must also be registered with the patent agency of the Russian Federation. If such patent registration is not obtained, the contract shall be deemed null and void. Article 1031 of the law provides that it is the franchisor's obligation to ensure the registration of the franchise agreement.

6. Spain

Article 62, Heading 2, provides that all persons who intend to carry out a franchise operation in Spain must enter the franchise in a registry. Franchisors must register with the Autonomous Government in the territory where they are headquartered. Each Autonomous Region maintains a register. A federal register is created pursuant to the regulations in addition to the registers maintained by each Autonomous Government. Franchisors whose registered offices are not in Spain may register directly on the federal register. The federal register exists to centralize franchisor data for franchisors that operate in more than one Autonomous Region.

Applications for inclusion in the register of franchisors must be accompanied by (1) the name, address, and identification number of the franchisor; (2) the intellectual property rights that will be licensed under the franchise agreement; and (3) a description of the franchised business including the number of franchisees and company-owned units stating the location of each unit as well as the number of franchisees who have ceased to be members of the franchised network in Spain during the past two years. If any of the above information changes subsequent to registration, the franchisor must so notify the registry. In addition, every year franchisors must notify the corresponding regional government of the closing or opening of franchised or company-owned businesses during the preceding year.

Practice Tip

Even though a particular country does not have a franchise-specific registration requirement, there may be other forms of registration or filing required. See Chapter 6 of this book for an overview of such requirements and consult local counsel for details.

C. LOGISTICS OF DISCLOSURE

1. Australia

The franchisor must give a copy of the required disclosure document along with a copy of the Code of Conduct to a prospective franchisee at least fourteen days before the prospect enters into a franchise agreement or pays nonrefundable money to the franchisor or an associate of the franchisor. The franchisor must also give a disclosure document to a franchisee at least fourteen days before renewal or extension of the existing franchise agreement. Additionally, Clause 19 of the Code of Conduct requires a franchisor to give an existing franchisee a copy of its current disclosure document within fourteen days after a written request by the franchisee. The franchisor must update its disclosure document for the benefit of its existing franchisees even if the franchisor is no longer selling new franchises. However, each franchisee may make such a request only once in a twelve-month period.

Also, a franchisor may not enter into, renew, or extend a franchise agreement or receive money unless the franchisor has received from the prospective franchisee a written statement that the prospective franchisee has received, read, and has had a reasonable opportunity to understand the disclosure document and the Code of Conduct. A franchisor must receive from a prospective franchisee a signed statement that the prospect has been given advice about the franchise by a legal, business. or accounting advisor, or a signed statement that the prospective franchisee has been told that he or she should seek such advice but has decided not to seek it. The June 28, 2001, regulations removed a provision that had required franchisees to deliver a short-form disclosure document prior to the transfer of an existing franchise.

Finally, upon request from a franchisee, Australia requires a franchisor to disclose to the franchisee the results of a required annual audit of the franchisor's advertising fund. The June 28, 2001, regulations added a notation to the Code of Conduct stating that, under Australia's Electronic Transactions Act 1999, obligations to provide information in writing under Australian law can be satisfied electronically if it is reasonable to expect that the information will be readily accessible and usable for subsequent reference and the recipient consents to receiving the information electronically.

2. Brazil

Article 4 of the Franchising Law provides that the franchise offering circular shall be delivered to the franchisee candidate at least ten days before the execution of the franchise agreement or the payment of any fee by the franchisee to the franchisor or to a company related to the franchisor.

3. Canada (Province of Alberta)

Section 4 of the act requires the franchisor to give every prospective franchisee a copy of the franchisor's disclosure document at least fourteen days before the prospective franchisee signs any agreement relating to the franchise, or pays any consideration relating to the franchise, whichever is earlier. The payment of any consideration relating to a franchise does not include the payment of a fully refundable deposit.

4. Canada (Province of Ontario)

Section 5 of the new disclosure act provides that the franchisor must provide to the prospective franchisee a disclosure document not less than fourteen days before the earlier of (1) the signing by the franchisee of the franchise agreement or any other agreement relating to the franchise, or (2) the payment of any other consideration relating to the franchise. A disclosure document may be delivered personally, by registered mail, or by any other prescribed method. The disclosure document must be given as one document at one time.

5. China

The Measures require a franchisor, at least ten days prior to the signing of the contract, to provide the disclosure document to the applicant.

6. France

Article 1 of the Doubin Law and Article 2 of the Implementing Regulations require that a disclosure document and the proposed franchise contract shall be delivered to the prospective franchisee at least twenty days before the execution of the contract or before the payment of any monies.

7. Indonesia

A franchisor is required to provide a franchisee with a disclosure document prior to signing a franchise agreement. No particular period is required for review of the disclosure document before signing an agreement. Article 9 of the law provides that "a franchisor from abroad must be in possession of a legal evidence from an authorized government agency in his country of origin and this legal evidence must be acknowledged by the local official of the representative office of the Republic of Indonesia."

8. Japan

The Retailers Law is worded rather vaguely and is often difficult to understand, at least in English translation. It provides that the franchisor must furnish the specified disclosures to a prospective member of a franchised retail chain "when entering a contract with a person who wants to join [the chain]."

9. Malaysia

Section 15 of the Franchise Act requires that a franchisor provide to a franchisee a copy of the franchise agreement and disclosure documents at least ten days before the franchisee signs the agreement.

10. Mexico

The obligation under the Law on Industrial Property is that the franchisor provide the disclosure document to the party to whom it intends to grant the franchise before entering into the franchise agreement.

11. Romania

Chapter 2, Article 2, of the ordinance requires a franchisor to provide a prospective franchisee a disclosure document before signing any contract to enable each of the parties to confirm its decision to enter into the agreement.

12. Russia

The Russian franchise law does not require presale disclosure to prospective franchisees.

13. South Korea

Articles 4 and 5 of the Franchising Regulations require franchisors to provide certain information about the franchise business to prospective franchisees. Article 4 requires the franchisor to make available to the franchisee the necessary information regarding the franchised business before entering into an agreement with a prospective franchisee. However, the regulations do not require that any specified amount of time must pass after disclosure and before the franchisee signs an agreement. The franchisor may not enter into a franchise agreement without complying with the prospective franchisee's request for further written information from the franchisor regarding the contents of the franchise agreement.

14. Spain

Article 3 of the regulations provides that the franchisor must provide the disclosure document to the franchisee at least twenty days before signing the agreement or payment of any consideration.

D. CONTENT OF DISCLOSURE DOCUMENTS

The prescribed contents of the various disclosure documents are summarized in the following paragraphs. Additionally, Exhibit B at the end of this chapter includes a chart comparing the various disclosure documents.

1. Australia

The Australian disclosure requirements are divided into two types of disclosure documents: extensive disclosure requirements applicable to most franchisors, and more limited disclosure requirements for the sale of a franchise where the franchisee's expected annual gross revenues are less than $50,000 Australian. Disclosure documents must include all required information, may include additional information, must be signed by a director or officer of the franchisor, and must be updated annually within three months after the end of each fiscal year of the franchisor. A franchisor must amend its disclosure document within sixty days after the change in a materially relevant fact. The Code of Conduct lists "materially relevant" changes. This list includes a change in control of the franchisor or the institution of or judgment in certain criminal or civil proceedings or arbitrations.

Matters to be disclosed are described, item by item, in Annexure 1 (for sale of most franchises) and Annexure 2 of the code (for the sale of franchises where franchisee revenues is not expected to exceed $50,000 Australian annually). Disclosure required under Annexure 1 covers a broad array of topics that are similar to U.S. disclosures, and include the following:

- franchisor's name, address, and ten-year business history;
- business history of officers and directors;
- litigation history;
- payments and financing;
- information about existing franchisees in Australia and franchisees who left the system;
- information about intellectual property;
- description of territorial rights, site selection, and supply restrictions;
- details of any advertising fund;
- estimate of the franchisee's investment; and
- summary of the contract obligations. Earnings information (if provided) is also regulated.

Annexure 2 eliminates some of these disclosure requirements, although a franchisee or prospective franchisee that receives a disclosure document in accordance with Annexure 2 is entitled to receive all of the Annexure 1 disclosures upon request unless it is reasonable for the franchisor to withhold the information under the circumstances. The Code of Conduct does not indicate what circumstances would justify withholding the information.

2. Brazil

Article 3 of the Franchising Law regulates the contents of the disclosure document, listing fifteen topics that must be addressed. Article 3 does not, on its face, require the document to be written in Portuguese. It requires only that it must be in "clear and comprehensible" language. The disclosure document must provide information about the franchised business, the franchisor, and the terms of the relationship. There is no specific provision about how and when the offering circular must be updated.

3. Canada (Province of Alberta)

The franchisor may use a disclosure document authorized under the franchise law of a jurisdiction outside Alberta as its disclosure document under the Franchises Act, if supplementary information is included that sets out any material changes to the document from its original jurisdiction to make it comply with the requirements of the Alberta regulations under the act. Many American franchisors take advantage of this option by using a special Alberta "wraparound" document that is added to their UFOC. At least two officers or directors of the franchisor must sign a certificate that must be included in the disclosure document. Financial statements prepared in accordance with generally accepted accounting principles for the jurisdiction in which the franchisor is based must be included, as well as the proposed agreements. The financial statements must be for the most recently completed fiscal year, and new statements for each fiscal year must replace the old statements within 180 days after the franchisor's fiscal year end. For the most part, the Alberta disclosure requirements cover the same topics as the U.S. requirements.

4. Canada (Province of Ontario)

Section 5(3) of the new disclosure act provides that the disclosure document will contain all material facts, financial statements, and copies of all agreements to be signed by the prospective franchisee. Additionally, the franchisor must provide the prospect with a written statement of any material change as soon as practicable after the change has occurred and before any agreements are signed or payments made.

The disclosure document must contain information on:

- the business background of the franchisor;
- the business background of the directors, general partners, and officers of the franchisor;
- litigation history of the franchisor and its associates, directors, general partners, and officers;
- bankruptcy or insolvency proceedings;
- financial statements;
- certain required franchisee protection statements;
- alternative dispute resolution processes;
- estimates of costs and fees, and the bases for cost estimates and any earnings claims;
- financing arrangements;
- training and other assistance programs;
- advertising fund provisions;
- restrictions on the franchisee's purchase and sale of goods and services;
- franchisor rebate policies;
- trademark information;
- governmental license, registration, and permit requirements for operation of the franchised business;
- personal participation requirements;
- territorial rights and encroachment policies;
- current and former franchisees;
- termination, renewal, and transfer restrictions; and
- a certificate certifying that the disclosure document contains no untrue information or excludes any material facts.

While the disclosure document requirements are similar to the U.S. UFOC Guidelines, they are not identical, and franchisors using a UFOC in the United States must supplement the UFOC to comply with the Ontario requirements. As discussed above, Alberta regulations under the Franchise Act specifically permits U.S. franchisors to use a wraparound document. Ontario law does not. It is not clear whether a U.S. franchisor will be permitted to simply supplement the UFOC to comply with the Ontario requirements. Therefore, some lawyers may be reluctant to use a wraparound document to comply with the disclosure requirements under Ontario law. Since the Ontario act is to be enforced by private action, it will be up to the judges, who may not be familiar with franchise laws, to decide the correct disclosure format under the Ontario Franchises Act.

5. China

The franchisor must provide to the applicant "true and basic information" about the franchise. Such information shall include, at a minimum: "the name and basic facts of the franchisor's enterprise, its business performance, business circumstances about its affiliated franchisees, the investment budget statement for the franchise network which is proved through practice, methods for collection of royalties and various charges, as well as the terms and restrictions for supply of articles and goods" (Article 12). There is no requirement in the Measures that the disclosure document be written in any particular language.

6. France

Although the Doubin Law does not explicitly require it, custom and practice is that the disclosure document be written in French. The required disclosure document covers, in broad terms, many of the same topics covered by the U.S. UFOC, but requires less detail. No disclosure of litigation history is required. One area of disclosure coverage not required by U.S. law is the disclosure of banking locations used by the franchisor. This information may be limited to the five principal banking locations used by the franchisor.

7. Indonesia

The disclosure document is not required to be in the Indonesian language; however, the franchise agreement must be in Indonesian and must be subject to Indonesian law. The disclosure document is required to contain:

- the identity of the franchisor along with information about its business activities;
- a balance sheet and profit and loss statement of the franchisor for the last two years;
- the description of the intellectual property, invention, or unique business characteristic constituting the object of the franchise;
- requirements that must be fulfilled by the franchisee;
- aid the franchisor offers the franchisee;
- rights and obligations of the franchisor and franchisee;

- the methods of and conditions for the expiration, termination, and extension of the franchise agreement; and
- other matters that the franchisee needs to know.

8. Japan

The Retailers Law requires disclosure of the following information:

- the amount of money to be paid to the franchisor and the method of calculation;
- the cost of fixtures;
- the due dates for all monies to be paid by the franchisee;
- the method of collection of such monies;
- if any monies are refundable, when and under what conditions they will be refunded;
- the types of goods to be sold to the franchisee;
- the method of payment for such goods;
- whether or not the franchisee will receive training at the time of joining the chain;
- the content of any training program;
- the method and frequency of managerial guidance to be providedto the franchisee on a continuous basis;
- the trademarks to be used by the franchisee;
- any conditions imposed on the franchisee's use of the trademark;
- the duration of the franchise agreement;
- the condition and procedure for renewal; and
- "any damages and other liabilities arising out of the termination of contract" *(sic)*.

9. Malaysia

The precise topics to be included in the disclosure document are not set forth in the law. The format of the disclosure document is prescribed in the implementing regulations. The format is set forth in Form 1 of the regulations and very closely follows the format of the U.S. UFOC. One notable difference in the Malaysia document as compared to the U.S. document is that, in addition to audited financial statements for three years, the franchisor must include financial forecasts for three years. The statute does not state whether this means a forecast of the franchisor's performance or that of the franchisee. The franchisor must also include an organization chart of its employees. The law does not specify the language of the disclosure document, but presumably it should be in Malaysian.

10. Mexico

Article 142 of the Law on Industrial Property provides that a franchisor must provide to the franchisee "information regarding the situation of the [franchisor's] business enterprise" prior to entering into a franchise agreement. Although the Industrial Property Law imposes a disclosure obligation on franchisors, it specifies only that information should be provided to the franchisee and does not list the specific items to be disclosed. Article 65 of the regulations provides a list of ten items that a franchisor must include in its disclosure document:

- the franchisor's name, domicile, and nationality;
- a description of the franchise;
- the amount of time the franchisor has been offering franchises or operating a business;
- the intellectual property rights involved in the franchise;
- the amount and types of payments that the franchisee must make to the franchisor;
- the type of service and assistance that the franchisor will provide to the franchisee;
- a definition of the territory in which the franchise will operate;
- the franchisee's right to grant subfranchises and, if the franchisee has that right, the requirements it must fulfill in doing so;
- the franchisee's obligation to maintain confidential information provided by the franchisor; and
- the franchisee's general rights and obligations under the franchise agreement.

Neither the statute nor the regulations states whether the disclosure document must be in Spanish.

11. Romania

Chapter 2, Article 2. requires a franchisor to provide a franchisee with a disclosure document that includes at least the following information:

- the franchisor's experience;
- the financial terms of the franchise agreement, including fees and royalties and required purchases;
- financial information that permits the franchisee to project its results and make a financial plan;
- the e exclusive territory granted to the franchisee; and
- the duration of the franchise agreement and the terms governing renewal, termination, and transfer of the agreement.

Government Ordinance 52/1997 does not specifically address whether the disclosure document must be in Romanian.

12. South Korea

Some basic information must be provided to every franchisee, such as "information relating to costs and fees." Presumably, this must be provided in Korean, although the statute does not specify. Other types of information must be provided to a prospective franchisee if he or she makes a specific written request for that information. A franchisee may request such information if it has difficulty understanding (based on the franchise agreement alone) the definite meaning of the agreement. The franchisee may request additional information about "the provision relating to goods and services, business instructions, method of payment, control of the business, cancellation, termination and conditions for renewal of the franchise agreement." The franchisor must also comply with the prospect's request for written information from the franchisor providing the details of "the business status of the shop to be operated by the prospective franchisee and how the sales are to be calculated in regards to the franchisor's anticipated sales for the franchised business." A franchisor is required to disclose any act that may interfere with the franchisee's business activities. If the franchisee requests it, the franchisor must provide "the necessary financial status relating to the franchised business, business history of the previous five years, and matters relating to ongoing actions with regard to the franchised business." The franchisor must allow the prospect sufficient time to fully review the data and information regarding the franchise agreement and all related documents.

13. Spain

Article 3 of the regulations provides seven categories of information that must be included in the disclosure document. Once again, the statute does not specify the language of the disclosure document, but custom and practice is to generally provide disclosure in Spanish. These seven categories expand upon the information required by the statute, which includes the identification of the franchise, a description of the commercial sector that is the subject of the franchise, the structure of the franchise network, and the essential elements of the franchise agreement. To these general categories, the regulations add the following details:

- name and address of the franchisor and the details about the franchisor that are included in the Register of Franchisors (foreign franchisors must identify their registrations in their country of origin);
- certificate of ownership or license of trademarks in Spain
- general description of the franchised business;
- experience of the franchisor, including date of incorporation and main stages of development of the company and the franchise network;
- explanation of the franchise system, including know-how and assistance to be provided, estimates of investments and expenses necessary for a typical business (sales forecasts and trading results must be based on experience or studies);
- structure and extent of franchise network in Spain, including number and location of existing units, number of franchisees who have ceased to be members of the network during the previous two years, and an explanation of whether the former franchisees left by virtue of expiration of franchise term or other reasons; and
- essential elements of the franchise agreement, including rights and obligations of parties, duration, conditions for renewal, any exclusivity, and restrictions on the franchisee's disposal of the business.

E. DELIVERY OF FRANCHISE AGREEMENT: COOLING-OFF PERIODS

1. Australia

Clause 13 of the Code of Conduct provides that a franchisee may terminate a franchise agreement within seven days after the earlier of: entering into the franchise agreement or paying any money under the agreement. However, this cooling-off period does not apply to the renewal, extension, or transfer of an existing franchise agreement. If a franchisee terminates his or her agreement during the cooling-off period, the franchisor must repay all the money paid by the franchisee within fourteen days after receiving notice that the franchisee intends to terminate the agreement. However, the franchisor may retain its reasonable expenses if the expenses or the method of calculation were set out in the franchise agreement.

2. *Malaysia*

Section 18(4) requires that every franchise agreement contain a cooling-off period, which shall be determined by the contracting parties but shall not be less than seven working days, during which the franchisee has the option to terminate the agreement. Upon termination of the franchise agreement during this cooling-off period, the franchisor must return all monies to the franchisee, but may keep an amount to cover its reasonable expenses incurred to prepare the agreement.

VII. Penalties for Noncompliance

A. GOVERNMENT-IMPOSED PENALTIES

Some of the disclosure laws provide for government-imposed penalties in the event of noncompliance. They are described below.

1. *Australia*

Both franchisees and the ACCC may bring an action for contravention of the Trade Practices Act. The Code of Conduct does not address sanctions. Sanctions arise under the Trade Practices Act and are discussed in Section B.1, below.

2. *Brazil*

The Brazil franchising law does not mention government-imposed civil penalties. Article 7 of the Franchising Law, when discussing applicable sanctions, states that it does not bar applicable criminal sanctions, but nothing further is mentioned in the law. One should look to the sections of the Brazilian Civil Code addressing civil liability for illegal acts and noncompliance with contractual obligations.

3. *France*

Under the regulations issued pursuant to the Doubin Law, failure to deliver the disclosure document is a quasi-criminal offense, subjecting a violator to a fine between 3,000 and 12,000 French francs and imprisonment from one to two months. Charges may be asserted by either a government prosecutor or a franchisee.

4. *Indonesia*

Articles 22 and 23 of the law describe sanctions that may be imposed upon a franchisee who has not obtained an STPUW, and in what instances the franchisee's STPUW may be suspended or revoked.

However, the franchise law does not contain information about sanctions imposed upon a franchisor for failure to comply with the Indonesia Franchise Law.

5. Japan

If a franchisor that falls under the Retailer's Law does not provide the specified disclosures, MITI may recommend that the franchisor do so. If the franchisor does not follow this recommendation, MITI may publicize the fact that the franchisor does not provide disclosures. This appears to be the only sanction for failure to disclose.

6. Malaysia

Section 79 of the Franchise Act provides that any person who commits an offense under the act shall, on conviction, be liable (1) for the first offense, a fine of not less than 5,000 ringgit and not more than 50,000 ringgit; and (2) for a second or subsequent offense, to a fine of not less than 10,000 ringgit or for a prison term not exceeding five years, or both. Upon sentencing a franchisor for a first offense, the court may declare the franchise agreement between the franchisor and any franchisee to be null and void. The court may also order that the franchisor refund any payment it has obtained from any franchisee or prohibit the franchisor from making any new franchise agreements. If an offense against any provision of the act was committed by a corporate entity, any person who at the time of commission of the offense was a director, manager, secretary, or similar officer, or was purporting to act in any such capacity, or was otherwise responsible for the management of the affairs of the corporation, shall be deemed to have committed the offense. However, such person may prove that the offense was committed without his or her knowledge or consent and that he or she took all reasonable precautions and exercised due diligence to prevent the commission of the offense.

7. Mexico

The Mexico Law on Industrial Property provides for both governmental and private enforcement of its requirements. The Ministry of Commerce and Industrial Development has the power to investigate and enforce violations of the law. Failure to comply with the disclosure and registration requirements may subject a franchisor to a variety of administrative penalties, including fines, temporary closure of the franchisor's business, and administrative arrest for up to thirty-six hours.

8. Spain

Article 65 of the statute provides that a violation by the franchisor of its obligation to register as a franchisor shall be considered a "serious infringement."

B. PRIVATE RIGHTS OF ACTION

1. Australia

Private individuals as well as the ACCC can bring court proceedings for breaches of the Code of Conduct. Sanctions under the Trade Practices Act include: an injunction to restrain breaches, monetary damages, and other court orders intended to compensate for the loss or damage suffered as a result of the breach.

The Code of Conduct contains a mandatory dispute resolution mechanism that provides a process for the resolution of disputes between a franchisor and a franchisee. The June 28, 2001, amendments to the Code of Conduct provide that the prescribed dispute resolution process must be conducted in Australia. All new franchise agreements entered into on or after October 1, 1998, must contain a dispute resolution process that complies with procedures specified in the Code of Conduct. The complaining party has the option of instituting the dispute resolution procedures prescribed by the Code of Conduct or bringing a lawsuit.

2. Brazil

A franchisee whose franchisor has failed to comply with the disclosure requirements may request the annulment of the franchise agreement and require the reimbursement of all amounts that the franchisee paid to the franchisor or to any party designated by the franchisor plus damages and losses. Article 7 of the Franchising Law also provides that the sanctions established in Article 4 apply also to a franchisor that includes untrue information in its disclosure document.

3. Canada (Province of Alberta)

If a franchisee suffers a loss because of a misrepresentation contained in a disclosure document, the franchisee has a right of action for damages against the franchisor and the directors and officers who signed the disclosure document. If a disclosure document contains a misrepresentation, the franchisee is deemed to have relied on the misrepresentation. However, if the franchisee had knowledge of the misrepresentation at the time he or she purchased the franchise, the franchisor may not be held liable. Section 13 of the Alberta Franchises Act provides that if a franchisor fails to give a franchisee the disclosure document in a timely manner, the franchisee may rescind all franchise agreements by giving notice of cancellation no later than sixty days after receiving the disclosure document or no later than two years after the franchisee was granted the franchise, whichever occurs first. Section 14 of the Alberta statute provides that if a franchisee cancels its franchise agreement as described above, the franchisor must, within thirty days of receiving the notice of cancellation, compensate the franchisee for any net losses that the franchisee has incurred in acquiring, setting up, and operating the franchised business. Section 15 of the Alberta statute also makes clear that the remedies specifically mentioned in the Alberta statute are in addition to and do not derogate from any other remedy the franchisee may have under the law. The Alberta statute does not provide for enforcement by the government.

4. Canada (Province of Ontario)

A franchisee may rescind a franchise agreement no later than sixty days after receiving the disclosure document if the franchisor failed to provide the disclosure document or a statement of material change, or if the contents of the disclosure documents do not comply with the act. A franchisee may rescind the franchise agreement no later than two years after entering into the agreement if the franchisor did not provide a disclosure document. Within sixty days after the effective date of rescission, the franchisor must refund all money it received from the franchisee, other than money for inventory, supplies, or equipment. The franchisor must also purchase from the franchisee any inventory the franchisee purchased pursuant to the franchise agreement at a price equal to the purchase price paid by the franchisee, and must purchase from the franchisee any supplies or equipment at a price equal to the purchase price paid by the franchisee. The franchisor must also compensate the franchisee for any losses that the franchisee incurred in acquiring, setting up, and operating the franchise, less the amounts paid to the franchisee pursuant to the repurchase requirements.

Additionally, if a franchisee suffers a loss because of a misrepresentation or the franchisor's failure to comply with the disclosure requirements of the act, the franchisee has a right of action for damages against the franchisor and the franchisor's agents, brokers, associates, and persons who signed the disclosure document. However, the person is not liable if he or she can prove that the franchisee acquired the franchise with knowledge of the misrepresentation.

5. *France*

The Doubin Law allows a private right of action by a licensee.

6. *Mexico*

A franchisee who did not receive the proper disclosure document may file a civil suit against the franchisor for a declaration invalidating the franchise agreement for and recovery of damages. Typically, however, noncompliance with the filing requirement will not affect the validity of the franchise agreement.

VIII. Exemptions from Disclosure Requirements

A. AUSTRALIA

The Australian Code of Conduct does not apply to a franchise agreement if the franchisor is resident, domiciled, or incorporated outside Australia and the franchisor grants only one franchise to be operated in Australia. A franchise agreement is also exempt from the code if another mandatory industry code prescribed under Section 51AE of the Trade Practices Act applies to it. Finally, the code is not applicable if (1) the franchise agreement is for goods or services that are substantially the same as those supplied by the franchisee before entering into the franchise agreement; (2) the franchisee has supplied those goods or services for at least two years immediately before entering into the franchise agreement; and (3) the sales under the franchise agreement are likely to provide no more than 20 percent of the franchisee's sales during the first year of the franchise. This exemption ceases to apply if the sales from the franchised goods and services constitute more than 20 percent of the franchisee's sales for three consecutive years and the franchisee so notifies the franchisor. Although the Code of Conduct does not specify the consequence if sales from the franchised business exceed 20 percent as described, the use of the phrase "ceases to apply" seems to indicate that the effect would be that the code applies from that point forward, rather than that the sale is retroactively tainted.

B. CANADA (PROVINCE OF ALBERTA)

Certain types of transactions are exempted from Section 4 of the Alberta Franchises Act, which requires the delivery of a disclosure document. These exemptions are automatic and require no application or disclosure. One such exemption is for the sale of a franchise by a franchisee if the franchisee is not the franchisor or a person related to the franchisor, the sale is for the franchisee's own account or, in the case of a master franchise, the entire franchise is sold and the sale is not effected by or through the franchisor. Also exempt is the sale of a franchise to a person who has been an officer or a director of the franchisor or an affiliate of the franchisor for at least six months. The sale of an additional franchise to an existing franchisee is exempt if that additional franchise is substantially the same as the existing franchise. Also exempt is a renewal or extension of an existing franchise agreement. The sale of a franchise is exempt if the franchisee is required to make a total annual investment of an amount that does not exceed $5,000 Canadian. The Alberta Franchises Act also contains exemptions similar to the leased business exemption and the fractional franchise exemption that are available under U.S. law. A regulation to the Alberta Franchises Act contains something similar to the U.S. large franchisor exemption. A franchisor who fits this large franchisor exemption must still comply with the disclosure obligation, but the franchisor is not required to include financial statements in its disclosure document. The exemption is available to franchisors with a net worth of $5 million Canadian according to the most recent audited financial statements and at least twenty-five franchisees at all times during the last five years or conduct by the franchisor of a similar business at all times for the preceding five years. The net worth portion of the large franchisor exemption may be fulfilled by a parent company that controls the franchisor if the franchisor has a net worth of $1 million Canadian. The controlling corporation must have a net worth of $5 million Canadian.

C. CANADA (PROVINCE OF ONTARIO)

The disclosure obligation does not apply to

- the sale of a franchise by a franchisee for its own account that is not effected through the franchisor;
- the grant of a franchise to a person who has been an officer or director of the franchisor or the franchisor's associate for at least six months;
- the grant of an additional franchise to an existing franchisee if that additional franchise is substantially the same as the existing franchise;
- fractional franchises;
- the renewal or extension of an existing franchise agreement; and

- a sophisticated franchisee (defined in terms of the size of the required initial investment).

D. MALAYSIA

Section 58 of the Franchise Law envisions that regulations may be adopted that exempt any person or class of persons or industry from any or all provisions of the Franchise Act. However, no such regulations have been established as of this writing.

Practice Tip

Consider the possibility of developing a "multinational" disclosure document using the UFOC format as a starting point; however, be sure to have it reviewed by local counsel for each transaction.

IX. Conclusion

Despite the variations in purpose, content, and origin of the varied disclosure laws discussed in this chapter, it should be feasible for U.S. franchisors to comply with most of these foreign disclosure laws by creating a template international disclosure document based on a U.S. UFOC format for the type of franchise being offered (that is, unit, area, or master franchise). This international disclosure document will need to be fine-tuned for use in each particular country, and some additional information may need to be added (either by addenda or to the body of the document), but there is significant overlap in the requirements of many of the disclosure laws. Since U.S. disclosure law is more comprehensive than most all of the foreign disclosure laws described in this chapter, U.S. franchisors may be able to prepare a disclosure document that is a suitable starting point for use in those countries having franchise disclosure requirements. Finally, it is beneficial when franchising in any foreign country for the first time for a franchisor to engage local counsel to review the disclosure document and to assist with the practicalities of any applicable registration process, as well as to provide input on local laws and customs and their impact on the proposed program.

Exhibit A: Summary of Out-of-State Sales Exemptions Under State Franchise Laws

State provides an out-of-state sales exemption or its functional equivalent where unit will not be located in state

State	No Exemption	Exemption Applies to Registration and Disclosure	Conditions Placed Upon the Exemption
California		X	Franchisee must not be "present" in state; franchisee not a resident of the state; and must comply with laws of other states and foreign jurisdictions.
Hawaii		X	Franchisee not a resident of the state.
Illinois		X	Franchisee not a resident of the state.
Indiana		X	Franchisee not a resident of the state.
Maryland		X[1]	Franchisee must not be "present" in state; and must comply with laws of other states and foreign jurisdictions.
Michigan		X	Franchisee not a resident of the state.
Minnesota		X	Franchisee must not be "present" in state' and must comply with laws of other states and foreign jurisdictions.
New York	X		
North Dakota	X		
Oregon	X		
Rhode Island	X		
South Dakota	X		
Virginia		X	
Washington		X	Must comply with laws of other states and foreign jurisdictions; offer must have been accepted outside of Washington.
Wisconsin		X	Franchisee not a resident of the state.

[1] Maryland provides an exemption from registration only.

Exhibit B:
Disclosure Document Contents

I. Disclosures About the Franchisor	Australia	Brazil	Canada (Alberta)	Canada (Ontario)	China (PRC)	France	Indonesia	Malaysia	Mexico	Romania	South Korea	Spain
1. Name/Address	Yes	Yes	Yes	Yes	Yes	Yes	Yes	Yes	Yes	R	Yes	Yes
2. Business description	R	Yes	Yes	Yes	Yes	Yes	R	Yes	Yes	No	Upon Request	R
3. Business experience	Yes	Yes	R	Yes	Yes	Yes	R	Yes	Yes	Yes	Upon Request	Yes
4. Background of key personnel	Yes	Yes	Yes	Yes	No	Yes	No	Yes	No	No	No	No
5. Litigation history	Yes	Yes	Yes	Yes	No	No	No	Yes	No	No	Upon Request	No
6. Bankruptcy history	Yes	No	Yes	Yes	No	No	No	Yes	No	No	No	No
7. Existing Franchisees' Locations	Yes	Yes	Yes	Yes	Yes	Yes	?	Yes	No	No	No	Yes
8. Former Franchisees	Yes	Yes	Yes	Yes	No	Yes	Yes	Yes	No	No	No	Yes
9. Bank Information	No	No	No	No	No	Yes	No	No	No	No	No	No
10. Financial Statements	Yes	Yes	Yes	Yes	R	Yes	Yes	Yes	No	No	No	No
II. Disclosure About the Franchise												
1. Payments	Yes	Yes	Yes	Yes	Yes	Yes	Yes	Yes	Yes	Yes	Yes	R
2. Suppliers	Yes	Yes	Yes	Yes	Yes	No	No	Yes	No	No	Upon Request	No
3. Site selection	Yes	Yes	No	No	No	No	No	Yes	No	No	No	No
4. Obligations of Franchisor/Franchisee	Yes	Yes	Yes	Yes	R	No	Yes	Yes	Yes	R	Yes	Yes
5. Territorial Rights	Yes	Yes	Yes	Yes	No	Yes	Yes	Yes	Yes	Yes	No	R
6. Training	Yes	Yes	No	Yes	No	No	Yes	Yes	No	No	No	R
7. Intellectual Property	Yes	Yes	Yes	Yes	No	Yes	Yes	Yes	Yes	No	No	Yes
8. Renewal/ termination	Yes	Yes	Yes	Yes	No	Yes	Yes	Yes	R	Yes	Upon Request	Yes
9. Franchisee's Investment	Yes	Yes	Yes	Yes	Yes	Yes	?	Yes	No	Yes	Upon Request	Yes

Yes = required No = not specifically required ? = unclear
R = general information required that could cover this topic, but not specifically required

Notes

Thanks for the very valuable contributions of Tara A. Cope and Amy Cheng Ware of Piper Marbury Rudnick & Wolfe.

1. 16 C.F.R. § 436.1.

2. California, Hawaii, Indiana, Illinois, Maryland, Michigan, Minnesota, New York, North Dakota, Oregon, Rhode Island, South Dakota, Virginia, Washington, and Wisconsin.

3. Bus. Franchise Guide (CCH) ¶ 5750.

4. However, if the franchisor did not have its financial statements audited for those years, or if it did not yet exist, the company may "phase in" its compliance by having its statement audited each year thereafter. *UFOC Guidelines*, Bus. Franchise Guide (CCH) ¶ 5773.

5. 15 U.S.C. 41 *et. seq*.

6. 178 F.3d 1126 (11th Cir. Fla. 1999), *cert. denied*, 120 S. Ct. 938 (U.S. 2000).

7. Florida Stat. Ann. §§501.201 to 501.211.

8. The court next compared the FTC Act with Title VII of the Civil Rights Act of 1964, noting the similarities between the statutes. Title VII stated that it applied to employers "engaged in an industry affecting commerce." Commerce was defined as "trade…among the several states; or between a state and any place outside thereof." The FTC Act states that it applies to unlawful unfair practices "in or affecting commerce," commerce being defined as "commerce among the several states or with foreign nations." Given the similarity of these definitions, the court reasoned that the scope of the FTC Act should be interpreted similarly—that because Title VII is not applied extraterritorially, the FTC Act should not be applied extraterritorially. Accordingly, the court held that the FTC Act does not authorize extraterritorial application of the FTC Rule.

9. Bus. Franchise Guide (CCH) ¶ 6502.

10. Many of the states have other types of exemptions from registration and, in some cases, disclosure.

11. The states are not bound by the FTC Interpretive Opinions discussed above.

CHAPTER ❖ 6

Impact of Other Local Laws

Joyce Mazero

I. Introduction

This chapter describes the legal issues common to most international franchise transactions, except for the more specific treatment of trademark, disclosure and tax considerations addressed in other chapters of this book. Whether a franchisor decides to have U.S. law, the law of the country in which franchised locations will operate, or any other country's law control the governance and interpretation of an international franchise agreement, U.S. franchise counsel should understand the impact and consequences of laws of the country in which the franchisee will operate to effectively evaluate and counsel a franchisor or franchisee client about an international transaction. Under any set of circumstances, the local law will play an important part in how the activities described in the agreement transpire in the real world. This can involve how the franchisor is paid; how a franchise can be terminated; whether trade secrets can be protected; whether noncompetition covenants can be enforced; whether prices can be predetermined; whether suppliers can be designated; whether disclosure, registration, or other government approval is required; and on and on.

To do justice to this effort, discussion of each of the legal topics chosen for this chapter focuses on how the issues may arise in a franchise context, how to recognize the issues, and what the issues practically mean to a franchisor or franchisee. There are many laws described in this chapter and many of them and related sources are cited for reference.[1]

It is also appropriate to note that the discussions, attributions, and conclusions reached in this chapter are based on the experiences of the author. Needless to say, other U.S. or foreign franchise counsels' experience or recommendations about the law or how to handle a particular issue may be different. This chapter is solely intended to highlight for U.S. franchise counsel important legal issues to consider in any international franchise transaction and is not intended to suggest that there are not alternative viewpoints to consider. Discussion and verification with local counsel about how any of these issues may relate to a specific transaction is a must.

II. Governmental Recordations, Registrations, or Approvals

A. WHAT IS THE ISSUE AND HOW WILL IT AFFECT YOUR CLIENT?

Most U.S. franchisors are familiar with the state franchise sales laws that exist in approximately one-third of the United States.[2] Generally, these laws are based on the state's strong public policy interest in protecting its consumers from being misled or deceived by an in-state or out-of-state franchisor. Essentially, these laws require that a franchisor either register or obtain an exemption for its franchise offering from the state franchise authorities before offering or selling a franchise in that state. In that regard, the state has the power to require the franchisor to comply with state franchise sales law requirements, including requirements relating to the preparation and content of a franchisor's financial statement, how a franchisor intends to resolve disputes with its franchisees, termination and nonrenewal of franchises, and so on.

Similarly, various foreign jurisdictions have registration, recordation, or government approval requirements that affect a franchisor's ability to offer or consummate the sale of a franchise. Because these requirements may be conditions to execution or enforcement of a franchise agreement in the jurisdiction, the importance of complying with these laws cannot be overstated.

These foreign government approval requirements typically are not unique to franchise transactions. Rather, they exist to foster a foreign jurisdiction's desire to control foreign business interests or activities within its borders. These requirements will normally pertain to and be known as foreign investment or technology/industry regulations, which restrict foreign investment in certain industries, technologies, or in real property; central bank approvals, which restrict certain types or amounts of currency exchange; competition authority approvals, which restrict certain competitive activity, including supplier, territorial, and noncompetition arrangements; trademark license filings or registrations (apart from the normally required registration to obtain a registered trademark in the foreign country); as well as in an increasing number of consumer protection/disclosure laws, which govern the offer and sale of franchises (more specifically addressed in Chapter 5 of this book).

B. WHAT IS THE LAW?

Depending on the jurisdiction, foreign governmental approval, recordation, and registration requirements take several different forms.

1. *Foreign Investment Approvals*

Perhaps the most burdensome form of government approval requirement relates to preapproval for foreign investment. Some franchisors may believe that these requirements will not affect them because they are neither interested in directly investing in the foreign franchisee entity, exercising a right of first refusal to acquire the franchisee's business in connection with a prospective transfer, nor exercising a post-termination option to acquire the foreign franchise business.[3] Although these types of overt opportunities for investment by the U.S. franchisor would be covered, these laws can also apply to a franchisor merely because it grants a franchise to a citizen of that country or the franchise concerns an industry that is regulated (protected) by the country. Obtaining these types of approvals are typically a prerequisite to having a valid franchise agreement or to permitting any foreign currency exchange.

For example, India and the People's Republic of China (PRC) retain many of the same bureaucratic regulatory practices that have long plagued their protective foreign investment structure. Approval processes will take time, patience, and money, and franchisors may endure bureaucratic meddling in the business and legal terms of a transaction, including questioning of the types and amounts of fees, choice of law provisions, and other business or legal terms to which the foreign franchisee may have previously agreed.

In the PRC, domestic PRC entities do not have the authority to enter into direct contracts with foreign franchisors unless such entities possess "foreign trade rights" pursuant to PRC laws and regulations. Foreign trade rights are normally only available to state-owned companies and foreign investment companies and, where the potential parties to the franchise agreement do not have such foreign trade rights, some PRC domestic entities use third-party foreign trade agents to act on their behalf to enter into contracts with foreign franchisors. However, this framework is imperfect, and it can be difficult to enforce rights against the real party in interest because the foreign trade agents are unlikely to guaranty or take on liability in any such transaction.[4]

Any franchise agreement involving technology transfers (which may include, among other things, the transfer of proprietary know-how, consulting services, or management services) must be submitted to the PRC government for approval after execution. Until the PRC government approves the franchise agreement, the franchise agreement is ineffective and not enforceable between the parties. Because the government often questions certain terms and conditions of a franchise agreement, many times appearing to negotiate on behalf of the PRC party, franchisors should be prepared to address demands for revisions that will delay the effectiveness of the franchise agreements and the franchisee's access to confidential information and training until such approval is granted.[5]

India has similar requirements. Franchise agreements must be approved by the Indian government before any fees may be collected by a foreign franchisor. Although there exists an expedited "automatic approval" process through the Reserve Bank of India (the RBI),[6] which can be started before execution for certain types of franchise agreements, there are fee and royalty limitations that may require the franchisor to seek approval through a more drawn-out process with the Secretariat of Industrial Approvals (the SIA).[7] In certain sectors such as tourism and hotels, the SIA allows certain higher royalty rates and marketing support fees. Agreements with payments in excess of the permitted royalty and fee limits require specific SIA approval, which is a discretionary approval process. The SIA process entails a written (and sometimes oral) "presentation" that consists of the terms of the letter of intent and supporting data that explains why fee payments exceed certain amounts allowed on an automatic basis. Once the SIA approval is granted, a filing must be made with the Central Bank, which evidences the SIA approval, and then the SIA and Central Bank approvals must be submitted to the investment or other bank that the franchisee uses to remit the payments abroad. The entire governmental approval and ancillary filings process can take at least four to six weeks.

2. *Trademark License Filings and Approvals*[8]

Perhaps the most widespread type of government approval, recordation, or registration requirement among international jurisdictions relates to the licensing of trademarks.

Several countries, including Mexico,[9] Brazil,[10] Columbia,[11] Lithuania,[12] and Peru,[13] have laws that require all trademark licensing agreements, such as franchise agreements, to be registered and approved by the respective national trademark office. There is no substantive review under the Mexican law, and the laws in Lithuania and Peru provide for a fairly ministerial review of the agreements. Failure to register, however, can hinder third-party trademark infringement actions in some cases.

Some of these laws are designed to protect local licensees and provide the local trademark authorities broad authority to scrutinize the substantive terms and conditions of an agreement. For instance, the Brazilian government enacted a 1997 law to simplify the trademark office approval process of franchise agreements.[14] Notwithstanding the simplification, basic trademark license agreements must be presented for recordation before the Brazilian trademark office if such agreements contain certain provisions related to the transfer of technology, and license agreements between commonly owned entities will be subject to royalty limitations.

There are various consequences of a failure to file. In many jurisdictions, the registration may benefit the franchisor by acting as prima facie evidence that the marks are being used in the country, thereby blocking any claim by the trademark office or a third party that the marks have been forfeited for nonuse. In the PRC, failure to register will render the trademark license portions of the franchise agreement ineffective.[15] In other jurisdictions, failure to register limits enforceability of other portions of the franchise agreement. For example, in Brazil, a franchise agreement must be filed with the National Institute of Industrial Property (INPI) before seeking Central Bank of Brazil approval. Without central bank approval, a franchisor is precluded from receiving payments from its franchisee. Some jurisdictions, such as Mexico and the PRC, require filing of additional license agreements if there is any variation between the entity that is the registered owner of the marks and the entity that will serve as the franchisor. In some jurisdictions, such as the PRC, registration is also a prerequisite to the granting of a valid trademark license. Other countries, such as England[16] and Germany,[17] permit but do not require recordation of a separate license agreement. Such recordation is normally for administrative purposes, but will allow the franchisee to move against a third-party infringer.

3. Central Bank Remittance Approvals and Filings

Countries such as India and Brazil have strong central banks that continue to require prior and ongoing approval of foreign currency remittances abroad,[18] although India has recently liberalized some of the more onerous restrictions related to routine payments. Several types of remittances, such as dividend and royalty payments that fall within the automatic approval route, are permitted to be remitted overseas without any prior approvals. Although currency or other remittance restrictions are generally being relaxed throughout the world, these restrictions can affect the structure and timing of a transaction in some cases because a franchisee may not be able to remit fees related to a letter of intent or other preliminary agreement until such central bank approval is granted. In Brazil, for example, such approval cannot be sought until after execution of a franchise agreement.[19]

Most franchisors require the franchisee to take all actions necessary to obtain appropriate approvals or file the appropriate documents with the government to satisfy the government requirement. As a result, many franchisees attempt to negotiate longer intervals between payments to compensate for these added burdens. Other franchisors attempt to avoid initial or ongoing central bank approvals by various alternative means. These include bypassing the central bank approvals by obtaining U.S. dollars from the so-called "grey" market of investment banks and other commercial interests[20] or by having monies wired from foreign accounts held by the franchisee or its principals.[21]

4. Franchise Registration and Disclosure Approvals and Filings

Many of those jurisdictions that have followed the lead of the U.S. and implemented some form of disclosure requirement have also implemented registration requirements that may or may not be tied to the disclosure obligation.[22] For example, Spain and Malaysia require prior registration and approval of the franchisor before the occurrence of a statutory "triggering event," which may be execution of a letter of intent or a franchise agreement or acceptance of money from a potential franchisee.[23] Malaysia also requires prior registration of a disclosure document if a foreign franchisor has licensed franchise rights in Malaysia to a master franchisee.[24]

Registration can take many different formats. In Spain, the franchisor must register itself before selling franchises there.[25] The franchise agreement itself need not be registered. In Malaysia, there are different forms of registration depending on the domicile of the franchisor and franchisee.[26] Also, foreign franchisors must seek approval to sell franchises in Malaysia and then must register the individual franchises once they are sold.

In Mexico[27] and Brazil,[28] which also require governmental filings related to trademarks,[29] there are registration obligations that are separate from the disclosure obligations. In these countries, for trademark protection purposes the franchise agreement (including a translation) must be submitted to the government soon after execution. The disclosure document need not be submitted to the government in Mexico while, in Brazil, a copy of the receipt of the disclosure document should be presented with the governmental filing of the franchise agreement at the Brazilian Trademark Office.

Several international disclosure or registration laws are newly enacted and/or vaguely written such that their application to international transactions and international franchisors may be unclear. As a consequence, international franchisors may not have the benefit of precedent to explain their compliance obligations. In these cases, franchisors normally must proceed on the guidance provided by experienced local counsel or nonbinding advisory opinions obtained from the local officials who interpret these laws. These opinions can be difficult to obtain and the official may not be in a position of power within the applicable governmental entity if a compliance issue or new interpretation arises.

Finally, some countries have implemented registration requirements that appear to serve solely an administrative purpose. For instance, Lithuania enacted a new Civil Code that took effect on July 1, 2001, and that contains a separate section on franchising. This new section merely requires that each new franchise agreement be registered with the Lithuanian government, apparently for administrative/statistical purposes. There is currently no substantive review or approval and the registry does not currently exist.

5. Miscellaneous Filings

Not all approvals, registrations, or recordations are mandatory. Several competition and antitrust laws allow preapproval. These laws are more specifically addressed in Section III of this chapter. Certain provisions in franchise agreements relating to suppliers, pricing, covenants against competition, or exclusivity may run afoul of these laws and potentially void the applicable franchise agreement provision or affect the enforceability of the franchise agreement. Several jurisdictions allow franchisors and other contracting parties to submit agreements to the local competition authority for an advisory or other form of opinion on the acceptability of the franchise agreement under applicable competition laws. This may be of particular importance in a country that has an active competition authority such as Korea or South Africa. Korea,[30] Ireland,[31] and South Africa[32] allow parties to submit contracts for review and a stamp of approval.

Practice Tip

Registration, approval, and disclosure requirements with early triggering events (that is, before offering a franchise or receiving payment of any fee) may create risk for franchisors in proceeding with the business aspects of the deal and then calling in the lawyers once the terms are set. Thus, it is a recommended practice to outline the significant legal issues in a country for the client before the letter of intent stage, and government approval requirements should be high on that list.

It is important for franchisors to maintain as much control over any required government approval or registration processes as is available, especially if changes to the agreements may be required by the government authorities. Depending on the jurisdiction, the franchise agreement should either (1) be terminable by the franchisor if registration or approval is not granted or (2) not become effective between the parties until such registration or approval is granted. In some cases, this may mean withholding training or confidential information until a post-execution approval or registration is granted. As a backstop, it may be possible to enter into separate confidentiality, noncompetition and indemnification agreements that are ancillary to the franchise agreement and that enable certain principals to go to training during a post-execution approval waiting period.

C. SAMPLE CLAUSES

Government Approval. Franchisor and Franchisee agree that, if required by applicable law, this Agreement will be registered or recorded with and approved by the appropriate governmental authorities. Franchisee's right to use the Proprietary Marks and the System to operate the Unit under this Agreement are subject to and conditioned upon such government approval, registration or recordation. Franchisor and Franchisee agree that they will share responsibility for obtaining and maintaining the approval, registration or recordation of this Agreement. Franchisor and Franchisee agree to cooperate with each other in connection with any dealings with all governmental authorities relating to this Agreement. Franchisor and Franchisee agree that neither will submit any information to governmental authorities with respect to this Agreement without the other's prior written approval, which approval will not be unreasonably withheld; provided that the foregoing restriction will not apply if formal or informal proceedings are instituted against a party or a dispute between the parties is submitted to any tribunal having jurisdiction over such matters. Franchisor and Franchisee agree to share equally the expense of registering, recording and obtaining approval of this Agreement, and any amendment hereto or thereto (including all legal and other professional expenses, except translation expenses, as noted in Section ___ and disbursements), with the appropriate governmental authorities.

Registered User. Franchisee agrees to cooperate fully with Franchisor in registering Franchisee in the Country as an authorized user of the Proprietary Marks with any governmental authority, if Franchisor deems such to be necessary, and also to cooperate in canceling such registration upon demand by Franchisor or upon termination or expiration of this Agreement. In connection herewith, Franchisee agrees to appoint the Trademark Representative identified in Attachment A or any other individual or firm designated by Franchisor in writing to obtain such registration or to terminate such registration as an authorized user of the Proprietary Marks in the Country. In furtherance of the foregoing, Franchisee hereby grants a Special Power of Attorney to Franchisor and the Trademark Representative to cancel the registration of Franchisee as an authorized user in the event of termination or expiration of this franchise and otherwise to terminate and cause the discontinuance of the license to use or the actual use of the Proprietary Marks as provided hereunder. Franchisee agrees that this Special Power of Attorney shall continue in full effect regardless of the termination or expiration of this franchise. Franchisee agrees to execute any and all further documents or instruments as Franchisor shall require to give full legal effect to the foregoing Special Power of Attorney. The cost of registration and cancellation of registration of Franchisee as an authorized user will be paid by Franchisee.

III. Competition Law/Covenants Against Competition/Confidentiality

A. WHAT IS THE ISSUE AND HOW WILL IT AFFECT YOUR CLIENT?

1. Competition Laws

Franchisors doing business in the United States are keenly aware of the potential antitrust implications of franchise relationships. Many of the questions that U.S. franchisors must ask themselves concerning the enforcement of price controls, territorial and customer restrictions, covenants restricting competition, monopolies and fairness, are also relevant to international franchise transactions. This section addresses two contractual restrictions especially important to franchisors.

2. Covenants Against Competition

Many franchisors desire to prevent franchisees from opening a competing unit during and after the term of the franchise agreement to maintain the value, identity, integrity, and reputation of the franchise granted. For the most part, the enforceability analysis of covenants internationally is similar to a U.S. state law analysis, focusing on whether the covenant, in-term or post-term, is reasonable in light of the scope of business covered, geographic scope, time limitations, the nature of competitive interests being protected, and whether a foreign court may reform covenants that are viewed as overly broad in one or more of these contexts.

3. Confidentiality Covenants

Another consideration for any international transaction is protecting the franchisor's confidential information, including manuals and other trade secrets, know-how, and business information. Some foreign jurisdictions are notorious for providing little or no legal protection for confidential information. Increasingly, many jurisdictions have enacted legislation protecting confidential information. However, these laws are generally untested and their practical effect remains questionable.

B. WHAT IS THE LAW?

1. Competition Laws

Competition laws that affect franchising generally apply to two forms of anti-competitive activities: (1) collusion by two parties that hinders consumers' choices regarding products and services and (2) abuse of a superior bargaining power that causes harm to another contracting party. Franchise agreement provisions that may run afoul of competition laws include exclusive supplier or purchase requirements, product tying requirements, resale price restrictions, restrictions on the right to contest the trademarks, restrictions on the geographic area in which the franchisee can conduct business, and self-help provisions that enable a franchisor to impose unilateral action upon a breach of the agreement. Although many of these issues are common to U.S. antitrust law, U.S. franchise counsel should not assume that the treatment or consequences of failure to comply with these laws is the same outside of the United States.

For example, Article 81 of the Treaty of Rome,[33] which applies to all European Union (EU) member nations,[34] prohibits any vertical agreements or behavior that has the effect of "preventing, restricting or distorting" competition within the European Union.[35] Franchisors who entered into agreements in the European Community (EC) in the past were shielded from Article 81 to some degree by the so-called Franchise Block Exemption Regulation,[36] which provided a safe harbor for franchisors whose franchise agreements did not contain certain blacklisted provisions, such as provisions on resale price maintenance, and restrictions on Internet Web sites, cross supply, or contesting the validity of the trademarks. The Franchise Block Exemption expired June 1, 2000.[37] As a consequence, franchise agreements need to be reviewed in connection with the replacement Vertical Restraints Regulation.[38] Although the new Vertical Restraints Regulation, which took effect June 1, 2000, protects franchisors from Article 81 if they have less than 30 percent market share and contracts that do not include certain enumerated vertical restraints, the new Vertical Restraints Regulation (and the accompanying guidelines[39]) may still limit a franchisor's ability to restrict a franchisee's ability to advertise its goods or services on the Internet, to protect its confidential information, and to protect against competition by its franchisees during and after the term of a franchise agreement. All EU countries also have their own competition laws, which will only apply, however, if EC competition law does not apply.

In particular, franchisors may be surprised to find that English counsel has advised that the EC competition authorities are currently interpreting Paragraph 51 of the Guidelines on Vertical Restraints to mean that a franchisor may not prohibit a franchisee from maintaining an independent Web site or even restrict a franchisee's Internet presence to an interior page or series of interior pages on the franchisor's Web site. A franchisor may not set unreasonable restrictions on a franchisee's use of the Internet under the guise of trademark control.

As a further example, franchisors should take particular caution to review a covenant against competition in Germany prior to any termination or expiration of a franchise agreement. Depending on whether the termination is for cause or if the franchise agreement will merely expire, a franchisee may be entitled to compensation if the franchisor does not act to withdraw a noncompetition covenant by a certain time period, depending on the circumstances of the termination or expiration.[40]

Outside of the EU, Argentina's antitrust law may be applicable to franchise agreements but only where the companies involved have significant revenues in Argentina and the price/value of the transferred company/assets in Argentina is significant.[41] Other countries, including the United Arab Emirates and Kuwait, have almost no competition laws. In these countries, the parties are generally free to set price controls and otherwise implement restrictions or take concerted actions that may otherwise run afoul of U.S. or other countries' competition laws.

Finally, other countries such as England,[42] Germany,[43] and Thailand[44] have laws that limit the enforceability of contracts that are viewed as contracts of adhesion. The Thai and British laws are particularly applicable to provisions that are not negotiated or to provisions perceived to be anticompetitive due to the lack of bargaining power on the part of the franchisee, such as choice of law provisions, dispute resolution provisions, or noncompetition provisions.

2. *Covenants Against Competition*

Similar to the United states, most jurisdictions allow enforcement of in-term and post-termination covenants against competition. The new EU Vertical Restraints Regulation referred to above limits in-term covenants against competition to five years. There are differing views among experts regarding the circumstances to which the five-year restriction will apply. However, one consideration is whether a franchisor can show that the information provided constitutes know-how under the regulation and that the contractual restriction is imposed to protect the identity and reputation of the franchise.[45] Under those circumstances, the franchisor may have a strong argument that the franchise agreement's in-term competition restriction falls outside both Article 81 and the regulation as a threshold matter.[46]

Many jurisdictions that enforce post-termination noncompetition covenants impose a reasonableness standard with respect to business and geographic scope and duration. Still other countries have additional requirements. For instance, in Germany, unless the covenant is withdrawn before termination, a franchisor may be required to pay the franchisee statutory compensation to enforce a post-termination or post-expiration noncompetition covenant, regardless of whether the franchise agreement provides for such compensation and regardless of the reason for termination.[47]

Several jurisdictions, including Mexico[48] and several regions of Brazil,[49] are highly critical of post-termination covenants against competition and consider the right to work a constitutional right, regardless of the apparent harm to be caused to a franchisor. Unless it is shown that the operation of the competing unit necessarily includes the use of confidential information, it may be difficult to enforce a covenant against competition in these countries, especially if the local franchisee complains that he or she is effectively shut out from earning a living as a result of the covenant.

Practice Tip

Franchise counsel can not take for granted that competition law in other countries will follow the U.S. model. Accordingly, U.S. franchise counsel should inquire about the effect of the competition law early on and make it part of a checklist of critical issues discussed earlier.

3. Confidentiality Covenants

Confidentiality covenants are generally enforceable through intellectual property laws related to trade secret protection.[50] In certain jurisdictions, however, such as Malaysia, Korea, and the PRC, protection may only be afforded for a limited time. For instance, Korea[51] and the PRC[52] have in the past taken the position that the rights in proprietary information provided to the franchisee inures to the franchisee after a certain time period and can be used after the term of the franchise agreement by the franchisee. In addition, the Malaysian franchise law[53] expressly states that the franchisee must keep confidential information confidential during the term of the agreement and for a period of two years thereafter, leaving open the issue of whether such information may be used at the end of the two-year period.

C. SAMPLE CLAUSES

1. Competition (European Union)

Franchisor, Franchisee and the Principals acknowledge that the License is granted on the assumption that this Agreement complies, and will continue to comply, with the Block Exemption Regulation for Vertical Agreements (EC No. 2790/1999) (the "Regulation") under Article 81 of the Treaty of Rome ("Article 81") and with the official and successor interpretative guidelines to the Regulation. If, at any time during the Term, questions arise concerning this Agreement's compliance with the Regulation, the parties agree to use their best efforts and to cooperate with each other to amend this Agreement either to bring it into conformity with the requirements of the Regulation or to seek an alternative way to comply with Article 81. If, in Franchisor's sole judgment, this Agreement cannot be modified to comply with EU competition law, including the Regulation, without undermining material elements of the franchise relationship, Franchisor may, at its option, without liability for such action or any further obligation to Franchisee, terminate this Agreement and the License upon 30 days' written notice to Franchisee. In such event, the post-termination obligations described in Section ___ of this Agreement will apply.

2. Covenants Against Competition

A. Competition During Term of Agreement. Franchisee and Franchisee's Principals specifically acknowledge that, pursuant to this Agreement, Franchisee will receive valuable specialized training and Confidential Information, including, without limitation, information regarding the operational, sales, promotional and marketing methods and techniques of Franchisor and the System. Franchisee and Franchisee's Principals, for as long as such Person is a Franchisee's Principal, covenant that during the term of this Agreement, Franchisee and Franchisee's Principals will not, either directly or indirectly, individually or through, on behalf of, or in conjunction with any Person:

Own, maintain, manage, operate, engage in, or have any financial or beneficial interest in, advise, assist or render services or make loans to, any Competitor;

Divert or attempt to divert any business or customer of the Restaurant to any Competitor, by direct or indirect inducement or otherwise, or do or perform, directly or indirectly, any other act injurious or prejudicial to the goodwill associated with the Proprietary Marks and the System; or

Employ or seek to employ any individual who is at that time, or was at any time during the prior twelve months, employed by Franchisor, its Affiliates or any other franchisee or developer of Franchisor, or otherwise directly or indirectly induce such individual to leave his or her employment.

B. Competition After Termination or Expiration of Agreement. Franchisee and Franchisee's Principals each covenant that for a period of two years from the date of termination or expiration of this Agreement or, with respect to a Franchisee's Principal, for a period of two years from the date the Franchisee's Principal ceases to be a Franchisee's Principal, they will not, at the Approved Location or within a 30 mile radius of (i) the Approved Location, (ii) any FRANCHISOR® restaurant or (iii) any other restaurant, however named, which uses the Proprietary Marks or the System, either directly or indirectly, individually or through, on behalf of, or in conjunction with any Person:

> own, maintain, manage, operate, engage in, or have any financial or beneficial interest in, advise, assist or render services or make loans to, any Competitor; or
>
> employ or seek to employ any individual who is at that time, or was at any time during the prior twelve months, employed by Franchisor, any Affiliate of Franchisor or any other franchisee or developer of Franchisor or otherwise directly or indirectly induce such individual to leave his or her employment.

3. Confidentiality Covenants

See the provision in Section VI of this chapter for a sample confidentiality covenant and the provision in Section XII of this chapter for a sample liquidated damages provision that could coincide with the confidentiality covenant.

IV. Currency Exchange Restrictions and Withholding Taxes

A. WHAT IS THE ISSUE AND HOW WILL IT AFFECT YOUR CLIENT?

Under current conditions, most developed nations allow their citizens to buy and remit payments with U.S. dollars. Franchisees in some nations, however, must obtain government approval before they can make payments with foreign currencies, and in a few instances franchisees are absolutely prohibited from paying in U.S. dollars. Such currency controls can, in some cases, be a tax. For example, in South Africa, the exportation of U.S. dollars and other hard currencies was strictly forbidden for many years up until 1995. The only currency that could be exported was a "financial rand," which had a value equivalent to 85 percent of the rand South Africans used internally. Foreign franchisors who were forced to accept financial rands in payment for royalties and other obligations therefore found themselves paying an involuntary 15 percent tax to the South African government.

Without an agreement specifying the currency in which franchisees will make their payments, a franchisee may justifiably assume that it may pay its obligations in its local currency or even with another currency that it selects. On occasion these risks can prove extraordinarily painful, such as the December 1994 devaluation of the Mexican peso. There is no assurance that U.S. dollars will retain their historical stability and value, but American franchisors with no experience in currency hedging are wise to demand a currency they know and trust.

In addition to currency risk issues, tax considerations must also be taken into account in evaluating impediments to a franchisor receiving the expected economic value from the transaction. Withholding tax, value added tax, and stamp tax are examples of the types of taxes that foreign countries impose on money leaving the country in the form of royalty or other payments.[54]

B. WHAT IS THE LAW?

1. *Currency Exchange*

Currency provisions should address three principal issues: (1) the currency in which the franchisee must pay its royalties and other fees;

(2) the exchange rate and conversion date on which the franchisee must purchase the required currency; and (3) the consequences of a change in local law or government policy concerning the purchase or remittance of the required currency.

Franchisors with multinational operations may prefer to receive payments in a foreign currency or in a foreign country. Such a franchisor may actively engage in currency trading as part of its treasury functions and may want the flexibility of obtaining payment in a specified foreign currency. Also, for tax and accounting reasons, a multinational organization with foreign-domiciled subsidiaries may want to defer movement of income into the United States.

Any currency conversion, however, carries risks. Exchange rates fluctuate daily, and different sources quote different prices for the same currency on a given day. The most effective way a franchisor can neutralize these risks is to designate the source from which exchange rate quotations will be obtained and to specify the date on which a currency transaction will be deemed to have occurred, whether or not it actually occurs on that date.

In some communist, socialist, or autocratic regimes, a central bank, which is either part of or controlled by the government, establishes the value of the local currency in relation to other currencies. In most capitalist countries, banks that engage in currency trading establish the rates by reference to market forces, although countries such as India and Chile that have strong central banks may step in to control fluctuation in some instances. Local practice will dictate the rate source a franchise agreement specifies in a particular country.

Typically, the date a periodic payment falls due is the currency conversion date. For expense reimbursements and other occasional payments, the selection typically relates to the date the franchisor incurs an expense or bills the related payment. The conversion date provision for delinquent payments should allow the franchisor to specify the date the payment was originally due or the date it is paid, whichever benefits the franchisor.

The agreement's currency provisions can also provide the franchisor discretion to change the currency in which payments are to be made, temporarily or permanently. These provisions can also allow the franchisor to terminate the relationship if the government freezes the outflow of money or bans the purchase or use of currencies acceptable to the franchisor. Similar provisions can provide for termination if a withholding or other tax rate rises above a certain level.

Practice Tip

Drafting precise, effective currency control provisions requires knowledge and understanding of a host country's laws and customs. U.S. franchise counsel should determine early in the process whether and how a country restricts a franchisee's ability to purchase and remit U.S. dollars abroad and, if so, the procedures a franchisee must follow to purchase U.S. dollars and to obtain any necessary government approval. The franchise agreement should expressly assign responsibility to the franchisee for obtaining required government approvals on time and at the franchisee's expense to create the best environment for making payments to the franchisor as contemplated by the franchise agreement. The agreement should also plot a realistic, alternative course of action if the law or government policy changes in ways that restrict payment in required currencies or increase the cost of currency transactions beyond the parties' expectations.

2. Tax Considerations

Even if the franchisee is able freely to remit payments to the franchisor, the amount of the payments may be significantly reduced by taxes imposed by the foreign jurisdiction.[55] Foreign withholding taxes potentially distort a franchisor's operating margins by subjecting the franchisor's income from foreign sources to a higher cumulative tax burden than the franchisor pays on its U.S. source income. Although a franchisor may be able to credit foreign taxes against U.S. income tax as discussed in detail in Chapter 4, there are numerous limitations on foreign tax credits, and the franchisor's reduction in revenue attributable to the withholding tax may not be offset by tax benefits. Further, a franchisor loses the use of funds that are withheld from its foreign source income between the time the taxes are withheld and the time its U.S. taxes are due.

Experienced franchisors often use two techniques to avoid the distortion that foreign withholding taxes can cause. The first is the so-called "tax gross-up" technique that involves shifting the burden of foreign withholding taxes to foreign franchisees. Most countries impose their withholding tax on the franchisee, who must withhold and pay the tax on its royalty and other obligations before remitting payment to a foreign franchisor. Through the tax gross-up technique, franchisors pass the withholding tax's economic and cash flow burden to their franchisees by requiring that franchisees both pay the withholding tax and pay royalties at the full contract rate.

Some franchisors try to buffer, with varying degrees of success, the technique's financial impact on franchisees by providing that if and when the franchisor receives the benefit of a tax credit against its U.S. income taxes for the withholding taxes a franchisee paid, the franchisor will refund to the franchisee an amount equal to the tax credit the franchisor received. There are a number of problems with this approach because of the complex calculation of the allowable foreign tax credit, however, as discussed in Chapter 4.[56]

Use of the tax gross-up technique is not practical in some countries that require government review of a franchise agreement's substantive provisions. The PRC, for example, will most likely delay, request language modifications, or reject registration of a technology transfer agreement that requires a PRC franchisee to pay royalties without regard to the withholding tax.[57]

Practice Tip

Foreign franchisees often doggedly resist tax gross-up provisions for reasons noted earlier. Counsel should prepare his or her client to evaluate and respond to a franchisee's arguments in advance of negotiations on the point. If the United States is a party to a favorable tax treaty with the target country and the franchisor can likely use the foreign tax credit fully and efficiently, the franchisor may be better served to forego or defer a gross-up requirement than to risk scuttling the relationship. If, on the other hand, a gross-up requirement is mandatory to preserve the relationship's economic integrity from the franchisor's perspective, counsel should be prepared to explain and demonstrate to the prospective franchisee why that is the case. Unless U.S. franchise counsel has experience in international taxation, he or she should seek the advice of a lawyer or accountant who can brief counsel on salient points and assist in structuring.

The second technique franchisors use to ease the burden of foreign withholding taxes is the so-called "allocation" or "unbundling" approach as discussed in Chapter 4. Many countries tax royalties and other "passive" income at materially different rates than taxes on fees for services such as training, field supervision, and business counseling. Which type of payment is taxed at a higher rate depends on the country and whether a tax treaty applies. Further, some countries exempt fees for services rendered outside their borders from withholding taxes. The unbundling technique involves separate treatment in the franchise agreement of the fee assessed for trademark and business system usage and the fees that compensate the franchisor for training, consultation, and other benefits or services the franchisor provides. It also requires documentation of the place where training and other assistance occurs to demonstrate eligibility for exemptions for revenues earned outside of the country.

Other countries attempt to impose income tax on the foreign franchisor. For example, Kuwait views royalty payments as income earned by the franchisor in Kuwait. The franchisor must make its own payment arrangements.[58] A Kuwaiti franchisee is obligated merely to hold back 5 percent of the royalty payments until the franchisor furnishes proof that it has paid the tax.[59] Upon receiving proof of payment, the franchisee may pay the balance of the obligation. One way to achieve a tax gross-up in this situation is for the franchisor to first claim a credit against its U.S. income tax for the Kuwait taxes it paid, calculate the net distortive impact of the Kuwait tax, and then request an equalizing payment from the Kuwaiti franchisee.

3. Governmental Approval

Governments in many developing nations, especially those that regard franchising as a variety of technology transfer, require government approval of a franchise arrangement's financial terms. Examples include India, Brazil, and the PRC,[60] which often limit the amount of royalties and other "soft" fees that a franchisor may charge and/or impose conditions on a franchisee's ability to obtain or make payments in a currency that is acceptable to the franchisor.[61] In countries that do not regulate a franchise arrangement's economic provisions, freedom of contract principles govern the parties' agreement with respect to currency provisions.

C. SAMPLE CLAUSES

1. Definitions

"Dollars" or "$" means United States dollars.

"Exchange Rate" means the rate for converting [the franchisee's local currency] into Dollars, [insert "as determined by the Central Bank", if a central bank controls exchange rates in the franchisee's country; otherwise, either insert "as published by an international bank with a branch in the franchised territory that is selected by or acceptable to Franchisor", or insert the name of a bank the Franchisor designates, such as Thomas Cook Bank, Citibank, or Barclay's Bank].

"Taxes" means any sales, remittance, stamp, use, service, occupation, excise, gross receipts, income, withholding, goods and services, and value added taxes and any levies, imposts, duties or other charges and taxes of whatsoever nature imposed upon any fees or payments payable to Franchisor under or in accordance with this Agreement, except U.S. taxes imposed on Franchisor's income.

2. *Currency Provisions*

(a) Designation of Currency; Determination of Payment Amount. Except as provided in Section 2(d), all payments to Franchisor under this Agreement will be calculated in [the franchisee's local currency], converted into Dollars in accordance with this Section 2 and paid in Dollars. The amount of Dollars that Franchisee owes for a particular payment will be calculated by using the Exchange Rate in effect on a conversion date, determined as follows:

(i) When calculating the Royalty [and any other monthly fee payable under the agreement], the conversion date will be the day on which a payment is due under Section [cite appropriate section of agreement], unless that day is not a Business Day, in which case the appropriate day will be the next Business Day.

(ii) When calculating the amount due for reimbursement of expenses that Franchisor paid in a currency other than Dollars, the conversion date will be either (i) the date on which the expenses were originally incurred, or (ii) the date of demand or billing by Franchisor, as designated by Franchisor in its discretion.

(iii) When calculating any other payment due under this Agreement (except past due payments), the conversion date will be the date of Franchisor's invoice or such other date as Franchisor reasonably designates.

(iv) When calculating past due payments and related interest, the conversion date will be either, at Franchisor's direction and in its discretion, (i) a date determined by reference to the preceding subsections (a), (b) or (c), or (ii) the day that Franchisee makes payment.

(b) Method of Payment. All payments shall be made by wire transfer of immediately available funds to a bank account that Franchisor designates, located either in the United States or elsewhere. Franchisor may change the designated account from time to time by notice to Franchisee.

(c) Transaction Costs. All fees, commissions and other costs of currency exchange and of electronic transfer of funds will be borne by Franchisee.

(d) Currency Restrictions. Franchisee will use all commercially reasonable efforts to obtain any consents or authorizations that may be necessary to permit timely payment in Dollars of all amounts payable under this Agreement. If any legal restrictions are ever imposed upon the purchase of Dollars in or the removal of Dollars from [the franchisee's country], Franchisee will notify Franchisor immediately. In this event Franchisor may direct Franchisee to make payment in such other currency and/or in such other jurisdiction as Franchisor may select. Franchisee will use commercially reasonable efforts to obtain any authorizations necessary to comply with Franchisor's directions.

(e) Consequences of Acceptance of Alternative Currency. Franchisor's acceptance of payment in a currency other than Dollars will not release Franchisee from an obligation to make future payments in Dollars to the extent permitted by applicable law.

(f) Franchisor's Election to Terminate. If, having used all available means to comply, Franchisee is unable to obtain authorization of a method and manner of payment reasonably acceptable to Franchisor, Franchisor, may by notice in writing to Franchisee, terminate this Agreement without any claim being made by either party against the other as a result of such termination (its being agreed that the termination of this Agreement in accordance with this Section 2(f) will not constitute or be deemed to arise from an event of default).

3. *Taxes*[62]

(a) Certain fees payable by Franchisee to Franchisor may be subject to Taxes. Each such payment and any other monies payable to Franchisor will be paid by Franchisee without deduction for any Taxes, its being the parties' intention that all payments due to Franchisor will be increased to the extent necessary to provide Franchisor with the same amount it would have received had no Taxes been applicable. Franchisee will (i) remit to the appropriate tax authorities, in a timely manner, all monies required to be withheld from payments to Franchisor, (ii) provide to Franchisor an official receipt issued by such authorities for payment of such Taxes within 30 days of such payment, and (iii) set forth in the regular monthly remittance report required by Franchisor pursuant to Section 7, the amount of such Taxes and the payments to which they relate.

(b) If Franchisor qualifies for and claims a foreign tax credit (regardless of the terminology used to refer to such credit) to reduce its United States federal income tax liability based on the Taxes that Franchisee paid in accordance with this Section 3, Franchisor will refund to Franchisee an amount representing the amount of foreign tax credit that Franchisor claimed as a result of Franchisee's payment of Taxes. The payment of any such refund in any year will be made by Franchisor within a reasonable time after Franchisor files its federal income tax return for the year in which it claims the foreign tax credit. The parties agree to make adjustments to any amount refunded to Franchisee as necessary to reflect changes in the amount of foreign tax credit allowed to Franchisor in the event of a federal income tax audit or amendment of its federal income tax returns.

*****

Severability. If a court or arbitrator enters a non-appealable order or binding award to the effect that any provision of this Agreement governing the payment of monies to Franchisor in Dollars or another currency acceptable to Franchisor is void, invalid or enforceable, Franchisor may terminate this Agreement immediately upon notice to Franchisee.

V. Restrictions on Transfer

A. WHAT IS THE ISSUE AND HOW WILL IT AFFECT YOUR CLIENT?

The legal issues affecting transfer restrictions typically fall into three categories: (1) the mechanism through which the restrictions are imposed (that is, the franchise agreement, the franchisee's organizational documents, or separate pledge agreements), (2) substantive content of the restrictions, and (3) enforcement of the restrictions.

With respect to the mechanism for imposing restrictions, transfer restrictions are typically contained within the franchise agreement. Franchisors may seek to incorporate similar restrictions into the franchisee's articles of incorporation or comparable organizational documents and in the franchisee's share certificates. This serves to put existing shareholders and prospective purchasers and other interested parties on notice of the existence of the restrictions, at least until the organizational documents and share certificates are changed. Other jurisdictions may require that, to effect the desired result, restrictions and rights of first refusal (which often serve to enable the franchisor to prevent an unacceptable transfer by itself acquiring the asset that is proposed to be transferred) must be formally contained in notarial deeds or pledge agreements.

With respect to the content of the restrictions, in most jurisdictions the parties are free to establish procedures for and conditions on the transfer of the franchisee, the franchise agreement, or all or substantially all of the assets of the franchised business, as long as such procedures and conditions are reasonable.

Regardless of mechanism employed and the content of the transfer restriction, the most frequent obstacle franchisors face in enforcing transfer restrictions is preventing an attempted or completed transfer. The inability to obtain injunctive or equitable relief will make it difficult, if not impossible, to prevent an improper transfer of, or encumbrance upon, an interest in the franchisee, the franchise agreement, or the franchisee's assets. The end result may be that the franchisor must either terminate the franchise agreement or find itself with a new, unapproved franchisee.

B. WHAT IS THE LAW?

1. Mechanism for Imposing Transfer Restrictions

Unless otherwise prohibited by local law, franchisors should consider requiring restrictions to be placed in a franchisee entity's articles of incorporation or association and bylaws, if such exist, to limit the ability to transfer to an innocent third party. In many countries, including Panama, Peru, and Nicaragua, this approach is recommended regardless of whether a franchisor desires enforcement of the restrictions or a right to obtain damages. For instance, Panamanian corporate law holds that articles of incorporation may include transfer restrictions; but any restriction providing for an absolute prohibition on share transfers shall be void. Similarly, the franchisee's articles of incorporation may not restrict transfer under the laws of Taiwan. Further, transfer restrictions contained in articles of incorporation are not customary in Australia and Malaysia. Measures that have been employed with some success in Costa Rica include: (1) requiring that the contract, specifically highlighting the transfer restrictions, be ratified and approved by resolution of the franchisee's shareholders; (2) duplicating such restrictions in the franchisee's corporate minute book; and (3) registering a note of the resolution in the shareholders' registry.

Several jurisdictions statutorily require (or local counsel recommends) that preemptive rights relating to the acquisition of real estate be contained in a notarial deed. Similarly, preemptive rights regarding personal property may have to be contained in a pledge agreement. Germany requires that agreements effecting real estate be executed in German before a German notary to be enforceable.[63] Additional protection of the real estate preemptive right can be obtained by registering the interest with the German Land Registry.[64] Many Latin American countries have similar laws regarding the filing of pledge agreements in the appropriate land or property registries. The benefits of making such filings must be weighed carefully. In Germany, failure to memorialize these preemptive rights in accordance with statutory requirements could result in the entire franchise agreement being declared void if a challenge to the preemptive rights is made successfully. In other cases, the only considerations are the time and cost of filing.

2. *Content of Transfer Restrictions*

Australia is an example of a country that has codified the right to impose reasonable transfer restrictions.[65] If the conditions are reasonable and any contractually mandated franchisor approval authority is not abused, the transfer restrictions will be upheld. Those statutory circumstances in which it is reasonable for the franchisor to withhold its consent include: (1) the transferee does not meet the selection criteria of the franchisor, (2) the franchisee has not paid all outstanding amounts owing to the franchisor, (3) the franchisee has breached the franchise agreement and not remedied the breach, and (4) the transferee does not meet a reasonable requirement contained in the franchise agreement.[66]

Korea employs a similar approach.[67] Although Korean law does not prohibit a franchisor from restricting a franchisee from transferring assets, like the law of Australia, if such restrictions are unreasonable and unnecessary for the proper management of the franchise system, or otherwise amount to an abuse of superior bargaining power by the franchisor, then the restrictions may be held to be an unfair trade practice.[68]

It may strengthen the enforceability of a transfer restriction in these jurisdictions to obtain, in the franchise agreement, an acknowledgment by the franchisee that the restrictions are reasonable and necessary for the proper management of the franchise system.

3. Enforcing Transfer Restrictions

Many countries effectively limit relief for the breach of a transfer restriction to termination of the franchise agreement or damages because injunctive or other equitable relief is unavailable or difficult to obtain. In some countries, such as Costa Rica, the power to restrict transfers of shares in a franchisee is limited based on a constitutionally granted right of each person to dispose of his property freely.

Several of the Middle East nations, including Egypt, Saudi Arabia, and the United Arab Emirates, have a long-standing judicial reluctance to grant injunctive or equitable relief. Interestingly, the new Egyptian Commercial Code effective in October 1999 expressly permits injunctive or equitable relief (in cases when the moving party can demonstrate the relief sought is paramount to a "legitimate and serious interest," under the Egyptian Commercial Code), although legal commentators in Egypt advise that it will most likely remain extraordinarily difficult to obtain such relief.[69]

At best, in some civil law jurisdictions, courts that are generally reluctant to grant immediate injunctive relief will require a full hearing on the merits of the case.

4. Special Situations

Other issues arise if the foreign country has created a complex regulatory scheme governing international transactions. The PRC is one notable example. In the PRC, if the franchisee is a joint venture, any attempt to realize a security interest with respect to the equity interest of the franchisee will be subject to the approval of the Ministry of Foreign Trade and Economic Cooperation (MOFTEC) and the consent by all other investors in the joint venture both at the time of the pledge and at the time of foreclosure.[70] Since PRC law requires any sale or transfer of equity interest in a joint venture be approved by MOFTEC, it is unlikely that a sale in violation of a pledge agreement that has been approved by MOFTEC will be approved. Before the execution of any pledge agreement, it should be verified with the State Administration of Industry and Commerce (SAIC) whether the joint venture interest in question has previously been encumbered.[71] In practice, it may be difficult to obtain a security interest over the joint venture's equity from the parties to the joint venture. However, a covenant by the parties to the joint venture not to transfer the interest in a joint venture does not require any government approval and can be included in the franchise agreement. In addition, it is usually advisable to include as an event of default in the franchise agreement or pledge agreement any substantial sale of the assets of the joint venture and the transfer of an interest in the joint venture.

Practice Tip

In many jurisdictions, a franchisor may be able to increase its chances of prohibiting an unapproved transfer by requiring the franchisee to incorporate the transfer restriction into its organizational documents to establish the agreement on this point by the franchisee entity and its owners and as notice to third parties. Many times this is not as legally effective as franchisor's counsel want it to be, but it can serve as a deterrent to transfers. Determining the effectiveness of transfer restrictions should be one of the goals of the issues checklist reviewed with local counsel.

C. SAMPLE CLAUSES

The laws noted above generally do not affect enforcement of the transfer provisions normally seen in U.S. franchise agreements. Therefore, typical domestic franchise agreements will not need to undergo significant revision. However, below is a typical transfer provision as well as a warranty and representation regarding transfer and a right of first refusal.

1. Transfer Provision

A. Transfer by Franchisor

Franchisor will have the right to transfer or assign this Agreement and all or any part of its rights or obligations to any Person. Specifically, and without limitation to the foregoing, Franchisee acknowledges and agrees that Franchisor may sell its assets, the Proprietary Marks or the System to a third party; may offer its securities privately or publicly; may merge, acquire other corporations or be acquired by another corporation; may undertake a refinancing, recapitalization, leveraged buyout or other economic or financial restructuring; or may terminate, cease to exist or dissolve; provided that with respect to any transfer that would result in the subsequent performance by the transferee of all or substantially all of the obligations of Franchisor hereunder, such transferee will be required to assume and undertake to perform such obligations in all material respects. With regard to any or all of the above sales, assignments and dispositions, Franchisee and each Franchisee's Principal expressly and specifically waive any claims, demands, or damages against Franchisor arising from or related to the transfer of the Proprietary Marks (or any variation thereof) or the System from Franchisor to any other party. Nothing contained in this Agreement will require Franchisor to offer any services or products, whether or not bearing the Proprietary Marks, to Franchisee, if Franchisor assigns or otherwise disposes of its rights in this Agreement. Franchisee acknowledges and agrees that Franchisor shall have no liability to Franchisee or any Principal after the effective date of such transfer; any such transfer shall constitute a release and novation with respect to this Agreement; and transferee shall be liable to Franchisee as if it had been an original party to this Agreement.

B. Transfers by Franchisee and Franchisee's Principals

1. Franchisee and each Franchisee's Principal understands and acknowledges that the rights and duties set forth in this Agreement are personal to Franchisee, and that Franchisor has granted the franchise in reliance on the business skill, financial capacity, and character of Franchisee, Franchisee's Principals and any guarantor of Franchisee's obligations. Accordingly, except as otherwise permitted herein, Franchisee will not sell, assign, transfer, convey, give away, hypothecate, pledge, encumber, alienate or otherwise dispose of any interest in the franchise, the Unit or any of the Unit's assets without Franchisor's prior written consent and compliance with all the conditions and requirements of this Section ___, except that Franchisor's consent will not be required for the sale of Unit inventory in the ordinary course of business or isolated sales of obsolete or worn out Unit furniture, fixtures and equipment. Further, no Franchisee's Principal will sell, assign, transfer, convey, give away, hypothecate, pledge, encumber, alienate or otherwise dispose of any direct or indirect equity or other interest in Franchisee without Franchisor's prior written consent and compliance with all the conditions and requirements of this Section ___. Any purported assignment or transfer, whether voluntary, involuntary or by operation of law, will be ineffective against Franchisor and will constitute a material breach of this Agreement for which Franchisor may terminate this Agreement without opportunity to cure pursuant to Section ___.

2. Franchisor will not unreasonably withhold its consent to an assignment of this Agreement and the franchise by Franchisee or to a sale of all or substantially all of Franchisee's assets (including the Unit) that would, by itself or in the aggregate, constitute a change of Control, provided that:

a. All of Franchisee's accrued monetary obligations and all other outstanding obligations to Franchisor and its Affiliates will have been satisfied;

b. Franchisee is currently in substantial compliance with all provisions of this Agreement and of any other agreement between Franchisee and Franchisor or its Affiliates;

c. Franchisee and each Franchisee's Principal have executed a general release and novation, in a form satisfactory to Franchisor, of any and all claims against Franchisor and its officers, directors, agents, shareholders, and employees, in their corporate and individual capacities;

d. The transferee and its principals have entered into a written agreement, in a form satisfactory to Franchisor, assuming and agreeing to discharge all obligations of Franchisee and Franchisee's Principals under this Agreement; and, if the obligations of Franchisee were guaranteed by a Person who has requested release from the guaranty, the transferee will arrange for a Person acceptable to Franchisor to guarantee all such obligations in writing in a form satisfactory to Franchisor;

e. The transferee has demonstrated to Franchisor's satisfaction that it meets Franchisor's educational, managerial, and business standards; possesses a good moral character, business reputation, and credit rating; has the experience, aptitude and ability to conduct the franchised business (as may be evidenced by prior related business experience or otherwise); has adequate financial resources and capital to operate the Unit; and is not a Competitor;

f. At Franchisor's option, the transferee and its principals will execute, for a term ending on the expiration date of this Agreement and with such renewal term as may be provided by this Agreement, the standard form International Unit Franchise Agreement that Franchisor is then offering to new international System franchisees, together with such ancillary agreements as Franchisor may require for the franchised business, which agreements will supersede this Agreement in all respects and the terms of which agreements may differ from the terms of this Agreement in ways that include, without limitation, a higher Monthly Royalty Fee and Marketing Expenditure; provided, that the transferee will not be required to pay an Initial Franchisee Fee;

g. The transferee, at its expense, will upgrade the Unit to conform to the then current Standards for __________® Units, and will complete the upgrading and other requirements within the time specified by Franchisor;

h. Franchisee will acknowledge in writing its continuing responsibility and liability for all of the obligations to Franchisor in connection with the franchised business before the effective date of the transfer and will execute any and all instruments reasonably requested by Franchisor to evidence such responsibility and liability;

i. Franchisee and each Franchisee's Principal will confirm in writing their obligation to comply with all restrictive covenants that survive the cessation of a party's interest in this Agreement and the franchise;

j. At the transferee's expense, the transferee, the transferee's managing partner and the transferee's operating partner will complete any training programs then in effect for franchisees upon such terms and conditions as Franchisor may reasonably require; and

k. Franchisee will reimburse Franchisor for its reasonable costs and expenses associated with reviewing the application to transfer, including, without limitation, legal and accounting fees and salaries of Franchisor's personnel.

3. If a transfer or series of prior, contemporaneous or proposed transfers of equity interests in Franchisee or a Franchisee's Principal would, in the aggregate, have the effect of transferring direct or indirect Control of Franchisee, Franchisor may, as a condition to approving any such transfer, require that Franchisee, the transferee and the transferor, as appropriate, satisfy any or all of the requirements of Section B.2 above.

4. If a transfer or series of prior, contemporaneous or proposed transfers of equity interests in Franchisee or a Franchisee's Principal would have the effect of transferring less than Control of Franchisee or a Franchisee's Principal, Franchisor may, as a condition to approving any such transfer, require that Franchisee, the transferee and the transferor, as appropriate, satisfy any or all of the conditions described in Section B above. In addition, each transferee must possess a good moral character and business reputation, acceptable credit rating and may not be a direct or indirect competitor of Franchisor, as determined by Franchisor.

C. Right of First Refusal

1. If Franchisee or any Franchisee's Principal (a "Transferor") wants to accept a bona fide offer to acquire Franchisee's interest in the franchise or the Unit's assets, or any part of a Franchisee's Principal's equity or other interest in Franchisee or of a Franchisee's Principal, the Transferor will, within five days of receipt of the offer and before its acceptance, provide a written Notice of Offer to Franchisor. The Notice of Offer will specify the Interest, the identity of the offeror, the purchase price and manner of payment, the treatment of any liabilities to which the Interest is subject and will include copies of all written communications from the offeror or Transferor containing or relating to the offer. The Transferor will also provide such other documents and information relating to the offeror and/or the offer as Franchisor requests. Further, if the Interest includes the franchise or the Unit's assets, the Transferor will provide Franchisor copies of all real estate and personal property leases and other encumbrances to which the Unit's assets are subject.

2. Upon receipt of a Notice of Offer, Franchisor will have the right and option to purchase, and the Transferor will be obligated to sell to Franchisor, the Interest upon the same terms and conditions contained in the Notice of Offer. In the event the consideration, terms and/or conditions contained in the Notice of Offer are such that Franchisor or its designee may not reasonably be required to furnish the same consideration, terms and/or conditions, Franchisor or its designee will notify the Transferor and Franchisor or its designee will have the right to substitute the reasonable cash equivalent; provided, that if in this case Franchisor or its designee and the Transferor cannot agree on the reasonable cash equivalent within fifteen days of receipt of the Notice of Offer, Franchisor (or its designee) and Franchisee will each appoint an independent, qualified appraiser to determine the reasonable cash equivalent of such consideration, terms and/or conditions. If the two appraisers so appointed cannot agree on the reasonable cash equivalent, they will appoint a third independent, qualified appraiser to determine the reasonable cash equivalent and the reasonable cash equivalent will be the average of the two closest appraisals. The determination of such appraisers will be final and binding on all parties.

3. Franchisor may exercise the purchase option granted in Section C.2 above by providing a written Notice of Exercise to the Transferor on or before the later of: (i) forty-five days from receipt of the Notice of Offer; (ii) thirty days from the date of receipt of all additional information and documents relating to the offeror and/or the offer requested by Franchisor or its designee pursuant to Section C.1 above; or (ii) thirty days from receipt of written determination by the appraiser of reasonable cash equivalent pursuant to Section C.2 above, if applicable.

4. The closing for any purchase by Franchisor or its designee under this Section 6 will be consummated and closed in Franchisor's (or its designee's) principal office or such other location designated by Franchisor or its designee at a mutually agreed upon date and time, provided that such closing will be held within ninety days from the date of Notice of Exercise. At the closing, the Transferor will execute and deliver to Franchisor or its designee such documents, affidavits and instruments as are necessary or appropriate, in the opinion of Franchisor's or its designee's counsel, to transfer good and marketable title in the Interest to Franchisor or its designee, free and clear of any lien, claim or encumbrance (except as otherwise specified in the Notice of Offer). The Transferor will execute and deliver to Franchisor or its designee such representation, warranties and indemnities as are customary or

appropriate, in the opinion of Franchisor's or its designee's counsel, in connection with the transfer of property of a kind similar to the Interest. Franchisor or its designee will deliver the purchase price to the Transferor in accordance with the Notice of Offer and/or determination of reasonable cash equivalent. If the Interest includes real property the Transferor will, at his expense, deliver to Franchisor or its designee an owner's marketability title insurance policy, or similar document, issued by a company acceptable to Franchisor's or its designee's counsel, insuring Franchisor's or its designee's title to the real property for the full amount of the purchase price without any exceptions or exclusions except for those acceptable to Franchisor. Franchisee will use his best efforts and due diligence to cure any title defects and the closing will be extended for a reasonable cure period. All costs, fees, document taxes and other expenses incurred in connection with the transfer of the Interest will be allocated in accordance with the Notice of Offer; any costs not allocated will be paid by the Transferor.

5. As to any particular Notice of Offer, if Franchisor or its designee does not exercise the purchase option within the time limit of Section C.3 above, or if Franchisor or its designee, through no fault of the Transferor, fails to close the purchase of the Interest within the time limit of Section C.4 above, then as to such particular Notice of Offer only, the Transferor will be free to transfer the Interest solely to the offeror named in the Notice of Offer upon the same terms and conditions contained in the Notice of Offer; provided however:

a. such transfer will be subject to compliance with all terms and provisions of Section B above; and

b. such transfer will be consummated and closed on or before the earlier of: (i) 90 days after compliance with and satisfaction of the terms and provisions of Section B above; or (ii) if Franchisor has not exercised its purchase option, 90 days from the expiration date for exercise of the purchase option pursuant to Section C.3 above; or (iii) if Franchisor has exercised the purchase option but failed to close through no fault of the Transferor, 90 days from the expiration date for closing pursuant to Section C.4 above.

6. Transferor will make no transfer of the Interest except to the offeror named in the Notice of Offer, on the same terms and conditions contained in the Notice of Offer and within the time limit specified in Section C.5 above. Any purported transfer not in strict compliance with all the requirements of the preceding sentence will be null and void. If the Transferor does not close and consummate the transfer of the Interest in strict accordance with the requirements of Section C.5 above, Franchisor's purchase option will again be exercisable and the Transferor will make no transfer of the Interest until he or she has again complied with all terms and provisions of this Section 6, including, without limitation, issuance of a new Notice of Offer. Any modification to an offer will constitute a new offer for which Franchisor's purchase option will again be exercisable and the Transferor will make no transfer pursuant to such modified offer until he or she has again complied with all terms and provisions of this Section 6 including, without limitation, issuance of a new Notice of Offer.

D. Non-Waiver of Claims

Franchisor's consent to a transfer of any interest in the franchise or in Franchisee granted now or in the future will not constitute a waiver of any claims it may have against the transferring party, nor will it be deemed a waiver of Franchisor's right to demand exact compliance with any of the terms of this Agreement by the transferee.

E. Transfers by Certain Principals

Notwithstanding Section B, if any Person holding an interest in Franchisee who satisfies the definition of a Franchisee's Principal, but does not execute this Agreement as a Franchisee's Principal, desires to transfer such interest or any part thereof, then Franchisee will promptly notify Franchisor of such proposed transfer in writing and will provide such information relative thereto as Franchisor may reasonably request before such transfer. Such transferee must possess a good moral character and business reputation, acceptable credit rating and may not be a competitor of Franchisor. Such transferee will be a Franchisee's Principal and as such will be required to execute a confidentiality agreement and ancillary covenants not to compete in the form then required by Franchisor, which form will be in substantially the same form attached hereto. Alternatively, Franchisor may also designate the transferee as a Franchisee's Principal who will be required to execute this Agreement or an addendum thereto as described in Section ___.

F. Control and Ownership Interests

As used in this Agreement, "Control" means possession (through one or more intermediaries) of the power to direct, or cause the direction of, the management or policies of any other entity, whether through the ownership of voting interest, by contract, or otherwise; but in all cases, fifteen percent or more of the Ownership Interest, directly or indirectly, in such entity will constitute Control. "Ownership Interests" means any ownership interest of any type, including (a) in relation to a company, the ownership of shares in the company; (b) in relation to a partnership, the ownership of a general or limited partnership interest; (c) in relation to a limited liability company, the ownership of a membership interest; or (d) in relation to a trust, the ownership of the beneficial interest of such trust.

2. *Warranties and Representation*

Franchisee will maintain stop transfer instructions against the transfer on its records of any equity securities. Unless expressly prohibited by applicable law, Franchisee's Charter Documents and each certificate representing an ownership interest in Franchisee will contain or have conspicuously endorsed upon its face a statement in a form satisfactory to Franchisor that all certificates evidencing ownership interests in Franchisee are held subject to, and that further assignment or transfer thereof is subject to, all restrictions imposed upon assignments by this Agreement.

VI. Trade Secret and Business Information Transfer

A. WHAT IS THE ISSUE AND HOW WILL IT AFFECT YOUR CLIENT?

The very essence of any franchise system is its trade secret and other confidential information. Typically, a franchisor's trade secrets constitute the methods, processes, materials, and recipes that the franchisor believes makes a particular system competitive and distinguishable. Trade secrets are often the result of substantial investments of time and money. Given the value associated with such trade secrets, especially for an established and recognizable brand, franchisors are loath to enter into markets where such secrets are susceptible to piracy, infringement, or widespread misuse.

The key element of trade secret information is secrecy. Statutory protection and remedies can deter franchisees, employees, and other participants in the franchise system from divulging trade secret information to the public, but franchisors cannot rely on this threat alone. Litigation's only practical effect is to punish the violator once the trade secret information is revealed, so franchisors should take preventative measures to ensure that their information remains secret.

B. WHAT IS THE LAW?

Generally, trade secrets can be defined as

> [I]nformation, including a formula, pattern, compilation, program, device, method, technique, or process, which: (1) derives independent economic value, actual or potential, from not being generally known to and not being readily ascertainable by proper means by other persons who can obtain economic value from its disclosure or use, and (2) is the subject of efforts that are reasonable under the circumstances to maintain its secrecy.[72]

There is no global law of trade secrets and, unlike patent, copyright, and trademark law, there are no comprehensive international treaties pertaining to trade secrets.[73]

Many countries, however, have enacted legislation to give greater protection to trade secrets. Nonetheless, identification of the law of trade secrets in foreign jurisdictions may be elusive.[74] This difficulty is compounded in the United States, because different states treat the protection of trade secrets differently. Also, legal protection of trade secrets in the United States is derived from many different legal theories as it is in other nations. A cause of action for misappropriation of trade secrets may lie in contract law, tort law, unfair competition law, criminal law, and the laws governing employee/employer relations and fiduciary obligations.

Some countries, such as the Philippines, provide no direct legal protection at all for trade secrets.[75] Some countries specifically address the protection of trade secret materials through specific legislation or through other business statutes. For instance, in Germany, trade secret protection is found in various places including the Unfair Competition Act, the Penal Code (relating to disclosure by professionals and fiduciaries), and the German agency law contained in the German Commercial Code,[76] which states that a commercial agent must not reveal business or trade secrets that were entrusted to him or that he or she acquired during his or her activity for the principal.[77] In Colombia, the violation of a trade secret statute constitutes a "disloyal competition practice"[78] for which a franchisor may bring an unfair competition action against the offending franchisee or third party. In Italy, trade secrets are protected under the penal code, the civil code regarding rules against unfair competition, and the patent code.[79] Chile is another example of a country that provides for trade secret protection in its penal code, which contains provisions that subject persons or entities that misuse trade secrets and other proprietary materials to up to three years in jail and a fine of approximately U.S. $1,000.[80]

Personal data about franchisees and employees can be viewed as trade secret or other protectable information. In this regard, it is useful to note that both the European Union[81] and the United Kingdom[82] have instituted data protection guidelines. Unlike any current regulation in place in the United States, these data protection acts establish registration and supervision requirements for personal information obtained in the European Community.[83]

Trade secret protection in Europe takes on added importance because of differences between the American and European patent systems. Technologies that are usually protected by patents in the United States may be more suited to trade secret protection in foreign jurisdictions.[84] Patent protection may not be available at all for some technologies in Europe. Accordingly, specific inquiry must be made about the most appropriate method of protection.

Recently, Japan has also seen the need to more adequately protect trade secrets. The Japanese Unfair Competition Law provides trade secret protection to any "manufacturing method, marketing method or other technical or business information useful in commercial activity."[85] This standard is similar to that of the Uniform Trade Secrets Act in the United States, but it is broader because it specifically protects business information.

The secrecy requirement in Japan may be stricter than in the United States as it is unclear whether reasonable efforts to maintain secrecy will be sufficient or whether absolute secrecy is required. Under the new Japanese law, a third party is liable for misappropriation of a trade secret if it knew or was *grossly negligent* in not knowing that an improper act was involved in acquiring the trade secret.[86] But if a third party acquires misappropriated information in good faith through a transaction, it may continue to use the information[87] and may also disclose the information to licensees or subcontractors.[88]

Notably, the new law expressly authorizes third-party liability and injunctions. Although punitive damages are not allowed, the law provides for compensatory damages and other remedies to restore goodwill are available, such as a public apology (a common form of relief in Japan).[89]

To assert a claim for trade secret misappropriation in Japan, however, it is necessary to disclose the trade secret without any procedural protection.[90] The Agreement on Trade-related Aspects of Intellectual Property Rights (TRIPS) agreement[91] explicitly requires that protective orders be available to protect trade secrets. Because international agreements ratified by Japan are self-executing and have the force of law in Japan, Japanese judges may now view TRIPS as a mandate to provide protection of trade secrets during court proceedings.[92]

As discussed in Chapter 3, business patents are a method increasingly being used as an alternative to trade secret protection. In the United States, patents give the patent owner the right to exclude others from practicing the claimed invention and close equivalents thereof for a period from patent issuance to twenty years from filing.[93] Presently, many foreign countries do not permit the filing of business method patents, but where they are available they can be an effective tool in protecting valuable assets of the franchisor.

Even when a patent is available on technology, sometimes it is still a more attractive alternative to protect it as a proprietary secret. To preserve foreign filing rights, it is important that a patent application be filed in all relevant jurisdictions before any public disclosure. In Europe, patent applications are published before issuance of the patent.[94] This publication gives competitors worldwide an opportunity to copy the technology.[95] "In addition, pre-issuance opposition procedures, long patent pendency after publication and poor enforcement of patents may all detract from the efficacy of patent protection under foreign patent systems."[96] In these situations, a franchisor may prefer to maintain the technology as a trade secret rather than have the technology subject to the public disclosure involved in obtaining patent protection. Moreover, although a patent is the possibility of perpetual protection. While a patent is limited by statute to a number of years, a trade secret will last indefinitely if not discovered.

Practice Tip

The most effective way to protect trade secret information is to monitor the dissemination of the information and to provide it to only those personnel whose job duties require that they have access to or know this information. To impress upon employees the importance and value of this information, franchisors should consider requiring key persons who have access to this information to sign a nondisclosure agreement in addition to any other employment documentation. A separate document that specifically outlines the employee's or other such person's obligations with respect to the trade secret information and the penalties for violating these obligations can convey the gravity of the topic and serve as a deterrent to would-be violators. Franchisees who have received these trade secrets should be required to employ these practices to ensure that the trade secrets that they have been entrusted with are protected.

Moreover, franchisors should ensure that their franchise agreements provide for the franchisor's right to seek injunctive or other equitable relief in any court having jurisdiction to protect its trade secrets and other business information. This carve-out from an arbitration clause may enable the franchisor to seek an expedited remedy for enforcement of post-termination obligations such as return of manuals and other proprietary information upon termination, if the franchisee fails to comply with its post-termination obligations. Although the actual procedures, timetables, and likelihood of success varies by country, many countries have procedures for obtaining such relief upon a prima facie showing of a right (that is, ownership of trade secret information and the termination of a franchise agreement) and irreparable harm (for example, loss of goodwill from continued operation of the unit under substandard conditions or risk of trade secret information being used in an unauthorized manner). By forcing the franchisee to cease operating as a unit of the franchise system, the franchisor can more readily limit the franchisee's ability to exploit the trade secret information acquired through the franchise relationship.

C. SAMPLE CLAUSES

Definitions

"Confidential Information" means all information and data relating to the business, trade practices, trade secrets, methods of operation, sales, promotion, marketing, technology, know-how or recipes of Franchisor, the System or operation of the Unit which may be communicated to Franchisee or Franchisee's Principals or of which Franchisee or Franchisee's Principals may be apprised by virtue of Franchisee's operation under the terms of this Agreement. The Confidential Information provided by Franchisor in connection with this Agreement constitutes valuable, essential, necessary and indispensable information that Franchisee requires and needs to perform under and offer the services described in, this Agreement. Each and all of the restrictions imposed on Franchisee in Sections _____ and _______ constitute measures necessary to maintain, the identity, integrity and reputation of the System.

"Controlling Principal" means the individual who supervises and oversees the operation of the Unit. If Franchisee is an individual, "Franchisee" and "Controlling Principal" have interchangeable meanings, and Franchisee shall perform all duties and obligations of the Controlling Principal. The first Controlling Principal is identified in Attachment ___.

"Proprietary Marks" means certain trade names, service marks, trademarks, logos and emblems, including, without limitation, the marks _______________®, and such other trade names, service marks, and trademarks as are now or hereafter designated by Franchisor in writing for use in connection with the System.

1. Confidential Information. Franchisee and Franchisee's Principals will not, during the term of this Agreement or at any time thereafter, communicate, publish, disclose, divulge, use, or authorize anyone else to communicate, publish, disclose, divulge or use, for the benefit of themselves (other than in connection with the operation of the Unit during the term of the franchise) or any other Person, any Confidential Information. Franchisee and Franchisee's Principals will divulge Confidential Information only to such of Franchisee's employees as must have access to it to operate the Unit. Any and all information, knowledge, know-how, and techniques provided or made available by Franchisor will be deemed Confidential Information for purposes of this Agreement, except information which Franchisee or any of Franchisee's Principals can demonstrate came to their attention before disclosure thereof by Franchisor; or which, at or after the time of disclosure by Franchisor to Franchisee or Franchisee's Principals, lawfully had become or later becomes a part of the public domain, through lawful publication or communication by others.

2. Franchisee will require and obtain execution of covenants similar to those set forth in this Section ____ (including covenants applicable upon the termination of an individual's employment with Franchisee) from all of Franchisee's personnel who have received or will have access to training or Confidential Information from Franchisor before the employment of such persons by Franchisee. Such covenants will be substantially in the form set forth in Attachment ___. All of Franchisee's Principals, including the Operating Partner and Managing Partner, except those Franchisee's Principals who have executed this Agreement, will also execute such covenants. Franchisor reserves the right, in its sole discretion, to decrease the period of time or geographic scope of the noncompetition covenant set forth in Attachment ___ or eliminate such noncompetition covenant altogether for any Person that is required to execute such covenants under this Section ___. Failure by Franchisee to obtain execution of a covenant required by this Section ___ will constitute a default under Section ___.

3. Other Proprietary Materials. Franchisee acknowledges and agrees that Franchisor may develop for use in the System other proprietary materials, including without limitation certain highly confidential secret recipe products which are trade secrets of Franchisor, and certain wearables and other products bearing the Proprietary Marks. Due to the importance of quality and uniformity of production and the significance of such products in the System, it is to the mutual benefit of the parties that Franchisor control the production and distribution of such products. Accordingly,

> Franchisee agrees that in the event such secret recipe products become a part of the System, Franchisee will use only Franchisor's secret recipe products and, if required by Franchisor, will purchase from Franchisor or from a source designated by Franchisor all of Franchisee's requirements of such products. In addition, Franchisee agrees to offer for sale at the Unit such wearables and other products bearing the Proprietary Marks as designated by Franchisor from time to time. Franchisee will carry an inventory of such wearables in such quantities and styles as may be required to meet consumer demand, as may be determined from time to time by Franchisor. If required by Franchisor, Franchisee will purchase all such requirements of wearables and other products bearing the Proprietary Marks only from a supplier designated by Franchisor. Franchisee acknowledges that Franchisor and its Affiliates have the right to offer and sell such secret recipe products, wearables and other products bearing the Proprietary Marks through any means other than a Unit, including at retail, on the Internet, or through catalogs (and Franchisor may require Franchisee to distribute copies of such catalogs to the customers of the Unit).

A liquidated damages clause similar to the sample clause in Section X of this chapter would also be appropriate in this provision.

VII. Labor/Immigration Issues

A. WHAT IS THE ISSUE AND HOW WILL IT AFFECT YOUR CLIENT?

It takes competent and motivated franchisees (with competent and motivated employees) to ensure the success of a franchise system no matter the prestige of the brand or the quality of the franchise system. Employees can be competent and motivated only if they are trained and understand their role in the franchise system as a whole. In many instances, newly signed franchisees and their employees or employees of the franchisor travel across national borders for training.

When franchisors and franchisees are training and hiring employees, immigration issues must be considered. For instance, having a franchisor's trainers in a country under an improper entrance certificate can create a dangerous situation for the trainer. The trainer could unintentionally be in violation of that country's law. Additionally, if a franchisor does not provide training in a timely manner, it may be in breach of a contractual duty to provide appropriate and necessary training to franchisees. Alternatively, if the franchisees or their employees are to be trained in the United States, the trainees will likely be required to obtain visas to enter the United States or special permission to leave their country of origin. Franchisees hiring employees in certain countries may also have to contend with special employee protection laws that provide certain protections against termination.

B. WHAT IS THE LAW?

1. Immigration Law

In most instances, the laws governing entrance into a country vary with respect to the purpose for entering the country. These different entrance requirements also carry with them different restrictions and privileges. The most obvious is the length of time that the individual can stay in the country and whether the person can become employed.

a. Inbound Immigration by Franchisee or Its Employees. In the United States, an alien having a residence in a foreign country that the alien has no intention of abandoning, and who is visiting the United States temporarily for business, may use a B-1 visa.[97] The B-1 visa may be used for legitimate temporary commercial or professional activities[98] for not more than one year with possible extensions of stay in increments of not more than six months that do not involve gainful employment, for example, consultation with business associates or clients, negotiation of contracts, or involvement in litigation.[99]

Aliens entering the United States "just using their passport" without a B-1 visa are entering under the Visa Waiver Pilot Program, often referred to as the Visa Waiver.[100] Any of the allowable activities and underlying requirements of the B-1 visitor for business also apply to nonimmigrants entering the United States under the Visa Waiver Pilot Program. There are additional specific requirements for nonimmigrants wishing to enter the United States under the Visa Waiver Pilot Program.[101]

Under the Visa Waiver Pilot Program, if the alien is from one of the specified countries, the alien may be admitted for a period of time not to exceed ninety days.[102] Generally, no extensions are available. However, in the event of an emergency that prevents the alien from departing within the allowable ninety days, the alien may apply for satisfactory departure at the Immigration and Naturalization Service (INS) District Office having jurisdiction over the place of the alien's temporary stay.[103] The INS District Director may—at his or her discretion—grant a period of satisfactory departure not to exceed thirty days. Other alternatives are available for individuals who want to remain in the United States for an extended period of time.

b. Outbound Immigration of Franchisor and Its Employees. For franchisors bringing trainers to a foreign jurisdiction or for franchisees hiring personnel in foreign jurisdictions, it is equally important to understand the immigration requirements. The following illustrates some of the country requirements that a franchisor will need to satisfy. In Australia, a Class 456 "Short Stay Business Visa" allows people to enter Australia for business purposes.[104] This visa is obtained by delegates to attend conferences, by employees to attend "in-house" training, and by businesspeople to attend meetings and participate in business discussions and negotiations. People are not eligible to apply for this class of visa who intend to engage in paid employment with an Australian company. Generally, applications for Australian visas must be filed with the overseas post (high commission, embassy, or consulate office) in the country in which the foreign person resides. However, a "Business ETA (Electronic Travel Authority) Visa" can be obtained from travel agents in most countries in the world.[105]

U.S. citizens can travel to Brazil for up to ninety days to participate in activities not involving gainful employment. However, if the U.S. citizen is required to stay for longer than ninety days and/or enter into employment, the rules change dramatically to include a lengthy bureaucratic process involving documentation from Brazil and the United States. It is interesting to note that this process is less burdensome for citizens of other countries. For instance, a citizen of Italy can travel to Brazil with relative ease and enter into temporary employment in Brazil with little extra processing.

Canada also has very specific guidelines that regulate travel across its borders. Any application made for a visitors' visa entitles the visa officer to assume that an applicant is an immigrant seeking permanent residence. Visitors must show proof that their visit is of a temporary nature. Visitors must also provide an immigration officer with evidence that they will be able to return to the country from which they sought entry, or continue on to some other country when their visit to Canada is completed.

If a U.S. citizen is going into Canada for activities not involving gainful employment, no visa is required and the U.S. citizen can participate in activities such as corporate training (which would include a franchisor's trainers), consultation with business associates or clients, involvement in litigation, and in some instances the negotiation of contracts. U.S. citizens can even obtain work authorizations in Canada under several categories without having to obtain a visa to enter Canada. The process to obtain a work authorization is reasonably easy and can be accomplished at the border upon entering Canada or through a Canadian Consulate in the United States.

Practice Tip

Whether the franchisor's training program contemplates the travel of franchisee's employees to the United States or the travel of franchisor's employees to a foreign jurisdiction to train franchisee's employees, failing to consider immigration issues early on could result in the traveler's trip being postponed for months beyond the planned date of arrival, could have dire legal consequences for the employer and employees, and could cause embarrassment and loss of credibility to the franchisor. When structuring an international franchise program, U.S. franchise counsel should obtain information about the need for cross-border travel and, if that is contemplated, ensure that immigration issues are addressed in the franchise agreement and built into the issues counsel will discuss with foreign counsel.

Labor laws primarily affect the franchisee's employment relationships. Unless the franchisor intends to have employees in the foreign jurisdiction, counsel should be able to address these issues in the franchise agreement by requiring the franchisee to comply with all laws and regulations, including the employment laws of the country.

2. Labor Laws

In addition to immigration laws, some countries have complex labor laws that can affect the franchisee's business and may require special language or treatment in the franchise agreement. For instance, in Mexico the Mexican Federal Labor Law sets forth a three-tiered minimum wage structure that differs by region.[106] More importantly, mandatory fringe benefits include profit sharing (10 percent of pretax profits spread among employees), vacation days, and Christmas bonuses.[107] Other requirements include mandatory contributions to the national workers housing institute, pension funds, and social security.[108] Mexico also regulates the termination of employees, providing for a tiered compensation structure for termination without cause.[109] The structure starts at three months' pay, plus twenty days additional pay in some cases, for every year employed and adds additional amounts if the employee was employed for greater than twelve years.[110]

C. SAMPLE CLAUSES

Training Costs. Franchisee or its employees will be responsible for any and all other expenses incurred by them in connection with any training programs hereunder, including, without limitation, the costs of transportation, insurance, visas and related expenses, lodging, meals, and wages.

Compliance with Law. Franchisee will comply with all applicable laws, rules, and regulations of the Country and each government authority that exercises jurisdiction over the Unit or Franchisee, and will timely obtain any and all permits, visas, certificates, or licenses necessary for the full and proper conduct of the Unit and training of employees, including, without limitation, licenses to do business, sales tax permits, environmental, safety and fire clearances, liquor licenses, and visas. In addition, Franchisee will comply with all requirements of applicable international treaties and conventions.

VIII. Imports/Duties/Customs

A. WHAT IS THE ISSUE AND HOW WILL IT AFFECT YOUR CLIENT?

Franchisors must review both U.S. and local laws regarding what can be imported or exported and what taxes or duties are required to be paid on those items shipped to and from the United States and the applicable country. For some business format or product franchises that require its franchisees to obtain specific ingredients, goods, or products for resale, a franchisor should understand the manner in which such goods may enter into the country where the franchised unit is located and how that country may assess or implement any import duties or customs requirements. A business format franchise system cannot function properly unless franchisors are able to ship training manuals, software, fixtures, and equipment into the various countries where their franchisees are located (and vice versa).

Many countries charge duties and taxes on imported goods to prevent imported goods from being sold at a much lower price than domestic goods. Governments want to support the industries within their own countries and do not want less expensive goods from abroad to undermine the growth and stability of local companies. As a result, duties and taxes on imports will vary based on the competitiveness of the particular domestic industry at the given time. Depending on the franchise system, import and export restrictions could have a great impact on the profitably of the business for franchisees.

B. WHAT IS THE LAW?

When considering restrictions on the transfer of goods and materials from the United States, a franchisor should consider export restrictions. The United States has very strict regulations on certain exports, especially computer software, hardware, and encryption technology. These export restrictions apply to re-export of items from one foreign country to another foreign country and can impose a duty or tax on items that are brought into the country and then sent out again. There are also rules that prohibit the export of any items to select countries, individuals, and entities without obtaining an export license.

For imports, countries have specific classifications, and these classifications determine the amount of duty that is to be paid on them. What is covered can be surprising. For example, in Thailand a services agreement is normally subject to stamp duty at the rate of 0.1 percent of the service fees.[111] However, the stamp duty may be exempted if all of the services under the agreement will be performed outside Thailand and the agreement is executed outside Thailand, or if all or part of the services under the agreement will be performed in Thailand, but the actual agreement is executed outside Thailand and is not brought into Thailand.[112] (One can bring a copy of the agreement into Thailand, but subject to payment of Baht 5 [U.S.$ 00.132661] per page.) These importation requirements vary by country and are affected by trade treaties like those required before accession into the World Trade Organization (WTO).

In Australia, the customs value of goods imported into Australia, on which import-tariff liability is calculated, is established in accordance with the World Trade Organization Valuation Agreement.[113] Australia uses a tariff-classification system that is based on the Harmonized Tariff of the World Customs Organization. Most Australian tariffs are ad valorem rates.[114] However, Australia provides preferential rates of duty for imports from various countries, which can permit the imports to come in duty-free. Preferential rates are applicable provided that the goods meet the requirements of Australia's Rules of Origin (ROO) for establishing whether particular goods are the "produce or manufacture" of the relevant country. Customs clearance is required on all goods entering Australia. Customs brokers are authorized to advise importers of specific regulations and controls applying to imports and to assist in meeting legal requirements.[115]

The PRC has recently undergone many changes with respect to its import/export regulations.[116] The PRC participates in the Information Technology Agreement, which eliminates all tariffs on high-technology products such as computers, telecommunications equipment, semiconductors, and computer equipment.[117] Despite tariff reductions,[118] consumption and value added taxes (VAT) significantly increase the overall effective tax rate on many imported items.[119] The PRC's import-tariff schedule gives minimum rates for countries with which it has reciprocal trade treaties or agreements, and general rates for countries without reciprocal trade treaties or agreements.[1203] In addition to quotas, the PRC also retains stringent regulatory control over imports through licensing, registration requirements, commodity inspection, and quarantine rules.[121] The Chinese regulations divide imports into three categories: (1) contraband goods, which may not be imported; (2) restricted goods, which require an import license; and (3) general goods, which do not require a license unless brought in by entities not specifically authorized to import that good.[122] If the imported products are in a restricted category, or if the company has previously violated customs regulations, the Chinese authorities also require that companies that import products for re-export place a deposit at a local bank equivalent to 28.7 percent of the value of the goods it plans to import.[123] No special taxes are assessed by the PRC on Chinese exports.[124]

Practice Tip

Franchise agreements should address who will pay the customs fees or duties that are placed on goods, software, equipment, or other products imported by foreign franchisees. The franchisor will normally prefer that the franchisee pay these additional costs because the payments diminish the franchisor's overall profit and the franchisee is in the country and will likely be more aware of what payments are required and how to avoid them. Franchisees argue that if they are required to pay all of these additional payments, they are essentially paying a higher royalty rate even if the franchisor is not receiving a higher royalty rate. Early knowledge of the relevant regulations will assist the franchisor in this negotiation, but the winner of this argument, as in most situations, is the party with the most bargaining power. A franchisee may be willing to split the costs of the broker if this issue is negotiated up front, as the outcome may be economically beneficial to both parties.

C. SAMPLE CLAUSE

> "Taxes" means any sales, remittance, stamp, use, service, occupation, excise, gross receipts, income, property withholding, goods and services and value added taxes and any levies, imposts, duties or other charges and taxes of whatsoever nature imposed upon any fees or payments payable to Franchisor (except taxes imposed on Franchisor's income) on the operation of the Unit under this Agreement or upon Franchisee.
>
> Certain fees and other payments described in this Franchise Agreement may be subject to Taxes. Franchisee shall be responsible for all Taxes unless otherwise agreed in writing by Franchisor or the applicable vendor or creditor of Franchisee... Notwithstanding this and specifically with respect to payments and any monies payable to the Franchisor, each such payment shall be paid to Franchisor without deduction for Taxes. . . . .

IX. Distributorship/Sales Agent/ Sales Representative Laws

A. WHAT IS THE ISSUE AND HOW WILL IT AFFECT YOUR CLIENT?

Under U.S. law, a franchise relationship is traditionally not considered an agency relationship and franchisors do not often deal with U.S. sales representative laws. An issue that may be unfamiliar to many U.S. franchisors is the existence and applicability of legislation designed to protect commercial sales agents or sales representatives who enter into principal/agency relationships to sell or promote goods or services in countries outside the United States. Among other things, these laws typically entitle a commercial agent to payment of reasonable compensation or indemnity upon the termination of the agency relationship unless, in some cases, such termination is proven to be for good cause as enumerated under the applicable jurisdictions' laws. Some of these laws also provide for such compensation or indemnity upon the expiration of an agency agreement. Still other laws limit the meaning of good cause so narrowly that an agent's right to compensation becomes almost inevitable upon termination or can make termination a significant or unreasonable risk for the terminating party.

B. WHAT IS THE LAW?

1. Application to Franchise Relationships

Franchisors do not want agency laws to apply to their franchise relationships because such laws may require the franchisor to compensate the franchisee in connection with termination or expiration of a franchise agreement. The threshold considerations are whether the applicable agency law applies to franchise relationships and how the agency law may be made applicable to the type of franchise relationship at issue.

Another issue is whether the agency law will apply to the sale of goods and services. The EC Directive for the Co-ordination of the Laws of Member States related to Self-employed Commercial Agents 1986[125] created a model commercial agents law that many members of the European Community have adopted in full or with modifications. The EC Directive defines a "commercial agent" as "a self-employed intermediary who has continuing authority to negotiate the sale or the purchase of goods on behalf of another person" or "to negotiate and conclude such transactions on behalf of and in the name of that [person]." Several countries have adopted this definition to limit application of the laws solely to the sale of goods.[126] Other EU countries have not so limited the scope of their agency laws.[127] For instance, in Italy the applicable law predates the EC Directive and covers "contracts," irrespective of whether such contracts related to the sale or purchase of goods or services.[128] Furthermore, although there are relatively few court decisions on the application of these laws to standard franchise relationships, courts more often side with the local agents, and several European legal commentators believe that their respective national courts would likely find these laws applicable to franchising.

2. *Government Filing Requirements*

Several jurisdictions require that a franchise or an agency agreement be filed with a governmental agency to be deemed a commercial agency agreement. For example, the U.A.E. Commercial Agencies Law requires that all agreements creating commercial agencies be registered with the U.A.E. Federal Ministry of Economy & Commerce and states that registration is a prerequisite to the agent taking advantage of the compensation provisions of the Commercial Agencies Law.[129] There are no penalties upon a foreign principal for nonregistration and the penalties for nonregistration by a local agent have not been uniformly enforced. Kuwait[130] and the Dominican Republic[131] have similar registration requirements. As a result, franchisors routinely refuse to permit or cooperate with registering of the franchise agreement with local government authorities to avoid application of the agency laws or block the ability of the franchisee to complete an agency law registration so that that the franchisor can avoid payment of compensation that would ordinarily be required under the agency law. Several of these approaches taken by franchisors are discussed below.

3. Formula for Measuring the Agent/Representative's Compensation

The formula for calculating compensation under the various agency laws varies by jurisdiction and is generally subject to the discretion of the court hearing the claim. Factors that are generally relevant in determining compensation include actual investment and reasonable expectation of future profits. However, courts normally look at all of the circumstances surrounding the agency agreement in making a compensation determination. Typical compensation is an amount equal to one years' total profits of the franchisee (averaged over a four- to five-year period), an amount for goodwill, and an amount for the repurchase of all unused inventory. However, it can be more. For instance, in the U.A.E., general compensation could be two to three times net annual profits or more if there is a long-term relationship and the agent can show extensive investment in the business.[132]

Most agency laws are considered to be mandatory laws that cannot be waived on the basis of public policy (Costa Rica[133] and the Dominican Republic[134] have particularly burdensome laws that cannot be waived). However, some agency laws, such as those of Guatemala[135] and Switzerland, are waivable.

Practice Tip

There are ways to protect against potential agency compensation claims. Examples of protective actions that have met with varying degrees of success include the following:

1. Requiring the franchisee to put up a letter of credit or provide a bank guaranty in an amount substantially similar to the amount likely to be obtained under the agency law
2. Imposing liquidated damages
3. Disclaiming the application of the agency law
4. Requiring agreement to contain covenants not to sue provisions
5. Including cross-default provisions (if the prospective franchisee is developing multiple units in multiple jurisdictions)
6. Structuring modifications, including requiring partial franchisor ownership of the franchisee entity or other foreign ownership
7. Including foreign choice of law provisions

In addition, where possible, ensuring that the prospective franchisee has assets outside the given jurisdiction will aid in both deterrence and enforcement of breaches of any covenants regarding the agency law.

C. SAMPLE CLAUSES

INDEPENDENT CONTRACTOR (For use in Spain)

A. Franchisee is an independent contractor. Nothing herein shall create the relationship of principal and agent, legal representative, joint venturers, partners, employee and employer or master and servant between the parties. No fiduciary duty is owed by, or exists between, the parties.

B. Franchisee, the Controlling Principals and the Principals acknowledge and agree that Spanish Agency Agreements Law (Law 12/1992 of May 27) shall not at any time during or subsequent to the Term of this Agreement, apply to this Agreement or to the relationship established herein and that Franchisor would not have entered into this Agreement were Spanish Agency Agreements Law (Law 12/1992 of May 27) or any successor thereto be applicable to this relationship. Without limiting the foregoing, in consideration of the rights granted herein: (1) Franchisee, the Controlling Principals and the Principals hereby agree to release and waive any rights of Franchisee, the Controlling Principals and the Principals and any obligations of Franchisor, if any, under Spanish Agency Agreements Law (Law 12/1992 of May 27) enacted in Spain, including the payment of any compensation to Franchisee, the Controlling Principals or the Principals upon the expiration or termination of this Agreement and shall defend and indemnify the Indemnitees with respect thereto; (2) Franchisee represents, warrants, and covenants that neither it, any Controlling Principal or any Principal, or any Affiliate or any principals thereof shall bring or attempt to bring an Action under Spanish Agency Agreements Law (Law 12/1992 of May 27) in any court, arbitration proceeding or before any other tribunal; and (3) Franchisee, the Controlling Principals and the Principals acknowledge and agree that any attempt to bring an action under Spanish Agency Agreements Law (Law 12/1992 of May 27) shall be an event of default under this Agreement, the Development Agreement and any other Franchise Agreement between Franchisor and Franchisee and their respective Affiliates. Franchisee, the Controlling Principals and the Principals agree to take any actions required by Franchisor to give effect to this Section 23.01.B.

C. Nothing herein authorizes Franchisee or any Principal to make any contract, agreement, warranty or representation or to incur any debt or obligation in Franchisor's name.

X. Indemnification

A. WHAT IS THE ISSUE AND HOW WILL IT AFFECT YOUR CLIENT?

Indemnification provisions are used in franchise agreements (both domestically and abroad) to allocate the burden of any losses and expenses that are incurred as a result of or that are ancillary to the franchise relationship. In most instances, the franchisor requires the franchisee to indemnify and hold harmless the franchisor for losses or expenses related to the operation of the unit. Such losses and expenses can result from lawsuits, dispute resolution proceedings, settlements, investigations, or legal fees and can cover breaches of the franchise agreement (including breaches of any covenants, warranties, or representations made in the franchise agreement related to issues pertinent to the franchisee organization, trademark protection, compliance with applicable laws, confidentiality, and noncompetition restrictions) or acts, errors, or omissions in the construction and operation of the franchised units (including customer, vendor, or other third-party claims regarding products or services offered at the franchised unit, or use of motor vehicles).

Some franchisors provide indemnification to franchisees for third-party actions related to the authorized use of the franchisor's trademarks.

In addition to determining the types of acts, errors, or omissions that will be covered by the indemnification, the parties need to agree on who will undertake (and who will pay for) the representation in any action in which the parties are involved, who will have final say over any settlements or dispute resolution tactics (the franchisor in most cases), whether the parties will be required to mitigate damages, and whether the indemnification obligations will survive the expiration or earlier termination of the franchise agreement.

B. WHAT IS THE LAW?

1. *Enforceability*

The extent to which a party may be indemnified for its own negligence, gross negligence, or intentional acts will depend on the law of the jurisdiction. In the United States, many states require that the agreement clearly state an intention to provide indemnification for the indemnitee's own negligence while other states allow such indemnification absent express language where to do otherwise would defeat the clear intent of the parties. Similar principles apply in jurisdictions outside of the United States, and indemnification provisions are generally upheld by courts in countries outside the United States to the extent that they are reasonable and do not attempt to indemnify parties for their own gross negligence or intentional acts. However, some countries limit the franchisor's right to choose its own legal counsel, disfavor damage awards that do not reflect the actual damages sustained by an aggrieved party, limit franchisor's right to choose its own legal counsel and also require franchisor to mitigate damages. For example, Italy applies general legal principles, such as the duty to mitigate damages, to limit a franchisor's right to recover excessive damages. This duty to mitigate damages limits costs for which a franchisor can hold a franchisee responsible through indemnification provisions.[136] In the PRC, a broad indemnification provision may be subject to a challenge by a PRC court and damages cannot exceed the loss that the breaching party foresaw or ought to have foreseen at the time of entering into the contract.[137]

Some countries have general contract laws that may impact the enforceability of indemnification provisions. For example, in Northern Ireland, the Unfair Contract Terms Act 1977 is a good faith and fairness act that can be used by a franchisee to avoid certain one-sided contract terms that attempt to exclude or restrict liability.[138] Some other countries apply similar principles of reasonableness, good faith, and fair dealing that are considered by the courts. The Republic of Ireland generally enforces indemnity provisions to the extent that they are reasonable. Thailand also generally enforces indemnification provisions, but a provision may be void and unenforceable if the provision is contrary to the public order or good morals of the people of Thailand.[139] In contrast, Indonesia does not use these standards, but limits enforceability to the extent that the underlying agreement is enforceable and valid.[140]

2. *Modification of Provision by Courts*

Although most courts uphold indemnification provisions to the extent that they meet reasonableness standards or other applicable good faith and fairness standards, some courts will modify the provisions to aid the franchisee in some situations. Italy generally enforces traditional indemnification provisions, but it may not enforce a franchisor's right (absent a conflict of interest) to choose its own counsel and charge the franchisee for the costs of the franchisor's legal counsel in a case in which the franchisee is also involved. By applying the general Italian legal principle of the duty to mitigate, the court may also reject a franchisor's waiver of its duty to mitigate damages if such failure exposes the franchisee to excessive additional costs.[141] Korea gives similar treatment to indemnification provisions. If a franchisor exercises its right to control the defense through counsel of its own choice at franchisee's expense, reimbursement will be limited to a reasonable amount.

Korean courts can also interpret the Korean Civil Code to require a franchisor to mitigate damages or losses, or else the franchisor's actions could be construed as an abuse of the franchisor's rights arising under the franchise agreement.[142]

3. *Permissibility of Coverage of Certain Types of Damages*

Most countries allow the parties to agree contractually to the types of damages covered by the indemnification provision, but several countries limit the types of damages that may be covered. The most common of those not covered are claims for damages for a franchisor's gross negligence, for willful misconduct,[143] or for punitive damages. For example, since German courts do not recognize punitive damages and will not enforce punitive damage awards, they only provide compensation for actual damages suffered and for pain and suffering.[144] Rather than limiting the types of damages that are recoverable, Malaysian law limits the franchisee's obligation to indemnify only to the franchisor itself, and not to its affiliates.[145]

4. Execution Formalities

Most countries do not require a specific format or wording for an indemnity provision, but it is always advisable to verify this with local counsel. Signing formalities are generally the same as those required for the franchise agreement as a whole. Notarization may be recommended but it is rarely required specifically for the indemnification provision. Indonesia has stricter execution formalities for indemnification provisions than most countries have. It requires spousal approval for an indemnity provided by a married person and an indemnity provided by a corporation or other business entity must be approved by the shareholders or partners of the franchisee.[146]

Practice Tip

The enforceability of indemnity provisions should be prominent in any discussion with local counsel. Issues will range from the types of damages recoverable, the effect of the duty to mitigate, the parties involved, and the execution of the indemnity. Nothing is too small to ask about the indemnity, particularly if liability under the indemnity is imposed on the individual principals of the franchisee, as this can be a contentious negotiation issue, but a very important one if the franchisee entity has few assets.

C. SAMPLE CLAUSES

1. Indemnification. Franchisee and each of Franchisee's Principals will, at all times, indemnify and hold harmless to the fullest extent permitted by law the Indemnitees from all Losses and Expenses[147] incurred in connection with any action, suit, proceeding, claim, demand, investigation or inquiry (formal or informal), or any settlement thereof (whether or not a formal proceeding or action has been instituted) which arises out of or is based upon any of the following:

a. The infringement, alleged infringement, or any other violation or alleged violation by Franchisee or any of Franchisee's Principals of any patent, mark or copyright or other proprietary right owned or controlled by third parties (except as such may occur with respect to any right to use the Proprietary Marks, any copyrights or other Confidential Information granted hereunder pursuant to this [franchise agreement];

b. The violation, breach or asserted violation or breach by Franchisee or any of Franchisee's Principals of any law, regulation, ruling, standard or directive or any industry standard, including any immigration, fire safety or other applicable laws;

c. Libel, slander or any other form of defamation of Franchisor, the System or any franchisee operating under the System, by Franchisee or by any of Franchisee's Principals;

d. The violation or breach by Franchisee or by any of Franchisee's Principals of any warranty, representation, agreement or obligation in this Agreement or in any other agreement between Franchisee or any of its Affiliates and Franchisor or any of its Affiliates, or their respective partners, or the officers, directors, shareholders, partners, agents, representatives, independent contractors, servants and employees of any of them; and

e. Acts, errors, or omissions of Franchisee, any of Franchisee's Affiliates and any of Franchisee's Principals and the officers, directors, shareholders, partners, agents, representatives, independent contractors and employees of Franchisee and its Affiliates or any other third parties with whom any of the foregoing may contract, regardless of purposes, in connection with the establishment and operation of the Unit, including, but not limited to, any acts, errors or omissions of any of the foregoing in the operation of any motor vehicle. With respect to all such acts, errors or omissions, such indemnification shall be without limitation and without regard to the cause or causes thereof or the strict liability or negligence of Franchisor or any other party or parties arising in connection therewith, and whether such negligence be sole, joint or concurrent, or active or passive. The parties understand and agree that Franchisor cannot and does not exercise control over the manner of operation of any motor vehicles used by, or on behalf of, Franchisee or any employee, agent or independent contractor of Franchisee and that the safe operation of any motor vehicle is, therefore, Franchisee's responsibility.

2. Franchisee and each of Franchisee's Principals agree to give Franchisor notice of any such action, suit, proceeding, claim, demand, inquiry, or investigation. At the expense and risk of Franchisee and each of the Franchisee's Principals, Franchisor may elect to assume (but under no circumstance is obligated to undertake) or associate counsel of its own choosing with respect to, the defense and/or settlement of any such action, suit, proceeding, claim, demand, inquiry or investigation. Such an undertaking by Franchisor will, in no manner or form, diminish the obligation of Franchisee and each of Franchisee's Principals to indemnify the Indemnitees and to hold them harmless.

3. To protect persons or property, or its reputation or goodwill, or the reputation or goodwill of others, Franchisor may, at any time and without notice, as it, in its judgment deems appropriate, consent or agree to settlements or take such other remedial or corrective action as it deems expedient with respect to the action, suit, proceeding, claim, demand, inquiry or investigation if, in Franchisor's sole judgment, there are reasonable grounds to believe that (a) any of the acts or circumstances enumerated in Sections 1. through 4. have occurred or; (b) any act, error, or omis-

sion as described in Section 5. may result directly or indirectly in damage, injury, or harm to any Person or any property.

4. All Losses and Expenses incurred under this Section will be chargeable to and paid by Franchisee or any of Franchisee's Principals pursuant to its obligations of indemnity under this Section, regardless of any actions, activity or defense undertaken by Franchisor or the subsequent success or failure of such actions, activity, or defense.

5. Under no circumstances will the Indemnitees be required or obligated to seek recovery from third parties or otherwise mitigate their losses to maintain a claim against Franchisee or any of Franchisee's Principals. Franchisee and each of Franchisee's Principals agree that the failure to pursue such recovery or mitigate loss will in no way reduce the amounts recoverable from Franchisee or any of Franchisee's Principals by the Indemnitees.

Franchisee agrees to refrain forever from bringing or asserting against Franchisor, its Affiliates, and their respective officers, directors, shareholders, agents, and employees, any suits, cause of action, proceeding, remedy, relief or other claims arising out of or based upon a business opportunity sales law or any other U.S. federal, state, or local franchise law, business opportunity law, or similar law, in connection with the offer or sale of this franchise.

6. Franchisee and Franchisee's Principals expressly agree that the terms of this Section will survive the termination, expiration or transfer of this Agreement or any interest in this Agreement.

XI. Guaranty

A. WHAT IS THE ISSUE AND HOW WILL IT AFFECT YOUR CLIENT?

Financial and performance guarantees are designed to ensure that the franchisee's obligations under the franchise agreement are fulfilled if the franchisee is unable to or refuses to perform. Guarantees can be important leverage in international transactions because arbitration or litigation of disputes is time-consuming and very expensive. Therefore, as in the United States, many times the existence of (and the threat of enforcement on) a personal or corporate guaranty will be the most viable method to encourage cooperation in a lawsuit where the franchisor is named and to deter violations of a franchise agreement, including nonpayment of fees or failure to de-identify upon termination or expiration of the franchise agreement. Personal guarantees are typically requested in international transactions. Many international franchisees are owned in some part by individuals with significant assets available for execution of a judgment. Corporate guarantees are also viable, but franchisors must bear the added burdens of ensuring that all applicable corporate consents and other formalities are followed and that the corporate entity maintains adequate capitalization to stand behind the guaranty. (The latter is obviously also true of personal guarantees.) Of course, the utility of any guaranty is dependent upon where and how difficult it will be to execute on the assets supporting the guaranty.

In some cases, it may be advisable to require a letter of credit or a bank guaranty that can be drawn down upon without having to conclusively prove damages or otherwise seek enforcement in the franchisee's home jurisdiction. This approach makes collection easier, but the cost to the franchisee can be high and can tie up capital that could be used for unit expansion.

In addition to structuring issues, there may be drafting and format requirements and execution formalities for guarantees. These requirements or recommendations may aid the franchisor in avoiding a determination that the guarantee is a contract of adhesion, that the guarantee is unconscionable, or that the guarantee is not authentic.[148]

B. WHAT IS THE LAW?

1. General Enforceability

Most jurisdictions permit guarantees in franchise agreements, but there are often local drafting or execution variations. For instance, Panama's Antitrust Act[149] provides that abusive clauses in adhesion contracts are void, including clauses under which an entity or individual renounces rights or waives personal notifications. To avoid this result, it is advisable to include an express acknowledgment in the guaranty that the guaranty has been negotiated and retain evidence of the changes made during the negotiation process. Because a requirement that the guarantor waive all demands and notices regarding the franchise agreement could amount to a one-sided contract of adhesion,[150] one point that is often negotiated (and documented) is a revision to require that a guarantor must be notified before the renewal, extension, modification, or amendment of any obligations to a franchisor under the franchise agreement. Many franchisors try to limit such notices to renewal or extensions of the guaranty and to the extent notice regarding modifications or amendments are negotiated, the parties may try to limit such notice to financial obligations.

Although many form guarantees specifically state that the franchisor need not pursue all remedies against the franchisee before attempting to enforce the guaranty, the Indonesian Civil Code, for example, provides a guarantor with additional protection by requiring that a debtor (that is, a franchisee) first settle any of its debts from its own assets before an Indonesian court will enforce a guaranty. Although this provision of the code may be waived, an Indonesian court may look past the waiver and determine that the guarantor is not a principal debtor or primary obligor.

Personal guarantees in the PRC are both rare and discouraged by the government. Personal guarantees must be approved by the government and, even if approval is given, enforcement will be very difficult.[151] Corporate guarantees by PRC entities are possible, but these too must be approved and are rare in practice.

In lieu of personal guarantees, franchisees may want to consider obtaining standby letters of credit or bank guarantees where guarantees will be difficult to enforce or there is the possibility that neither the franchisee nor the guarantor will have significant assets if the franchised business fails. A standby letter of credit permits the franchisor, upon the submission of an affidavit or other documentation required by the issuing bank, to draw directly from the line of credit without having to pursue remedies against the underlying primary obligor. Further, in international transactions, the franchisor can generally turn to a local, confirming bank to draw on amounts due. The confirming bank then looks to the issuing bank for payment, bearing the risk of loss if the issuing bank refuses to honor the underlying letter of credit.

Alternatively, franchisors faced with a franchisee who refuses to sign a personal guarantee or provide a letter of credit may request a bank guaranty. Bank guarantees are generally less valuable than letters of credit because they require the franchisor to exhaust its remedies against the primary obligor before the issuing bank will honor the bank guarantee. Banks usually require significant deposits and fees, however, in connection with letters of credit and bank guarantees.

As with personal guarantees, issuing banks will generally impose their own forms of letter of credit or bank guarantee. However, franchisors should provide their own forms of guarantee in an attempt to persuade the issuing bank to agree to the documentation necessary upon presentment.

2. *Form of Execution*

Often, a local counsel will urge a U.S. franchisor to use a particular form of guaranty as opposed to the franchisor's general form contained in its form of franchise agreement.

a. Particular Form and Wording. Spanish law requires specific wording to uphold a guaranty as enforceable.[152] Thailand provides guarantors certain statutory rights and protections and a franchisor will be required to obtain the guarantor's express waiver of such statutory rights or protections to avoid having to comply with them. These rights and protections relate to a guarantor's waiver of presentment, of demand for payment, and of any right to require that proceedings be brought first against the franchisee or another third party as well as guarantor's right to utilize certain defenses that the franchisee may have against franchisor. Provisions prohibiting guarantors from being discharged from their obligations under the guaranty may also be included.

To be enforceable in Guatemala, the guarantee will have to be translated into Spanish before submission to a local court, although the guarantee need not be executed in Spanish from the beginning.[153]

In Argentina, the guarantee should state that the guarantor agrees to pay any applicable debts as first and principal payor and should expressly waive certain provisions of the Argentine Civil Code[154] and of the Commercial Code[155] to ensure ability to proceed against the guarantor without first exhausting all remedies against the franchisee entity or individual itself.

Some countries offer alternate ways to meet the form or wording requirements by giving notice or warning to the guarantor. In Germany, if the financial guarantee is prepared in German in the format provided for by German Civil Code, it does not need any particular warning to the guarantor. If a guarantee is given in the form of a cumulative assumption of debts of the franchisee, such as the franchisee undertaking to buy goods regularly from the franchisor, and if the franchise agreement as such requires a written warning, then the guarantor also needs to receive a written warning in a particular form. General guarantees or undertakings that include nonfinancial obligations do not need to contain warnings or be in German.[156]

b. Notarization. Notarization requirements vary by country. Generally, the same execution or notarization formalities required for the franchise agreement itself are adequate, although it may be advisable for the signatures on a guarantee to be witnessed by at one least one or two unrelated third parties. For instance, in Guatemala guarantors' signatures should be legalized by a notary public and then by the Guatemalan Consulate to ensure its enforceability.[157] In Spain, a guaranty of the franchisee's obligations is enforceable in Spain as long as it is executed before a stock exchange broker.[158]

Requirements may vary also if the guarantor is a corporation rather than an individual. For example, in the Republic of Ireland guarantees are generally enforceable, but any guarantee executed by an Irish corporation should be executed under seal. Similarly, in many

Asian countries guarantees should be accompanied by a company chop (that is, a registered symbol for the company that acts as a seal or other confirmation of authority for execution).

c. Execution by Spouse. Spousal execution is also required in some countries and recommended by local counsel in others because of laws substantially similar to U.S. marital laws and to deter any transferring or hiding of assets with the spouse. In Spain and Peru it is recommended that a guarantor's spouse should also execute. If a Swiss guarantee qualifies as a bond under the Swiss Code of Obligations, it must be notarized and executed by a spouse.

Taiwan has other regulations requiring that a corporation acting as guarantor must state that the articles of incorporation provide that the corporation has the right to offer guarantees. The articles of incorporation should also be closely scrutinized to ensure that there are no limits on the corporation's ability to provide guarantees and to determine whether the provision of a guaranty requires board or shareholder approval. Taiwanese law also requires a corporate guarantor that is a public company listed on a stock exchange to file its guarantee restrictions with the Taiwanese Securities and Futures Commission. Many of the foregoing are commonsense requirements and should apply to any review of a corporation's ability to provide a guaranty.

Practice Tip

It may be necessary to prepare a guaranty so that it complies with the laws of several different jurisdictions to ensure flexibility with respect to enforcement against assets in multiple jurisdictions. It will be important as a matter of due diligence to know the guarantor's financial position and where the guarantor's assets are located. The guaranty can be a legally "sensitive" document that can require greater compliance with internal laws than the other agreements that make up the transaction.

d. Effect of Changes in the Agreement. As discussed above, it may be necessary to notify a guarantor of any material changes or amendments to the franchise agreement because this could render the guaranty unenforceable or could discharge the guarantor from issues raised subsequent to the amendment in many countries. These notice requirements protect the guarantor from liability from changes to the franchise agreement that were not agreed upon or are unknown to the guarantor, but in the real world are very difficult for a busy franchisor to provide.[159]

In Panama, a guarantor must be notified before the renewal, extension, modification, or amendment of any substantial obligations, and failure to do so can render the guaranty unenforceable under the antitrust law. Malaysian law holds that changes made without the debtor's consent or knowledge could discharge the guarantor from issues raised after an amendment to the franchise agreement.[160]

C. SAMPLE CLAUSES

1. *Principals' Undertaking and Guaranty.* The Controlling Principal and certain other of Franchisee's Principals designated by Franchisor will jointly and severally (a) bind themselves to the terms of this Agreement pursuant to the attached Principals' Undertakings, and (b) guarantee Franchisee's performance of this Agreement pursuant to the attached Guaranty. Upon request by Franchisor, and in the event of a material amendment to this Agreement or any material change to the relationship created by this Agreement, the Controlling Principal and such other of Franchisee's Principals who have executed the Guaranty and/or the Principals' Undertaking shall execute a new Guaranty or Principals' Undertaking, as applicable, in substantially the same form attached to this Agreement. In addition, or in lieu thereof, Franchisor may require Franchisee and Franchisee's Principals to provide an additional or alternative form of guarantee of Franchisee's performance of its obligations under this Agreement, including, without limitation, the following:

Franchisor may require Franchisee or Franchisee's Principals to obtain and maintain during the term of this Agreement a Standby Letter of Credit from a bank acceptable to Franchisor for the benefit of Franchisor and for such face amount and subject to such other conditions as Franchisor, in its sole discretion, may determine. In the event that the bank issuing the Standby Letter of Credit is not a U.S. bank, payment of the Standby Letter of Credit must be confirmed by a U.S. bank to permit Franchisor to present the requisite documentation to the confirming bank and receive immediate payment thereon. Franchisee and/or Franchisee's Principals may be required to maintain the Standby Letter of Credit on an ongoing basis during the term of this Agreement and in such case must require the bank issuing the Standby Letter of Credit to provide Franchisor 45 days prior written notice in the event any such bank elects not to renew the Standby Letter of Credit at any time.

Franchisor may require Franchisee or Franchisee's Principals to obtain a demand guaranty from a bank approved by Franchisor and subject to such terms and conditions as Franchisor, in its discretion, may determine.

Sample Guaranty For the Republic of Ireland
(for execution by an individual)[161]

GUARANTY (Republic of Ireland)

This Guaranty is entered into this _________ day of _________, 2000

BETWEEN:

(1) ______________, of ______, Republic of Ireland (the "Guarantor"); and

(2) ______________, a ___________ corporation having its principal office at _________________________ (the "Franchisor")

WHEREAS:

(A) The Guarantor is related to and in business with __________ (the "Franchisee"); and

(B) Simultaneously with the execution of this Guaranty, the Franchisor has granted to the Franchisee a franchise (the "Franchise") to operate an ____________________ (the "Unit") under a Franchise Agreement of even date herewith (the "Franchise Agreement"); and

(C) It is a term of the Franchise Agreement that the Guarantor enters into this Guaranty.

WHEREBY IT IS AGREED as follows:

1. The Guaranty - Interpretation

In this Guaranty, which is a continuing security securing the ultimate balance due to the Franchisor by the Guarantor from time to time:

1.1 words and expressions defined in the Franchise Agreement shall have the same meanings when used in this Guaranty unless they are otherwise defined now or unless the context otherwise requires; and

1.2 masculine includes the feminine and the singular the plural and vice versa and obligations undertaken by more than a single person, including a company or firm, are joint and separate obligations.

2. Covenants of Guarantor

In consideration of the Franchisor granting the Franchisee a Franchise, the Guarantor hereby covenants and undertakes with the Franchisor:

2.1 that, except as expressly stated to the contrary in Section 5 of this Guaranty, the Franchisee will duly observe and perform all the obligations contained in the Franchise Agreement including without limitation the obligation to pay the fees to the Franchisor set out in Section 3 of the Franchise Agreement;

2.2 that, except as expressly stated to the contrary in Section 5 of this Guaranty, if the Franchisee shall fail to observe or perform any of the said obligations or fail to pay for any products, materials, advertising or promotional materials or services supplied to the Franchisee by the Franchisor, or any other sums which may be payable by the Franchisee under the Franchise Agreement, the Guarantor will be liable for such default and shall make payment of any sums so due upon demand being made by the Franchisor;

2.3 that, except as expressly stated to the contrary in Section 5 of this Guaranty, he or she will (as a distinct and separate obligation) render harmless the Franchisor in respect of all losses, damages, claims, costs and expenses which the Franchisor may incur or suffer by reason of its entry into, continuance of, or termination (in any way) of the Franchise Agreement;

2.4 that he or she will not seek to enforce repayment from the Franchisee, or exercise any other rights or remedies of any kind which may accrue to him in respect of any monies paid pursuant to the terms of this Guaranty and/or in respect of any other monies from time to time due to him from the Franchisee on or after the date of any demand made pursuant to the terms of this Guaranty until such demand has been fully satisfied and all other debts of the Franchisee to the Franchisor have been fully satisfied.

3. Parties

If there are two (2) or more persons who are parties to this Guaranty as Guarantor, all covenants and Agreements on the part of the Guarantor shall be deemed to be in joint and several covenants on their part.

4. Other Rights

4.1 This Guaranty is in addition to and not in substitution for any other rights which the Franchisor may have or security which it may hold for the payment of monies due to it under or by virtue of the Franchise Agreement and may be enforced without first having recourse to any such rights or securities and without first taking any steps or proceedings against the Franchisee.

4.2 This Guaranty is a continuing Guaranty and will extend to the ultimate balance of all sums guaranteed hereunder regardless of any intermediate payment or discharge in whole or in part.

4.3 This Guaranty is and shall remain a continuing security for the Franchisee's obligations to the Franchisor detailed in Clause 2 above at any time and shall not be satisfied or otherwise affected by any repayment or recovery from time to time of the whole or any part of any amount which may then be due and owing from the Franchisee to the Franchisor.

4.4 This Guaranty shall remain in force notwithstanding the death of the Guarantor, and shall be binding on his personal representatives.

4.5 This Guaranty shall continue and shall be enforceable notwithstanding any change in the name or the constitution of the Franchisor or Franchisee.

4.6 The Guarantor shall not in competition with or in priority to the Franchisor seek to enforce repayment or to exercise any other rights or legal remedies of whatsoever kind which may accrue to him or her in respect of any amount which may have been paid by the Guarantor to the Franchisor hereunder, and in particular (without prejudice to the generality of the foregoing) shall not make any claim against the Franchisee nor make any claim in the bankruptcy or liquidation of the Franchisee nor enforce any security from or against the Franchisee.

4.7 The Guarantor agrees to pay interest to the Franchisor on all sums demanded under this Guaranty from the date of demand until the date of payment (after judgment as well as before it) at four percent per annum above the published base rate of Bank of Ireland from time to time. Such interest shall accrue on a day-to-day basis and be calculated on the basis of a three hundred and sixty-five (365) day year and shall be compounded (in accordance with the Franchisor's usual practice) (but this Clause shall not prejudice the right of the Franchisor to require payment of such interest when due).

4.8 The Guarantor's obligations under this Guaranty are those of a primary obligor and exist irrespective of any total or partial invalidity of any purported obligation or liability of the Franchisee to the Franchisor.

4.9 As a separate and independent stipulation the Guarantor agrees that if any sum arising or purportedly arising under the guarantees contained in this Guaranty is not or would not be recoverable on the footing of a guarantee for any reason whatsoever, whether or not known to the Franchisor, such sum shall nevertheless be recoverable from the Guarantor as a sole principal debtor and shall be paid by the Guarantor to the Franchisor on demand.

4.10 The Guarantor acknowledges and agrees that, except as expressly stated to the contrary in Section 5 of this Guaranty, none of its liabilities under this Guaranty shall be reduced, discharged or otherwise adversely affected by:

(a) any variation, extension, release, discharge, compromise, dealing with, exchange or renewal of any security and of any other right or remedy which the Franchisor may now or at any time have from or against the

Franchisee or any other person in respect of any of the obligations and liabilities of the Franchisee or any other person;

(b) any act or omission by the Franchisor or any other person in taking up, preserving, perfecting or enforcing any security from or against the Franchisee or any other person;

(c) any termination, amendment, variation, novation or supplement of or to any agreement (oral or in writing), accommodation or transaction with or in connection with the Franchisee or any other person;

(d) the insolvency, bankruptcy, liquidation, administration, winding-up, voluntary agreement with creditors, incapacity, limitation, disability, discharge by operation of law, change in the constitution, name and style of the Franchisee or any other person;

(e) any security or other right or remedy held by or available to the Franchisor being or becoming void, voidable or unenforceable on any ground whatsoever and whether in whole or in part;

(f) any claim or enforcement of payment from the Franchisee or any other person;

(g) any grant of time, indulgence, waiver, or concession to the Franchisee or any other person; or

(h) any act or omission which would not have discharged or affected the liability of a sole principal debtor instead of a guarantor or by anything done or omitted to be done by the Franchisor or any other person or by any other act matter or thing which but for this provision might operate to exonerate or discharge the Guarantor or otherwise reduce or extinguish its liability under this Guaranty.

4.11 The Franchisor may enforce this Guaranty whether or not it has first:

(a) taken action or obtained judgment in any court against the Franchisee or any other person;

(b) made or filed any claim in a bankruptcy, liquidation, administration or insolvency of the Franchisee or any other person; or

(c) made demand upon, or enforced any claim, right or remedy against the Franchisee or any other person.

4.12 This Guaranty is freely assignable or transferable by the Franchisor in whole or in part and the Guarantor agrees to take such action as is necessary to effect the novation of any rights it has under it. The Franchisor may disclose any information about the Guarantor to any person to whom the Franchisor reasonably considers it to be relevant.

5. Limitation of Risk

5.1 Notwithstanding any term or provision of this Guaranty to the contrary, Guarantor shall not have liability for any failure by Franchisee to observe or perform any obligation under the Franchise Agreement that is caused by or directly attributable to a condition or event of Force Majeure, as defined in Section _______ of the Franchise Agreement.

5.2 Franchisor acknowledges that it claims no lien or security interest in Guarantor's family home as security for the performance of Guarantor's obligations under this Guaranty.

6. Severability

If any item or provision contained in this Guaranty or any part thereof (in this Clause called the "offending provision") shall be declared or become unenforceable invalid or illegal for any reason whatsoever including, but not detracting from the generality of the foregoing, a decision by the competent domestic or European courts, an act of Parliament, European Union legislation or any statutory or other bye-laws or regulations or any other requirements having the force of law, the other terms and provisions of this Guaranty shall remain in full force and effect as if this Guaranty had been executed without the offending provision appearing in this Guaranty.

7. Notices
Any notice (the "Notice") required to be given for the purposes of this Guaranty shall be given in writing by sending the same by courier delivery, facsimile or personal delivery to the following addresses or such other address as shall have been notified (in accordance with this Clause) by the party concerned as being its address for the purposes of this Clause:

Notices to Franchisor:

****

Notices to Guarantor:

****

Any Notice sent by courier shall be deemed to have been served three (3) working days after the date of dispatch. Any Notice sent by personal delivery shall be deemed to have been given upon delivery. Any Notice sent by facsimile shall be deemed to have been served on actual receipt by the recipient as proved by a facsimile confirmation sheet.

8. Approvals
Any approval or consent given under this Guaranty will only be valid if given in writing by one of the Franchisors' officers.

9. Waiver
Neither the failure of the Franchisor to exercise any power given to it hereunder or to insist upon strict compliance by the Franchisee with any obligation hereunder nor any custom or practice of the parties shall constitute any waiver of any of the Franchisor's rights under this Guaranty. Waiver by the Franchisor of any particular default by the Franchisee must be in writing and shall not affect or impair the Franchisor's rights in respect of any subsequent default of any kind by the Franchisee nor shall any delay by or omission of the Franchisor to exercise any rights arising from any default of the Franchisee effect or impair the Franchisor's rights in respect of the said default or any default of any kind.

10. Rights of Third Parties
It is the intention that no term of this Guaranty may be enforced by any person who is not a party to this Guaranty (a "third party"), notwithstanding that any such term of this Guaranty may purport to confer, or may be construed as conferring, any benefit on such third party and irrespective of whether such third party is identified in this Guaranty.

IN WITNESS whereof the Guaranty has been duly executed as a deed on the date first written above by the parties hereto.

Signed, Sealed and Delivered by

____

__________ "Guarantor" in the presence of:

____

Executed as a Deed

By ____

by ____

title ____

XII. Liquidated Damages

A. WHAT IS THE ISSUE AND HOW WILL IT AFFECT YOUR CLIENT?

Liquidated damages provisions (called penal clauses in many jurisdictions) are routinely used in international franchise transactions because of the difficulty of proving damages in a foreign court or obtaining other relief. These provisions also serve as a deterrent to possible breach of contract. In the franchise context, liquidated damages provisions are typically used to set a reasonably enforceable amount to be paid upon breach of covenants covering competition restrictions, confidentiality requirements, transfer restrictions, trademark or other intellectual property protections, and in connection with the enforcement of post-termination or expiration obligations.

The availability of liquidated damages as a remedy may provide franchisors with additional leverage to ensure the opportunity for continued protection and safeguarding of the fundamental aspects of its system. The existence of such provisions in franchise agreements sends a message to a prospective franchisee that certain covenants will create the right to terminate the relationship and to collect money damages. However, liquidated damages provisions do not give franchisors carte blanche to impose monetary damages arbitrarily. In fact, most foreign jurisdictions that allow liquidated damages will scrutinize either the amount requested (if the amount is set) or the formula used in calculating such damages.

Inquiry should be made about whether such damages are commensurate with the actual damages suffered by the aggrieved party. If the amount of damages provided in a liquidated damages provision acts more as a penalty rather than as compensation, then the court or other tribunal will generally reduce the award to a reasonable amount, if such reduction is permitted in the jurisdiction. In determining whether to use liquidated damages, franchise counsel should also consider whether the jurisdiction has historically permitted the recovery of significant actual damages such as the fees that would have been payable during the remaining term of the franchise agreement (reduced to present value) or whether a reasonable approximation of the damages is so difficult to determine that the provision will almost certainly fail.

B. WHAT IS THE LAW?

Most jurisdictions permit liquidated damages provisions to be included in franchise agreements. However, jurisdictions vary widely in their review and enforcement of such provisions. Generally, courts will look at the breadth of the provision and assess whether the amount provided as liquidated damages (1) is clearly provided for in the agreement, as is the case in Malaysia[162]; (2) acts as a penalty, in which case the amount will be unenforceable and reduced to a reasonable amount, such as is the case in Egypt[163] and Italy[164]; (3) is unduly onerous and is a penalty, and will be unenforceable in its entirety as is the case in Singapore; or (4) is a reasonable approximation of damages to compensate the franchisor for a breach of a material provision of the franchise agreement, in which case the amount will likely be enforceable as is the case in Bahrain.[165] In Germany, liquidated damages amounts must be a reasonable approximation of actual damages and the defending party must be given the right to show that the damages actually suffered are lower than the amount agreed upon.[166] In the U.A.E., a court may decide either to disregard the liquidated damages if determined to be unreasonable, or decrease the amount to correspond to the actual loss.[167]

Since jurisdictions favor a particular form of liquidated damages provision (that is, a set amount or an amount based on a formula tied to gross sales), or use the liquidated damages as a cap for damages if the amount itself is not upheld. For example, the Italian Civil Code[168] permits an Italian judge to scrutinize the amount or calculation method used in determining the amount of damages, and reduce it to a reasonable amount.

The Dominican Republic is an example of a jurisdiction where a court may find that the liquidated damages provision acts as a cap on damages for a breach related to the applicable provision.[169] When a contract contains a clause that fixes a determined amount of damages to be paid by the breaching party as damages, such amount cannot be increased or decreased. Consequently, a Dominican Republic judge cannot scrutinize the amount of damages provided in a liquidated damages provision, essentially allowing the franchisor to set an amount that may act as a penalty.

In contrast, liquidated damages provisions as a whole are generally disfavored in the United Kingdom, where courts prefer to base damages on the direct or actual harm suffered by the aggrieved party. A court would likely review the liquidated damages clause and deem the liquidated sum to be either a penalty or a cap on damages if the franchisor is required to prove actual damages anyway.

In countries that permit liquidated damages provisions and allow a judge to scrutinize the amount and method of calculation of such clauses, proof of their validity shifts to the party asserting their invalidity. This shift is beneficial to the franchisor since it becomes the duty of the franchisee to prove that the amount of damages provided are unfair. In addition to providing for liquidated damages, a franchisor should always retain the right to terminate the franchise relationship in the event a court determines that a liquidated damages provision is invalid.

Practice Tip

Before requiring liquidated damages, review the jurisdictions' history of awarding actual damages for breaches of a franchise agreement to which the liquidated damages provisions would ordinarily apply and the confidence that a franchisor has in its damage estimation. In jurisdictions where a court has broad discretion in evaluating liquidated damages, ensure that any liquidated damages provision is reasonable to avoid a judge striking the clause in its entirety or reducing the award.

C. SAMPLE CLAUSES

a. For breach of the obligations undertaken by franchisee and franchisee's principals in this Section _____ (transfer), in consideration of the specialized training, confidential information and value of the system provided hereunder, and due to the difficulty of establishing the precise amount of damages for breach of these covenants, in addition to the other remedies provided for in this agreement or otherwise available to franchisor, franchisee and franchisee's principals who committed such breach jointly and severally agree to pay franchisor monetary damages in the amount of $5,000 per day for each day the breach continues.

b. For breach of the covenants in Sections ___. (relating to Confidential Information) and ___ (relating to Non-Competition), which are made in consideration of the specialized training and Confidential Information described above, and due to the difficulty of establishing the precise amount of damages for breach of these covenants, in addition to the other remedies provided for in this Agreement or otherwise available to Company, Franchisee and Franchisee's Principal Owners who commit any breach thereof, jointly and severally agree to pay Company an amount for each day that any breach remains uncured by Franchisee to Company's satisfaction equal to: (1) the average Royalty Fees due and payable by Franchisee under all Franchise Agreements executed pursuant to the Development Agreement over the twelve months before the occurrence of the breach (or lesser time period, if none of the Stores operated pursuant to such Franchise Agreements has been open and in operation at least twelve months) divided by 360 (or the number of calendar days within such lesser time period); or (2) $5,000 U.S. Dollars per day, whichever amount is greater.

XIII. Foreign Ownership Restrictions and Local Ownership Requirements

A. WHAT IS THE ISSUE AND HOW WILL IT AFFECT YOUR CLIENT?

The United States encourages investment from outside sources. Similarly, many countries do not impose legal restrictions on foreign ownership of businesses, including franchises. However, there are certain countries that continue to limit and strictly control investment by foreigners. In such countries, franchisors may be limited to granting franchises to either local individuals, locally created entities, or foreign entities that have a certain percentage of local ownership. The practical result for franchisors in these countries is that it may be more difficult to sign up a multicountry development agreement with a single individual or entity or a franchisor may find itself working with or relying on third-party investors or "agents" who serve as surrogate parties for purposes of meeting local ownership requirements. In addition, local ownership requirements limit a franchisor's ability to exercise purchase options and rights of first refusal under its franchise agreements, unless such options are specifically tailored to specific local ownership requirements.

B. WHAT IS THE LAW?

Local ownership requirements can come in various forms, but the most common are: (1) the requirement that the actual franchisee be a local individual or local entity (Indonesia[170]); (2) local ownership is determined by the nature of the business being franchised (Bahamas, Korea[171]); and (3) the franchisee entity be composed of at least a certain percentage of local ownership (U.A.E.[172] or the Bahamas[173]).

In many cases, these local ownership requirements do not directly pertain to franchising, but arise from a country's desire to control the amount and source of foreign investment. Such is apparent in countries that limit certain industries to local ownership, while allowing foreign ownership in certain other businesses. For example, in the PRC generally, a wholly foreign-owned entity will not be permitted to own a hotel because the hotel industry is normally not open to wholly foreign-owned investment.[174] Similarly, in Aruba and the Bahamas, as noted above, local ownership requirements are dictated by the type and nature of the business being franchised. Presently, restaurant franchises owned and operated in the Bahamas are exclusively reserved to Bahamians,[175] for example, provided that specialty, gourmet, or ethnic restaurants, as well as restaurants operated in hotels and resorts, may be owned and operated by non-Bahamians.[176] In Aruba, a company must be granted a business license by the Minister of Economic Affairs, Commerce and Industry to legally conduct business in Aruba.[177] Similar to the Bahamas, the existing guidelines provide that business licenses are only granted to businesses in which the majority of the shares are held by Aruban shareholders unless the investment required cannot be provided by local investors or the business requires special expertise that is not available locally. In Korea, if the franchised business involves the wholesaling of meat products, then the entity receiving the rights under the franchise must be at least 51 percent locally owned. However, if the franchised business involves the hotel industry, there are no local ownership requirements.

Under a recently enacted Thai law, the rights of non-Thai individuals and entities to enter into certain businesses in which Thais are not yet prepared to compete with aliens were restricted.[178] One of these businesses is the sale of food and beverages. Aliens may engage in these businesses only with the permission of the Director-General of the Department of Commercial Registration, Ministry of Commerce, and with the approval of the Foreign Business Operation Board. This approval will allow 100 percent foreign ownership of the alien entity. The statute also appears to require a non-Thai individual or entity to obtain permission before conducting any business-related activities in Thailand, and may prevent a foreign franchisor from exercising a right of first refusal with respect to an existing Thai franchised business.[179]

In the U.A.E., local ownership in a franchise is mandatory, regardless of the nature of the business.[180] Article 22 of the Federal Company Law requires that U.A.E. nationals own at least a 51 percent interest in any company established in the U.A.E., including those operating or owning a franchised business in the U.A.E.

Practice Tip

The existence of local ownership requirements creates an additional hurdle franchisors must overcome very early in negotiations to determine whether they are able to grant franchises in countries with such requirements. Franchisors who grant a franchisee a multicountry development agreement, permitting the developer to open a certain number of units in various countries, will also need to understand to what extent the franchisee entity in each country will have to be locally owned.

Local ownership requirements also apply during and at the end of a franchise relationship when the parties propose a transfer to a third party or even a repurchase by the franchisor. The parties' plan may be hindered by the passage of a new local ownership law or policy statement that may not have been in existence when the relationship was consummated, but that would preclude a repurchase by the foreign franchisor or an existing franchisee from a neighboring country. It is important that the franchisor research this issue before terminating a franchise or responding to a request for a transfer or the franchisor may find itself effectively shut out from a country that may have been profitable.

C. SAMPLE CLAUSE

Permission to Operate (Thailand)

Before franchisor will grant its permission for franchisee to open the restaurant, franchisee shall pursuant to the Foreign Business Act, B.E. 2542 (A.D. 1999), obtain the necessary permission and approvals from the Director-General of the Department of Commercial Registration, Ministry of Commerce and the Foreign Business Operation Board to operate a restaurant and sell food and beverages in Thailand. If franchisee is unable to obtain such permission and approvals, it will designate a Thai business entity or individual to act as its surrogate for purposes of complying with the Foreign Business Act.

XIV. Religious or Other Customary Laws That Affect the Enforceability of the Franchise Agreement or the Operation of the Contemplated Business

A. WHAT IS THE ISSUE AND HOW WILL IT AFFECT YOUR CLIENT?

Religious and other customary laws that affect the enforceability of franchise agreements or the operation of a franchise business are common in the Middle East and countries with strict religious laws (such as many Islamic countries). Many of the laws regarding religious practices are recommendations as opposed to mandatory practices and are generally applicable to food service franchises. Franchisors need to be cognizant of the existence of religious customs and restrictions to ensure that a franchisee complies with any approvals or certifications necessary to operate the franchise. More importantly however, franchisors need to be sensitive to religious and customary laws to successfully promote the franchise in such country.

For example, certain agencies in countries with laws governing restaurants and other food service businesses can recommend that certain certifications or approvals be obtained once a restaurant is open to the public. Certifications generally require that a government-appointed agency or private agency approve the methods and operations of the kitchen of a restaurant to ensure that (1) the cook is apprised of any requirements for food preparation, (2) certain meat products are prepared in a manner that complies with religious custom, and (3) menu items and descriptions are specific enough to allow customers with religious requirements to understand the methods used in food preparation.

B. WHAT IS THE LAW?

Religious laws and laws that govern the operation of a franchised business vary from country to country. For example, under the laws of Kuwait, during the holy month of Ramadan it is not permissible to serve food or drinks to customers for consumption on the premises between fajr (approximately one hour before sunrise) and sunset (this provision of the law is not applicable to service restaurants located in hotels).[181] In addition to observance of religious holidays, Kuwaiti law prohibits the sale of all pork products[182] and alcoholic beverages.[183]

In Indonesia, there are no specific religious or other laws that restrict the operations of a franchise. However, for practical purposes it is advised that in the case of restaurants, clear and precise information should be provided regarding the services it provides (especially with respect to food menus). Although not mandatory, as a matter of course, certification of "halal" foods is easily obtained for restaurants not serving pork products.[184] Halal certification can serve to heighten customer awareness and can make a restaurant more appealing to those potential customers who observe such religious practices.[185]

Malaysia also does not have any particular laws that would affect the operation of a franchise there.[186] However, as with Indonesia, it is advisable that if halal food is being served at a restaurant, certification is required but is somewhat more arduous to obtain than in Indonesia.[187]

Not all religious laws or customs pertain to the certification of food. In Israel, religious (Jewish) customs and rabbinate institutions regulate certain industries, including the hotel industry. Hotels in Israel are operated under strict guidelines and supervision of institutions, but are excepted from the requirement of being closed in recognition of the Sabbath, which is recognized in Israel from sundown on Friday to sundown on Saturday. Special restrictions relate to the fifty-two Sabbath days each year and to approximately twenty days of religious holidays throughout the year. These rabbinate restrictions provide rules that affect the manner of providing service both to guests of the hotel and to the public (manner of operation of swimming pools, health clubs, stores, restaurants, and so forth).

Practice Tip

Generally, it is the duty of the franchisee to ensure compliance with local laws and customs. However, because a failure to recognize such laws and customs can reduce customer recognition and satisfaction, franchisors may consider requiring franchisees to receive and display certifications or approvals that reflect compliance.

C. SAMPLE CLAUSES

A general compliance with laws provision should suffice for purposes of compliance with any religious law. Accordingly, we have not added any formal sample clauses for this section of the chapter.

XV. Execution Formalities

A. WHAT IS THE ISSUE AND HOW WILL IT AFFECT YOUR CLIENT?

U.S. franchisors familiar with domestic notarization procedures or requirements may be surprised by some of the more complicated execution formalities that exist in some international jurisdictions, depending on whether the franchise agreements are executed in or outside of the applicable jurisdiction. Execution formalities can include witness requirements, spousal execution requirements, notarization requirements, legalization requirements, or payment of stamp duties. In many cases, notarization can involve review or translation in the applicable jurisdiction by a licensed notary who, in many cases, is a lawyer and who may have substantive comments on a franchise agreement.

B. WHAT IS THE LAW?

Execution formalities differ from country to country and many times the applicability of such formalities is contingent upon where a franchise agreement will be executed. For example, under the laws of the PRC, PRC parties must follow certain formalities in executing franchise and ancillary agreements. All documents that need to be presented for governmental approval must be translated and executed in Chinese (there may be an English version as well). Additionally, in executing franchise agreements and other documents, the legal representative of the PRC franchisee should execute such documents and apply the appropriate enterprise seal. Other Asian countries require the affixation of a chop or other form of company seal. Although some of these formalities are not mandatory, in a subsequent attack of the agreement, the franchisor can use the chop or notarization as further proof of the validity of the relationship.

Franchisors should ensure that franchise agreements with franchisees in the U.A.E.[188] or Kuwait are not notarized! A franchisor's failure to notarize a franchise agreement may effectively block the ability of the franchisee to register the franchise agreement under the Kuwaiti agency law. As previously noted in Section VII of this chapter, a franchisor should be particularly sensitive to agency laws as they generally entitle franchisees to receive certain benefits upon termination or early expiration of the franchise relationship that they would not otherwise receive. Similarly, in the U.A.E., franchise agreements that are notarized and translated into Arabic are more capable of registration under the U.A.E. Commercial Agency Law.[189] Further, if a franchisee is required to sign a guaranty that would need to be enforced in the U.A.E., the guaranty should be notarized and translated into Arabic.

Many Latin American countries require that agreements that are executed in the United States be "legalized" either through the nearest country consulate or through the Hague Convention on Apostille.[190] For example, the failure to have a franchise agreement legalized in El Salvador (or alternatively having an apostille affixed to the agreement) can render the agreement invalid in El Salvador.[191]

In addition, many countries have certain requirements that must be met if a franchise agreement is signed within such countries' borders. In Costa Rica, the franchise agreement should be witnessed by two individuals and notarized before a Costa Rican notary.[192] In Japan, a minimal stamp tax of ¥4000 will be imposed if the franchise agreement is signed in Japan,[193] and in India franchise agreements will need to be stamped before execution if executed in India or within three months of execution if executed outside of India.[194] In Argentina, payment of a stamp tax will be due unless the agreement is to be performed entirely in certain local jurisdictions (for example, if the franchised location is in the city of Buenos Aires).[195] Interestingly, in Lithuania there are two separate laws that, by way of implication, require development agreements and franchise agreements to be translated into Lithuanian. The translated copies do not need to be executed and are required solely for purposes of assisting the tax authorities in determining the taxes applicable under the agreements.[196]

In Germany, franchise agreements that contain preemptive rights relating to the acquisition of real estate property[197] or shares in a GmbH[198] must be contained in a notarial deed executed in German before a German notary to be enforceable. A German notary will scrutinize those provisions that will be notarized and will notarize them only if they comply in all regards with any German mandatory laws. In addition, there are different opinions on whether the whole franchise agreement or only the portion concerning the preemptive right must be notarized. It may be difficult to find a German notary who will notarize only a portion of the franchise agreement as opposed to the entire agreement or a significant portion of it. As noted in Section V of this chapter, failure to obtain a notarial deed in relation to rights in real property may render the entire franchise agreement void in certain circumstances where it can be proven that the party attempting to void the franchise agreement would not have executed the franchise agreement had it known the rights to real property were not valid. This could occur despite the presence of a severability clause.

Many countries impose execution requirements if a franchise agreement is executed outside its borders. If a franchise agreement is signed outside Argentina, the signatures of the persons signing the agreement should be certified by a notary public and the document must be legalized with the Apostille of the Hague.[199] Similarly, in Brazil, if a franchise agreement is signed outside its borders, the franchise agreement must be executed by the parties before a notary public and legalized at the nearest Brazilian Consulate.[200]

Practice Tip

Translations, notarizations, legalizations, and other execution formalities are straightforward but may be costly. Therefore, franchisors should become familiar with the existence of such requirement to defray some or all of the cost onto the franchisee. Provisions may be incorporated in franchise agreements to allow the costs of translations either to be split by the franchisor and the franchisee, or borne entirely by the franchisee.

XVI. Termination and Nonrenewal

A. WHAT IS THE ISSUE AND HOW WILL IT AFFECT YOUR CLIENT?

Most U.S. franchisors are familiar with state-mandated restrictions on their ability to terminate or refuse to renew existing franchise relationships. Such laws typically provide that the franchisor must have "good cause" to terminate or refuse renewal, that the franchisor provide the franchisee with prior notice of the termination or nonrenewal, and that in most instances it offer the franchisee an opportunity to cure. Many foreign jurisdictions have enacted similar legislation, typically in the form of a general agency law, noted below and in Section VII of this chapter or through laws specifically aimed at the franchise relationship. These franchise-specific laws tend to require that the franchisor have good cause and provide the franchisee with prior notice and an opportunity to cure before the franchisor may lawfully terminate or refuse to renew the franchise agreement.

B. WHAT IS THE LAW?

Among the countries that have enacted legislation (or that have trade associations that have enacted rules of conduct) affecting a franchisor's right to terminate or refuse to renew a franchise agreement are: Australia, Italy, Malaysia, Romania, and Russia. Most of these laws or rules contain one or more of the restrictions noted above, typically requiring good cause and notice of termination.

The law varies significantly from country to country. However, it may be useful to explore a few examples for illustrative purposes.

1. *Australia*

Clauses 21 through 23 of the Australia Franchising Code of Conduct,[201] a mandatory code established under the Australian Trade Practices Act, expressly governs franchisor terminations resulting from a breach by the franchisee, no breach by the franchisee, and "special circumstances." For terminations resulting from a breach of the franchise agreement by the franchisee, the franchisor must (1) provide reasonable notice, (2) inform the franchisee about what must be done to remedy the breach, and (3) allow the franchisee a reasonable time to remedy the breach, which need not be more than thirty days. The code further provides that for franchisor terminations that are not premised upon a breach of the franchise agreement by the franchisee, the franchisor must provide the franchisee with reasonable notice and the reasons for the termination. The dispute resolution provisions of the code will also apply to a franchisor termination not premised upon a franchisee breach. The franchisor is not compelled to comply with the requirements described above where "special circumstances" exist. These include the franchisee's bankruptcy or insolvency, abandonment, fraud, and conviction for a serious offense.

2. *Italy*[202]

The Italian Franchise Association's regulations[203] provide that the franchise agreement must clearly indicate the grounds for termination.[204] Any automatic termination that is based on the breach of an obligation contained in the franchise agreement must be limited to clauses of objectively great importance. When the termination is based on the breach of a franchise agreement provision that is not of great importance, the agreement must provide for a notice to be given to the defaulting party and an opportunity to cure. Finally, the franchise agreement must contain express provisions covering post-termination obligations.

3. *Malaysia*

Section 31 of the Malaysia Franchise Act of 1998[205] provides that franchisors must have good cause lawfully to terminate a franchise agreement and must provide notice and an opportunity to cure, which shall not be less than fourteen days. Good cause includes the franchisee's failure to comply with the franchise agreement. Grounds for termination that do not require the franchisor to provide notice and an opportunity to cure include the franchisee's assignment for the benefit of creditors, abandonment, fraud, conviction of a criminal offense, and repeated failure to comply with the franchise agreement.

Section 32 of the Malaysia Franchise Act[206] provides that a franchisor must compensate the franchisee if the franchisor refuses to renew the franchise agreement and either (1) the franchisee is bound by a noncompetition agreement that prohibits the franchisee from continuing to conduct substantially the same business under another mark in the same area subsequent to the termination, or (2) the franchisee was not given a written notice of the franchisor's intent not to renew at least six months before the expiration of the franchise agreement. The Malaysia Franchise Act also requires a mandatory cooling-off period after execution of the franchise agreement, during which the franchisee may terminate the franchise agreement.[207]

4. Romania

Articles 5 through 8 of the Romanian Ordinance Regarding the Legal Status of Franchise[208] governs the termination of franchise agreements. Article 5 provides that the franchise agreement must describe the conditions governing termination. Article 6 requires the franchisor to notify the franchisee of its intention not to renew the agreement and requires that the franchise agreement contain a precise description of the conditions allowing termination without notice. Article 7 states that the franchisor must provide the franchisee with a written notice and opportunity to cure each breach of the franchise agreement. Finally, Article 8 states that post-termination relations will be based upon the rules of fair competition.

5. Russia

Articles 1035 and 1037 of the Russia Franchise Act[209] govern renewal and termination of franchise agreements. Article 1035 provides the franchisee with a right of renewal, where the franchisee properly performed during the term. Article 1037 further provides that termination before the expiration of the franchise agreement must be registered by the franchisor and that franchise agreements with an unlimited term may be terminated by either party upon six months' advance notice.

C. SAMPLE CLAUSE

The laws noted above are consistent with the termination and nonrenewal provisions generally seen in U.S. franchise agreements. Therefore, we anticipate that most domestic franchise agreements that are prepared by experienced U.S. franchise counsel will not need to undergo significant revision. Notwithstanding this, the following sample clause is an example of a specifically tailored revision to general termination provisions.

MALAYSIA

Cooling-Off Period. Franchisee shall have 7 Business Days after the date Franchisor signs this Agreement to terminate it without cause upon written notice to Franchisor. If Franchisee terminates this Agreement within the 7 day period, Franchisor will promptly refund the initial franchise fee set forth in Section 3.A and all other amounts that Franchisee previously paid Franchisor, except that Franchisor will deduct, at cost, all out-of-pocket expenses that Franchisor incurred through the date of termination in connection with examining Franchisee's application to become a franchisee and in preparing this Agreement.

Notes

The author of this chapter would like to thank Charles Cannon, Jan Gilbert, Brian Cole, Robert Lauer, Claude Rich, Jay Strimel, and Kenya Scott from Jenkens & Gilchrist and the following international lawyers for their invaluable assistance with the preparation of this chapter: Osvaldo Marzorati and Adriana de Florio, Allende & Brea; Penny Ward, Baker & McKenzie; Herbert S. Wolfson, Law Offices of Herbert S. Wolfson; Luiz Henrique do Amaral, Dannemann, Siemsen, Bigler & Ipanema Moreira; Raul Toro, Del Rio Morgan Peralta & Toro; Howard Chao and Nan Wang, O'Melveny & Myers; Carlos Umaña, Brigard & Urrutia; Zia Mody and Anu Iyer, Chambers of Zia Mody; Galinar R. Kartakusuma and Ricky Firman, Makarim & Taira S.; Patricia McGovern and Derval O'Halloran, L.K. Shields, Solicitors; Salvador Jiménez Mariscal, Gomez-Acebo & Pombo; Dr. C. Mark Bruppacher, Bruppacher Hug & Partner; Corin Trandifir, Herzfeld & Rubin (Romania) S.R.L.; P. Mark Abell and Babette Marzheuser-Wood, Field Fisher Waterhouse; Albrecht Schulz, CMS Hasche Sigle Eschenlohr Peltzer; Claudia Pereira, Mayora & Mayora; Aldo Frignani, Frignani E Associati; Sam Habbas and Rob Little, Al Sarraf & Al Ruwayeh; Egidijus Bernotas and Urge Navikamskaite, Advokatfirman Glimstedt; Mohamed Bustaman Haji Abdullah and Suat Gaik Yeoh, Bustaman & Company; Carlos Müggenburg, Creel, Garcia-Cuèllar y Müggenburg; Yavel Francis Lanuza, Sucre, Arias, Castro & Reyes; Jean Paul Chabeneix, Rodrigo, Elias & Medrano Abogados; and Francois Terblanche, Edward Nathan & Friedland Inc.

1. The citation form is informal in many cases, in part because such cites are not easily available and, in part, because in the author's view, more formal

citation form would not be helpful to U.S. franchise counsel using this information as a reference source. Rather, knowing the fact that the laws exist, their name, how current the laws are, and where to find the laws or related topical information is the focus of the citation form used because this is critical information that U.S. franchise counsel will need to evaluate and discuss with local counsel and the client. Therefore, out of necessity and practicality, cites in this chapter have been so limited.

2. *See* Chapter 5 regarding Disclosure Issues.

3. *See* Section XIII of this chapter, which discusses foreign investment restrictions.

4. PRC Administrative Regulations on Technology Import Contracts (5/20/85); Detailed Rules for the Implementation of the PRC Administrative Regulations on Technology Import Contracts (1/20/88); Guiding Principles for Signing and Approving Technology Import Contracts (1/22/92); Administration of Trade In Importation of Technology and Equipment Tentative Procedures, 3/26/96).

5. PRC Administrative Regulations on Technology Import Contracts (5/20/85); Detailed Rules for the Implementation of the PRC Administrative Regulations on Technology Import Contracts (1/20/88); Guiding Principles for Signing and Approving Technology Import Contracts (1/22/92); Administration of Trade In Importation of Technology and Equipment Tentative Procedures (3/26/96).

6. Foreign Exchange Management Act, 1999 (replacing Foreign Exchange Regulation Act, 1973).

7. Foreign Exchange Regulation Act, 1973.

8. *See* Chapter 3, which addresses protection of trademarks and related intellectual property rights.

9. 1991 Industrial Property Law of Mexico, dated June 17, 1991, and August 2, 1994, Federal Oficial Gazette (Diario Oficial de la Federación).

10. The Brazilian Industrial Property Law (Law No 9,279/96).

11. Decision 486 of the Cartagena Agreement. According to Colombian Industrial Property Law, all trademark licenses must be registered before the Colombian Trademark Office (The Office of the Superintendent of Industry and Commerce) for such licenses to be binding on third parties. The trademark office review focuses on a licensee's compliance with regulations on unfair competition.

12. Lithuanian Intellectual Property Law.

13. Decision 486 of the Andean Community; Legislative Decree 823 (abrogating DL 26017, 1992) and implemented by the National Institute for the Defense of Competition and Protection of Industrial Property (INDECOPI).

14. Normative Act No. 135 of April 15, 1997, issued by the Brazilian Trademark Office.

15. PRC Trademark Law, published March 1, 1983.

16. Trade Marks Act (1994).

17. Trademark Act (1968).

18. *See also* Section IV of this chapter relating to currency restrictions.

19. Normative Act No. 135 of April 15, 1997, issued by the Brazilian Trademark Office.

20. Brazil is one country that has an extensive "grey" market that exists outside the central bank framework.

21. Until recently, in India, some franchisors set up accounts whereby amounts paid to the unit in foreign currencies were set aside in a so-called EEFC account and used to pay all fees. A Foreign Exchange Management Act notification dated March 30, 2001, altered this practice by revoking the ability to make payments from these EEFC accounts. All franchise fees must now gain prior RBI approval.

22. Countries that currently have franchise-specific disclosure obligations include Australia, Brazil, Alberta and Ontario Provinces in Canada, Indonesia, Malaysia, Mexico, People's Republic of China, Romania, Russia, South Africa, Spain, and Taiwan. Other countries have voluntary codes of conduct that include disclosure obligations. Disclosure obligations are addressed in depth in Chapter 5 of this book.

23. Royal Decree 2485/1998 of the 13th November, For the Development of Article 62 of Act 7/1996, of 15th January, On the Regulation of Retail Trading, In Relation to Regulation of the Franchise Regime, and the Creation of a Register of Franchisors Law; Franchise Act 1998 (act 590 given Royal Assent December 24, 1998, published December 31, 1998).

24. Franchise Act 1998 (act 590 given Royal Assent December 24, 1998, published December 31, 1998).

25. Royal Decree 2485/1998 of the 13th November, For the Development of Article 62 of Act 7/1996, of 15th January, On the Regulation of Retail Trading, In Relation to Regulation of the Franchise Regime, and the Creation of a Register of Franchisors Law.

26. Franchise Act 1998 (act 590 given Royal Assent December 24, 1998, published December 31, 1998), Sections 6 and 55.

27. 1991 Industrial Property Law of Mexico (Article 136 of the Industrial Property Law); 1994 Regulations to the Industrial Property Law (Federal Office Gazette Diario Oficial de la Federación of November 23, 1994).

28. Normative Act No. 135 of April 15, 1997.

29. Section II, above.

30. Monopoly Regulation and Fair Trade Act (as administered by the Korean Fair Trade Commission).

31. Competition Acts of 1991–1996.

32. Competition Act of 1998 (effective September 1, 1999, repealing and replacing the Maintenance and Promotion of Competition Act of 1979).

33. The Treaty of Rome, establishing the (then) European Community, came into force on January 1, 1958. The contents of Article 81 were originally contained in Article 85, but the treaty was subsequently renumbered.

34. The fifteen countries that currently are members of the EU are Austria, Belgium, the Netherlands, Luxemberg, Denmark, Finland, France, Germany, Greece, Ireland, Italy, Portugal, Spain, Sweden, and the United Kingdom.

35. Article 81 specifically prohibits acts that "(a) directly or indirectly fix purchase or selling prices or any other trading conditions; (b) limit or control production, markets, technical development, or investment; (c) share markets or sources of supply; (d) apply dissimilar conditions to equivalent transactions with other trading parties, thereby placing them at a competitive disadvantage; or (e) make the conclusion of contracts subject to acceptance by the other parties of supplementary obligations which, by their nature or according to commercial usage, have no connection with the subject of such contracts."

36. Regulation EC4087/88.

37. Agreements entered into before May 31, 2000, are grandfathered under Regulation EC4087/88 until December 31, 2001.

38. Regulation EC2790/1999.

39. The commission issued its Commission Regulation Guidelines for the application of the Vertical Restraints Regulation in May 2000, and were published in the OJ C29/1, October 13, 2000.

40. Section 90a, German Commercial Code.

41. Decree 391/2001 revised the parameters for notification such that notification is necessary only where (a) the combined turnover (net sales) of the involved companies exceed U.S. $200 million in Argentina alone, and (b) the value of the assets of the Argentine company that is being transferred "or" the price of the transaction (prorated for the Argentine portion if necessary) exceed U.S. $20 million.

42. Unfair Contract Terms Act 1977.

43. German Standard Terms of Contracts Act.

44. Unfair Contract Terms Act.

45. Commission Notice: Guidelines on Vertical Restraints, ¶ 200 (May 2000).

46. *See* Commission Notice: Guidelines on Vertical Restraints, ¶ 200 (May 2000); Pronuptia de Paris GmbH, Frankfurt am Main v. Pronuptia de Paris Irmgard Schillgalis, Hamburg, Court of Justice of the European Communities Case No. 161/84 (Jan 28, 1986); Notice Pursuant to Article 19(3) of Council Regulation 17/62 Concerning Case IV/30937—Pronuptia, Commission of the European Communities (July 16, 1986).

47. Section 90a of the German Commercial Code.

48. *See generally* Article 5 of the Mexican Constitution (Constitución Política de los Estados Unidos Mexicanos Artículo 5).

49. Unreported cases.

50. *See* Section VI of this chapter relating to trade secret protection.

51. *See generally* Korea Trademark Law.

52. PRC Trademark Law, published March 1, 1983.

53. Franchise Act 1998 (Malaysia), Section 26.

54. *See* Chapter 4 addressing tax implications of international franchise transactions.

55. *See* Chapter 4 for an in-depth discussion of the tax ramifications of international franchise relationships.

56. See the discussion of gross-up provisions and foreign tax credits in Chapter 4 for a more in-depth discussion of tax planning.

57. 1991 Unified Tax Law.

58. Decree No. 3 of 1955, as amended by Decree No. 2 of 1957.

59. Ministerial Order No. 44 of 1985.

60. *See* Section II of this chapter addressing governmental approvals.

61. Section II of this chapter (Governmental Recordations, Regulations, and Approvals) refers to the governmental approval requirements and compliance procedures of several key nations, including those covering a franchise agreement's currency provisions, and will not be repeated here.

62. Tax gross-up clauses similar to those described in subsection (b) of the sample are often difficult to administer because of the complex calculation of the allowable foreign tax credit for U.S. income tax purposes.

63. Article 313 of the German Civil Code.

64. The land registry is called the Grundbuch and recordations are made before a presiding judge or notary, called a Auflassung.

65. *See* Franchising Code of Conduct, Clause 20.

66. *Id.*

67. In Korea, the Monopoly Regulation and Fair Trade Act (MRFTA) governs fair trade issues generally. The MRFTA is largely untested in the franchise context.

68. Article 23 of the MRFTA. *See* Notice No. 1997-4 of the Federal Trade Commission.

69. *See* Egyptian Commercial Code, issued May 17, 1999.

70. *See Several Provisions Regarding Changes in Equity Interest of Investors in Foreign Investment Enterprises* (1997).

71. *Id.*

72. UNIFORM TRADE SECRETS ACT § (4) (1985) (The original UTSA was adopted in 1979 by the National Conference of Commissioners on Uniform State Laws, and was amended in 1985).

73. Karen Magri, *International Aspects of Trade Secrets Law* at http://www.carolinapatents.com/ts_articles/trade_secret3.htm. NAFTA (Art. 1711) and TRIPS (Art. 39) provide only brief attention to the topic. Article 10*bis* of the Paris Convention (covering unfair competition) has provided a potential source of support for international standards of trade secret protection, but the language has traditionally been viewed as insufficiently addressing the issue.

74. *Id.*

75. Karen Magri, *International Aspects of Trade Secrets Law* at http://www.carolinapatents.com/ts_articles/trade_secret3.htm.

76. *See* §§ 89b and 90s, German Commercial Code; §§ 17 *et. seq.*, Unfair Competition Act; §§ 203 *et. seq.*, German Penal Code.

77. *See* Richard Kemp, *International Considerations in IP Licensing*, 576 PLI/Pat 461 (1999). The commercial agent must also keep these secrets confidential and must not use or communicate them after termination of the contract in line with "professional ethics of a proper merchant". See *also* Section 90s, German Commercial Code.

78. Section 262, Decision 486 of the Cartagena Agreement.

79. Patent Code, Article 6 bis. *See* Aldo Frignani, *Know-how and Trade Secrets*, INTERNATIONAL JOURNAL OF FRANCHISING AND DISTRIBUTION LAW, p. 59–67 (1996).

80. Section 284, Chilean Penal Code.

81. Directive 95/46/EC on the protection of individuals with regard to the processing of personal data and on the free movement of such data. *See* Henry J. Peritt, Jr. and Margaret G. Stewart, *False Alarm?,* 51 FED. COMM. J.L. 911 (1999).

82. Data Protection Act 1998. Chris Swindells and Kay Henderson, *Legal Regulation of Electronic Commerce,* THE JOURNAL OF INFORMATION LAW AND TECHNOLOGY, October 30, 1998.

83. For instance, under the UK law, U.S. franchisors could be subject to criminal sanctions if the franchisor compiles information on a prospect in the United Kingdom and uses that information in the United States without implementing the necessary safeguards required under the UK law. These safeguards include keeping registrations up to date and organizing databases for ease of access upon request by the data subject while maintaining security and secrecy.

84. Karen Magri, *International Aspects of Trade Secrets Law* at http://www.carolinapatents.com/ts_articles/trade_secret3.htm.

85. Article 1(3) the Japanese Trade Secrets Act, an amendment of the Unfair Competition Prevention Act (118th Diet, 66th Act 1990).

86. Japanese Trade Secrets Act.

87. *Id.*

88. *Id.*

89. *Id.*

90. The law makes no provision for protecting trade secrets during litigation. There is no provision in Japanese law for protective orders or other means of maintaining the confidentiality of the information. *Id.*

91. The Agreement on Trade-related Aspects of Intellectual Property Rights (TRIPS) came into effect in January 1995. The TRIPS Agreement is administered by the World Trade Organization (WTO) and provides rules concerning trade-related intellectual property rights, covering basic principles of previous intellectual property conventions, standards regarding availability, scope, and use of intellectual property rights, effective and appropriate enforcement, multilateral dispute settlement procedures, and transitional arrangements for developing nations.

92. *Id.*

93. 35 USCS § 154 (2000).

94. Karen Magri, *International Aspects of Trade Secrets Law* at http://www.carolinapatents.com/ts_articles/trade_secret3.htm.

95. *Id.*

96. *Id.*

97. The Immigration and Naturalization Act, 8 U.S.C. § 1101(a)(15)(B). The criteria include (1) residence in a foreign country that is their actual dwelling place in fact; (2) no intention of abandoning their foreign residence (i.e., they must have a clear intent to continue their foreign residence at the end of their temporary business visit to the United States); (3) be coming to the United States to engage in legitimate temporary business activities; (4) all salary and benefits must come from the alien's employer abroad, however, incidental expenses may be covered by a U.S. entity; (5) alien's principal place

of business must be predominantly in a foreign country; (6) alien must be able to show adequate financial ability to carry out the purpose of the business visit; (7) alien must show an intent to depart the United States at the end of the requested stay (this intention may be evidenced by ties the alien has to a foreign country, such as principal place of employment, family, social ties, etc.); and (8) alien must have permission to enter a foreign country at the end of the stay in the United States.

98. *Id.* A B-1 visa is not available for the purpose of study or of performing skilled or unskilled labor or as a representative of foreign press, radio, film, or other foreign information media coming to engage in such vocation.

99. *Id.*

100. Normally, any nonimmigrant who is not in possession of a valid nonimmigrant visa or border-crossing identification card at the time of application for admission to the United States, is inadmissible. This requirement of a valid nonimmigrant visa is "waived" for citizens of certain specified countries who are entering the United States as either visitors or for business. 8 U.S.C. § 1187.

101. *Id.*

102. *Id.*

103. *Id.*

104. The Economist Intelligence Unit, Investing, Licensing & Trading in Australia, § 6.0 (2000).

105. A Business ETA, which is almost identical to the Short Stay Business Visa, is a new category of visa introduced by the Australian government to facilitate business travel by passport holders of designated countries such as the United States, United Kingdom, Canada, Hong Kong, Singapore, Malaysia, and most Western European countries.

106. See Article 11 of the Mexican Federal Labor Law (Ley Federal del Trabajo Artículo 11).

107. *Id.*

108. *Id.*

109. *Id.*

110. *Id.*

111. *Taxation in Thailand*, at http://www.tcc.or.th/thailand/tax.html [last visited 08/10/00].

112. *Id.*

113. The Economist Intelligence Unit, Investing, Licensing & Trading in Australia, § 11.0 (2000).

114. This rate varies for some products, such as alcoholic beverages and certain tobacco products, where the rates are a combination of ad valorem and a fixed-dollar amount per liter or kilogram. The rate of duty for general merchandising goods is at zero or 5 percent. Special industry rates apply to certain items such as imported passenger motor vehicles, certain passenger motor-vehicle components, and to textiles, clothing, and footwear.

115. Two systems of tariff concessions are available to help lower costs on goods to be used in domestic industries: (1) The Tariff Concession System allows an importer to apply for a tariff concession order (TCO), which permits

the import of goods at reduced tariffs in instances where substitutable goods are not produced in Australia; and (2) The Project By-law Scheme provides duty-free entry for certain capital equipment for use in the mining, resources processing, agriculture, food processing, and food packaging industries if it is more technologically advanced, productive, or efficient than equipment made in Australia. *Id.*

116. The PRC is continuing its policies of granting export-tax rebates for certain sectors. Following a round of tax rebates taking effect at the beginning of 1999, the average tax rebate for exporters now stands at 12.56 percent.

117. The Economist Intelligence Unit, Investing, Licensing & Trading in China, 11.0 (2000).

118. *Id.* Effective October 1, 1997, the PRC reduced tariffs for 4,874 commodities—73 percent of those subject to tariffs. This reduction brought the PRC's average tariff rate down from 23 percent to 17 percent. Under those tariff reductions, the average tariff for machinery and electronic raw materials, parts, and finished products stands, respectively, at 8.94 percent, 10.76 percent, and 14.92 percent.

119. *See generally* PRC Administrative Regulations on Technology Import Contracts (5/20/85); Detailed Rules for the Implementation of the PRC Administrative Regulations on Technology Import Contracts (1/20/88); Guiding Principles for Signing and Approving Technology Import Contracts (1/22/92); Administration of Trade In Importation of Technology and Equipment Tentative Procedures (3/26/96).

120. Import quotas for machinery and electronic products are set and allocated by the Machinery and Electronics Product Import and Export Office under the State Economic and Trade Commission. *Id.*

121. *Id.*

122. *Id.*

123. *Id.*

124. *Id.* Amendments to the PRC's value added tax (VAT) law have clarified that under the VAT system, exports produced by foreign investment enterprises in the PRC are tax exempt rather than zero rated. VAT paid on domestically bought raw materials can only be partially recovered. VAT rebates on domestically produced raw materials used in producing exports were reduced from the full 17 percent rate to 14 percent in July 1995. Under tax measures announced in late 1995, the VAT rebate was further reduced to 9 percent for most items with effect from the start of 1996.

125. Council Directive 86/653/EEC.

126. England and Finland are examples of countries that have adopted the definition verbatim so as to limit application to the sale of goods.

127. Austria, Germany, Spain, and Portugal are examples of countries that have not adopted the definition verbatim such that application of these agency laws apply to the sale of services as well as to the sale of goods.

128. Italian Civil Code, Article 1742.

129. U.A.E. Federal Law No. 18 of 1981 Regulating Commercial Agencies, as amended, Article 3.

130. Law on Commerce of Kuwait.

131. Law No. 173, Official Gazette No. 8979, Dated April 1966, Law Concerning the Protection to Importing Agents of Merchandise and/or Product.

132. *See generally* U.A.E. Federal Law No. 18 of 1981 Regulating Commercial Agencies, as amended, Article 3.

133. Law 6209, Protection for Representatives and Distributors of Foreign Companies.

134. Law No. 173, Official Gazette No. 8979, Dated April 1966, Law Concerning the Protection to Importing Agents of Merchandise and/or Product.

135. See Articles 290 and 291, Decree No. 8-98 (modifying Commerce Code of the Republic of Guatemala Decree Number 2-70 of the Congress of the Republic).

136. Italian Civil Code, Article 1227.

137. Article 113, PRC Contract Law. Other provisions in the PRC Contract Law seem to suggest that indirect damages may be limited.

138. Unfair Contract Terms Act 1977. A valid choice of law provision may insulate the franchisor from this provision.

139. Thai Civil Code.

140. Indonesian Civil Code, Articles 1315 and 1316.

141. Italian Civil Code, Article 1227.

142. Korean Civil Code.

143. An indemnification will generally not cover willful misconduct in Kuwait. Further, in Italy a franchisor cannot require the franchisee to indemnify the franchisor for its own willful misconduct or gross negligence. Any such requirement will be null and void under Article 1229 of the Italian Civil Code.

144. *See generally* §§ 765 *et. seq.*, German Civil Code; The maximum amount awarded so far in Germany for pain and suffering is DEM 500,000.

145. Malaysian Contracts Act 1950, Section 78.

146. *See generally* Articles 1315 and 1316 of the Indonesian Civil Code.

147. A sample definition for the phrase "Losses and Expenses" would be "without limitation, all losses, compensatory, exemplary or punitive damages, fines, charges, costs, expenses, lost profits, reasonable attorneys' fees, court costs, settlement amounts, judgments, compensation for damages to the Franchisor's reputation and goodwill, costs of or resulting from delays, financing, costs of marketing materials and media time/space, and costs of changing, substituting or replacing the same, and any and all expenses of recall, refunds, compensation, public notices and other such amounts incurred in connection with the matters described."

148. *See generally* Panama Antitrust Act; Unfair Contract Terms Act 1977 (Northern Ireland)

149. *See* Panama Antitrust Act.

150. *Id.*

151. *See* PRC Contract Law.

152. *See* Article 349 *et seq.*, of the Spanish Commercial Code; Articles 1144, 1822, 1825, 1831, 1837, and 1855 of the Spanish Civil Code.

153. See Article 11 of Decree 2-89 of the Congress of the Republic—Judicial Branch Law, which establishes that the official language is Spanish; Article 37 of Decree 2-89 of the Congress of the Republic—Judicial Branch Law, which states that a document that comes from abroad must be legalized by the Ministry of Foreign Affairs to be admmisible and that all documents written in a foreign language must be translated to Spanish by a sworn translator authorized for use in the Republic of Guatemala.

154. Sections 2012, 2020, 2021 and 2022, Argentine Civil Code.

155. Sections 480, last paragraph, and 482, Argentine Commercial Code.

156. Sections 765 *et seq.*, of the German Civil Code.

157. *See generally* Hague Legalization Convention, 527 U.N.T.S. 189, T.I.A.S. 10072, 20 I.L.M. 1405, 1407.

158. In Spain, stockbrokers act essentially as notaries. The Spanish notary framework was modified in January 2001 to merge the Spanish notary and stock exchange broker frameworks into one concept.

159. See the discussion above in subsection 1 regarding waiver of presentment and notices with regard to modifications or amendments of the franchise agreement.

160. Malaysia Contracts Act 1950, Section 86.

161. This form of guaranty is for use by an individual guarantor. Guarantees executed by corporate entities should reflect authority to enter into guarantees granted under the entities' Memorandum and Articles of Incorporation as well as evidence that all other restrictions on the granting of guarantees under the Companies Acts, 1963 to 1999 have not been contravened. If the Guaranty is governed by Irish law, the execution should be preceded by the following: "Present when the common seal of the Company was affixed hereto:"

162. *See* Section 75 of the Malaysia Contracts Act 1950, which specifically provides the following: "when a contract has been broken, if a sum is named in the contract as the amount to be paid in cases of such breach, or if the contract contains any other stipulation by way of penalty, the party complaining of the breach is entitled, whether or not actual damage or loss is proved to have been cause thereby, to receive from the party who has broken the contract reasonable compensation not exceeding the amount so named or, as the case may be, the penalty stipulated for."

163. *See* Egyptian Commercial Code (October 1999).

164. *See* Italian Civil Code, Articles 1382 and 1384.

165. *See* Bahrain Contract Law of 1969, Article 94.

166. *See* The German Standard Terms of Contract Act § 11.

167. *See* Article 390 of U.A.E. Federal Law No. 5 of 1985 Concerning Civil Transactions, as amended, which states (1) "The contracting parties may fix the amount of compensation in advance by making a provision therefor in the contract or in a subsequent agreement, subject to the provisions of the law"; and (2) "The judge may in all cases, upon the application of either of the parties, vary such agreement so as to make the compensation equal to the loss, and any agreement to the contrary shall be void."

168. Article 1384.

169. Article 1152 of the Civil Code.

170. *See* the Company Law (Law 1/1995), enacted March 7, 1996. Interestingly, in relation to franchisee entities, there is no requirement that the entity itself be owned by Indonesians, only that the entity be organized under the laws of Indonesia.

171. *See* Foreign Investment Promotion Act (November 1998).

172. See U.A.E. Federal Law No. 8 of 1984 Concerning Commercial Companies, as amended, Articles 22 *et seq*.

173. *See* Bahamian National Investments Policy, interpreted by the Bahamian Investments Authority.

174. *See* the Provisional Regulations Concerning Investment in and Establishment of Investment Companies by Foreign Business Entities, Promulgated by the Ministry of Foreign Trade and Economic Co-Operation.

175. National Investment Policy, issued and regulated by the Bahamian Investments Authority; *See Doing Business in the Bahamas*, Higgs and Johnson.

176. The Bahamian government will strictly scrutinize any attempt to set up a superficial nominee arrangement (for example, where the Bahamian nominee merely holds the shares of a company and does not accrue the revenue generated from the restaurant) and reject such an arrangement.

177. The guidelines are issued periodically by the Department of Economic Affairs, Commerce and Industry.

178. *See* Foreign Business Act, passed October 1999, effective March 3, 2000.

179. *Id.*

180. *See* U.A.E. Federal Law No. 8 of 1984 Concerning Commercial Companies, as amended, Article 22.

181. Article 1 of the Law No. 44 of 1968 on Eating Publicly During Fasting Time in Ramadan issued on November 2, 1968. Although not codified, there is in practice an exception for room service provided in hotels.

182. Article 1 of Amiri Decree issued on April 20, 1977 on Slaughterhouses.

183. Article 206 of the Penal Law No. 16 of 1960 issued on June 2, 1960.

184. Certification is granted by the Indonesian Uelemas Counsel. Decree of the Indonesian Ministry of Heath. *See generally* Indonesian Consumer Protection Law (March 30, 1999). With respect to the hours a restaurant or other business may operate, the Directorate General of Tourism is responsible for issuing business licenses that, among other things, governs the hours of operation.

185. The relevant Islamic law is the Hukum Syarak. The definition of halal can be found in the Trade Descriptions Act of 1972.

186. *See generally* The Muslim Food Board at www.halal.demon.co.uk; Muis Services at www.muia.gov.sg; and www.sinteccom.org.

187. Certification requires the submission of a formal application to Ilham Daya Sdn Bhd, a private company that inspects the restaurant premises to make an assessment that the individual(s) in charge of preparing the food is aware of the halal guidelines and that the meat being served is supplied by a

certified slaughterhouse (there is a list of approved U.S. slaughterhouses). Upon inspection, the officer submits his report to the Islamic Development Department of Malaysia for recommendation of approval. If approved, a halal certificate is issued to the restaurant upon the payment of a certification fee.

188. *See* U.A.E. Federal Law No. 18 of 1981 Regulating Commercial Agencies. A franchise agreement must be registered with the U.A.E. Federal Ministry of Economy and Commerce for a franchisee to invoke the statutory protections of Federal Law No. 18. A prerequisite to registering the agreement with the Ministry of Economy and Commerce is that the signature of the parties be notarized. Note, however, that courts have occasionally ordered registration where the foreign party withheld notarization in bad faith.

189. *Id.*

190. *See generally* Hague Legalization Convention, 527 U.N.T.S. 189, T.I.A.S. 10072, 20 I.L.M. 1405, 1407.

191. Civil Code Articles 17, 18; Code of Civil Procedure 261; Notaries Law 218 of Dec. 6, 1962, as amended.

192. Law 7764 of April 17, 1998.

193. *See* Revenues Stamp Law.

194. Stamp duties are generally regulated by the Indian Stamp Act, 1899. Stamps can be purchased at a local Stamp Office in Bombay and if an agreement that contains an indemnification provision is executed in Bombay, it should be stamped with approximately 120 Rs. (about $3).

195. The amount of the stamp tax will vary by Province but normally ranges from 1 percent to 1.5 percent of all payments to the franchisor and is usually paid up front within 10 or 15 days from the execution of the franchise agreement. If the franchised location will be operated within the Province of Buenos Aires (i.e., outside the city), the stamp tax percentage may be reduced to 0.35 percent by paying such tax at the Commercial Chamber of La Plata.

196. The Law on Language (1991) is a remnant of Lithuania's independence from Russia and requires that all official documents and all agreements or contracts with foreign entities be translated into Lithuanian and confirmed by a Lithuanian notary. The Lithuanian translations need not be executed and the English version of the agreements will control in the event of a dispute. The Lithuanian Law on Tax Administration requires that agreements (including any development agreement or franchise agreement) be translated into Lithuanian to enable the franchisee to file any withholding or income taxes applicable under such agreements.

197. Article 313, German Civil Code.

198. Article 13(3), German Companies Act. A GmbH is a preferred organizational structure for many German companies.

199. *See* Law 23,458, published on the Official Gazette on April 21, 1987 (passing the Hague Convention).

200. *See* Decree 88451 of Jan. 31, 1980.

201. The Australia Franchising Code of Conduct became effective July 1, 1998, and was updated effective June 28, 2001.

202. We note that, at present, there are approximately five proposed franchise bills in the Italian Parliament. However, it is unsure if such bills will be passed.

203. The Italian Franchise Association regulations took effect January 1, 1995, but are only applicable to franchisors who voluntarily seek membership.

204. Article 11 of the Italian Franchise Association regulations states "[f]inally, the agreement must contain specific provisions concerning the obligations of the parties on the termination of the agreement, in particular with reference to the ceasing of the use by the franchisee of any distinctive signs of the franchisor and the resale of any remaining goods, or the possible repurchase of them by the franchisor should that resale not be possible or the franchisor prefers to do so for the protection of the franchise system."

205. Act 590, given Royal Assent December 24, 1998; published in the Gazette December 31, 1998.

206. *Id.*

207. Section 18(4), Franchise Act 1998. *See* sample provision below.

208. Government Ordinance no. 52/1997 Regarding the Legal Status of Franchise (G.O. 52), adopted by the Government of Romania on August 28, 1997, and published in the Official Gazette of Romania (in Romanian, Monitorul Oficial al Romaniei (M.Of.) no. 224/30.08.1997. G.O. 52 was later approved and amended by the Parliament through Law no. 79, April 9, 1998 (published in M.Of. 147. April 13, 1998) and republished in M.Of. 180, May 14, 1998. The republished version represents the current and reference version of G.O. 52.

209. Chapter 54 of Part II of the Russian Civil Code, enacted January 1996.

CHAPTER ❖ 7

Dispute Resolution: Choice of Law and Forum

ERIK B. WULFF

I. Introduction

The dramatic increase in international franchising is but part of a much broader trend of globalization of commercial activity. One need not travel far abroad to realize that many consumer brands originating from the United States are also present in other countries. Conversely, many popular consumer brands in the United States are of foreign origin. Many companies, particularly in consumer product markets, are pursuing global branding strategies.

Taking one's brand to another shore often requires significant involvement by other parties, particularly those with a local strategic presence, to successfully develop those markets. Their involvement may vary considerably, including participation as joint venture partners, master franchisees, multiunit developers, or single-unit franchisees. In this context, it is important to have a clear understanding of the parties' respective rights and obligations and to know which laws will govern the parties' performance and how disputes will be resolved, should any arise.

The clear expression of the parties' rights and obligations is primarily a function of a well-drafted, comprehensive agreement, although sometimes it is more customary to cover the principal business terms only and to let applicable commercial law provide the overall framework of the relationship. How a party's performance will be evaluated, should the other party be dissatisfied, is heavily influenced by the law that governs the relationship and the forum that will resolve disputes. Although not considered part of the "business deal," the choice of law and the procedural mechanisms by which the parties choose to resolve disputes are critically important elements to an international agreement.

Choice of law and choice of forum are topics of considerable complexity worthy of in-depth analysis. In fact, numerous treatises have been written just about international arbitration, the most common choice of forum in international transactions.[1] This chapter is not intended to provide a comprehensive treatment of these complex issues; instead, it is intended to provide a practical framework of some of the more important considerations for a U.S. franchisor venturing abroad, with references to relevant materials.

Section II of this chapter will cover considerations regarding choice of law. Section III will deal with choice of forum, including international arbitration, adjudication through national court systems, as well as nonbinding dispute resolution mechanisms. We will also compare various alternative arbitral organizations commonly used to resolve international disputes.

II. Choice of Law Governing the Relationship

In the absence of a contractual choice of law, the law governing the parties' relationship is determined by the particular forum resolving the parties' dispute, using its own particular choice of law principles. A failure to have a choice of law in a domestic franchise agreement leads to uncertainty, and that uncertainty is greatly magnified in an international relationship due to the potential for vastly differing treatment of the agreement under the diverse legal regimes of countries around the world. Accordingly, to foster predictability it is critically important to have a choice of law in an international agreement. In fact, the importance is highlighted by the widespread support of the parties' contractual choice of law.[2]

As a practical matter, the choice of law in international franchise relationships often is a choice between the laws of the franchisor's home country (for the purposes of this chapter, we assume that to be the United States) or the laws of the country where the franchise will operate, that is, the host country. In the context of negotiating the agreement, the choice of law can come down to a simplistic assertion of "my law" versus "your law" and can become a contentious point of negotiation. When approached in this vein, the choice of law is then often dictated by the party who is perceived to have the greatest leverage in the negotiations, oftentimes the U.S. franchisor.

Practice Tip

Even with a U.S. choice of law in the agreement, local counsel needs to be retained to advise on "transactional" laws and mandatory laws in the host country.

Yet, the choice of law on the interpretation of the contract is only one aspect of a broad range of laws that may govern or affect the parties' conduct. Franchising, after all, consists of granting a bundle of intellectual property rights, including the right to use trademarks, in addition to providing the services and assistance to properly exploit them. Intellectual property rights are generally conferred by national law and consequently, the franchisor is licensing property rights granted and recognized by the host country. If a franchisor chooses to have U.S. law govern the contract, that choice has no effect on the nature, extent, or protectability of the licensed intellectual property rights, which will be governed by the laws of the host country and, in some instances and to a lesser extent, international treaties. Additionally, host country currency control restrictions, nonresident withholding taxes, franchise disclosure, or relationship laws and competition laws (just to name a few of the more common host country laws applicable to franchise transactions) typically will not be displaced by the contractual choice of law. Most countries have "mandatory" laws or laws reflecting strong public policies, including competition laws, franchisee protection laws, and so forth, that will override the parties' choice of law (and, indeed, may even invalidate an otherwise enforceable arbitration award). On the other hand, there are a number of U.S. laws that may govern or affect the parties' conduct even with a host country choice of law, including the Foreign Corrupt Practices Act, foreign asset control regulations, antitrust laws, RICO, and state franchise disclosure laws.[3] There are also supranational laws, such as European Community (EC) competition regulations, that will apply regardless of the parties' choice of law. The parties also may be engaged in conduct that violates the laws of the home country or host country, unaffected by the choice of law governing the contract, such as laws against fraud or deceptive practices. Thus, the choice of "my law" or "your law" has only a limited effect on the overall legal regime that will be applicable to the agreement and the relationship.

Furthermore, one should also critically examine one's natural bias in favoring one's own law over the laws of the host country. There now

Practice Tip

Do not simply assume that your state's laws will always be more favorable than the laws of the host country.

are an increasing number of U.S. states that have statutes and a common law that perceive an imbalance in franchise relationships and therefore are distinctly protective of franchisee interests.[4] If the franchisor is located in one of those states, the host country's laws may be preferable.

It should be apparent from the foregoing that a U.S. franchisor needs to understand, at least at some level, the laws of the host country, even if the choice of law in the agreement is the law of the franchisor's home state in the United States. One should understand the laws that establish and define the intellectual property rights that are licensed, the commercial "transactional" laws, such as currency controls, nonresident withholding taxes and customs regulations, and mandatory laws or public policies, such as competition laws and laws restricting terminations of franchises or requiring compensation on termination. In addition, before acceding to a request that the host country law govern the contractual relationship, a U.S. franchisor should determine the implications of that choice, including the formalities of contract formation, rules of construction, nature of relationship created (that is, independent contractor or agency and the potential of vicarious liability), implied obligations, language requirements, and so forth.

If a U.S. franchisor is unwilling to accommodate a request that the host country law govern the contractual relationship (for example, legitimate reasons would include an inadequately developed body of commercial law) and the prospective franchisee is equally leery of U.S. law (often, there is great trepidation about the complexity of U.S. law), one still has several choices to pursue. First, the parties could agree to the laws of a third country with which both parties are familiar. In doing so, one should be aware that the laws of some countries impose limits on the enforceability of choice of law provisions when the chosen law lacks a reasonable relationship to the party's transaction.[5] In this respect, the considerations leading to the choice of a neutral situs for arbitration may lead to the same choice of governing law for the contract. After all, if arbitration is chosen to be held in a neutral third country, that country's procedural laws relating to arbitrations, as supplemented by the procedural rules of the arbitration organization or the ad hoc procedural rules, will be implicated.

Second, the agreement can remain silent on the governing law of the contractual relationship and rely on the tribunal that hears disputes between the parties to determine what law to apply. For obvious reasons, this is not a very satisfactory solution, for it will likely result in significant argument about the applicability of the home country law versus the host country law and may create uncertainty about the parties' respective rights and obligations. In the context of a franchise relationship, there is a significant risk that a tribunal, at least one that sits outside the United States, would conclude, by virtue of its own choice of law principles, that the host country's laws have the greatest connection to the transaction and therefore should govern.

Finally, one can also choose, in the context of international arbitration, that the arbitrators be guided by what they deem just and equitable without reference to any particular law, that is, to decide the case *ex æquo et bono*.[6] Again, a certain measure of predictability is then lost.

In sum, the choice of law is more complicated than an arm wrestling contest of "my law" versus "your law." One should not immediately assume that the other party's law is less favorable and, even so, there may be other viable alternatives to insisting that the choice will be "my law."

III. Choice of Forum to Resolve Disputes

Like the choice of law considerations, the choice of forum considerations in an international franchise context are complex. First, the same considerations as in a domestic context are present. For example, the convenience and familiarity factors that lead one to choose the courts in one's home state are also present. The factors in weighing whether one should choose litigation or arbitration are also relevant in an international context. However, the further complications to these decisions arise from the fact that one is dealing with a foreign national about a business transaction that involves his or her use of the franchisor's intellectual property rights in a foreign country. Thus, commencing an action in one's local court raises potential procedural issues relating to the court's jurisdiction, including personal jurisdiction over the franchisee. Moreover, if the franchisee, whether reactively or otherwise, files a parallel action in a court of the host country, it is entirely possible that such action would proceed on a parallel basis because there may be no

Practice Tip

The normal preference to choose your home state courts does not work well in international franchising because generally there is no mandate that the host country courts recognize those home state proceedings and enforce their judgments.

requirement that the foreign court dismiss the action or hold it in abeyance pending resolution of the matter in the United States. After all, the U.S. constitutional concept of "full faith and credit" does not carryover into the international arena, where such matters are determined on a discretionary basis under the concept of international comity.

Even if a franchisor obtains jurisdiction over the franchisee in a U.S. court and prevails in the action, it needs to consider the ability to enforce that judgment. Unless the franchisee has assets in the United States that can be attached to satisfy the judgment, the U.S. franchisor would need to obtain enforcement in the host country or possibly even other countries. Since the United States is not a party to any treaties regarding the enforcement of foreign judgments,[7] the enforcement of a U.S. judgment in the host country is a matter of international comity.[8] Particularly if the foreign franchisee has not appeared in the U.S. action, there is substantial risk that the judgment would not be enforced at least without relitigating parts of the merits of the case.

The uncertainty about the enforcement of a U.S. judgment abroad is magnified when the judgment also contains injunctive relief, which is often the case in franchise termination litigation to force the discontinuance of the use of trademarks and other intellectual property rights and to stop competitive activities. Consequently, litigating termination disputes with foreign franchisees in one's home state may be a very difficult and uncertain undertaking.

The foregoing discussion is a microcosm of the broader difficulties of dispute resolution in international commercial transactions. They are not unique to franchising and affect myriad international commercial relations. Additionally, just as much as the U.S. party is likely to be unwilling to subject itself to the unfamiliar judicial procedures in the national court systems of the host country, the foreign party is likely to have the same concerns about the U.S. court system. Indeed, given the U.S. reputation for litigousness, a prospective foreign franchisee may be unwilling to proceed with the transaction at all if he or she is to be subjected to those risks. Accordingly, in international franchise transactions, as well as other international commercial transactions, parties often choose other dispute resolution mechanisms, such as international arbitration.

A. ARBITRATION OF DISPUTES

Arbitration has become the preferred means of resolving international commercial disputes. Arbitration of disputes in international commercial relationships has long been promoted by numerous international bodies, including the United Nations. The United Nations Convention on the Recognition and Enforcement of Foreign Arbitral Awards (the New York Convention) has now been embraced by 126 countries, including the United States and virtually all developed nations. As a result of the globalization of economies and the general preference for using arbitration as the means to resolve disputes, all three of the major international arbitration institutions—the International Court of Arbitration of the International Chamber of Commerce (ICC), the American Arbitration Association (AAA), and the London Court of International Arbitration (LCIA)—have experienced steady increases in the number of international arbitrations, with the ICC and AAA now each handling approximately 500 international arbitration filings per year.

Practice Tip

Arbitration generally is the preferred way to resolve international commercial disputes, including franchise disputes, because of the widespread adoption of the New York Convention throughout the world.

The forces driving arbitration as the preferred method of resolving disputes in international commercial relations include neutrality of forum and, as a result of the New York Convention, assurance that the arbitration proceedings will be recognized as the only forum in which to resolve the dispute (less potential for duplicative parallel legal proceedings in both countries), and that the arbitration award will be recognized and enforced with a minimum of judicial interference.

International arbitration is very similar to domestic arbitration in that it is a consensual means of dispute resolution by a nongovernmental decision-maker that results in a legally binding and enforceable ruling. As a result of its widespread acceptance in many countries by their adoption of the New York Convention, parties are able to avoid the often protracted and expensive proceedings arising in connection with judicial resolution of disputes relating to the jurisdiction of the courts and parallel proceedings in different countries.

As mentioned above, one of the perceived advantages of international arbitration is that it offers a genuinely neutral forum. Although many developed nations have court systems that are generally competent and unbiased, the lack of familiarity with the procedures can give the domestic party an advantage over the foreign party. Moreover, beyond the major industrialized nations, many national court systems lack the experience and competence to handle the complexities of a typical franchise case and may not have the tradition of evenhandedness with respect to foreigners. International arbitration offers a neutral forum that is unattached to either side or to national governmental authorities. Moreover, by carefully selecting the arbitrators based on their experience, one can have assurance of a level of competency in handling the matter.

A second advantage of arbitration is that, as a general proposition, arbitration agreements and awards are more easily and reliably enforced in other countries. As noted above, the New York Convention has been widely adopted. In contrast, there are few bilateral or multilateral treaties, and in fact the United States is not a party to any treaties dealing with the recognition and enforcement of foreign judicial awards. As a result of the perceived enforceability of arbitral awards, it has been observed that there is a relatively high level of voluntary compliance with the awards.

The parties also have great flexibility in establishing the procedural rules for the arbitration. Although the rules of arbitration of the three major international arbitration organizations (ICC, AAA, and LCIA) are generally similar, the parties have the ability, even when choosing one of these institutions, to modify or supplement those rules. This is also true for so-called *ad hoc* arbitrations, such as those conducted under the United Nations Commission on International Trade Law (UNCITRAL) rules.

Practice Tip

Parties have great flexibility to establish their own procedural rules for the arbitration proceedings even if conducted under the auspices of one of the major international arbitrations institutions.

International arbitration involves significantly less discovery than is commonly experienced in U.S. court actions. Lack of comprehensive discovery can be an advantage or disadvantage, depending on the circumstances of a particular case. If desired, one can provide for more extensive discovery by modifying the procedural rules of the arbitration, subject to the arbitrator's ability to compel discovery. As will be discussed below, the International Bar Association has adopted supplementary rules regarding discovery and evidence that the parties can choose to follow.

As with domestic arbitrations, the proceedings are confidential and do not establish precedent. Again, depending on the circumstances, this may be advantageous or disadvantageous.

Like domestic arbitrations, international arbitrations generally are conducted only among the parties to the particular agreement. Hence, international arbitration can defeat efforts of multiple foreign franchisees seeking to leverage their legal positions by filing consolidated cases.

Finally, although it is often said that arbitration is less costly than litigation, the fees payable to international arbitration organizations and to the arbitrators themselves can be very substantial. In fact, the high cost of arbitrating international disputes for both parties can be a powerful incentive to resolve differences through private negotiations or mediation. Other major disadvantages of arbitration are that the tribunal is not bound by legal precedent, lending to unpredictable results, and the awards are generally not appealable, even in the face of significant errors.

In sum, international arbitration is often viewed as the lesser of two evils. As noted above, it can be extremely expensive, the results can be unpredictable, and errors are generally not appealable. Yet, when compared to litigation in national courts, it is often viewed as the preferred method.

B. LAWS GOVERNING INTERNATIONAL ARBITRATION

Arbitration proceedings are governed by both substantive law and procedural law. Oftentimes, the governing law of the agreement also represents the substantive law of the arbitration, although as mentioned above, the laws of home country and host country may be implicated, notwithstanding the choice of law.[9] Procedural law consists primarily of the procedural rules of the arbitration. Those procedural rules can be the comprehensive rules of the chosen international arbitration organization or the rules the parties have chosen for themselves in an *ad hoc* arbitration proceeding (that is, one that is not administered by an organization), the most common of which are the UNCITRAL rules. In both instances, these procedural rules can be modified or supplemented by the parties, such as stipulating the qualifications and methods of selecting arbitrators. This "private" procedural framework then needs to be considered in light of the laws on arbitration in the country where the arbitration proceedings are to be conducted, as well as the interpretation of the enforcement convention in the countries where an award is likely to have to be enforced.

1. International Arbitration Conventions

The principal arbitration conventions from a U.S. perspective are the New York Convention and the Panama Convention.[10] Drafted by a United Nations conference and signed in 1958, the New York Convention has now been adopted by 126 countries.[11] It was designed to "encourage the recognition and enforcement of commercial arbitration agreements in international contracts and to unify the standards by which agreements to arbitrate are observed and arbitral awards are enforced in the signatory countries."[12]

In general terms, the New York Convention requires courts of signatory nations to recognize and enforce foreign arbitral awards, subject to certain limited exceptions described below. It also requires courts of signatory nations to recognize the validity of arbitration agreements, again subject to certain limited exceptions, and requires them to refer parties to arbitration when they have entered into valid arbitration agreements subject to the convention. To enforce an arbitral award under the New York Convention, the successful party need only provide the appropriate national court the original or certified copy of the award and the arbitration agreement. The party against whom the award is rendered has the burden of proving that the award is unenforceable by showing one of five grounds for blocking the award. By limiting these grounds, the convention seeks to eliminate wasteful duplicative litigation following resolution of the dispute. These grounds are as follows:

1. The arbitration agreement is invalid due to the incapacity of a party or because the agreement is not valid under applicable law.
2. A party lacked notice or opportunity to present its case.
3. The award deals with a matter beyond the submission.
4. The composition of the tribunal or its procedure fails to follow the arbitral agreement or the law of the place of arbitration.
5. The award is not yet binding or has been set aside or suspended in the country where it was made.

The New York Convention also permits a court to refuse to enforce the award if the subject of the dispute is not capable of settlement by arbitration in the enforcement jurisdiction or the award is against public policy of the country where the award is sought to be enforced.

U.S. courts have generally been reluctant to void an arbitral award and narrowly construe the defenses permitted under the New York Convention. The same is true for most of the other countries that are signatories to the convention.[13]

In 1975, the United States and most South American nations signed the Inter-American Convention on International Commercial Arbitration, also known as the Panama Convention. Signatories to this convention include Argentina, Bolivia, Brazil, Chile, Columbia, Costa Rica, the Dominican Republic, Ecuador, El Salvador, Guatemala, Honduras, Mexico, Nicaragua, Panama, Paraguay, Peru, the United States, Uruguay, and Venezuela. This convention provides for the general enforceability of arbitration agreements and arbitral awards subject to specified exceptions that are similar to those found in the New York Convention. The Panama Convention contains a fallback on procedural rules that is not found in the New York Convention. Where the parties have not expressly agreed to any institutional or other arbitration rules, the rules of the "Inter-American Commercial Arbitration Commission" will govern. These rules are essentially the same as the UNCITRAL arbitration rules, described below. The Federal Arbitration Act, which is the implementation legislation in the United States with respect to both the New York Convention and the Panama Convention, provides that if both the New York and Panama Conventions apply, the Panama Convention will govern.

2. National Laws on Arbitration

Most countries that are signatories to the New York Convention have implemented the convention through national legislation. The manner in which the convention is implemented is therefore dependent on such national legislation and its judicial interpretation. Thus, it is important to know not only whether the host country is a signatory to

Practice Tip

In choosing the country where the arbitration will be conducted, those countries that restrict judicial interference the most are preferred.

the New York Convention, but also how its implementation legislation works.

In addition, it is important to review the arbitration laws of the country of the situs of arbitration. As noted above, the laws of the country where the arbitration takes place can have a significant procedural impact on the manner in which the arbitration will be conducted. One should determine the degree of sanctioned judicial interference into the arbitration process and the flexibility conferred on the parties in establishing the manner in which the arbitration will be conducted.[14] In general, it is preferable to be in a country that severely limits the role of the courts in the arbitration process and provides the parties with significant autonomy in the manner in which the arbitration is conducted.

In the United States, the implementation legislation for the New York Convention has been incorporated into the Federal Arbitration Act, which reflects a strong policy favoring arbitration proceedings and enforcing arbitral awards. Likewise, many developed countries have adopted legislation providing for effective support of the arbitral process. These countries include Austria, Belgium, England, France, Spain, The Netherlands and Switzerland. However, other countries still remain suspicious toward international commercial arbitration, particularly countries in Latin America and the Middle East. To promote international commercial arbitration, UNCITRAL has adopted a model law on international commercial arbitration, which has been adopted by a number of countries.

a. Federal Arbitration Act. In the United States, international arbitrations are governed by the Federal Arbitration Act of 1947, 9 U.S.C. §§ 1–6 (FAA), a copy of which is included as Appendix 3 at the end of this chapter. The FAA was amended in 1970 to implement the New York Convention and in 1990 to implement the Panama Convention. The purpose of the FAA is to ensure that U.S. courts recognize and enforce arbitration agreements. Under the FAA, parties have autonomy to craft their own procedures for arbitrations, including choice of law, the number of arbitrators, situs of the arbitration, and the election, if any, of an administrative arbitral agency.

The FAA applies to both domestic and international arbitrations. It provides that arbitration agreements "shall be valid, irrevocable, and enforceable, save upon such grounds as exist at law or in equity for the revocation of any contract."[15] The FAA requires "any court of the United States" to stay proceedings if they involve issues that are "referrable to arbitration" and requires U.S. District Courts to issue orders compelling arbitration under appropriate circumstances. The act also permits U.S. District Courts to issue a compulsory process to assist arbitrators in taking evidence.

While there are arbitration statutes in virtually all U.S. states, their impact on arbitration matters is limited due to the broad preemptive effect given to the FAA.[16] Several states, including California, Connecticut, Oregon, and Texas, have adopted the UNCITRAL Model Law, described below, to fill the gaps in the FAA.

b. Arbitration Laws of Foreign Countries. Many countries have enacted arbitration regulations with varying degrees of judicial interference. The most common arbitration law enacted outside the U.S. is the model arbitration law drafted by UNCITRAL and adopted by the United Nations General Assembly in December 1985. The UNCITRAL Model Law, in considerable detail, supplements the New York Convention and provides a consistent framework for the UNCITRAL Arbitration Rules, described below. It is intended to harmonize international commercial arbitration, and has been adopted by a number of countries, including Australia, Bahrain, Bermuda, Bulgaria, Canada, Cyprus, Egypt, Germany, Guatemala, Hong Kong, Hungary, India, Islamic Republic of Iran, Kenya, Lithuania, Malta, Mexico, New Zealand, Nigeria, Oman, Peru, Russian Federation, Scotland, Singapore, Slovenia, Sri Lanka, Tunisia, Ukraine, and Zimbabwe. The UNCITRAL Model Law is also more comprehensive than the FAA, leading a number of states to adopt it to fill in the gaps left in the FAA.

Although the model law's impact on promoting international commercial arbitration will ultimately depend on its interpretation by national courts, it supplements the New York Convention with a detailed legal framework for international arbitration that clarifies the grounds for vacating awards and clearly defines the scope of national court interference in, and assistance to, the arbitration process. The model law contains provisions concerning the scope of permissible judicial intervention (Chapter I, Article 5); the enforcement of arbitration agreements and the provision of interim court measures (Chapter II); the composition of arbitral tribunals and grounds and procedures for challenges (Chapter III); the competence of the arbitral tribunal to rule on its own jurisdiction and to order interim measures (Chapter IV); the manner in which arbitral proceedings are conducted, including court assistance in taking evidence (Chapter V); the issuance of the award (Chapter VI); recourse against an award (Chapter VII); and recognition and enforcement of the award, including grounds for refusal (Chapter VIII).

C. ARBITRATION PROCEDURES (INSTITUTIONAL ADMINISTRATION VERSUS *AD HOC*)

As in the selection of the governing law, the parties are free to select the procedural rules that are to govern the arbitration proceeding. In doing so, the parties may either elect to obtain assistance from one of many administrative institutions or to establish their own *ad hoc* procedures.

In determining the procedural law, parties may agree to use the services of an institutional arbitration agency or organization such as the AAA, the LCIA, or the ICC, as well as others, such as the World Intellectual Property Organization (WIPO) or the Stockholm Chamber of Commerce (SCC). More recently, The Center for Public Resources (CPR) has entered the field of international mediation and arbitration.

These organizations, with their own procedural rules, are particularly helpful to those companies with little or no international arbitration experience. The assistance these organizations may provide includes the selection and establishment of an arbitral tribunal and administrative functions such as establishing the location, date, and time for the arbitration proceeding. Another significant consideration is that these organizations may add legitimacy to an arbitration proceeding, facilitating the enforcement of an arbitral award.

Practice Tip

The parties need to weigh the advantages and disadvantages of institutional and *ad hoc* arbitration proceedings, as well as the various international arbitration institutions.

The ICC, headquartered in Paris, is the most commonly used institution for international arbitrations. It also provides the greatest institutional involvement in the arbitration proceedings and, accordingly, has a significant fee structure in addition to the fees to be paid to the arbitrators. The ICC reviews the final award to ensure its enforceability.

Although the AAA is known primarily for domestic arbitrations, it has become very active in international arbitrations and now has separate rules for international commercial arbitrations, which are different from the domestic commercial arbitration rules. The fee structure for the AAA is considerably less than the ICC, but some have suggested that the quality of the organizationally selected arbitrators, in the event the parties are unable to agree, is generally better with the ICC.

The LCIA, headquartered in London, is the oldest international arbitration organization. The LCIA historically has been steeped in British traditions, but has more recently moved more toward becoming a truly global institution with arbitrators from around the world. Its administrative involvement is less than the ICC. It also does not have quite the volume of arbitration filings as either the ICC or the AAA.

WIPO, established in 1994, is a relatively newer arbitration center. Its rules of arbitration are very similar to the ICC. One of the major advantages to using the WIPO in connection with international arbitrations relating to intellectual property is that the arbitrators, listed in their database, have expertise in intellectual property matters. In 1999, the WIPO handled one arbitration. As of August 2000, over 1,000 arbitration claims had been filed with the WIPO.

Finally, CPR, based in New York, has become active in international mediations and published its international arbitration rules in September 2000. Unlike the other organizations, CPR is less involved in administrative oversight and acts more as an appointing authority for arbitrators in the event the parties themselves cannot agree. In this respect, CPR may be an appropriate candidate to serve as the appointing authority in connection with ad hoc arbitrations.

An alternative to the rules associated with an institutional arbitration is an *ad hoc* arbitration. An ad hoc arbitration is a proceeding in which the parties themselves structure the procedural rules of the arbitration. Such structure can range from a totally custom-crafted proceeding to a proceeding that relies on institutional rules, such as the UNCITRAL Arbitration Rules. Most ad hoc arbitration proceedings use the UNCITRAL Arbitration Rules.

D. OTHER ISSUES IMPACTING INTERNATIONAL ARBITRATION

1. Arbitration Situs

The site of the arbitration proceeding is a significant decision for several reasons. First, as noted above, the FAA will only recognize awards rendered in those countries that are signatories to the New York Convention or the Panama Convention. Second, some national courts might interfere with, or may not support, the arbitration proceeding. Such interference can include mandatory requirements for interlocutory judicial resolution of issues of law, or interference in such matters as procedural rules or selection of arbitral situs. Alternatively, the court might refuse to enforce the order of an arbitrator to turn over certain factual materials. Third, some nations require that a local lawyer of the country participate in the international arbitration proceeding.[17] Finally, the availability of air, rail, and road transportation, hotels, and the law of the nation in which the arbitration is to be held may impact the arbitration itself.

2. *Separability*

The "separability" doctrine is widely recognized throughout the world. It provides that an arbitration clause is separate and autonomous from the agreement that is the subject of arbitration. According to the Supreme Court's decision in *Prima Paint Corp. v. Flood & Conklin Manufacturing Co.*,[18] "except where the parties otherwise intend . . . arbitration clauses as a matter of federal law are 'separable' from the contracts in which they are embedded. . . ." The rationale is that the parties' agreement to arbitrate "formed a quid pro quo of one another and constitute a separable and enforceable part of the agreement."[19] Accordingly, the fact that the enforceability of an agreement may be tainted by fraud, for example, does not mean that the arbitration provision in the agreement would necessarily also be tainted.

The doctrine of "'Kompetenz-Kompetenz' concerns the allocation of authority between arbitrators and national courts over the interpretation and enforceability of the parties' arbitration agreement."[20] Many of the international arbitral bodies and national laws have provided for arbitrators to determine their own jurisdiction.[21] At a minimum, the doctrine means that arbitrators can determine their own jurisdiction, and do not need to request a judicial decision.

The applicability of the Kompetenz-Kompetenz doctrine is not clear in the United States. The Supreme Court in *AT&T Technologies, Inc. v. Communications Workers of America*, held that:

> [u]nder our decisions, whether or not the company was bound to arbitrate, as well as what issues it must arbitrate, is a matter to be determine by the Court on the basis of the contract entered into by the parties. . . . The duty to arbitrate being of contractual origin, a compulsory submission to arbitration cannot precede judicial determination that the collective bargaining agreement does in fact create such a duty.[22]

This language clearly states that the question of arbitration is one for the judiciary and not the arbitrator. However, a number of lower courts have concluded that the *AT&T Technologies* holding was limited to the labor context and not applicable to the FAA.[23] As a result, lower courts are divided over the applicability of the doctrine.

3. The Number and Selection of Arbitrators

One of the most important decisions a party will make in an arbitration proceeding is the selection and size of the arbitration tribunal. The number of arbitrators may be written in the contract. Typically, an arbitration tribunal consists of one or three arbitrators. There are a number of considerations to take into account when selecting the size of the tribunal.

The advantage in selecting a single arbitrator is the cost. Obviously, the arbitrator fees will be higher with more arbitrators. Scheduling may also be more difficult with a larger arbitration tribunal. On the other hand, a single arbitrator raises the concern of a greater risk of an erroneous award. It is generally believed that multiple arbitrators tend to provide a better-balanced decision.

Once the size of the tribunal is chosen, the selection of the arbitrators can be vital. Arbitrators will govern the management of the case, decide on discovery requests, and make the final decision. If a party needs discovery to assist in its fact-finding, that party is more likely to choose an arbitrator from a common law nation. A party wanting to limit discovery might choose an arbitrator from a civil law nation.

To ensure competency of arbitrators, the parties may establish minimum qualifications and experience that an arbitrator must meet. Additionally, some arbitration organizations will discourage the use of an arbitrator that is from the same nation as any of the parties.

4. Discovery

The extensive discovery tools used in U.S. litigation (for example, depositions, interrogatories, and document production) are seldom available in an arbitration proceeding. Generally, the decision to order discovery and the extent of such discovery is left to the discretion of the arbitrator. Two factors, the arbitrator's experience with discovery and the arbitrator's interest, affect this decision. If an arbitrator's experience in litigation and arbitration matters is limited to the production of documents, the arbitrator may not be inclined to provide for depositions or interrogatories. Arbitrators from civil law nations in which party-initiated discovery is not the norm are reluctant to order such discovery. Common law lawyers, particularly those from the United

States, are more accustomed to a party-directed adversarial process and freewheeling discovery. Where the arbitrators and lawyers are from such countries, some measure of discovery is not uncommon. An arbitral tribunal's interest in discovery may also be limited because it generally lacks the direct authority to sanction disobedience and the resources to supervise the process.

To develop a more consistent approach on discovery and presentation of evidence in international arbitrations, the International Bar Association has adopted the "Supplementary Rules Governing the Presentation and Reception of Evidence in International Commercial Arbitration." These rules provide a blend of civil law and common law approaches to discovery and evidentiary presentation and can be incorporated by reference in an arbitration clause to enhance the certainty of the manner in which the arbitration will be conducted.

5. Types of Awards

Monetary relief is the typical award in arbitrations; however, injunctive relief may also be possible. In the United States, courts have recognized an arbitrator's award that includes injunctive or equitable relief. In *Island Creek Coal Sales v. City of Gainesville*, the court held that "[t]he Agreement here does not provide any specific limitations on the power of the arbitrators under [AAA] Rule 43, and we are required to give deference to the arbitrators' interpretation of the Rule and the Agreement unless they have clearly exceeded this authority."[24] One needs to consult the rules of the particular arbitration organization selected and the laws of the jurisdiction where the arbitration will be conducted and enforced to determine whether the arbitral tribunal has the authority to issue injunctive relief.

E. COMPARISON OF THE RULES OF THE MAJOR ARBITRATION INSTITUTIONS

The following is a summary of a comparison of the procedural rules of the ICC, AAA, LCIA, and UNCITRAL. (See Appendix 4 at the end of this chapter for a detailed comparison).

Neutrality. All four administrative bodies require the arbitrator to be impartial and neutral. Each organization reserves the right to disqualify or remove an arbitrator if challenged by a party. In addition, the AAA, LCIA, and UNCITRAL rules impose a duty upon the arbitrator to disclose any possible partiality.

Number. The ICC, LCIA, and the AAA rules provide for the appointment of one arbitrator unless the parties have agreed differently or the administrator determines that three are necessary. The UNCITRAL rules provide for three arbitrators, but the parties may agree to one arbitrator.

Nationality of Arbitrators. All four administrative bodies consider the nationality of the arbitrator. The AAA rules state that upon the request of any party, the appointed arbitrator may be a national of a country other than that of any of the parties. The ICC rules provide that the arbitrator will be of a different nationality from any of the parties unless it is determined that the circumstances of the dispute permit an arbitrator that is the nationality of any party to be chosen provided neither party objects. The LCIA prohibits the chairperson of the tribunal or the sole arbitrator to share the same nationality of either party, unless the party not of the same nationality agrees in writing.

Defining Conflict (Change of Claims). All four administrative bodies allow for parties to amend or supplement their claims. However, UNCITRAL and the AAA allow the administrator to consider whether the amendment or supplement is appropriate. In addition, the ICC does not allow any amendments or supplements after the terms of reference have been signed and approved by the court unless authorized by the court.

Discovery. The UNCITRAL, LCIA, and AAA rules specifically state that the arbitrator may require the parties to produce any documents, exhibits, or other evidence during the arbitration. The ICC rules simply state that the arbitrator will use the least amount of time possible to determine the facts of the case. The breadth of discovery under the ICC rules is unclear.

Possible Use of Mediation. The ICC and AAA state in the foreword and introduction to their respective rules that parties may wish to consider mediation (conciliation) but are not required to do so. The LCIA and UNCITRAL rules do not address the possible use of mediation.

Consolidation of Existing Claims. The UNCITRAL and AAA rules state that a party may amend or supplement its claim during the arbitral proceedings provided that the amendment or supplement does not fall outside the scope of the arbitration agreement. The ICC rules state that once the terms of reference are defined, the submission of new claims or counterclaims is prohibited unless authorized by the court. Under the LCIA rules, the arbitrator has the power to allow a party to amend its case, defense, or reply upon application by the party or by the arbitrator's own motion. However, such amendments may not be permitted until *after* a hearing or receipt of representations by both parties.

Timing. The ICC rules state the arbitral tribunal must render its award within six months from the signing of the terms of reference. This time limit may be extended by the court upon a request from the arbitral tribunal. The UNCITRAL, LCIA, and AAA rules do not address the time frame within which a decision must be rendered.

Default of Judgment. The ICC, LCIA, and AAA rules permit the arbitral tribunal to continue with the arbitration should a party fail to take part in the arbitration (for example, failing to file a statement of defense or failing to appear at a hearing).

Severability of Issues/Awards. The UNCITRAL, LCIA, and AAA rules provide for the arbitral tribunal's right to make interim, interlocutory, or partial orders or awards. The ICC rules do not address this issue.

Mechanics (Stenographic Report of Hearing). The UNCITRAL rules state that the arbitral tribunal will make arrangements for a record of the hearing if it is deemed necessary or if the parties have so agreed. The ICC, LCIA, and AAA do not address the mechanics of the hearings.

Language. The ICC, LCIA, and UNCITRAL rules provide that, subject to any agreement between the parties, the language of the arbitration will be determined by the arbitral tribunal. The AAA rules state that unless otherwise agreed by the parties, the language of the arbitration will be that of the documents containing the arbitration agreement.

Interpreters. The UNCITRAL, LCIA, and AAA rules provide for the translation or interpretation of documents and oral statements if it is deemed necessary. The ICC rules do not have such a provision.

Time Extensions. The UNCITRAL and AAA rules state that the time periods for the communication of written statements may be extended by the arbitral tribunal. The LCIA rules permit the arbitrators to extend or abbreviate any time limit. The ICC rules do not discuss time extensions with respect to the parties' written statements; however they do provide for the extension of the six-month time limit for the submission of the award by the arbitral tribunal.

Ad Hoc. The UNCITRAL rules were established for ad hoc arbitration. The ICC, AAA, and LCIA rules were established for administered, rather than ad hoc, arbitration.

F. JUDICIAL RESOLUTION OF DISPUTES

While modern legal developments have provided alternative means of dispute resolution, traditional court action is still the ultimate means to resolve disputes. In an international context, the quality of courts can vary dramatically from country to country, which may affect a party's willingness to select judicial resolution over other forms of dispute resolution.[25] When a country's court system provides a reasonably speedy and fair trial, there are often clear advantages of adjudication over other forms of dispute resolution.

Practice Tip

Despite giving the franchisee the "local court" advantage, consideration should be given to judicial resolution in the host country if its judiciary has a reputation for competence and fairness.

Perhaps most importantly, a decision of a court is backed by the enforcement mechanisms of the government of the nation in which it is rendered. Thus, if there is nonpayment of debt and no justifiable reason for nonpayment, a court proceeding may be the best way to ensure enforcement of a ruling in favor of the unpaid party.[26] Furthermore, decisions of courts are appealable, which protects parties against arbitrary rulings inconsistent with precedent. Litigation can also be attractive to a party who wants to take advantage of the public aspects of a trial.[27] Parties to litigation generally also have greater assurance of due process protections and procedural restraints, such as rules of evidence.[28] Generally, as a court is governed by established procedures, precedent, and public norms, it is a more predictable means of dispute resolution than are others.

There are, however, definite disadvantages to litigation. Commencing litigation in one's home country has the disadvantages that were discussed in the introduction to the choice of forum section of this chapter. On the other hand, if the host country has a judicial system with a reputation for competence and evenhandedness, choosing the host country's courts as the forum for resolving disputes may be a viable alternative to international arbitration. As a practical matter, in connection with a franchise termination, a U.S. franchisor may have no choice but to ultimately proceed through the court system of the host country. Even if the agreement provides for binding international arbitration and the arbitral tribunal has issued injunctive relief to prohibit continued use of intellectual property rights or to prohibit competitive activities, that order, if not voluntarily complied with, would need to be enforced through the courts of the host country.

Of course, one should avoid using judicial resolution of an international dispute in a host country that does not have a developed body of commercial law or a judiciary that does not have a reputation for competence and evenhandedness.

G. OTHER DISPUTE RESOLUTION MECHANISMS: NEGOTIATION AND MEDIATION

Given the myriad cultures and legal regimes, as well as the costs and interests of the parties, the selection of a dispute resolution method in each transaction should be carefully considered. Some forms of dispute resolution are culturally disfavored, while others are preferred. In China and Japan for example, where litigating a dispute is considered dishonorable, conciliation and compromise are the preferred means of dispute resolution.

Moreover, even if litigation or arbitration are acceptable means to resolve a dispute, and the appropriate mechanisms have been provided for in the agreement, negotiation and mediation are often the principal means to resolve a dispute in an international commercial relationship. As noted above, there are distinct disadvantages to both binding dispute resolution mechanisms that can adversely impact both parties. These disadvantages provide a strong incentive for parties to try to resolve their differences voluntarily. In this author's view, international franchise disputes are therefore much less likely than domestic franchise disputes to end up in litigation or arbitration. A vast majority of these disputes are resolved through private negotiations with or without the assistance of mediators.

Mediation is a private, nonbinding, voluntary, and informal method of dispute resolution. Mediation involves the use of a neutral third-party mediator to assist disputing parties in reaching a voluntary resolution of their conflict. It differs from arbitration and litigation in that the conflict is not resolved by a neutral third-party (that is, the arbitrator or judge) but rather by the parties themselves with the assistance of the mediator.[29] The entire mediation process is noncompulsory, and it can be terminated by either party if a mutual agreement appears unlikely.

Accordingly, parties who believe mutual agreement to a resolution is possible frequently use mediation. It may be especially attractive (1) if the parties have an ongoing relationship that will extend beyond the duration of the conflict; (2) in instances where arbitration or litigation resolution is problematic; or (3) in countries where the culture encourages conciliation and compromise.

Internationally, various organizations such as UNCITRAL, the ICC, CPR, and the International Council for Societies of Industrial Design (ICSID) supply guidelines that parties electing mediation may adopt. Parties insert an appropriate clause in their contracts electing to mediate future disputes under the guidelines of a particular organization. Of course, not having such a clause does not mean that the parties cannot initially agree to involve such procedures when a dispute arises.

A benefit of mediation over litigation is that it takes place in a nonpublic forum, which may be attractive to parties in situations where privacy is valuable. Further, through mediation parties have more control over the resolution of the dispute than in either litigation or arbitration because the mediator, unlike the judge or arbitrator, lacks authority to resolve the situation. Another benefit of mediation, relative to other forms of dispute resolution, is the relative lack of formal procedural restraints such as rules of evidence. The lack of formal procedural restraints can enhance communication between the parties and lead to innovative solutions. Perhaps the most attractive aspect of mediation over litigation or arbitration, however, is the cost savings realized as a result of avoiding costly legal or arbitration processes.

There are, however, reasons that a party would opt against mediation. First, mediation is likely to be successful only where the parties are indeed interested in resolving the dispute. Second, as the mediator has no power to impose a settlement, mediation is a process that will not necessarily result in a resolution, despite the time and expense dedicated to the process. Third, mediated resolutions are nonbinding and unenforceable. Fourth, the lack of procedural restraints, while a benefit in some circumstances, can also work against parties, as it may restrict access to information and deprive parties of due process safeguards.

IV. Issues, Choices, and Considerations

The following is a brief outline of dispute resolution issues, the choices that might be selected, and considerations in making such decisions.

A. CHOICE OF LAW

- Home state law:
  - provides certainty
  - familiar to franchisor
  - unfamiliar to franchisee
- Host country law:
  - is there a developed body of commercial law?
  - how are franchise relationships treated?
  - familiar to franchisee
  - unfamiliar to franchisor
- Neutral country law:
  - is there a developed body of commercial law?
  - how are franchise relationships treated?
  - unfamiliar to franchisor and franchisee
  - does the transaction meet a reasonable relationship test?
- Law of another state in the United States where there is a sophisticated body of commercial law (for example, New York):
  - does the transaction meet a reasonable relationship test?
  - provides certainty
  - familiar to franchisor
  - unfamiliar to franchisee
- *Ex æquo et bono:*
  - uncertainty for both franchisor and franchisee
  - requires a reasonable and sophisticated arbitrator
- No choice of law:
  - uncertainty as to the parties' rights and obligations

B. CHOICE OF FORUM: LITIGATION OR ARBITRATION

- Require parties to litigate in the home state:
  - jurisdiction over defendant
  - enforcement of judgment: in the United States, and in host country unless there is a treaty
  - enforcement is discretionary under international principles of comity
  - does it prevent the defendant from starting a parallel action in the host country?
- Require parties to litigate in the host country:
  - judiciary with a reputation for sophistication and neutrality?

enforcement of adverse judgment in the United States?

- Require binding arbitration:
  recognition and enforcement in 126 countries
  avoids protracted and potentially expensive proceedings
  availability of the New York Convention and other conventions for recognition and enforcement
  arbitration law of the country where the arbitration is conducted; extent of judicial intervention?
  host country enabling legislation
  practical experience in enforcement

C. ARBITRATION ISSUES

- Place of arbitration:
  home: convenient to franchisor; inconvenient to franchisee
  host: inconvenient to franchisor; convenient to franchisee; extent of judicial intervention
  third-country neutral: convenience to the parties; extent of judicial intervention; impact of host country laws on arbitration proceeding or choice of law
- Arbitral Bodies/Rules
  for a comparison of the four major arbitral bodies, see Appendix 4 to this chapter
  for sample arbitration clauses, see Appendix 5 to this chapter
- Number of Arbitrators
  single arbitrator: cost advantages; greater risk of an erroneous award
  multiple arbitrators: better-balanced decision; greater costs
- Types of relief
  limited to monetary awards: insufficient protection for trademark and intellectual property; permits recovery of fees and payments
  including injunctive relief: prohibits improper use of trademark and intellectual property; Does the arbitrator have the authority? Will an injunction be enforceable in the host country?

Notes

The author wishes to express his appreciation for the valuable contributions of Christopher A. Nowak, an associate at Hogan & Hartson, L.L.P.

1. *See, e.g.*, GARY B. BORN, INTERNATIONAL COMMERCIAL ARBITRATION IN THE UNITED STATES 120 (1994); INTERNATIONAL ALTERNATIVE DISPUTE RESOLUTION (William A. Hancock ed., Business Laws, Inc.) (1997); MARTIN DOMKE, DOMKE ON COMMERCIAL ARBITRATION (1999).

2. AAA International Rules Art. 28(1), at http://www.adr.org/; LCIA Rules Art. 22.3 at http://www.lcia-arbitration.com/lcia/rulecost/english.htm; ICC Rules Art. 17(1) at http://www.iccwbo.org/court/english/arbitration/rules.asp; UNCITRAL Rules Art. 33(1) at http://www.uncitral.org/en-index.htm; RESTATEMENT (SECOND) CONFLICT OF LAWS § 187 (1969 and Supp. 1988).

3. John R. F. Baer et. al., *Application of U.S. Franchise Laws to International Franchise Sales*, 15 FRAN. L.J. 41 (1995); John R. F. Baer, et. al., *Application of U.S. Franchise Laws to International Franchise Sales*, 15 FRAN. L.J. 107 (1996).

4. *E.g.*, California and New Jersey. *See, e.g.*, Vylene Enterprises, Inc. v. Naugles, Inc., 90 F.3d 1472 (9th Cir. 1996); Postal Instant Press v. Sealy, 51 Cal. Rptr. 2d 365 (Cal. Ct. App. 1996); Sons of Thunder v. Borden, Inc., 690 A.2d 575 (N.J. 1997).

5. RESTATEMENT (SECOND) CONFLICT OF LAWS § 187.

6. *See, e.g.*, ICC Rules Art. 18(3).

7. Multilateral and bilateral treaties on the enforcement of foreign judgments are not common. The most prominent treaty in that regard is the Treaty of Brussels regarding enforcement of judgments within the European countries.

8. *See*, Hilton v. Guyst, 159 U.S. 113 (1895). Several states have codified the principles of comity set forth in *Hilton* by adopting the Uniform Foreign Money Judgments Recognition Act.

9. One should also be aware that some countries may have mandatory laws or laws reflecting strong public policy that may not be arbitrated. For example, competition law issues may not be arbitrated in Germany.

10. Copies of the New York Convention and the Panama Convention are at the end of this chapter as Appendix 1 and Appendix 2 respectively.

11. As of January 17, 2001, the following countries and territories have signed the New York Convention: Algeria, Antigua and Barbuda, Argentina, Armenia, Australia, Austria, Azerbaijan, Bahrain, Bangladesh, Barbados, Belarus, Belgium, Benin, Bermuda, Bolivia, Bosnia and Herzegovina, Botswana, Brunei Darussalam, Bulgaria, Burkina Faso, Cambodia, Cameroon, Canada, Central African Republic, Chile, China, Colombia, Costa Rica, Côte d'Ivoire, Croatia, Cuba, Cyprus, Czech Republic, Denmark, Djibouti, Dominica, Ecuador, Egypt, El Salvador, Estonia, Finland, France, Georgia, Germany, Ghana, Greece, Guatemala, Guinea, Haiti, Holy See, Honduras, Hungary, India, Indonesia, Ireland, Israel, Italy, Japan, Jordan, Kazakhstan, Kenya, Kuwait, Kyrgyzstan, Lao People's Democratic Republic, Latvia, Lebanon, Lesotho, Lithuania, Luxembourg, Madagascar, Malaysia, Mali, Malta, Mauritania, Mauritius, Mexico, Moldova, Monaco, Mongolia, Morocco, Mozambique, Nepal, The Netherlands, New Zealand, Niger, Nigeria, Norway, Oman, Pak-

istan, Panama, Paraguay, Peru, Philippines, Poland, Portugal, Republic of Korea, Romania, Russian Federation, Saint Vincent and the Grenadines, San Marino, Saudi Arabia, Senegal, Singapore, Slovakia, Slovenia, South Africa, Spain, Sri Lanka, Sweden, Switzerland, Syrian Arab Republic, Thailand, The former Yugoslav Republic of Macedonia, Trinidad and Tobago, Tunisia, Turkey, Uganda, Ukraine, United Kingdom of Great Britain and Northern Ireland, United Republic of Tanzania, United States of America, Uruguay, Uzbekistan, Venezuela, Vietnam, Yugoslavia, Zimbabwe.

12. Scherk v. Alberto-Culver Co., 417 U.S. 506, 520 (1974).

13. However, a few countries, such as China, Indonesia, and India, have refused arbitral awards on grounds not delineated in the New York Convention. While reforms in China and India have begun, enforcement of arbitral awards in these countries is questionable.

14. *Cf.* In Re Chromalloy Aeroservices, 939 F. Supp. 907 (D.D.C. 1996) (enforcing an award that was set aside by an Egyptian court on the basis that the parties in the case (including the Egyptian government itself) had agreed in the contract that there would be "no appeal or other recourse" against the award).

15. 9 U.S.C. § 2.

16. *See, e.g.*, Southland Corp. v. Keating, 465 U.S. 1 (1984); Volt Info. Sciences, Inc. v. Board of Trustees, 489 U.S. 468, 479 (1989); Mastrobuono v. Shearson Lehman Hutton, Inc., 514 U.S. 52 (1995).

17. *See* Builders Federal (Hong Kong) Ltd. v. Turner Construction, 1987 WL 15122 (S.D.N.Y. July 28, 1987) (Singapore court enjoined a U.S. law firm from representing the respondents in an arbitration sited in Singapore. Subsequently altered by legislation, but still requires Singapore counsel's participation.); Born, *supra* note 1, at 74 n. 156.

18. Prima Paint Corp. v. Flood & Conklin Mfg. Co., 388 U.S. 395, 402 (1967).

19. *Id.*

20. *See* BORN, *supra* note 1, at 193.

21. *See* UNCITRAL Rules Art. 21; AAA International Rules Art. 15; European Convention on International Commercial Arbitration, Apr. 21, 1961, art. V(3), 484 U.S.T. 364.

22. AT&T Tech., Inc. v. Communications Workers of America, 475 U.S. 643, 649 (1986).

23. Dougherty v. Mieczkowski, 661 F. Supp. 267 (D. Del. 1987); *see also* Galt v. Libbey-Owens-Ford Glass Co., 397 F.2d 439, 441–42 (7th Cir.) *cert. denied*, 393 U.S. 925 (1968) ("Questions of arbitrability are initially for the arbitrators.").

24. Island Creek Coal Sales v. City of Gainesville, 729 F.2d 1046, 1049 (6th Cir. 1984).

25. *See* Michael Pryles, *Assessing Dispute Resolution Procedures*, 7 AM. REV. INT'L ARB. 267, 275 (1996).

26. *Id.* at 275.

27. *See* JOHN W. COOLEY, MEDIATION ADVOCACY 5–8 (1996).

28. *Id.* at 8.

29. *Id.* at 2.

Appendix 1
United Nations Convention on the Recognition and Enforcement of Foreign Arbitral Awards (New York Convention)

Article I

1. This Convention shall apply to the recognition and enforcement of arbitral awards made in the territory of a State other than the State where the recognition and enforcement of such awards are sought, and arising out of differences between persons, whether physical or legal. It shall also apply to arbitral awards not considered as domestic awards in the State where their cognition and enforcement are sought.

2. The term "arbitral awards" shall include not only awards made by arbitrators appointed for each case but also those made by permanent arbitral bodies to which the parties have submitted.

3. When signing, ratifying or acceding to this Convention, or notifying extension under article X hereof, any State may on the basis of reciprocity declare that it will apply the Convention to the cognition and enforcement of awards made only in the territory of another Contracting State. It may also declare that it will apply the Convention only to differences arising out of legal relationships, whether contractual or not, which are considered as commercial under the national law of the State making such declaration.

Article II

1. Each contracting State shall recognize an agreement in writing under which the parties undertake to submit to arbitration all or any differences which have arisen or which may arise between them in respect of a defined legal relationship, whether contractual or not, concerning a subject matter capable of settlement by arbitration.

2. The term "agreement in writing" shall include an arbitral clause in a contract or an arbitration agreement, signed by the parties or contained in an exchange of letters or telegrams.

3. The court of a Contracting State, when seized of an action in a matter in respect of which the parties have made an agreement within the meaning of this article, shall, at the request of one of the parties, refer the parties to arbitration, unless it finds that the said agreement is null and void, inoperative or incapable of being performed.

Article III

Each Contracting State shall recognize arbitral awards as binding and enforce them in accordance with the rules of procedure of the territory where the award is relied upon, under the conditions laid down in the following articles. There shall not be imposed substantially more onerous conditions or higher fees or charges on the recognition or enforcement of arbitral awards to which this Convention applies that are imposed on the recognition or enforcement of domestic arbitral awards.

Article IV

1. To obtain the recognition and enforcement mentioned in the preceding article, the party applying for recognition and enforcement shall, at the time of the application, supply:

(a) The duly authenticated original award or a duly certified copy thereof;

(b) The original agreement referred to in article II or a duly certified copy thereof.

2. If the said award or agreement is not made in an official language of the country in which the award is relied upon, the party applying for recognition and enforcement of the award shall produce a translation of these documents into such language. The translation shall be certified by an official or sworn translator or by a diplomatic or consular agent.

Article V

1. Recognition and enforcement of the award may be refused, at the request of the party against whom it is invoked, only if that party furnishes to the competent authority where the recognition and enforcement is sought, proof that:

(a) The parties to the agreement referred to in article II were, under the law applicable to them, under some incapacity, or the said agreement is not valid under the law to which the parties have subjected it or, failing any indication thereon, under the law of the country where the award was made; or

(b) The party against whom the award is invoked was not given proper notice of the appointment of the arbitrator or of the arbitration proceedings or was otherwise unable to present his case; or

(c) The award deals with a difference not contemplated by or not falling within the terms of the submission to arbitration, or it contains decisions on matters beyond the scope of the submission to arbitration, provided that, if the decisions on matters submitted to arbitration can be separated from those not so submitted, that part of the award which contain decisions on matters submitted to arbitration may be recognized and enforced; or

(d) The composition of the arbitral authority or the arbitral procedure was not in accordance with the agreement of the parties, or, failing such agreement, was not in accordance with the law of the country where the arbitration took place; or

(e) The award has not yet become binding on the parties, or has been set aside or suspended by a competent authority of the country in which, or under the law of which, that award was made.

2. Recognition and enforcement of an arbitral award may also be refused if the competent authority in the country where recognition and enforcement is sought finds that:

(a) The subject matter of the difference is not capable of settlement by arbitration under the law of that county; or

(b) The recognition or enforcement of the award would be contrary to the public policy of that country.

Article VI

If an application for the setting aside or suspension of the award has been made to a competent authority referred to in article V(1)(e), the authority before which the award is sought to be relied upon may, if it considers it proper, adjourn the decision on the enforcement of the award and may also, on the application of the party claiming enforcement of the award, order the other party to give suitable security.

Article VII

1. The provisions of the present Convention shall not affect the validity of multilateral or bilateral agreements concerning the recognition and enforcement of arbitral awards entered into by the Contracting States nor deprive any interested party of any right he may have to avail himself of an arbitral award in the manner and to the extent allowed by the law or the treaties of the country where such award is sought to be relied upon.

2. The Geneva Protocol on Arbitration Clauses of 1923 and the Geneva Convention on the Execution of Foreign Arbitral Awards of 1927 [27 LNTS 157; 92 LNTS 301] shall cease to have effect between Contracting States on their becoming bound and to the extent that they become bound, by this Convention.

Article VIII

1. This Convention shall be open until 31 December 1958 for signature on behalf of any Member of the United Nations and also on behalf of any other State which is or hereafter becomes a member of any specialized agency of the United Nations, or which is or hereafter becomes a party to the Statute of the International Court of Justice [T.S. 993; 59 Stat. 1055], or any other State to which an invitation has been addressed by the General Assembly of the United Nations.

2. This Convention shall be ratified and the instrument of ratification shall be deposited with the Secretary-General of the United Nations.

Article IX

1. This Convention shall be open for accession to all States referred to in article VIII.

2. Accession shall be effected by the deposit of an instrument of accession with the Secretary-General of the United Nations.

Article X

1. Any State may, at the time of signature, ratification or accession, declare that this Convention shall extend to all or any of the territories for the international relations of which it is responsible. Such a declaration shall take effect when the Convention enters into force for the State concerned.

2. At any time thereafter any such extension shall be made by notification addressed to the Secretary-General of the United Nations and shall take effect as from the ninetieth day after the day of receipt by the Secretary-General of the United Nations of this notification, or as from the date of entry into force of the Convention for the State concerned, whichever is the later.

3. With respect to those territories to which this Convention is not extended at the time of signature, ratification or accession, each New York Convention State concerned shall consider the possibility of taking the necessary steps in order to extend the application of this Convention to such territories subject, where necessary for constitutional reasons, to the consent of the Governments of such territories.

Article XI

In the case of a federal or non-unitary State, the following provisions shall apply:

(a) With respect to those articles of this Convention that come within the legislative jurisdiction of the federal authority, the obligations of the Federal Government shall to this extent be the same as those of Contracting States which are not federal States;

(b) With respect to those articles of this Convention that come within the legislative jurisdiction of constituent states or provinces which are not, under the constitutional system of the federation, bound to take legislative action, the federal Government shall bring such articles with a favourable recommendation to the notice of the appropriate authorities of constituent states or provinces at the earliest possible moment;

(c) A federal State Party to this Convention shall, at the request of any other Contracting State transmitted through the Secretary General of the United Nations, supply a statement of the law and practice of the federation and its constituent units in regard to any particular provision of this Convention, showing the extent to which effect has been given to that provision by legislative or other action.

Article XII

1. This Convention shall come into force on the ninetieth day following the date of deposit of the third instrument of ratification or accession.

2. For each State ratifying or acceding to this Convention after the deposit of the third instrument of ratification or accession, this Convention shall enter into force on the ninetieth day after deposit by such State of its instrument of ratification or accession.

Article XIII

1. Any Contracting State may denounce this Convention by a written notification to the Secretary-General of the United Nations. Denunciation shall take effect one year after the date of receipt of the notification by the Secretary-General.

2. Any State which has made a declaration or notification under article X may, at any time thereafter, by notification to the Secretary-General of the United Nations, declare that this Convention shall cease to extend to the territory concerned one year after the date of the receipt of the notification by the Secretary-General.

3. This Convention shall continue to be applicable to arbitral awards in respect of which recognition or enforcement proceedings have been instituted before the denunciation takes effect.

Article XIV

A Contracting State shall not be entitled to avail itself of the present Convention against other Contracting States except to the extent that it is itself bound to apply the Convention.

Article XV

The Secretary-General of the United Nations shall notify the States contemplated in article VIII of the following:

(a) Signatures and ratifications in accordance with article VIII;

(b) Accessions in accordance with article IX;

(c) Declarations and notifications under articles I, X and XI;

(d) The date upon which this Convention enters into force in accordance with article XII;

(e) Denunciations and notifications in accordance with article XIII.

Article XVI

1. This Convention, of which the Chinese, English, French, Russian and Spanish texts shall be equally authentic, shall be deposited in the archives of the United Nations.

2. The Secretary-General of the United Nations shall transmit a certified copy of this Convention to the States contemplated in article VIII.

Done at New York June 10, 1958.

(List of signatories)

Appendix 2
Inter-American Convention on International Commercial Arbitration (Panama Convention)

Preamble

The Government of the Members States of the Organization of American States, desirous of concluding a convention on international commercial arbitration, have agreed as follows:

Article 1

An agreement in which the parties undertake to submit to arbitral decision any differences that may arise or have arisen between them with respect to a commercial transaction is valid. The agreement shall be set forth in an instrument signed by the parties, or in the form of an exchange of letters, telegrams, or telex communications.

Article 2

Arbitrators shall be appointed in the manner agreed upon by the parties. Their appointment may be delegated to a third party, whether a natural or juridical person. Arbitrators may be nationals or foreigners.

Article 3

In the absence of an express agreement between the parties, the arbitration shall be conducted in accordance with the Rules of Procedure of the Inter-American Commercial Arbitration Commission.

Article 4

An arbitral decision or award that is not appealable under the applicable law or procedural rules shall have the force of a final judicial judgment. Its execution or recognition may be ordered in the same manner as that of decisions handed down by national or foreign ordinary courts, in accordance with the procedural laws of the country where it is to be executed and the provision of international treaties.

Article 5

1. The recognition and execution of the decision may be refused, at the request of the party against which it is made, only if such party is able to prove to the competent authority of the State in which recognition and execution are requested:

a. That the parties to the agreement were subject to some incapacity under the applicable law or that the agreement is not valid under the law to which the parties have submitted it, or if such law is not specified, under the law of the State in which the decision was made; or

b. That the party against which the arbitral decision has been made was not duly notified of the appointment of the arbitrator or of the arbitration procedure to be followed, or was unable, for any other reason, to present his defense; or

c. That the decision concerns a dispute not envisaged in the agreement between the parties to submit to arbitration; nevertheless, if the provisions of the decision that refer to issues submitted to arbitration can be separated from those not submitted to arbitration, the former may be recognized and executed; or

d. That the constitution of the arbitral tribunal or the arbitration procedure has not been carried out in accordance with the terms of the agreement signed by the parties or, in the absence of such agreement, that the constitution of the arbitral tribunal or the arbitration .procedure has not been carried out in accordance with the law of the State where the arbitration took place; or

e. That the decision is not yet binding on the parties or has been annulled or suspended by a competent authority of the State in which, or according to the law of which, the decision has been made.

2. The recognition and execution of an arbitral decision may also be refused if the competent authority of the State in which the recognition and execution is requested finds:

a. That the subject of the dispute cannot be settled by arbitration under the law of that State; or

b. That the recognition or execution of the decision would be contrary to the public policy ("order public") of that State.

Article 6

If the competent authority mentioned in article 5.1.e has been requested to annul or suspend the arbitral decision, the authority before which such decision is invoked may, if it deems it appropriate, postpone a decision on the execution of the arbitral decision and, at the request of the party requesting execution, may also instruct the other party to provide appropriate guaranties.

Article 7

This Convention shall be open for signature by the Members States of the Organization of American States.

Article 8

This Convention is subject to ratification. The instruments of ratification shall be deposited with the General Secretariat of the Organization of American States.

Article 9

The Convention shall remain open for accession by any other State. The instruments of accession shall be deposited with the General Secretariat of the Organization of American States.

Article 10

This Convention shall enter into force on the thirtieth day following the date of deposit of the second instrument of ratification.

Article 11

If a State Party has two or more territorial units in which different systems of law apply in relation to the matters dealt with in this Convention, it may, at the time of signature, ratification or accession declare that this Convention shall extend to all its territorial units or only to one or more of them.

Such declaration may be modified by subsequent declarations, which shall expressly indicate the territorial unit or units to which the Convention applies. Such subsequent declarations shall be transmitted to the General Secretariat of the Organization of American States, and shall become effective thirty days after the date of their receipt.

Article 12

This Convention shall remain in force indefinitely, but any of the States' Parties may denounce it. The instrument of denunciation shall be deposited with the General Secretariat of the Organization of American States. After one year from the date of deposit of the instrument of denunciation, the Convention shall no longer be in effect for the denouncing State, but shall remain in effect for the other States' Parties.

Article 13

The original instrument of this Convention, the English, French, Portuguese and Spanish texts of which are equally authentic, shall be deposited with the General Secretariat of the Organization of American States. The Secretariat shall notify the Member States of the Organization of American States and the States that have acceded to the Convention of the signatures, deposits of instruments of ratification, accession, and denunciation as well as of reservations, if any. It shall also transmit the declarations referred to in Article 11 of this Convention.

IN WITNESS WHEREOF the undersigned Plenipotentiaries, being duly authorized thereto by their respective Governments, have signed this Convention.

DONE AT PANAMA CITY, Republic of Panama, this thirtieth day or January one thousand nine hundred and seventy five.

ADOPTED AT: PANAMA, PANAMA

DATE: 01/30/75

CONF/ASSEM/MEETING: INTER-AMERICAN SPECIALIZED CONFERENCE ON PRIVATE INTERNATIONAL LAW

ENTRY INTO FORCE: 06/16/76 IN ACCORDANCE WITH ARTICLE 10 OF THE CONVENTION.

DEPOSITORY: GENERAL SECRETARIAT, OAS (ORIGINAL INSTRUMENT AND RATIFICATIONS).

TEXT: OAS, TREATY SERIES, NO. 42.

UN REGISTRATION: 03/20/89 No. 24384 Vol.

OBSERVATIONS: This Convention shall remain open for signature by the Member States of the OAS and for accession by any other State.

GENERAL INFORMATION OF THE TREATY

SIGNATORY COUNTRIES	SIGNATURE	RA/AC/AD	DEPOSIT	INST	INFORMA
Argentina	05/15/91	11/03/94	01/05/95	RA	/ /
Bolivia	08/02/83	10/08/98	04/29/99	RA	/ /
Brazil	01/30/75	08/31/95	11/27/95	RA	/ /
Chile	01/30/75	04/08/76	05/17/76	RA	/ /
Colombia	01/30/75	11/18/86	12/29/86	RA	/ /
Costa Rica	01/30/75	01/02/78	01/20/78	RA	/ /
Dominican Republic	04/18/77	/ /	/ /		/ /
Ecuador	01/30/75	08/06/91	10/23/91	RA	/ /
El Salvador	01/30/75	06/27/80	08/11/80	RA	/ /
Guatemala	01/30/75	07/07/86	08/20/86	RA	/ /
Honduras	01/30/75	01/08/76	03/22/79	RA	/ /
Mexico[1]	10/27/77	02/15/78	03/27/78	RA	/ /
Nicaragua	01/30/75	/ /	/ /		/ /
Panama	01/30/75	11/11/75	12/17/75	RA	/ /
Paraguay[1]	08/26/75	12/02/76	12/15/76	RA	/ /
Peru	04/21/88	05/02/89	05/22/89	RA	/ /
United States[a]	06/09/78	11/10/86	09/27/90	RA	/ /
Uruguay	01/30/75	03/29/77	04/25/77	RA	/ /
Venezuela	01/30/75	03/22/85	05/16/85	RA	/ /

REF = REFERENCE
INST = TYPE OF INSTRUMENT
D = DECLARATION
RA = RATIFICATION
R = RESERVATION
AC = ACCEPTANCE
AD = ACCESSION
INFORMA = INFORMATION REQUIRED BY THE TREATY

NOTES:

1. Mexico, Paraguay:

Signed ad referendum.

a. United States:

(Reservations made at the time of ratification)

In accordance with Article 8 of the Convention, the instrument of ratification of the government of the United States of America was deposited with the Secretary General of the Organization of American States on September 27, 1990.

In ratifying the Convention, the government of the United States of America made the following reservations.

"1. Unless there is an express agreement among the parties to an arbitration agreement to the contrary, where the requirements for application of both the Inter-american Convention on International Commercial Arbitration and the Convention on the Recognition and Enforcement of Foreign Arbitral Awards are met, if a majority of such parties are citizens of a state or states that have ratified or acceded to the Inter-american Convention and are member states of the Organization of American States, the Inter-american Convention shall apply. In all other cases, the Convention on the Recognition and Enforcement of Foreign Arbitral Awards shall apply.

2. The United States of America will apply the rules of procedure of the Inter-American Commercial Arbitration Commission which are in effect on the date that the United States of America deposits its instrument of ratification, unless the United States of America makes a later official determination to adopt and apply subsequent amendments to such rules.

3. The United States of America will apply the Convention, on the basis of reciprocity, to the recognition and enforcement of only those awards made in the territory of another Contracting State."

Appendix 3
U.S. Federal Arbitration Act (FAA)

Title 9, US Code, Section 1–14, was first enacted February 12, 1925 (43 Stat. 883), codified July 30, 1947 (61 Stat. 669), and amended September 3, 1954 (68 Stat. 1233). Chapter 2 was added July 31, 1970 (84 Stat. 692), two new Sections were passed by the Congress in October of 1988 and renumbered on December 1, 1990 (PLS 669 and 702); Chapter 3 was added on August 15, 1990 (PL 101-369); and Section 10 was amended on November 15.

Arbitration

Chapter 1. GENERAL PROVISIONS

Section 1. "Maritime transactions" and "commerce" defined; exceptions to operation of title

Section 2. Validity, irrevocability, and enforcement of agreements to arbitrate

Section 3. Stay of proceedings where issue therein referable to arbitration

Section 4. Failure to arbitrate under agreement; petition to United States court having jurisdiction for order to compel arbitration; notice and service thereof; hearing and determination

Section 5. Appointment of arbitrators or umpire

Section 6. Application heard as motion

Section 7. Witnesses before arbitrators; fees; compelling attendance

Section 8. Proceedings begun by libel in admiralty and seizure of vessel or property

Section 9. Award of arbitrators; confirmation; jurisdiction; procedure

Section 10. Same; vacation; grounds; rehearing.

Section 11. Same; modification or correction; grounds; order

Section 12. Notice of motions to vacate or modify; service; stay of proceedings

Section 13. Papers filed with order on motions; judgment; docketing; force and effect; enforcement

Section 14. Contracts not affected

Section 15. Inapplicability of the Act of State doctrine

Section 16. Appeals

Chapter 2. CONVENTION ON THE RECOGNITION AND ENFORCEMENT OF FOREIGN ARBITRAL AWARDS

Section 201. Enforcement of Convention

Section 202. Agreement or award falling under the Convention

Section 203. Jurisdiction; amount in controversy

Section 204. Venue

Section 205. Removal of cases from State courts

Section 206. Order to compel arbitration; appointment of arbitrators

Section 207. Award of arbitrators; confirmation; jurisdiction; proceeding

Section 208. Chapter 1; residual application

Chapter 3. INTER-AMERICAN CONVENTION ON INTERNATIONAL COMMERCIAL ARBITRATION

Section 301. Enforcement of Convention

Section 302. Incorporation by reference

Section 303. Order to compel arbitration; appointment of arbitrators; locale

Section 304. Recognition and enforcement of foreign arbitral decisions and awards; reciprocity

Section 305. Relationship between the Inter-American Convention and the Convention on the Recognition and Enforcement of Foreign Arbitral Awards of June 10, 1958

Section 306. Applicable rules of Inter-American Commercial Arbitration Commission

Section 307. Chapter 1; residual application

Chapter 1. GENERAL PROVISIONS

Section 1. "Maritime transactions" and "commerce" defined; exceptions to operation of title

"Maritime transaction," as herein defined, means charter parties, bills of lading of water carriers, agreements relating to wharfage, supplies furnished vessels or repairs to vessels, collisions, or any other matters in foreign commerce which, if the subject of controversy, would be embraced within admiralty jurisdiction; "commerce," as herein defined, means commerce among the several States or with foreign nations, or in any Territory of the United States or in the District of Columbia, or between any such Territory and another, or between any such Territory and any State or foreign nation, or between the District of Columbia and any State or Territory or foreign nation, but nothing herein contained shall apply to contracts of employment of seamen, railroad employees, or any other class of workers engaged in foreign or interstate commerce.

Section 2. Validity, irrevocability, and enforcement of agreements to arbitrate

A written provision in any maritime transaction or a contract evidencing a transaction involving commerce to settle by arbitration a controversy thereafter arising out of such contract or transaction, or the refusal to perform the whole or any part thereof, or an agreement in writing to submit to arbitration an existing controversy arising out of such a contract, transaction, or refusal, shall be valid, irrevocable, and enforceable, save upon such grounds as exist at law or in equity for the revocation of any contract.

Section 3. Stay of proceedings where issue therein referable to arbitration

If any suit or proceeding be brought in any of the courts of the United States upon any issue referable to arbitration under an agreement in writing for such arbitration, the court in which such suit is pending, upon being satisfied that the issue involved in such suit or proceeding is referable to arbitration under such an agreement, shall on application of one of the parties stay the trial of the action until such arbitration has been had in accordance with the terms of the agreement, providing the applicant for the stay is not in default in proceeding with such arbitration.

Section 4. Failure to arbitrate under agreement; petition to United States court having jurisdiction for order to compel arbitration; notice and service thereof; hearing and determination

A party aggrieved by the alleged failure, neglect, or refusal of another to arbitrate under a written agreement for arbitration may petition any United States district court which, save for such agreement, would have jurisdiction under Title 28, in a civil action or in admiralty of the subject matter of a suit arising out of the controversy between the parties, for an order directing that such arbitration proceed in the manner provided for in such agreement. Five days' notice in writing of such application shall be served upon the party in default. Service thereof shall be made in the manner provided by the Federal Rules of Civil Procedure. The court shall hear the parties, and upon being satisfied that the making of the agreement for arbitration or the failure to comply therewith is not in issue, the court shall make an order directing the parties to proceed to arbitration in accordance with the terms of the agreement. The hearing and proceedings, under such agreement, shall be within the district in which the petition for an order directing such arbitration is filed. If the making of the arbitration agreement or the failure, neglect, or refusal to perform the same be in issue, the court shall proceed summarily to the trial thereof. If no jury trial be demanded by the party alleged to be in default, or if the matter in dispute is within admiralty jurisdiction, the court shall hear and determine such issue. Where such an issue is raised, the party alleged to be in default may, except in cases of admiralty, on or before the return day of the notice of application, demand a jury trial of such issue, and upon such demand the court shall make an order referring the issue or issues to a jury in the manner provided by the

Federal Rules of Civil Procedure, or may specially call a jury for that purpose. If the jury find that no agreement in writing for arbitration was made or that there is no default in proceeding thereunder, the proceeding shall be dismissed. If the jury find that an agreement for arbitration was made in writing and that there is a default in proceeding thereunder, the court shall make an order summarily directing the parties to proceed with the arbitration in accordance with the terms thereof.

Section 5. Appointment of arbitrators or umpire

If in the agreement provision be made for a method of naming or appointing an arbitrator or arbitrators or an umpire, such method shall be followed; but if no method be provided therein, or if a method be provided and any party thereto shall fail to avail himself of such method, or if for any other reason there shall be a lapse in the naming of an arbitrator or arbitrators or umpire, or in filling a vacancy, then upon the application of either party to the controversy the court shall designate and appoint an arbitrator or arbitrators or umpire, as the case may require, who shall act under the said agreement with the same force and effect as if he or they had been specifically named therein; and unless otherwise provided in the agreement the arbitration shall be by a single arbitrator.

Section 6. Application heard as motion

Any application to the court hereunder shall be made and heard in the manner provided by law for the making and hearing of motions, except as otherwise herein expressly provided.

Section 7. Witnesses before arbitrators; fees; compelling attendance

The arbitrators selected either as prescribed in this title or otherwise, or a majority of them, may summon in writing any person to attend before them or any of them as a witness and in a proper case to bring with him or them any book, record, document, or paper which may be deemed material as evidence in the case. The fees for such attendance shall be the same as the fees of witnesses before masters of the United States courts. Said summons shall issue in the name of the arbitrator or arbitrators, or a majority of them, and shall be signed by the arbitrators, or a majority of them, and shall be directed to the said person and shall be served in the same manner as subpoenas to appear and testify before the court; if any person or persons so summoned to testify shall refuse or neglect to obey said summons, upon petition the United States district court for the district in which such arbitrators, or a majority of them, are sitting may compel the attendance of such person or persons before said arbitrator or arbitrators, or punish said person or persons for contempt in the same manner provided by law for securing the attendance of witnesses or their punishment for neglect or refusal to attend in the courts of the United States.

Section 8. Proceedings begun by libel in admiralty and seizure of vessel or property

If the basis of jurisdiction be a cause of action otherwise justiciable in admiralty, then, notwithstanding anything herein to the contrary, the party claiming to be aggrieved may begin his proceeding hereunder by seizure of the vessel or other property of the other party according to the usual course of admiralty proceedings, and the court shall then have jurisdiction to direct the parties to proceed with the arbitration and shall retain jurisdiction to enter its decree upon the award.

Section 9. Award of arbitrators; confirmation; jurisdiction; procedure

If the parties in their agreement have agreed that a judgment of the court shall be entered upon the award made pursuant to the arbitration, and shall specify the court, then at any time within one year after the award is made any party to the arbitration may apply to the court so specified for an order confirming the award, and thereupon the court must grant such an order unless the award is vacated, modified, or corrected as prescribed in sections 10 and 11 of this title. If no court is specified in the agreement of the parties, then such application may be made to the United States court in and for the district within which such award was made. Notice of the application shall be served upon the adverse party, and thereupon the court shall have jurisdiction of such party as though he had appeared generally in the proceeding. If the adverse party is a resident of the district within which the award was made, such service shall be made upon the adverse party or his attorney as prescribed by law for service of notice of motion in an action in the same court. If the adverse party shall be a nonresident, then the notice of the application shall be served by the marshal of any district within which the adverse party may be found in like manner as other process of the court.

Section 10. Same; vacation; grounds; rehearing

a. In any of the following cases the United States court in and for the district wherein the award was made may make an order vacating the award upon the application of any party to the arbitration
   1. Where the award was procured by corruption, fraud, or undue means.
   2. Where there was evident partiality or corruption in the arbitrators, or either of them.
   3. Where the arbitrators were guilty of misconduct in refusing to postpone the hearing, upon sufficient cause shown, or in refusing to hear evidence pertinent and material to the controversy; or of any other misbehavior by which the rights of any party have been prejudiced.
   4. Where the arbitrators exceeded their powers, or so imperfectly executed them that a mutual, final, and definite award upon the subject matter submitted was not made.

5. Where an award is vacated and the time within which the agreement required the award to be made has not expired the court may, in its discretion, direct a rehearing by the arbitrators.

b. The United States district court for the district wherein an award was made that was issued pursuant to section 590 of title 5 may make an order vacating the award upon the application of a person, other than a party to the arbitration, who is adversely affected or aggrieved by the award, if the use of arbitration or the award is clearly inconsistent with the factors set forth in section 582 of title 5.

Section 11. Same; modification or correction; grounds; order

In either of the following cases the United States court in and for the district wherein the award was made may make an order modifying or correcting the award upon the application of any party to the arbitration –

a. Where there was an evident material miscalculation of figures or an evident material mistake in the description of any person, thing, or property referred to in the award.
b. Where the arbitrators have awarded upon a matter not submitted to them, unless it is a matter not affecting the merits of the decision upon the matter submitted.
c. Where the award is imperfect in matter of form not affecting the merits of the controversy.

The order may modify and correct the award, so as to effect the intent thereof and promote justice between the parties.

Section 12. Notice of motions to vacate or modify; service; stay of proceedings

Notice of a motion to vacate, modify, or correct an award must be served upon the adverse party or his attorney within three months after the award is filed or delivered. If the adverse party is a resident of the district within which the award was made, such service shall be made upon the adverse party or his attorney as prescribed by law for service of notice of motion in an action in the same court. If the adverse party shall be a nonresident then the notice of the application shall be served by the marshal of any district within which the adverse party may be found in like manner as other process of the court. For the purposes of the motion any judge who might make an order to stay the proceedings in an action brought in the same court may make an order, to be served with the notice of motion, staying the proceedings of the adverse party to enforce the award.

Section 13. Papers filed with order on motions; judgment; docketing; force and effect; enforcement

The party moving for an order confirming, modifying, or correcting an award shall, at the time such order is filed with the clerk for the entry of judgment thereon, also file the following papers with the clerk:

a. The agreement; the selection or appointment, if any, of an additional arbitrator or umpire; and each written extension of the time, if any, within which to make the award.

b. The award.

c. Each notice, affidavit, or other paper used upon an application to confirm, modify, or correct the award, and a copy of each order of the court upon such an application.

The judgment shall be docketed as if it was rendered in an action.

The judgment so entered shall have the same force and effect, in all respects, as, and be subject to all the provisions of law relating to, a judgment in an action; and it may be enforced as if it had been rendered in an action in the court in which it is entered.

Section 14. Contracts not affected

This title shall not apply to contracts made prior to January 1, 1926.

Section 15. Inapplicability of the Act of State doctrine

Enforcement of arbitral agreements, confirmation of arbitral awards, and execution upon judgments based on orders confirming such awards shall not be refused on the basis of the Act of State doctrine.

Section 16. Appeals

a. An appeal may be taken from
   1. an order –
      A. refusing a stay of any action under section 3 of this title,
      B. denying a petition under section 4 of this title to order arbitration to proceed,
      C. denying an application under section 206 of this title to compel arbitration,
      D. confirming or denying confirmation of an award or partial award, or
      E. modifying, correcting, or vacating an award;
   2. an interlocutory order granting, continuing, or modifying an injunction against an arbitration that is subject to this title; or
   3. a final decision with respect to an arbitration that is subject to this title.

b. Except as otherwise provided in section 1292(b) of title 28, an appeal may not be taken from an interlocutory order
   1. granting a stay of any action under section 3 of this title;
   2. directing arbitration to proceed under section 4 of this title;
   3. compelling arbitration under section 206 of this title; or
   4. refusing to enjoin an arbitration that is subject to this title.

Chapter 2. CONVENTION ON THE RECOGNITION AND ENFORCEMENT OF FOREIGN ARBITRAL AWARDS

Section 201. Enforcement of Convention

The Convention on the Recognition and Enforcement of Foreign Arbitral Awards of June 10, 1958, shall be enforced in United States courts in accordance with this chapter.

Section 202. Agreement or award falling under the Convention

An arbitration agreement or arbitral award arising out of a legal relationship, whether contractual or not, which is considered as commercial, including a transaction, contract, or agreement described in section 2 of this title, falls under the Convention. An agreement or award arising out of such a relationship which is entirely between citizens of the United States shall be deemed not to fall under the Convention unless that relationship involves property located abroad, envisages performance or enforcement abroad, or has some other reasonable relation with one or more foreign states. For the purpose of this section a corporation is a citizen of the United States if it is incorporated or has its principal place of business in the United States.

Section 203. Jurisdiction; amount in controversy

An action or proceeding falling under the Convention shall be deemed to arise under the laws and treaties of the United States. The district courts of the United States (including the courts enumerated in section 460 of title 28) shall have original jurisdiction over such an action or proceeding, regardless of the amount in controversy.

Section 204. Venue

An action or proceeding over which the district courts have jurisdiction pursuant to section 203 of this title may be brought in any such court in which save for the arbitration agreement an action or proceeding with respect to the controversy between the parties could be brought, or in such court for the district and division which embraces the place designated in the agreement as the place of arbitration if such place is within the United States.

Section 205. Removal of cases from State courts

Where the subject matter of an action or proceeding pending in a State court relates to an arbitration agreement or award falling under the Convention, the defendant or the defendants may, at any time before the trial thereof, remove such action or proceeding to the district court of the United States for the district and division embracing the place where the action or proceeding is pending. The procedure for removal of causes otherwise provided by law shall apply, except that the ground for removal provided in this section need not appear on the face of the complaint but may be shown in the petition for removal. For the purposes of Chapter 1 of this title any action or proceeding removed under this section shall be deemed to have been brought in the district court to which it is removed.

Section 206. Order to compel arbitration; appointment of arbitrators

A court having jurisdiction under this chapter may direct that arbitration be held in accordance with the agreement at any place therein provided for, whether that place is within or without the United States. Such court may also appoint arbitrators in accordance with the provisions of the agreement.

Section 207. Award of arbitrators; confirmation; jurisdiction; proceeding

Within three years after an arbitral award falling under the Convention is made, any party to the arbitration may apply to any court having jurisdiction under this chapter for an order confirming the award as against any other party to the arbitration. The court shall confirm the award unless it finds one of the grounds for refusal or deferral of recognition or enforcement of the award specified in the said Convention.

Section 208. Chapter 1; residual application

Chapter 1 applies to actions and proceedings brought under this chapter to the extent that chapter is not in conflict with this chapter or the Convention as ratified by the United States.

Chapter 3. INTER-AMERICAN CONVENTION ON INTERNATIONAL COMMERCIAL ARBITRATION

Section 301. Enforcement of Convention

The Inter-American Convention on International Commercial Arbitration of January 30, 1975, shall be enforced in United States courts in accordance with this chapter.

Section 302. Incorporation by reference

Sections 202, 203, 204, 205, and 207 of this title shall apply to this chapter as if specifically set forth herein, except that for the purposes of this chapter "the Convention" shall mean the Inter-American Convention.

Section 303. Order to compel arbitration; appointment of arbitrators; locale

(a) A court having jurisdiction under this chapter may direct that arbitration be held in accordance with the agreement at any place therein provided for, whether that place is within or without the United States. The court may also appoint arbitrators in accordance with the provisions of the agreement.

(b) In the event the agreement does not make provision for the place of arbitration or the appointment of arbitrators, the court shall direct that the arbitration shall be held and the arbitrators be appointed in accordance with Article 3 of the Inter-American Convention.

Section 304. Recognition and enforcement of foreign arbitral decisions and awards; reciprocity

Arbitral decisions or awards made in the territory of a foreign State shall, on the basis of reciprocity, be recognized and enforced under this chapter only if that State has ratified or acceded to the Inter-American Convention.

Section 305. Relationship between the Inter-American Convention and the Convention on the Recognition and Enforcement of Foreign Arbitral Awards of June 10, 1958

When the requirements for application of both the Inter-American Convention and the Convention on the Recognition and Enforcement of Foreign Arbitral Awards of June 10, 1958, are met, determination as to which Convention applies shall, unless otherwise expressly agreed, be made as follows:

1. If a majority of the parties to the arbitration agreement are citizens of a State or States that have ratified or acceded to the Inter-American Convention and are member States of the Organization of American States, the Inter-American Convention shall apply.
2. In all other cases the Convention on the Recognition and Enforcement of Foreign Arbitral Awards of June 10, 1958, shall apply.

Section 306. Applicable rules of Inter-American Commercial Arbitration Commission

a. For the purposes of this chapter the rules of procedure of the Inter-American Commercial Arbitration Commission referred to in Article 3 of the Inter-American Convention shall, subject to subsection (b) of this section, be those rules as promulgated by the Commission on July 1, 1988.
b. In the event the rules of procedure of the Inter-American Commercial Arbitration Commission are modified or amended in accordance with the procedures for amendment of the rules of that Commission, the Secretary of State, by regulation in accordance with section 553 of title 5, consistent with the aims and purposes of this Convention, may prescribe that such modifications or amendments shall be effective for purposes of this chapter.

Section 307. Chapter 1; residual application

Chapter 1 applies to actions and proceedings brought under this chapter to the extent chapter 1 is not in conflict with this chapter or the Inter-American Convention as ratified by the United States.

Appendix 4
Comparison of ICC/UNCITRAL/AAA/LCIA Rules

ROLE OF ADMINISTRATIVE BODY

ICC Court of Arbitration of the International Chamber of Commerce "is to provide for the settlement by arbitration." Art. 1(1). Court appoints or confirms appointment of arbitrators. Art. 9. Court is sole judge on a challenge of an arbitrator. Art. 11. Court may replace arbitrator if he fails to timely perform. Art. 12(2). Court does not settle disputes, rather it "has the function of ensuring the application of the [ICC] Rules." Art. 1(2).

UNCITRAL Secretary-General of the Permanent Court of Arbitration at The Hague will designate an appointing authority if the parties cannot agree to an appointing authority or if the chosen appointing authority refuses to act. Art. 6(2).

AAA AAA is an active administrator. Art. 1(3). AAA acts as a clearinghouse for initial service. Art. 2. AAA may choose the site of arbitration if the parties fail to agree. Art. 13. If parties fail to select arbitrator, AAA may appoint one. Art. 6. AAA may determine that more than one arbitrator is needed. Art. 5.

LCIA LCIA (the court) receives initial service. Art. 1.1 The court may select and appoint arbitrators. Art. 5. If any arbitrator, after an appointment, becomes unable or unfit to act, the court will, upon request, appoint another arbitrator in his place. Art. 11. Arbitrator's fees are established by the court. Art. 28.

ARBITRATOR POOL

ICC No pool is maintained. The arbitrator(s) are either nominated by the parties or, in the absence of nomination, appointed by the court. Art. 8(3).

UNCITRAL Rules defer to appointing authority. Art. 6-7.

AAA No pool maintained. Arbitrators are designated by the parties or appointed by AAA. Art. 6.

LCIA No pool is maintained. The arbitrator(s) are either nominated by the parties, or if the parties fail to agree, appointed by the court. Art. 5, 7.

SELECTION OF ARBITRATORS BY THE PARTIES

ICC Parties may nominate a single arbitrator for confirmation by the court. Art. 8(3). If there are three arbitrators, each party may nominate one arbitrator for confirmation by the court. The court will appoint the third arbitrator who will act as chairman. Art.

8(4). If the parties fail to nominate an arbitrator, the court will appoint one. Art. 8(3), 8(4).

UNCITRAL Parties may mutually agree to a sole arbitrator and to an appointing authority. Art. 6(1). Secretary General of the Permanent Court of Arbitration at The Hague will designate an appointing authority upon default. Art. 6-7. Appointing authority shall appoint sole arbitrator by supplying parties with identical lists of at least three names—parties can strike and rank the suggested arbitrators. Art. 6(3). If three arbitrators are to be used, each party appoints one and the arbitrators jointly choose chairperson. Default to appointing authority. Art. 7.

AAA Parties may mutually agree on an arbitrator with or without the assistance of AAA. Art. 6(2).

LCIA The court will select and appoint an arbitrator to determine the dispute. Art. 5. The parties may nominate an arbitrator, however, only the court can appoint an arbitrator and the court may refuse to appoint any nominee if it determines that the nominee is not suitable, independent, or impartial. Art. 7.1. The court will appoint one of the arbitrators, not nominated by any party, as the chairperson. Art. 7.2

NEUTRALITY

ICC "Every arbitrator must be and remains independent of the parties involved in the arbitration." Art 7(1). Court can disqualify or replace an arbitrator when challenged by a party. Art. 11, 12(1).

UNCITRAL "Any arbitrator may be challenged if circumstances exist that give rise to justifiable doubts as to the arbitrator's impartiality or independence." Art. 10(1). "[A]ppointing authority shall have regard to such considerations as are likely to secure the appointment of an independent and impartial arbitrator . . ." Art. 6(4). Arbitrator has duty to disclose partiality. Art. 9.

AAA Arbitrators shall be impartial and neutral. Arbitrator has the duty to disclose partiality. Art. 7.

LCIA All arbitrators conducting an arbitration under the rules shall be and remain at all times wholly independent and impartial, and shall not act as advocates for any party. Arbitrator has the obligation to disclose partiality. Art. 5.3.

DISQUALIFICATION OF ARBITRATORS

ICC An arbitrator shall be replaced upon acceptance by the court of a challenge, upon request of all the parties, or upon the court's decision that he is unable or unwilling to fulfill his function in accordance with the rules or within the prescribed time limits. Art. 12(1), 12(2).

UNCITRAL "If the other party does not agree to the challenge and the challenged arbitrator does not withdraw, the decision on the challenge will be made by the appointing authority." Art. 12(1).

AAA If the other party does not agree to the challenge or the arbitrator does not withdraw, AAA shall make the decision on the challenge. Art. 9.

LCIA An arbitrator may be challenged by any party if circumstances give rise to justifiable doubts about the arbitrator's impartiality or independence. Unless the challenged arbitrator withdraws or the other parties agree to the challenge, the court will decide. Art. 10.

COMPENSATION

ICC The court fixes the fees and expenses of the arbitrators in accordance with the scale provided in the appendix to the rules. The court may adjust these fees in exceptional circumstances. Art. 31(1), 31(2).

UNCITRAL "The Arbitral Tribunal shall fix the costs of arbitration in its award. The term 'costs' includes . . . the fees of the Arbitral Tribunal . . ." Art. 38. "The fees of the Arbitral Tribunal shall be reasonable in amount . . ." Art. 39(1). Fee schedules issued by the appointing authority shall be taken into account by the Arbitral Tribunal in fixing its fees. Art. 39(2).

AAA Arbitrators are compensated based on their amount of service. AAA will arrange a daily and hourly rate. If the parties cannot agree on the terms of compensation, AAA will establish an appropriate rate and communicate it in writing to the parties. Art. 32.

LCIA Arbitrators fees will be calculated by reference to the work done in connection with the arbitration, and will be charged at rates approximate to the particular circumstances of the case, including the complexity, and any special qualifications of the arbitrator. These rates will be established by the court after consultation with the parties and before the appointment of the arbitrator. Schedule of Fees and Costs 4(a). Administration charges will also apply.

NUMBER

ICC One or three arbitrators. Art. 8(1). If the number is not designated, the court will appoint one, or three if warranted. Art. 8(2).

UNCITRAL Three normally. Parties may stipulate one. Art. 5.

AAA If the parties do not agree differently, then one arbitrator shall handle the dispute. AAA can, in its discretion, direct that three be appointed. Art. 5.

LCIA Unless agreed otherwise by the parties, one arbitrator will be appointed unless the court determines that a three-member tribunal is more appropriate. Art. 5.4.

NATIONALITY OF ARBITRATORS

ICC Regard is given to nationality when arbitrators are considered. Art. 9(1). "The sole arbitrator or the chairman of the Arbitral Tribunal shall be of a nationality other than those of the parties. However, in suitable circumstances and provided that neither of the parties objects within the time limit fixed by the Court, the sole arbitrator or the chairman of the Arbitral Tribunal may be chosen from a country of which any of the parties is a national." Art. 9(5).

UNCITRAL "[A]ppointing authority shall have regard to such considerations as are likely to secure the appointment of an independent and impartial arbitrator and shall take into account as well the advisability of appointing an arbitrator of a nationality other than the nationalities of the parties." Art. 6(4).

AAA "At the request of any party or on its own initiative, [AAA] may appoint nationals of a country other than that of any of the parties." Art. 6(4).

LCIA "Where the parties are of different nationalities, a sole arbitrator or Chairman shall not have the same nationality as any party unless the parties who are not of the same nationality as the proposed appointee agree in writing otherwise." Art. 6.

INITIATION OF ARBITRATION (NOTICE OF ISSUES, PLEADINGS, TERMS OF REFERENCE)

ICC The request for arbitration shall, inter alia, include: names, descriptions, and addresses of the parties; a statement of the claimant's case; the relevant agreements, and such documentation as will clearly establish the circumstances of the case; a statement of the relief sought; and all relevant particulars concerning the number of arbitrators and their choice. Art. 4(3).

UNCITRAL "The party initiating recourse to arbitration . . . shall give to the other party . . . a notice of arbitration" containing: a demand that the dispute be referred to arbitration, the names and addresses of the parties, a reference to the arbitration clause or the separate arbitration agreement that is invoked, a reference to the contract out of or in relation to which the dispute arises, the general nature of the claim and an indication of the amounts involved, the relief or remedies sought, and a proposal as to the number of arbitrators if the parties have not previously agreed thereon. Art. 3.

AAA The party initiating arbitration shall give written notice to the AAA and the other party containing: a demand that the dispute be referred to arbitration; the names and addresses of the parties; a reference to the arbitration clause or agreement that is invoked; a reference to any contract out of or in relation to which the dispute arises; a description of the claim and an indication of the facts supporting it; the relief or remedy sought and the amount claimed; and a proposal as to the number of arbitrators, the place of arbitration, and the language of the arbitration. Art. 2

LCIA Any party wishing to commence an arbitration shall send to the Register of the Court a written request for arbitration including: the names and addresses of the parties to the arbitration, copies of the contractual documents under which the arbitration arises, any separate submission or reference to the arbitration, a brief statement of the nature and circumstances of the dispute, a statement of any matters on which the parties have previously agreed as to the conduct of the arbitration, and the fee prescribed in the Schedule of Costs. Art. 1.

DEFINING CONFLICT (CHANGE OF CLAIMS)

ICC "After the Terms of Reference have been signed or approved by the Court, no party shall make new claims or counterclaims which fall outside the limits of the Terms of Reference unless it has been authorized to do so by the Arbitral Tribunal, which shall consider the nature of such new claims or counterclaims, the stage of the arbitration and other relevant considerations." Art. 19.

UNCITRAL "During the course of the arbitral proceedings either party may amend or supplement his claim or defense unless the Arbitral Tribunal considers it inappropriate to allow such amendment having regard to the delay in making it or prejudice to the other party or other circumstances." Art. 20.

AAA "During the arbitral proceedings, any party may amend or supplement its claim, counterclaim or defense, unless the tribunal considers it inappropriate to allow such amendment or supplement. . . . A party may not amend . . . if the amendment or supplement would fall outside the scope of the agreement to arbitrate." Art. 4.

LCIA	Unless the parties agree otherwise, the arbitrator may allow parties to amend the statement of the case, defense, or reply, upon a motion and after hearing or receiving any representations from the parties concerned. Art. 22.1(a).

ARBITRATOR AS INVESTIGATOR

ICC	"The Arbitral Tribunal shall proceed within as short a time as possible to establish the facts of the case by all appropriate means." Art. 20(1). Arbitrator may request to hear parties and may decide to hear any other person. Art. 20(2), 20(3). The arbitrator may "appoint one or more experts, define their terms of reference and receive their reports." Art. 20(4).
UNCITRAL	"The Arbitral Tribunal may meet at any place it deems appropriate for the inspection of goods, other property or documents." Art. 16(3). "The parties shall give the [arbitrator-appointed] expert any relevant information or produce for his inspection any relevant documents or goods that he may require of them." Art. 27(2).
AAA	The arbitrator may appoint one or more experts to report to it in writing on specific issues designated by the parties and communicated to the parties. Art. 22(1). At any other time the arbitrator may order parties to produce other documents, exhibits, or other evidence it deems necessary or appropriate. Art. 19.
LCIA	The arbitrator may order any party to furnish him with such further details of its case, in fact or law, as he may require. Art. 22.1.

DISCOVERY

ICC	"The Arbitral Tribunal shall proceed within as short a time as possible to establish the facts of the case by all appropriate means." Art. 20(1).
UNCITRAL	"At any time during the arbitral proceedings the Arbitral Tribunal may require the parties to produce documents, exhibits, or other evidence. . . ." Art. 24(3).
AAA	The arbitrator shall conduct the proceedings with a view to expedite the resolution of the dispute. Art. 16(2). Each party has the burden of proving the facts relied on in supporting its claim or defense. The arbitrator may order the parties to deliver a summary of the documents and other evidence that the party intends to use in support of its claim. At any other time the arbitrator may order parties to produce other documents, exhibits, or other evidence it deems necessary or appropriate. Art. 19.

LCIA The arbitrator may order any party to furnish him with such further details of its case, in fact or law, as he may require. Art. 22.1.

CROSS-EXAMINATION

ICC At the request of the parties or on his own initiative, the arbitrator "shall hear the parties together in person. . . ." Art. 20(2).

UNCITRAL "The Arbitral Tribunal is free to determine the manner in which witnesses are examined." Art. 25(4). Experts appointed by the arbitral tribunal are subject to interrogation upon request of either party. Art. 27(4).

AAA The arbitrator determines the manner in which the witnesses are examined. Art. 20(4). Parties shall be given the opportunity to question the arbitrator-appointed expert at the hearing. Art. 22(4).

LCIA Any witness who gives oral evidence at a hearing before the arbitral tribunal may be questioned by each of the parties under the control of the tribunal. The tribunal may ask questions at any stage of the evidence. Art. 20.5.

DEFINING SCOPE OF ISSUES

ICC "As soon as it has received the file from the Secretariat, the Arbitral Tribunal shall draw up, on the basis of documents or in the presence of the parties and in light of their most recent submissions, a document defining it Terms of Reference." This document should include, among other things, a summary of the parties' respective claims and a list of the issues to be determined. Art. 18(1).

UNCITRAL Statement of claim will contain the points at issue and the relief sought. Art. 18(2). Arbitrators may require further written statements. Art. 22.

AAA The statement of claim should include a summary of the parties' respective claims. Art. 2, 3. "The arbitrator may conduct a preparatory conference with the parties for the purpose of organizing, scheduling, and agreeing to procedures to expedite subsequent proceedings." Art. 16(2).

LCIA "Any party wishing to commence an arbitration shall send a written request for arbitration, including . . . a brief statement of the nature and circumstances of the dispute." Art. 1.1(c).

RESOLVING CONFLICT (SUBMISSION OF EXISTING DISPUTE TO ARBITRATION)

ICC If the defendant does not file an answer within 30 days, the "Court may decide . . . that the arbitration shall proceed if it is

	prima facie satisfied that an arbitration agreement under the Rules may exist." Art. 6(2).
UNCITRAL	"Where the parties to a contract have agreed in writing that disputes in relation to that contract shall be referred to arbitration . . ." Art. 1(1).
AAA	If a party fails to appear at a hearing without showing sufficient cause for such failure, the tribunal may proceed with the arbitration. Art. 23(2).
LCIA	Existing disputes may be submitted to arbitration where an agreement or reference has provided for arbitration under the rules. Foreword.

SUBMISSION OF FUTURE DISPUTE TO ARBITRATION

ICC	To specify that disputes arising in connection with a contract will be finally settled under the Rules of Conciliation and Arbitration of the ICC, reference to a standard clause in the arbitration contract is recommended.
UNCITRAL	Future disputes may be submitted to arbitration "[w]here the parties to a contract have agreed in writing that disputes in relation to that contract shall be referred to arbitration under the UNCITRAL Arbitration Rules. . . ." Art. 1(1).
AAA	Parties can arbitrate future disputes under the AAA rules by inserting a standard arbitration clause into their contracts. Introduction.
LCIA	Future disputes may be submitted to arbitration in advance by agreement, submission, or reference providing for arbitration under the rules, and one or more parties habitually resides, carries on business, or is incorporated, managed, or controlled outside the United Kingdom. Foreword.

POSSIBLE USE OF MEDIATION IN ADDITION TO ARBITRATION

ICC	Conciliation remains entirely optional unless the parties have otherwise agreed. The ICC Rules of Arbitration do not require the parties to attempt conciliation prior to commencing an arbitration. So, too, the rules permit conciliation to be attempted without requiring that the dispute be referred to arbitration thereafter if the conciliation effort is unsuccessful. Foreword..
UNCITRAL	No provision as of the most recent revision.
AAA	Parties may wish to consider the possibility of mediation or conciliation, which they may discuss with the AAA. Introduction.
LCIA	No provision as of the most current revision.

EVIDENCE

ICC "The Arbitral Tribunal shall proceed within as short a time as possible to establish the facts of the case by all appropriate means." Art. 20(1).

UNCITRAL "If either party so requests . . . the Arbitral Tribunal shall hold hearings for the presentation of evidence by witnesses, including expert witnesses, or for oral argument. In the absence of such a request, the Arbitral Tribunal shall decide whether to hold such hearings or whether the proceedings shall be conducted on the basis of documents and other materials." Art. 15(2). "The Arbitral Tribunal shall determine the admissibility, relevance, materiality, and weight of the evidence offered." Art. 25(6).

AAA Each party has the burden of proving the facts relied upon in stating its claim or defense. The tribunal may order a party to produce any other documents, exhibits, or other evidence it deems necessary or appropriate. Art. 19.

LCIA The arbitrator may order any party to produce any documents or classes of documents in their possession, custody, or power that the tribunal considers relevant. The tribunal may also decide whether to apply any strict rules of evidence and determine the time, manner, and form in which the material will be exchanged between the parties and produced to the tribunal. Art. 22.1(e),(f).

HEARING

ICC Arbitrator shall "hear parties together in person if any of them so requests or, failing such a request, it may of its own motion decide to hear them." Art. 20(2). The arbitral tribunal "may decide the case solely on the documents submitted by the parties unless any of the parties requests a hearing." Art. 20(6). Parties are entitled to be present during hearings. Art. 21(3).

UNCITRAL "If either party so requests at any stage of the proceedings, the Arbitral Tribunal shall hold hearings for the presentation of evidence. . . ." Art. 15(2).

AAA The arbitrator shall set the date, time, and place of the initial oral hearing. Other hearings may be held for the presentation of evidence throughout the resolution of the dispute. Art. 20.

LCIA The arbitrator will fix the date, time, and location of any meetings and hearings in the arbitration and will give the parties advance notice unless the parties have agreed in writing on document-only arbitration. Art. 19.2

SECRECY

ICC	"Save with the approval of the Arbitral Tribunal and the parties, persons not involved in the proceedings shall not be admitted." Art. 21(3). Copies of the award are not available to nonparties. Art. 28(2). "The work of the Court is of a confidential nature and must be respected by everyone who participates in that work in whatever capacity." Appendix I, Art. 6.
UNCITRAL	"Hearings shall be held *in camera* unless the parties agree otherwise. The Arbitral Tribunal may require the retirement of any witness or witnesses during the testimony of other witnesses." Art. 25(4). "The award may be made public only with the consent of both parties." Art. 32(5).
AAA	"Hearings are private unless the parties agree otherwise or the law provides to the contrary." Art. 20(4).
LCIA	All meetings and hearings will be in private unless the parties agree otherwise. Art. 19.4

SEQUESTRATION OF WITNESSES

ICC	"[T]he Arbitral Tribunal shall hear the parties together in person if any of them so requests or, failing such a request, it may of its own motion decide to hear them." Art. 20(2). In addition, "[t]he Arbitral Tribunal may decide to hear . . . any other person, in the presence of the parties, or in their absence provided they have been duly summoned." Art. 20(3). "The Arbitral Tribunal shall be in full charge of the hearings, at which all the parties shall be entitled to be present. Save with the approval of the Arbitral Tribunal and the parties, persons not involved in the proceedings shall not be admitted." Art. 21(3).
UNCITRAL	"Hearings shall be held *in camera* unless the parties agree otherwise. The Arbitral Tribunal may require the retirement of any witness or witnesses during the testimony other witnesses. The Arbitral Tribunal is free to determine the manner in which witnesses are examined." Art. 25(4).
AAA	"The tribunal may require any witness or witnesses to retire during the testimony of other witnesses." Art. 20(4).
LCIA	No provision as of the most current revision.

RULE INTERPRETATION

ICC	"The proceedings before the Arbitral Tribunal shall be governed by these Rules, and, where these Rules are silent, by any rules which the parties, or failing them, the Arbitral Tribunal may settle on, whether or not reference is thereby made to the rules of

	procedure of a national law to be applied to the arbitration." Art. 15(1).
UNCITRAL	"These Rules shall govern the arbitration except that where any of these Rules is in conflict with the provision of the law applicable to the arbitration from which the parties cannot derogate, that provision shall prevail." Art. 1(2). "Subject to these Rules, the Arbitral Tribunal may conduct the arbitration in such manner as it considers appropriate, provided that the parties are treated with equality and that at any stage of the proceedings, each party is given a full opportunity of presenting his case." Art. 15(1).
AAA	The tribunal shall interpret and apply the rules insofar as they relate to its powers and duties. The AAA shall interpret and apply all other rules. Art. 36.
LCIA	No provision as of the most current revision.

REPRESENTATION

ICC	"The parties may appear in person or through duly authorized representatives. In addition, they may be assisted by advisors." Art. 21(4).
UNCITRAL	"The parties may be represented or assisted by persons of their choice." Art. 4.
AAA	Any party may be represented in the arbitration. Art. 12.
LCIA	Any party may be represented by legal representatives or any other representatives. The representative may be required to produce proof of authority. Art. 18.

INTERIM RELIEF

ICC	"Before the file is transmitted to the Arbitral Tribunal, and in appropriate circumstances even thereafter, the parties may apply to any competent judicial authority for interim or conservatory measures." Art. 23(2).
UNCITRAL	"At the request of either party, the Arbitral Tribunal may take interim measures it deems necessary in respect of the subject-matter of the dispute. . . . Such interim measures may be established in the form of an interim award. . . . A request for interim measures addressed by any party to a judicial authority shall not be deemed incompatible with the agreement to arbitrate, or as a waiver of that agreement." Art. 26.
AAA	At the request of either party, the tribunal may take whatever interim measures it deems necessary, including injunctive relief and measures for the protection or conservation of property. Art. 21(1).

LCIA The arbitrator shall have the jurisdiction to take interim or conservatory measures. Art. 25.

EXPEDITED PROCEDURE

ICC No provision as of the most current revision.
UNCITRAL No provision as of the most current revision.
AAA No provision as of the most current revision.
LCIA No provision as of the most current revision.

CONSOLIDATION OF EXISTING CLAIMS

ICC "After the Terms of Reference have been signed or approved by the Court, no party shall make new claims or counterclaims which fall outside the limits of the Terms of Reference unless it has been authorized to do so by the Arbitral Tribunal, which shall consider the nature of such new claims or counterclaims, the stage of the arbitration and other relevant circumstances." Art. 19.

UNCITRAL "During the course of the arbitral proceedings either party may amend or supplement his claim or defense unless the Arbitral Tribunal considers it inappropriate to allow such amendment having regard to the delay in making it or prejudice to the other party or any other circumstances. However, a claim may not be amended in such a manner that the amended claim falls outside the scope of the arbitration clause or separate arbitration agreement." Art. 20.

AAA "During the arbitral proceedings, any party may amend or supplement its claim, counterclaim or defense, unless the tribunal considers it inappropriate to allow such amendment or supplement. . . . A party may not amend . . . if the amendment or supplement would fall outside the scope of the agreement to arbitrate." Art. 4.

LCIA Unless the parties otherwise agree, the arbitrator shall have the power, upon the application of any of the parties or his own motion, but in either case only after hearing or receiving any representations from the parties concerned, to allow the amendment of any party's case, defense, or reply. Art. 22(1).

ARBITRATOR AS CASE MANAGER

ICC "The Arbitral Tribunal shall proceed within as short a time as possible to establish the facts of the case by all appropriate means." Art. 20(1).

UNCITRAL "Subject to these Rules, the Arbitral Tribunal may conduct the arbitration in such manner as it considers appropriate provided that the parties are treated with equality . . ." Art. 15(1).

AAA "The tribunal may conduct the arbitration in whatever manner it considers appropriate, provided that the parties are treated with equality and that each party has the right to be heard and is given a fair opportunity to present its case." Art. 16(1).

LCIA The tribunal may conduct inquiries that in the tribunal's opinion, are necessary or expedient, including whether and to what extent the tribunal should take the initiative in identifying the issues and ascertaining the relevant facts and the law(s) or rules of law applicable to the arbitration, the merits of the parties' dispute, and the arbitration agreement. Art. 22.1(c).

APPLICABLE LAW

ICC "The parties shall be free to agree upon the rules of law to be applied by the Arbitral Tribunal to the merits of the dispute. In the absence of any such agreement, the Arbitral Tribunal shall apply the rules of law which it determines to be appropriate." Art. 17(1).

UNCITRAL "The Arbitral Tribunal shall apply the law designated by the parties as applicable to the substance of the dispute. Failing such designation by the parties, the Arbitral Tribunal shall apply the law determined by the conflict of laws rules which it considers applicable." Art. 33(1).

AAA "The tribunal shall apply the substantive law(s) or rules of law designated by the parties as applicable to the dispute. Failing such a designation by the parties, the tribunal shall apply such law(s) or rules of law as it determines to be appropriate." Art. 28(1).

LCIA The dispute shall be decided in accordance with the law or rules of law chosen by the parties, or if no such choice was made, the tribunal shall apply the law(s) or rules of law that it considers appropriate. Art. 22.3.

LAW OF FORUM VS. SUBSTANTIAL JUSTICE

ICC "In all matters not expressly provided for in these Rules, the Court and the Arbitral Tribunal shall act in the spirit of these Rules and shall make every effort to make sure that the Award is enforceable at law." Art. 35.

UNCITRAL "The Arbitral Tribunal shall decide as *amiable compositeur* or *ex æquo et bono* only if the parties have expressly authorized the Arbitral Tribunal to do so and if the law applicable to the arbitral procedure permits such arbitration." Art. 33(2).

AAA The tribunal shall not act as "amiable compositeur" or "ex æquo et bono" unless the parties have expressly authorized it to do so. Art. 28(3).

LCIA The Tribunal "shall only apply to the merits of the dispute principles deriving from *'ex æquo et bono,'* 'amiable composition' or 'honourable engagement' where the parties have so agreed expressly in writing." Art. 22.4.

WHO DETERMINES JURISDICTION OF ARBITRATOR

ICC Court of Arbitration makes a preliminary determination as to whether there is a prima facie case for the existence of an arbitration agreement. If so, "arbitration shall proceed. . . . In such a case, any decision as to the jurisdiction of the Arbitral Tribunal shall be taken by the Arbitral Tribunal itself." Art. 6(2).

UNCITRAL "The Arbitral Tribunal shall have the power to rule on objections that it has no jurisdiction, including any objections with respect to the existence or validity of the arbitration clause. . . . The Arbitral Tribunal shall have the power to determine the existence or the validity of the contract of which an arbitration clause forms a part." Art. 21.

AAA "The tribunal shall have the power to rule on its own jurisdiction, including any objections with respect to the existence, scope or validity of the arbitration agreement." Art. 15(1).

LCIA The arbitral tribunal shall have the power to rule on its own jurisdiction, including any objection to the initial or continuing existence, validity, or effectiveness of the arbitration agreement. Art. 23.1.

AWARD (FORM)

ICC "The final Award shall fix the costs of the arbitration and decide which of the parties shall bear them or in what proportion they shall be borne by the parties." Art. 31(3).

UNCITRAL "The Arbitral Tribunal shall state the reasons upon which the award is based, unless the parties agree that no reasons are to be given." Art. 32(3). "[E]ither party . . . may request that the Arbitral Tribunal give an interpretation of the award." Art. 35(1).

AAA The award will be made in writing and copies of the award will be given to the parties by AAA. The award will be made public only with the consent of all parties. Art. 27.

LCIA The arbitral tribunal will make its award in writing. Art. 26.1.

REASONED VS. NAKED AWARD

ICC "[An] award shall state the reasons upon which it is based." Art. 25(2).

UNCITRAL "The Arbitral Tribunal shall state the reasons upon which the award is based, unless the parties have agreed that no reasons are to be given." Art. 32(3).

AAA "The tribunal shall state the reasons upon which the award is based, unless the parties have agreed that no reasons need be given." Art. 27(2).

LCIA The award shall state the reasons upon which it was based, unless otherwise agreed upon by the parties. Art. 26.1.

REVIEW

ICC "Before signing any Award, the Arbitral Tribunal shall submit it in draft form to the Court. The Court may lay down modifications as to the form of the Award and, without affecting the Arbitral Tribunal's liberty of decision, may also draw its attention to points of substance." Art. 27.

UNCITRAL Parties may request that the arbitral tribunal interpret the award. Art. 35(1).

AAA Within thirty days of receipt of the award, any party may request the tribunal to interpret the award, correct any clerical errors, or make an additional award as to claims presented but omitted from the award. Art. 30(1).

LCIA Within thirty days of receipt of any award, a party may submit written notice to the Registrar of the Court requesting the tribunal to correct any errors in computation and clerical or typographical errors. Art. 27.1.

TIMING

ICC The award must be submitted six months from the signing of the "Terms of Reference." Art. 24(1). In exceptional circumstances the court may extend the time limit. Art. 24(2).

UNCITRAL No provision as of the most current revision.

AAA No provision as of the most current revision.

LCIA No provision as of the most current revision.

SEVERABILITY OF ARBITRATION CLAUSE FROM ARBITRATION CONTRACT

ICC "Unless otherwise agreed, the Arbitral Tribunal shall not cease to have jurisdiction by reason of any claim that the contract is null and void or allegation that is non-existent provided that the Arbitral Tribunal upholds the validity of the arbitration agreement. The Arbitral Tribunal shall continue to have jurisdiction to determine the respective rights of the parties and to adjudicate their claims and pleas even though the contract itself may be non-existent or null and void." Art. 6(4).

UNCITRAL "A decision by the Arbitral Tribunal that the contract is null and void shall not entail *ipso jure* the invalidity of the arbitration clause." Art. 21(2).

AAA "The tribunal shall have the power to determine the existence or validity of a contract of which an arbitration clause forms a part. Such an arbitration clause shall be treated as an agreement independent of the other terms of the contract. A decision by the tribunal that the contract is null and void shall not for that reason alone render invalid the arbitration clause." Art. 15(2).

LCIA An arbitration clause which forms or was intended to form part of another agreement shall be treated as an arbitration agreement independent of the other agreement. A decision by the tribunal that the other agreement is nonexistent, invalid, or ineffective does not for that reason alone render the arbitration clause invalid. Art. 23.1.

CONFIRMATION OF SETTLEMENT AGREEMENT

ICC "If the parties reach a settlement after the file has been transmitted to the Arbitral Tribunal . . . the settlement shall be recorded in the form of an Award made by consent of the parties if so requested by the parties and if the Arbitral Tribunal agrees to do so." Art. 26.

UNCITRAL "If, before the award is made, the parties agree on a settlement of the dispute, the Arbitral Tribunal shall either issue an order or the termination of the arbitral proceedings or, if requested by both parties and accepted by the Tribunal, record the settlement in the form of an arbitral award on agreed terms." Art. 34(1).

AAA If settlement is reached before an award is made, the tribunal will terminate the arbitration and, if requested, record the settlement in the form of an award on agreed terms. Art. 29(1).

LCIA If settlement is reached, the tribunal may render an award recording the settlement, if requested by the parties, provided that the award contains an express statement that it is an award made with the parties' consent. Art. 26.8.

DEFAULT JUDGMENT

ICC "If any of the parties refuses or fails to take part in the arbitration or any stage thereof, the arbitration shall proceed notwithstanding such refusal or failure." Art. 6(3) "If any of the parties, although duly summoned, fails to appear without valid excuse, the Arbitral Tribunal shall have the power to proceed with the hearing." Art. 21(2).

UNCITRAL If claimant fails to present his or her claims in a timely manner—dismissal. If respondent fails to respond in a timely manner—proceedings continue. Art. 28(1).

AAA If party fails to file a statement of defense or fails to appear at a hearing, the arbitration will continue. If a party fails to produce evidence within the time established by the tribunal, the tribunal may make the award on the evidence before it. Art. 23.

LCIA If the respondent fails to submit a statement of defense or the claimant fails to submit a statement of defense of a counterclaim, or if at any point any party fails to present its case, the tribunal may proceed with the arbitration and make an award. Art. 15.8.

COSTS

ICC "The final Award shall fix the costs of the arbitration and decide which of the parties shall bear them or in what proportion they shall be borne by the parties." Art. 31(3).

UNCITRAL "[C]osts of arbitration shall in principle be borne by the unsuccessful party. However, the Arbitral Tribunal may apportion each of such costs between the parties if it determines that apportionment is reasonable, taking into account the circumstances of the case." Art. 40(1).

AAA "The tribunal shall fix the costs of the arbitration in its award. The tribunal may apportion such costs among the parties if it determines such apportionment is reasonable, taking into account the circumstances of the case." Art. 31.

LCIA The court sets the costs of the arbitration. The tribunal specifies the total amount of costs in its award and unless otherwise agreed, determines the proportions in which the parties shall bear all or part of the arbitration costs. Art. 28.

FINALITY

ICC "Every Award shall be binding on the parties. By submitting the dispute to arbitration under these Rules, the parties undertake to carry out any Award without delay and shall be deemed to have waived their right to any form of recourse insofar as such waiver can validly be made." Art. 28(6).

UNCITRAL "The award shall be . . . final and binding on the parties. The parties undertake to carry out the award without delay." Art. 32(2).

AAA The award shall be final and binding on the parties and the parties undertake to carry out the award without delay. Art. 27(1).

LCIA All awards shall be final and binding on the parties, and by agreeing to arbitration, the parties agree to carry out the award immediately and without delay. Art. 26.9.

MAJORITY

ICC "When the Arbitral Tribunal is composed of more than one arbitrator, an Award is given by a majority decision. If there be no majority, the Award shall be made by the chairman of the Arbitral Tribunal alone." Art. 25(1).

UNCITRAL "When there are three arbitrators, any award or other decision of the Arbitral Tribunal shall be made by a majority of the arbitrators." Art. 31(1).

AAA "Where there is more than one arbitrator, any award, decision or ruling of the arbitral tribunal shall be made by the majority of the arbitrators. Art. 26(1).

LCIA Where there are three arbitrators and the arbitral tribunal fails to agree on any issue, the arbitrators shall decide that issue by a majority. Failing a majority decision on any issue, the chairperson of the tribunal shall decide. Art. 26.3.

SEVERABILITY OF ISSUES/AWARDS

ICC No provision as of the most recent revision.

UNCITRAL "In addition to making a final award, the Arbitral Tribunal shall be entitled to make interim, interlocutory, or partial awards." Art. 32(1).

AAA In addition to the final award, the tribunal may make interim, interlocutory, or partial orders or awards. Art. 27(7).

LCIA The tribunal may make separate awards on different issues at different times. Art. 26.7.

MECHANICS (STENOGRAPHIC REPORT OF HEARING)

ICC No provision as of the most recent revision.

UNCITRAL "The Arbitral Tribunal shall make arrangements for . . . a record of the hearing . . ." if deemed necessary or if the parties so agree. Art. 25(3).

AAA No provision as of the most recent revision.

LCIA No provision as of the most recent revision.

LANGUAGE

ICC "In the absence of an agreement by the parties, the Arbitral Tribunal shall determine the language or languages of the arbitration, due regard being given to all relevant circumstances, including the language of the contract." Art. 16.

UNCITRAL "Subject to an agreement by the parties, the Arbitral Tribunal shall . . . determine the language or languages to be used . . ." Art. 17(1).

AAA If not agreed otherwise, the language of the arbitration shall be that of the documents containing the arbitration agreement, subject to the power of the tribunal to determine otherwise based upon the contentions of the parties and circumstances of the arbitration. Art. 14.

LCIA The initial language of the arbitration shall be the language of the arbitration agreement. Upon the formation of the tribunal, the arbitrators may decide what language shall be the language of the arbitration after giving the parties an opportunity to make written comments and taking into account the initial language. Art. 17.1, 17.2.

INTERPRETERS

ICC No provision as of the most recent revision.

UNCITRAL "The Arbitral Tribunal shall make arrangements for the translation of oral statements made at a hearing . . . if . . . deemed necessary . . ." Art. 25(3).

AAA The tribunal may order that documents delivered in another language shall be accompanied by a translation into the language(s) of the arbitration. Art. 14. "At the request of the tribunal or pursuant to mutual agreement of the parties, the [AAA] shall make arrangements for the interpretation of oral testimony or for a record of the hearing." Art. 20(3)

LCIA The tribunal may order documents delivered in another language to be translated. Art. 17.4.

LOCATION

ICC "The place of the arbitration shall be fixed by the Court unless agreed upon by the parties." Art. 14(1).

UNCITRAL "Unless the parties have agreed upon the place where the arbitration is to be held, such place shall be determined by the Arbitral Tribunal. . . ." Art. 16(1).

AAA "If the parties disagree as to the place of arbitration, the administrator may initially determine the place of arbitration, subject to the power of the tribunal to determine finally the place of arbitration within 60 days after its constitution." Art. 13(1).

LCIA The parties may agree on the place of arbitration. If there is no such agreement, the location shall be in London, unless and until the court determines that another location is more appropriate. Art. 16.1.

TIME EXTENSIONS

ICC "The Court may extend [the time limit for rendering a final Award] pursuant to a reasoned request from the Arbitral Tribunal or on its own initiative if it decides it is necessary to do so." Art. 24(2).

UNCITRAL Time periods for communication of written statements may be extended by the arbitral tribunal. Art. 23.

AAA Time periods for communication of written statements may be extended by the tribunal. Art. 17(2).

LCIA The tribunal may extend or abbreviate any time limit provided by the arbitration agreement or the rules for the conduct of the arbitration or by the tribunal's orders. Art. 22.1(b).

MISCELLANEOUS (LIMITATIONS ON APPLICATION OF RULES)

ICC "The function of the Court is to provide for the settlement by arbitration of business disputes of an international character. . . . If so empowered by an arbitration agreement, the Court shall also provide for the settlement by arbitration in accordance with these Rules of business disputes not of an international character." Art. 1(1).

UNCITRAL "These Rules shall govern the arbitration except that where any of these Rules is in conflict with the provision of the law applicable to the arbitration from which the parties cannot derogate, that provision shall prevail." Art. 1(2).

AAA "These rules govern the arbitration, except that, where any such rule is in conflict with any provision of the law applicable to the arbitration from which the parties cannot derogate, that provision shall prevail." Art. 1(2).

LCIA In all matters not expressly provided for in these rules, the LCIA Court, the arbitral tribunal, and the parties shall act in the spirit of these rules and shall make every reasonable effort to ensure that an award is legally enforceable. Art. 32.2.

AD HOC

ICC The ICC rules were established for administered, rather than ad hoc, arbitration.

UNCITRAL UNCITRAL rules were established for ad hoc arbitration. Resolution 31/98.

AAA Administered, rather than ad hoc, arbitration.

LCIA The LCIA rules were established for administered, rather than ad hoc, arbitration.

SUBMISSION TO COURT'S JURISDICTION

ICC "Before the file is transmitted to the Arbitral Tribunal, and in appropriate circumstances even thereafter, the parties may apply to any competent judicial authority for interim or conservatory measures." Art. 23(2).

UNCITRAL "A request for interim measures addressed by any party to a judicial authority shall not be deemed incompatible with the agreement to arbitrate, or as a waiver of that agreement." Art. 26(3).

AAA "A request for interim measures addressed by a party to a judicial authority shall not be deemed incompatible with the agreement to arbitrate or a waiver of the right to arbitrate." Art. 21(3).

LCIA "By agreeing to arbitrate under the [LCIA] rules, the parties shall be treated as having agreed not to apply to any state court or other judicial authority for any order available from the Arbitral Tribunal, except with written agreement of all parties." Art. 22.2.

Appendix 5
Sample Arbitration Clauses

NEGOTIATED ARBITRATION PROVISION

Arbitration. [Subject to the provision regarding injunctive relief, and] upon written notice to all parties, all controversies, disputes or claims arising between Franchisor, any of its affiliates or any of their respective officers, directors, agents, employees and attorneys and Master Franchisee, any of its affiliates or any of their respective officers, directors and shareholders, arising out of or related to the relationship of the parties hereto or this Agreement (the "Dispute") shall be settled by binding arbitration in accordance with the then-current UNCITRAL Arbitration Rules, in the municipality in which Franchisor has its principal place of business. Such arbitration proceedings shall be conducted by one (1) neutral arbitrator appointed by the CPR Institute for Dispute Resolution. This provision shall be governed by, and enforced in accordance with, the United States Arbitration Act (9 U.S.C. §§ 1-16) (the "Federal Arbitration Act"). The arbitration proceedings shall be conducted on an individual basis and not on a multi-plaintiff, consolidated or class-wide basis.

The arbitrator shall be bound by, and shall strictly enforce the terms of this Agreement and shall not limit, expand or otherwise modify its terms. The arbitrator shall have sole authority to resolve any and all issues as to the arbitrability of any Dispute, including the application or running of any statute of limitations and all questions involving issue preclusion. The arbitrator shall have the power to determine the nature and extent of any discovery and to resolve all issues of admissibility of evidence. The arbitrator shall not have the power to award damages in connection with any Dispute in excess of actual compensatory damages, which may include interest on unpaid amounts from date due, and consequential damages. The arbitrator shall not have the power to award punitive damages or to multiply actual damages. The arbitrator shall be permitted, where warranted, to also award specific performance and/or injunctive relief.

The decision and award of the arbitrator shall be in writing and state the reasons for such decision and award. The decision and award shall be conclusive and binding upon all parties and judgment upon the award may be entered in any court of competent jurisdiction. The arbitrator, the parties, their representatives and participants shall hold the existence, contents and result of any arbitration in confidence, except to the limited extent necessary to enforce a final settlement agreement, to obtain enforcement of the arbitrator's decision and award, or as otherwise required by law. Franchisor, its Affiliates and their respective officers, directors, agents, employees and attorneys and Master Franchisee, and its Affiliates and their respective officers, directors and shareholders hereby waive any right to contest the validity or enforceability of such award, except as provided in the Federal Arbitration Act. This provision shall continue in full force and effect subsequent to and notwithstanding expiration or termination of this Agreement.

AAA STANDARD ARBITRATION CLAUSE

"Any controversy or claim arising out of or relating to this contract shall be determined by arbitration in accordance with the International Arbitration Rules of the American Arbitration Association."

The parties may wish to consider adding

"The number of arbitrators shall be (one or three)";
"The place of arbitration shall be (city and/or country)"; or
"The language(s) of the arbitration shall be ______________________."

Parties are encouraged, when writing their contracts or when a dispute arises, to request a conference, in person or by telephone, with the AAA, to discuss an appropriate method for selection of arbitrators or any other matter that might facilitate efficient arbitration of the dispute.

UNCITRAL MODEL ARBITRATION CLAUSE

Any dispute, controversy or claim arising out of or relating to this contract, or the breach, termination or invalidity thereof, shall be settled by arbitration in accordance with the UNCITRAL Arbitration Rules as presently in force.

Parties may wish to consider adding:

(a) The appointing authority shall be ... (name of institution or person);
(b) The number of arbitrators shall be ... (one or three);
(c) The place of arbitration shall be ... (town or country);
(d) The language(s) to be used in the arbitral proceedings shall be ...

LCIA STANDARD ARBITRATION DISPUTE

Future Disputes:

Any dispute arising out of or in connection with this contract, including any question regarding its existence, validity or termination, shall be referred to and finally resolved by arbitration under the LCIA Rules, which Rules are deemed to be incorporated by reference into this clause:

The number of arbitrators shall be [one / three].

The seat, or legal place, of arbitration shall be [City and / or Country].

The language to be used in the arbitral proceedings shall be [ ].

The governing law of the contract shall be the substantive law of [ ].

WIPO ARBITRATION CLAUSE

Arbitration Clause

"Any dispute, controversy or claim arising under, out of or relating to this contract and any subsequent amendments of this contract, including, without limitation, its formation, validity, binding effect, interpretation, performance, breach or termination, as well as non-contractual claims, shall be referred to and finally determined by arbitration in accordance with the WIPO Arbitration Rules. The arbitral tribunal shall consist of [three arbitrators][a sole arbitrator]. The place of arbitration shall be . . . The language to be used in the arbitral proceedings shall be . . . The dispute, controversy or claim shall be decided in accordance with the law of . . ."

Expedited Arbitration Clause
"Any dispute, controversy or claim arising under, out of or relating to this contract and any subsequent amendments of this contract, including, without limitation, its formation, validity, binding effect, interpretation, performance, breach or termination, as well as non-contractual claims, shall be referred to and finally determined by arbitration in accordance with the WIPO Expedited Arbitration Rules. The place of arbitration shall be . . . The language to be used in the arbitral proceedings shall be . . . The dispute, controversy or claim shall be decided in accordance with the law of . . ."

CPR ARBITRATION CLAUSE

"Any dispute arising out of or relating to, this contract, including the breach, termination or validity thereof, shall be finally resolved by arbitration in accordance with the CPR Institute for Dispute Resolution Rules for Non-Administered Arbitration of International Disputes, by (a sole arbitrator) (three arbitrators, of whom each party shall appoint one) (three arbitrators, none of whom shall be appointed by either party). Judgment upon the award rendered by the arbitrator(s) may be entered by any court having jurisdiction thereof. The seat of the arbitration shall be (city, country). The arbitration shall be conducted in (language). The Neutral Organization designated to perform the functions specified in Rules 5, 6 and 7 shall be (name of CPR or other organization)."

CHAPTER ❖ 8

Research, Resources, and Treaties

ANDREW P. LOEWINGER

This chapter discusses the availability of resources and treaties on international franchise projects and the most effective use of them by

U.S. counsel. Section I addresses the initial spotting of the issues in any international franchise project and the most effective ways to research issues and integrate its use efficiently with local counsel, including identifying the principal types of legal issues and specific research materials available for international franchising. Section II discusses relevant international treaties.

I. International Franchise Resources: Finding "The Right Stuff"

There are numerous international resource materials available. The challenge for the franchise practitioner is to find materials that have a particular relevance for international franchising. Those materials that are most relevant to international franchising are those that specifically address franchising, trademarks, trade secret information, other intellectual property issues, dispute resolution, contract law, tax law issues, corporate law issues, and competition (or antitrust) law issues. These materials are presented in Sections I.A and B, below, with a brief summary of their scope.

Material is available in periodicals, books, treatises and, increasingly, on the World Wide Web. Moreover, international treaties are particularly important to consult on a variety of issues in international franchising. Although there are no international treaties that relate specifically to franchising, there are many multilateral and bilateral treaties that directly affect international franchise arrangements in such areas as dispute resolution, trademarks and other intellectual property issues, international sales of goods, and tax issues. These are discussed in more detail in Section II, below.

Although international franchising is still relatively young, there are myriad resources available to the practitioner. These resources are of two types: research materials and organizational resources. Research materials are available through traditional sources such as treatises and other publications as well as through the World Wide Web. Materials and resources from organizations that are most relevant to franchising are those organizations, committees, or sections specifically devoted to franchising.

We identify below some of the principal sources of materials that are useful for various categories of information. Our list is designed to be more illustrative than exhaustive.

A. RESOURCE MATERIALS

We describe below available materials by subject matter. Clearly, the most immediately useful materials and information for the franchise practitioner are those that relate directly to franchising.

1. *Franchise Materials*

a. Books and Treatises. We describe below those international franchise materials we have found to be most useful.

Business Franchise Guide (CCH) (CCH, Inc., 2000, www.cch.com).

The *Business Franchise Guide,* at paragraphs 7000–7256, presents information on the franchise laws and regulations in Australia, Brazil, Canada, China, France, Indonesia, Italy, Malaysia, Mexico, Romania, Russia, South Korea, Spain, and the European Union. Relevant sections of the laws and regulations of each of these jurisdictions is presented, as is an overview of franchising in each jurisdiction.

Disclosure Requirements in International Transactions, Business. Franchise Guide (CCH) (CCH, Inc., Issue No. 229, Sept. 9, 1998).

This publication, prepared for the International Bar Association's 27th Biennial Conference, in September 1998, provides information on the disclosure requirements for fourteen countries: Australia, Brazil, Canada, China, France, Indonesia, Italy, Japan, Malaysia, Mexico, South Africa, South Korea, Spain, and the United States.

The International Encyclopaedia of Franchising (Martin Mendelsohn and Michael G. Brennan, eds., Kluwer Law International, 2000, www.kluwerlaw.com).

This treatise includes information relating to international franchising in fourteen jurisdictions: Australia, Austria, Canada, Denmark, Germany, Israel, Italy, New Zealand, South Korea, Sweden, Switzerland, the United Kingdom, the United States, and the European Union. The encyclopaedia also includes *The International Franchise Law Bibliography* (Andrew P. Loewinger, ed.), (see below).

The International Franchise Law Bibliography (Andrew P. Loewinger, ed., Kluwer Law International, 2001, www.kluwerlaw.com).

Compiled under the auspices of Committee X (International Franchising) of the International Bar Association, this bibliography references a body of legal materials specifically related to international franchising, including primary legal materials (laws and regulations), secondary legal materials (books and treatises), articles from legal journals and other periodicals, and various legal symposia materials. Jurisdictions for which materials are referenced include Argentina, Australia, Austria, Brazil, China, Croatia, England, the European Community, Finland, France, Greece, Hong Kong, Italy, Japan, Malaysia, the Netherlands, New Zealand, Norway, the Philippines, Portugal, Scotland, South Korea, Spain, Sweden, Switzerland, Thailand, and Turkey.

International Franchising (Alex S. Konigsberg, Q.C., ed., 2d ed., Juris Publishing, 2000, www.jurispub.com).

This book provides extensive analysis on the topic of international franchising, including (1) the types of laws governing international franchising, including specific franchise legislation; (2) the different alternatives available to the franchisor who is considering franchising abroad, with a consideration of relevant business and legal factors; (3) the different agreements commonly used in international franchise transactions; (4) difficulties associated with international franchising and suggestions to avoid these problems; (5) negotiation of agreements; (6) the fiscal implications of international franchising; and (7) trademark matters in the international setting.

International Franchising Law (Dennis Campbell, ed., Lexis Publishing, 2000, www.lexis.com).

This treatise presents an introduction to and the pros and cons of international franchising. The two-volume work has contributions from country authors on international franchising in fifty-nine countries. Topics included in each country section vary slightly, but generally include the country's legal system and its applicability to franchising, intellectual property, restrictive trade practices, licensing and technology transfer, and taxation. These and many other issues discussed are useful to the franchise practitioner working in other countries.

Guide to International Master Franchise Arrangements (International Institute for the Unification of Private Law (UNIDROIT), 1998, www.unidroit.org).

The *UNIDROIT Guide* offers an examination of many of the issues involved in international franchising, including the advantages and disadvantages of master franchise arrangements and other commercial vehicles available to a franchisor, negotiation and drafting of the master franchise agreement and associated agreements, subfranchising, regulatory issues, fees and other financial issues, advertising and supply issues, intellectual property concerns, issues raised by changes in the franchise system, transfer and termination of agreements, and dispute resolution. The UNIDROIT Web site, www.unidroit.org/english/franchising/main.htm, may also provide useful information.

Survey of Foreign Laws and Regulations Affecting International Franchising (Philip F. Zeidman, ed., 2d ed., Franchising Committee, Section of Antitrust Law, American Bar Association, 1989, www.abanet.org,).

This survey presents information on the laws and regulations affecting franchising in twenty-five countries. Topics covered include the business climate and franchising; legislation affecting franchising; antitrust law; trademarks; forms of doing business; tax aspects of foreign franchising; investment incentives; customs and import-export controls; labor issues; and real estate. Although somewhat dated, it provides a useful structure for analyzing issues impacting international franchising.

Franchising Law: Practice and Forms (Fern, Asbill, Costello, and Scott, eds., Specialty Technical Publishers, Inc., 2001, www.stpub.com, Bus. Franchise Guide (CCH) (CD-ROM)).

Chapter 22 of the Franchisor Volume and its Appendix contains useful charts for the franchise practitioner dealing with selected countries. The first set of charts is a comparison of disclosure mechanics, either required by statute in eleven countries or part of pending legislation or codes of ethics in eight jurisdictions. International franchise laws relationship requirements in eleven countries are included.

A second set of charts compares items to be disclosed in various countries to the items required by the UFOC guidelines and includes endnotes. The chart contains a comparison of International Franchising Disclosure Requirements with UFOC requirements in Australia, Brazil, Canada (Alberta and Ontario), China, France, Indonesia, Malaysia, Mexico, Romania, Russia, South Korea, Spain, and Taiwan.

Franchise Law Bibliography (Michael J. Lockerby, ed., 2d ed., Franchising Committee, Section of Antitrust Law, American Bar Association, 1993 www.abanet.org).

The *Franchise Law Bibliography* contains an annotated listing by title of publications on franchise law, franchising, and related topics.

b. Periodicals

International Journal of Franchising and Distribution Law (Martin Mendelsohn, ed., Kluwer Law International, www.kluwerlaw.com).

This quarterly publication assembles articles and materials for the international franchising practitioner, including news items; examinations of changes in the law in individual countries; worldwide case reports with analysis; reports from world conferences; and a range of topical articles.

Country Commerce (The Economist Intelligence Unit, Ltd., www.eiu.com).

This publication (formerly entitled *Investing, Licensing & Trading*), is issued annually, and provides a guide to operating conditions, commercial laws, and business regulations in numerous countries. It addresses such issues as investment restrictions, licensing requirements, and taxation.

2. *Trademark Materials*

Trademarks Throughout the World (Jeanine M. Politi, ed., West Group, 1999, www.westgroup.com).

A treatise on trademark laws worldwide, covering over 200 countries.

International Trademark Treaties and Agreements (Frederick W. Mostert, ed., International Trademark Association, 1998, www.inta.org).

This is a comprehensive resource for global trademark treaties and agreements. It discusses seventeen treaties, agreements, and policy statements concerning trademarks and contains the full text of the Paris Convention, Madrid Agreement, Madrid Protocol, TRIPS Agreement, and NSI Domain Name Dispute Policy, among others.

Trademark Law and the Internet: Issues, Case Law and Practice Tips (Lisa E. Cristal and Neal S. Greenfield, eds., International Trademark Association, 2000, www.inta.org).

This reference provides commentary and analysis on the use and protection of trademarks on the Internet. Issues discussed include domain names; registry policies; dispute resolution, use, and affixation; U.S. Patent and Trademark Office practice; searching; policing; enforcement; jurisdiction; linking, framing, and metatagging; agreements; applicable laws, rules, regulations, and guidelines; and evolving case law.

Country Guides: Basic Information on Trademark Registration Worldwide (John Hornick, et. al., eds., 2d ed., International Trademark Association, 1998, www.inta.org).

This resource provides information on trademark filing, prosecution, registration, maintenance, and enforcement in over seventy-four jurisdictions and defines thirty-three commonly used trademark terms in glossaries that are translated into seven languages: English, Chinese, French, German, Japanese, Russian, and Spanish. The section for each country provides concise answers to thirty common questions of trademark owners and lawyers.

1999 Trademark Law Handbook: U.S. and International (Anthony L. Fletcher, et. al., eds., International Trademark Association, 1999, www.inta.org).

This publication is updated annually to reflect developments in trademark law and practice in the United States and abroad. Volume I covers the United States and includes analyses of noteworthy decisions, highlights of changes in procedure and practice, issue reviews, and federal court defenses and remedies. Volume II covers international developments and selected cases, and commentaries on various issues prepared by practitioners in over sixty jurisdictions.

3. *International Tax Materials*

Tax Management (BNA, 2000)

This service covers all aspects of U.S. federal tax, and includes the *Foreign Income Series*, which is more relevant to matters dealing with international franchising. The *Foreign Income Series* consists of portfolios dealing with U.S. law governing cross-border tax issues and the "Business Operations" portfolios, dealing with various aspects of the legal system in over thirty countries, in addition to tax regimes in each jurisdiction within the European Community. The Tax Management portfolios are available to subscribers in print, CD-ROM, and via the Internet. The Internet product features access to the text of U.S. bilateral tax treaties, with commentary. For a list of portfolios, go to www.bna.com/tmweb/catalog/tmfi.html.

International Bureau of Fiscal Documentation

The International Bureau of Fiscal Documentation (IBFD) publishes a series of loose-leaf products that provide information on the tax regimes of many countries. Information is grouped by region (for example, Europe, Latin America, and Asia-Pacific) or by subject matter (for example, corporate taxes and VAT). Among the resources available from the IBFD is the actual text, in English, of various bilateral tax agreements for the avoidance of double taxation. This service is available in print and on CD-ROM. To see a description of these products, go to www.ibfd.com/IBFDCat.htm.

Tax Analysts

Tax Analysts' Web product, "TaxBase," is a comprehensive database of tax documents and news items. TaxBase's Worldwide Tax Treaties collection includes over 3,500 tax treaties, amending protocols, and similar documents from over 181 jurisdictions. For more information regarding TaxBase, see www.taxbase.tax.org/.

4. Dispute Resolution Materials

Domke, The Law of Practice of Commercial Arbitration (Gabriel M. Wilner, ed., West Group, 1999, www.westgroup.com).

Volume I of the *Domke* treatise addresses topics including the nature of commercial arbitration, the development of commercial arbitration law, the arbitration agreement, initiation of arbitration, statutory enforcement of arbitration agreements, the arbitrator and arbitration hearings, cost and expenses of arbitration, interstate enforcement of awards, and the enforcement of arbitration agreements and awards in international transactions. Volume II provides further information on the international enforcement of agreements and awards.

5. Antitrust Materials

Block Exemption on Vertical Agreements

The European Commission has replaced the 1989 "block exemption" from European Union competition law for franchising with a broader regulation governing all vertical restraints. Text of the new regulation appears at Bus. Franchise Guide (CCH) ¶ 7101 and at the European Union's Web site, europa.eu.int/eur-lex/en/lif/dat/2000/en_300R2658.html.

The vertical restraints regulation became effective June 1, 2000, and is set to expire on May 31, 2010. To avert a legal vacuum, the "block exemption" for franchising, which was scheduled to expire on December 31, 1999, was extended through May 31, 2000. Existing agreements will continue to benefit from the "block exemption" for franchising until the end of 2001.

The new rule is the product of an ongoing review of competition policy on vertical restraints. In January 1997, the European Commission initiated the process by issuing a Green Paper on Vertical Restraints (*see* Bus. Franchise Guide (CCH) ¶ 7358), which analyzed the current law and invited public comment on a number of alternatives. In September 1998, the commission released a Communication (*see* Bus. Franchise Guide (CCH) ¶ 7371) proposing a regime similar to the new regulation.

According to the European Commission, the new regulation indicates a shift from the formalistic regulatory approach embodied by the old "block exemption" toward a more economics-based approach. The basic aim of the new approach is to simplify the rules applicable to supply and distribution agreements and to reduce the regulatory burden, while ensuring more effective control of agreements entered into by companies holding significant market power.

In May 2000, the commission issued guidelines ("Block Exemption Guidelines") explaining the new regulation (Commission Notice, Guidelines on Vertical Restraints). Specifically, the guidelines explain, among other things, (1) which vertical agreements benefit from the "safe harbor" created by the new regulation; (2) the important concept of market share and the calculation of a company's market share; and (3) the commission's enforcement policy for agreements not covered by the new regulation. The commission intends to revise the Block Exemption Guidelines in 2004 in light of the experience gained in applying the regulation and the Block Exemption Guidelines.

Guide to the EU Block Exemption for Vertical Agreements (Martin Mendelsohn and Stephen Rose, eds., Kluwer Law International, 2000, www.kluwerlaw.com).

This work provides a comprehensive review of recent European Union policy application of competition law to vertical agreements. A full text of the block exemption regulation, accompanying guidelines, and other commission notices are included. Other issues include a background to European Union competition law; an in-depth analysis of the provisions of the block exemption regulation; and an examination of how the rules apply to exclusive distribution, exclusive purchasing, selective distribution, franchising, and agency agreements.

B. ORGANIZATIONAL RESOURCES

Organizational materials available on international franchise matters are of two types: associations of lawyers, such as the International Bar

Association's International Franchising Committee (Committee X) and the American Bar Association's Forum on Franchising; and franchise organizations such as the International Franchise Association and national franchise associations.

1. Legal Associations

International Bar Association's International Franchising Committee (Committee X)

The International Franchising Committee (Committee X) of the International Bar Association (IBA) holds meetings twice a year on international franchise matters, publishes a newsletter and other franchise publications, and operates an e-mail ListServe.

Each year the committee conducts programs at the annual IBA Conference. The annual 2001 conference, Cancun 2001, is scheduled for October–November 2001 in Cancun, Mexico. The 2002 conference will be in Durban, South Africa. For further information, and for a complete listing of all IBA publications available for purchase or download, visit the IBA Web site at www.ibanet.org.

Through the committee's newsletter, *International Franchising*, com mittee members are kept up-to-date on legal developments around the world, seminars, and publications of interest. For more information, contact Richard M. Asbill, Chair, SBL Committee X, at rickasbill@paulhastings.com or sbl@int-bar.org, 271 Regent Street, London W1R 7PA, England. IBA's ListServe allows subscribers to exchange information regarding international franchising and other topics via e-mail with contacts around the world. To subscribe to the ListServe, which is free of charge, and for details on the activities and resources of Committee X, consult the IBA Web site at www.ibanet.org.

Subscribing to the ListServe requires IBA membership but is otherwise free of charge. To subscribe, follow these six steps:

1. Log onto the IBA home page (www.ibanet.org).
2. Click on the box saying "login now" in the top right-hand corner.
3. Insert your IBA member number in the box labeled "logon ID."
4. Insert your family name in the "password" box and click "logon."
5. Click on category labeled "Committee Index."
6. Click on "International Franchising (SBL-X)."

American Bar Association's Forum on Franchising

The Forum on Franchising holds an annual conference that regularly includes programs on international franchising; publishes the *Franchise Law Journal* and *The Franchise Lawyer*, which contain articles on international franchising, and on a variety of other franchise-related matters; and operates an e-mail ListServe allowing franchise practitioners to exchange information and ideas via e-mail. A selection of the papers presented at prior conferences are available on the Web site at www.abanet.org/forums/franchising/frprogpap. In addition, the Web site at www.abanet.org/forums/franchising/frjournal2000, contains an index to the *Franchise Law Journal* articles.

To join the ListServe, which is free of charge to Forum members, or for further information on the resources and activities of the Forum on Franchising, see the ABA Web site at www.abanet.org/forums/franchising.

A sample listing of useful papers dealing with international franchising from past conferences of the Forum on Franchising are provided below.

1993: E. Lynn Perry and David C. Gryce, "Trademarks and Copyright Issues in the International Arena," ABA Forum on Franchising (1993).

This paper focuses on trademark and copyright issues that U.S. companies (franchisors) may encounter when seeking to do business overseas. The papers note the complexities of obtaining a trademark registration in other countries and identifies countries having "first to register," "first to use," or "cautionary" notice trademark laws, and includes research on the advantages of registration; international treaties and related materials affecting trademarks (Paris Convention, Convention establishing the World Intellectual Property Organization, Madrid Agreement (and amendments), Trademark Registration Treaty, Madrid Protocol, Pending U.S. Implementation Legislation, and so forth); Common Market Protection; Changes in Eastern Europe; International Searching; The Registration Process; After Registration; and Copyright.

1994: Michael G. Brennan, Alex S. Konigsberg, Q.C., and Philip F. Zeidman, "Globetrotting: Successful Strategies for Launching and Protecting U.S. Franchisors Abroad," ABA Forum on Franchising (1994).

This paper explores functions of franchise counsel, specifically those representing U.S. franchisors expanding internationally. Key topics include discussions on counsel; an examination of traditional methods used by U.S. franchisors expanding abroad and other options; and drafting international franchise agreements.

1995: Andrew P. Loewinger and Thomas M. Pitegoff, "Avoiding the Long Arm of the Law in International Franchising: Issues and Approaches," ABA. Forum on Franchising (1995).

This paper addresses requirements for registration and disclosure under federal and state law in the United States and in Brazil, France, Mexico, and Australia. It addresses the jurisdictional reach of such laws and the means to avoid jurisdiction of such laws.

1996: Gary R. Duvall, Andrea Oricchio Kirsh, and Mark Abell, "Foreign Policy: Shaping International Franchise Legislation," ABA Forum on Franchising (1996).

This paper provides an introduction to international franchising on a variety of related topics, including specific franchise laws; voluntary codes, local trade regulations, foreign currency, and repatriation limitations; supranational organizations; information pertaining to Central and South American markets; trends in franchising (Argentina, Colombia, and Brazil); and an overview of European franchise legislation and notes on member-state franchise laws.

1997: Catherine Riesterer and Frank Zaid, "The Basics of International Franchising," ABA Forum on Franchising (1997).

This paper addresses some of the initial considerations of international franchising, such as expansion strategy, choosing a market, picking the right partner, intellectual property and tax implications, forms of franchising, and various other legal issues.

1998: Anne-Marie Gauthier, Lou Hedrik Jones, Kenneth Kaplan, and Frank Zaid, "Fundamentals of International Franchising," ABA Forum on Franchising (1998).

This publication discusses issues related to fundamentals of international franchising, such as structures for international franchising, currency control provisions, and choice of law considerations.

1999: Gary R. Duvall, Jane LaFranchi, and Paul Jones, "Planning for International Enforcement of Franchise Agreements," ABA Forum on Franchising (1999).

This paper discusses the enforcement of franchise agreements in Brazil, France, Japan, Mexico, and South Korea, in addition to preparing franchise agreements for enforcement in the transitional economies of the People's Republic of China and the Russian Federation.

2000: Richard M. Asbill, Michael G. Brennan, William A. Finkelstein, Steven M. Goldman, Kenneth S. Kaplan, Andrew P. Loewinger, Joyce G. Mazero, Cathy A. Riesterer, T. Timothy Tuerff, and Erik B. Wulff, *A Practical Guide for International Franchising*, ABA Forum on Franchising (2000).

This collection of papers addresses all relevant topics on international franchising, including effective use of local counsel, protection of trademarks and related intellectual property rights, a franchisor's organizational and business considerations, contractual structures, U.S. tax considerations related to cross-border franchise transactions, disclosure issues, local legal issues and sample "international clauses," dispute resolution, and resources and treaties in the international franchising process, and was the initial source for this book.

2. *Franchise Associations*

International Franchise Association (IFA)

Founded in 1960, the IFA is an organization of franchisors, franchisees, and suppliers. The IFA has legal programs from time to time on international franchising. For more information on the legal activities and resources of the IFA, contact: Matthew R. Shay, Executive Vice President at matthew@franchise.org, International Franchise Association, 1350 New York Avenue, NW Suite 900, Washington, D.C. 20005-4709. Phone: (202) 628-8000. Fax: (202) 628-0812, or consult the IFA Web site, www.franchise.org.

Annually, in May, the International Bar Association Section on Business Law's International Franchising Committee (Committee X) and the IFA jointly sponsor a program on international franchising in Washington, D.C. A sample listing of topics from past joint programs is provided below.

1997: The 1997 program, "Key Issues in the Life Cycle of an International Franchise Relationship," addressed disclosure and registration in the international context; arbitration, litigation, and mediation in international networks; developing and enhancing communication and support in an international network; establishing and maintaining a healthy franchise relationship; and termination of the franchise relationship.

1998: The 1998 program, "International Franchising: Traditional Issues and New Challenges," covered multiconcept and co-branding arrangements in international franchising; a realistic approach to international marketing and advertising; hot issues in international disclosure; and franchising and the Internet.

1999: The 1999 program, "The Continuing Challenges of Franchising in the Global Marketplace," included discussions in international arbitration of franchise disputes; the European Union competition law and franchising; basics of international franchise agreements; disclosure requirements for international franchising; and international acquisitions of franchising companies.

2000: The 2000 program, "Practical Advice for International Franchising in the New Millennium," addressed managing the international reach of U.S. laws; current strategies for protecting a franchisor's intellectual property, especially with the development of the Internet; what happens to the subfranchisee when a master franchise agreement is transferred or terminated; the Internet's impact on exclusive territories in international franchising; and changes to franchising in Europe following the new block exemption.

2001: The 2001 program, "Emerging Trends and Difficult Issues in International Franchising" addressed business aspects of an international franchise transaction; what to disclose when there is no disclosure law; the Internet and international franchising; and bringing franchise systems to the United States.

Country Franchise Associations

Franchise associations exist in fifty-two countries around the world. Although these associations are not designed specifically to provide legal resources, they can be a useful source of information on issues relating to franchising in their countries and can provide contacts to knowledgeable individuals within those countries. A list of franchise associations in fifty-two countries, with contact information, is included as Exhibit A and the end of this chapter. This list is provided courtesy of the IFA.

3. Other Associations

International Trademark Association

The International Trademark Association educates business, the media, and the public on the proper use of trademarks and actively pursues public policy matters concerning trademarks. For details on the resources and materials available through the International Trademark Association, consult the association's Web site, www.inta.org.

II. International Treaties Affecting Franchising

An important part of any international research relates to international treaties. There are a variety of treaties that affect international franchising. These include dispute resolution treaties (such as the New York Convention on arbitration); significant treaties addressing intellectual property matters or tax matters; and the United Nations Convention on the International Sales of Goods.

A. GENERAL TREATY INFORMATION

There are several very useful general resources for international treaties. For example, the following are available on the Internet:

U.S. Department of Commerce, Trade Compliance Center

This U.S. Department of Commerce Web site offers a trade and related agreements database that includes the full texts of over 250 international agreements to which the United States is party, including categories for service industries and goods industries. For more information, go to www.mac.doc.gov\tcc.

Law Library of Congress

The Guide to Law Online, prepared by the U.S. Law Library of Congress for the Global Legal Information Network (GLIN), is an annotated hypertext guide to sources of information worldwide on government and law available on-line without charge. It includes links only to the most useful and reliable sites for legal information available for each of the world's nations. As such sites come on-line, they will be linked directly to the GLIN database and will additionally receive special recognition in the Guide. To access the GLIN, go to www.lcweb2.loc.gov/glinhome.html.

Organization of American States Inter-American System of Legal Information Secretariat for Legal Affairs Department of Legal Cooperation and Information

The Department of Legal Cooperation and Information of the Secretariat for Legal Affairs develops and disseminates legal information both in conventional and electronic format. Of particular interest is a database of international treaties, featuring a United Nations Treaty Database, the Treaty Database of the Fletcher School of Law and Diplomacy, The Political Database of the Americas, and the GLIN. For more information, go to www.oas.org/En/prog/juridico/english/otherdat.html.

B. FRANCHISE TREATIES

There are no bilateral or multilateral treaties devoted to franchise matters.

C. TRADEMARK AND INTELLECTUAL PROPERTY TREATIES

The Paris Convention

Most nations of the world are members of the International Convention for the Protection of Industrial Property, typically referred to as the "Paris Convention." Generally speaking, the Paris Convention sets out minimum standards for the protection of patents, trademarks, and other proprietary property among member nations. The convention does not, however, provide for a worldwide trademark right and does not harmonize the laws of member nations. Under the Paris Convention, no member nation of the convention may implement a bifurcated system of trademark or patent administration favoring its citizens over foreign nationals. For the full text, go to the World Intellectual Property Organization (WIPO) Web site at www.wipo.int/treaties/ip/paris/index.html.

The Madrid Agreement

The Agreement of Madrid for the International Registration of Trademarks (Madrid Agreement) has approximately thirty members, mostly European nations. Notably, the United States, Great Britain, and Japan are not members. The Madrid Agreement, administered by the World Intellectual Property Organization (WIPO), creates a system whereby a single trademark registration application filed with the WIPO is considered equivalent to an application in each member country. The applicant must obtain a valid registration of its trademark in one of the member nations prior to filing with the WIPO. Further, as with the Paris Convention, the Madrid Agreement does not harmonize the laws of member nations. Each application filed with the WIPO is subject to review and rejection under the specific laws of each member nation. For the full text, go to the World Intellectual Property Organization (WIPO) Web site at www.wipo.int/treaties/registration/madrid/index.html.

The Madrid Protocol

The failure of the Madrid Agreement to gain the acceptance of nations such as the United States, Great Britain, and Japan led to the creation of the Protocol Relating to the Madrid Agreement Concerning the International Registration of Marks (Madrid Protocol). Generally speaking, the Madrid Protocol fine-tuned the Madrid Agreement and removed many of the burdens imposed by it. To date, the Madrid Protocol has not been ratified by the U.S. Congress, although ratification is expected soon and should make it much easier to obtain international trademark registrations. For the full text of the treaty, visit the World Intellectual Property Organization (WIPO) Web site at www.wipo.int/treaties/registration/protocol-madrid/index.html.

Berne Convention for the Protection of Literary and Artistic Works

The Berne Convention provides copyright protection for authors of literary or artistic works. For the full text, the World Intellectual Property Organization (WIPO) Web site at www.wipo.int/treaties/ip/berne/index.html.

World Intellectual Property Organization (WIPO) Copyright Treaty

This treaty is a supplement to the Berne Convention. Essentially, it extends the copyright protection provided by the Berne Convention to, among other things, computer programs and databases. For the full text, go to the WIPO Web site at www.wipo.int/treaties/ip/copyright/index.html.

Patent Cooperation Treaty

The Patent Cooperation Treaty is administered through the WIPO. The treaty creates a system for a unitary patent filing. It covers substantially all of the industrialized countries of the world, with the exception of Taiwan. For the full text, visit the WIPO Web site at www.wipo.int/treaties/registration/pct/index.html.

See also Chapter 3 of this book for a discussion of trademark and intellectual property issues.

D. TAX TREATIES

In the tax area, treaties are generally negotiated on a bilateral basis. Resources containing the text of U.S. treaties are described in Chapter 4 of this book.

E. DISPUTE RESOLUTION TREATIES

United Nations Convention on the Recognition and Enforcement of Foreign Arbitral Awards

To date, 126 countries and territories have ratified the 1958 United Nations Convention on the Recognition and Enforcement of Foreign Arbitral Awards (the New York Convention), which provides the basis for enforcing most international arbitration awards in commercial matters. The New York Convention requires the enforcement of arbitration agreements by member nations and provides for the mutual recognition and enforcement of arbitral awards by those nations, with only certain limited defenses provided to the enforcement of such an award. For the full text, visit the United Nations Commission on International Trade Law (UNCITRAL) Web site at www.uncitral.org/english/texts/arbconc/58conv.htm.

Inter-American Convention on International Commercial Arbitration

To date, nineteen nations of the western hemisphere, including the United States, Mexico, Brazil, and Argentina, have ratified the Inter-American Convention on International Commercial Arbitration (the Panama Convention). The Panama Convention is very similar to the New York Convention, but does provide different procedures for the enforcement of an award rendered in a member nation. For the full text, visit the Inter-American System of Legal Information Web site at www.oas.org/juridico/english/treaties/b-35.htm.

Inter-American Convention on Extraterritorial Validity of Foreign Judgments and Arbitral Awards

To date, Argentina, Brazil, Colombia, Ecuador, Mexico, Paraguay, Peru, Uruguay, and Venezuela have ratified the Inter-American Convention on Extraterritorial Validity of Foreign Judgments and Arbitral

Awards. Under this convention, judgments rendered in civil, commercial, or labor proceedings in one member state will be enforceable in another member state, provided certain conditions are met. In addition, the Convention on Extraterritorial Validity of Foreign Judgments and Arbitral Awards applies to all arbitral awards rendered in matters not covered by the Inter-American Convention. For the full text, visit the Inter-American System of Legal Information Web site at www.oas.org/juridico/english/treaties/b-41.htm.

Convention on Jurisdiction and the Enforcement of Judgments in Civil and Commercial Matters

The European Community's Convention on Jurisdiction and the Enforcement of Judgments in Civil and Commercial Matters (the Brussels Convention) entered into force for the original signatory nations on February 1, 1973. The fifteen current member-states of the European Community were either original signatories or have acceded to the Brussels Convention. Under the Brussels Convention, with certain limited exceptions, a judgment rendered in one member state will be recognized in any other member state. In addition, the convention mandates, with certain exceptions, that a national of a member state must be sued in the state where he or she is domiciled, irrespective of his or her nationality. For the full text, visit the Lex Mercatoria Web site at www.jus.uio.no/lm/ec.jurisdiction.enforcement.judgements.civil.commercial.matters.convention.brussels.1968/doc.html.

Lugano Convention on Jurisdiction and the Enforcement of Judgments in Civil and Commercial Matters

In the mid-1980s, Sweden, Switzerland, and other nations of the European Free Trade Association entered into talks with the members of the European Community to create a convention similar to the Brussels Convention. As a result, in 1988 the Lugano Convention on Jurisdiction and the Enforcement of Judgments in Civil and Commercial Matters was opened for signature. At least eighteen Western European nations are parties to the Lugano Convention, which, generally speaking, allows the rules and obligations of the Brussels Convention to be extended to any signatory nation. For the full text, see the Lex Mercatoria Web site at www.jus.uio.no/lm/ec.efta.jurisdiction.enforcement.judgements.civil._commercial.matters.lugano.convention.1968/doc.html.

See also Chapter 7 of this book for a discussion of dispute resolution issues.

F. AGREEMENTS FOR TRADING OF GOODS

North American Free Trade Agreement (NAFTA)

The North American Free Trade Agreement (NAFTA) was built upon the 1989 U.S.-Canada Free Trade Agreement (CFTA). Portions of the treaty that may be relevant for the franchise practitioner include Part Five (investment, services, and related matters), Part Six (intellectual property), and Part Seven (administrative and institutional provisions). Visit www.199.88.185.106/tcc/data/commerce_html/TCC_/NAFTA/toc.htm. for the full text.

Treaty Establishing the European Economic Community, March 25, 1957, Office for Official Publication of the European Communities, Treaties Establishing the European Communities (1978).

The treaty establishing the European Economic Community—The Treaty of Rome—is the EU's form of government and its constitutional law. For the full text, see www.tufts.edu/departments/fletcher/multi/texts/rome/contents.html.

United Nations Convention on Contracts for the International Sale of Goods (Vienna, 1980)

This convention provides uniform rules that govern contracts for the international sale of goods, akin to Article 2 of the Uniform Commercial Code. The convention applies to contracts for the sale of goods between parties whose places of business are in different countries, and its provisions govern contract formation, the obligations of the seller and buyer, and the remedies available upon either parties' breach of contract. To date, fifty-four countries are signatories. For the full text of the treaty, visit the United Nations Commission on International Trade Law (UNCITRAL) Web site at www.uncitral.org/english/texts/sales/salescon.htm.

See also the 1994 IBA/IFA Joint Seminar on International Franchising program materials "The Sale of Goods in International Franchising - The Impact of the UN Convention on Contracts for the International Sale of Goods," as well as the article of the same title published in the *Journal of International Franchising and Distribution Law* (Vol. 8, No. 4, 1994), both authored by John R.F. Baer.

United Mexican States – European Community Free Trade Agreement

Adopted in March 2000, the United Mexican States - European Community Free Trade Agreement officially entered into force on July

1, 2000. This bilateral agreement includes provisions similar to those found in NAFTA, and provides for the entry into force of the chapters on public procurement, competition, and dispute settlement, any of which may be relevant to the franchise practitioner. For the full text, visit http://europa.eu.int/comm/trade/bilateral/mexico/fta.htm.

G. ANTITRUST TREATIES

Treaty of Rome

Most vertical restraints, with the exception of minimum price-fixing and territorial customer restraints, are no longer regarded as per se suspicious or *per se* anticompetitive. An analysis of market structure is now essential for determining the impact of vertical restraints. Under the current view of the European Commission, anticompetitive effects are likely to exist only where interbrand competition is weak and barriers to entry exist.

The EU has replaced the 1989 "block exemption" from EU competition law for franchising with a broader regulation governing all vertical restraints. Text of the new regulation appears at paragraph 7101 of the *Business Franchise Guide* (CCH) and at the European Union's Web site, europa.eu.int/eur-lex/en/lif/dat/2000/en_300R2658.html. See Section II.A.5 in this chapter, above, for a discussion of the accompanying Block Exemption Guidelines.

EXHIBIT A
LIST OF COUNTRY FRANCHISE ASSOCIATIONS
(January 1, 2001)

ARGENTINA Franchise Association
General Manager (currently Mr. Jose Fernandez)
Av. Libertador 222, 7th - A
Buenos Aires (1001ABP), Argentina
TEL/FAX: (54-11) 4394-3318/8107
Web site: www.aafranchising.com
E-mail: info@aafranchising.com

AUSTRALIA Franchise Council
Chief Executive (currently Mr. Jim McCracken)
Level 14 / 461 Bourke Street
Melbourne 3000, Australia
TEL: (61-3) 9602-4568
FAX: (61-3) 9602-3414
Web site: www.fca.com.au
E-mail: info@fca.com.au

AUSTRIA Franchise Association
Chairman (currently Mr. Martin Knoll)
Bayerhamerstrasse 12, 1st Floor,
A-5020, Salzburg - Austria
TEL: (43-662) 874-2360
FAX: (43-662) 874-2365
Web site: franchise.at
E-mail: oefr@franchise.at

BELGIUM Franchise Federation
Chairman (currently Mr. Pierre Jeanmart)
Boulevard de L'Humanite, 116/2,
B-1070 Brussels, Belgium
TEL: (32-2) 523-9707
FAX: (32-2) 523-3510
Web site: www.fbf-bff.be
E-mail: belgian.franchisefederation@euronet.be

BRAZIL Franchise Association
President (currently Mr. Ricardo Young)
Alameda Irae, 276, Moema
SP 04075-000 - Sao Paulo, Brazil
TEL: (55-11) 5051-9496
FAX: (55-11) 5051-5590
Web site: www.abf.com.br
E-mail: abf@cyberspace.com.br

BRITISH Franchise Association
Director General (currently Mr. Brian Smart)
Thames View, Newtown Road
Henley-on-Thames
Oxforshire RG9 1HG, Great Britain
TEL: (44) 1491-578-050
FAX: (44) 1491-573-517
Web site: www.british-franchise.org.uk
E-mail: mailroom@british-franchise.org.uk

BULGARIA Franchise Association
President (currently Ms. Lubka Kolarova)
P.O. Box 20,
Varna 9010, Bulgaria
TEL / FAX: (359-52) 600-724
E-mail: wan3vn@mbox.digsys.bg

CANADA Franchise Association
President (currently Mr. Richard Cunningham)
2585 Skymark Avenue, suite 300
Mississauga L4W 4L5
Ontario, Canada
TEL: (905) 625-2896
FAX: (905) 625-9076
Web site: http://www.cfa.ca
E-mail: info@cfa.ca

CHILE Franchise Association
President (currently Mr. Fernando Kaminetsky)
Rafael Canas 16, of. I
Providencia, Santiago - Chile
TEL: (56-2) 236-3622
FAX: (56-2) 264-9134
E-mail: entrepre@chilesat.net

CHINA Chain-Store & Franchise Association
President (currently Ms. Guo Geping)
No.25 Yuetan North St.
Beijing 100834 - P.R. China
TEL.: (86-10) 6839-2260
FAX: (86-10) 6839-2210
Web site: www.ccfa.org.cn
E-mail: chainsch@public.east_on.net

CHINA International Franchisors Association
General Counsel (William A. Wright, Attorney)
Lehman, Lee & Xu
China Lawyers, Patent & Trademark Agents
Suite 188, Beijing International Club
21 Jianguomenwai Dajie
100020 Beijing, China
TEL. (86-10) 6532-3861
FAX (86-10) 6532-3877
Web site: www.chinalaw.cc
E-mail: wwright@chinalaw.cc

COLOMBIA Franchise Association
President (currently Mr. Jorge Barragan)
Cra. 100 11-90 Torre Lili, of. 606
Cali, Colombia
TEL: (57-2) 339-2163
FAX: (57-2) 339-2166
Web site: www.centercourt.com/acolfran
E-mail: jbarragan@telesat.com.co

CZECH Franchise Association
President (currently Gosef Fidler)
Rytirska 18-20, P.O. Box 706
11000 Prague - Czech Republic
TEL: (42-2) 2423-0566
FAX: (42-2) 2421-5099

DENMARK Franchise Association
Executive Director (currently Mr. Finn Birkegaard)
Lyngbyvej 20
DK-2100 Copenhagen - Denmark
TEL: (45) 3678-5822
FAX: (45) 3649-9898
Web site: www.dk-franchise.dk
E-mail: info@dk-franchise.dk

DOMINICAN REPUBLIC Franchise Association
Executive Director (currently Mr. Oscar Luis Monzon)
Plibio Diaz #74, apt. c-1
Edificio Alfonso X, Cuaristo Morales
Santo Domingo, Dominican Republic
TEL: (809) 549-6383
FAX : (809) 563-1916
E-mail: c.nacional@codetel.net.do

ECUADOR Franchise Association
Director (currently Dr. Leonidas Villagran-Cepeda)
P. O. Box 579
Guayaquil, Ecuador
TEL/FAX: (593-4) 305-799
E-mail: Leonidas@Samerica.com

EGYPT Franchise Association
Chairman (currently Dr. Aly Tolba)
1191 Corniche El Nil St., 15th floor
Cairo, Egypt
TEL: (20-2) 578-6260
FAX: (20-2) 240-8937
E-mail: atolba@intouch.com

EUROPEAN Franchise Federation
Executive Director (currently Ms. Carol Chopra)
Boulevard de l'Humanite 116/2
Brussels, Belgium
TEL: (32-2) 520-1607
FAX: (32-2) 520-1735
Web site: www.eff-franchise.com
E-mail: eff-franchise@euronet.be

FINLAND Franchise Association
Executive Officer (currently Mr. Rolf Granstrom)
Laurinkatu 47
08100 Lohja, Finland
TEL: (358) 19-331-195
FAX: (358) 19-331-075
Web site: www.franchising.fi
E-mail: sfy@sfy.pp.fi

FRANCE Franchise Federation
Executive Director (currently Ms. Chantal Zimmer)
60, rue La Boetie
Paris 75008, France
TEL: (33-1) 53-75-22-25
FAX: (33-1) 53-75-22-20
Web site: www.franchise-fff.com
E-mail: info@franchise-fff.com

GERMANY Franchise Association
President (currently Mr. Prof.Dr. Utho Creusen)
Paul Heyse Str. 33-35,
Munchen 80336, Germany
TEL: (49) 89-53-07-140
FAX: (49) 89-53-13-23
Web site: www.dfv-franchise.de
E-mail: info@dfv-franchise.de

GREECE Franchise Association
Secretary (currently Ms. Anna Trigetta)
Skoufou 10
105 57 Athens - Greece
TEL: (30-1) 323 -4620
FAX: (30-1) 323-8865
Web site: www.franchising.gr
E-mail: info@franchising.gr

HONG KONG Franchise Association
Senior Manager (currently Ms. Charlotte Chow)
22/F Unit A United Centre
95 Queensway, Hong Kong
TEL: (852) 2529-9229
FAX: (852) 2527-9843
Web site: www.franchise.org.hk
E-mail: hfka@franchise.org.hk

HUNGARY Franchise Association
CEO (currently Dr. Istvan Kiss)
POB. 446
Budapest H-1537, Hungary
TEL: (36-1) 212-4124
FAX: (36-1) 212-5712
Web site: www.datanet.hu/mfsz
E-mail: franchise.ass@mail.datanet.hu

IBERO AMERICAN Franchise Federation (FIAF)
Secretary General (currently Mr. Xavier Vallhonrat)
Avda. de las Ferias S/N
P.O. Box 476
46035 Valencia, SPAIN
TEL: (34-96) 386-1123
FAX: (34-96) 363-6111

INDIA Franchise Association
Chairman SIG (currently Mr. C. Yoginder Pal)
1-C, Vulcan Insurance Bldg.
Veer Nariman Road
Churchgate, Mumbai 400-020 / INDIA
TEL: (91-22) 282-1413
FAX: (91-22) 204-6141
E-mail: iacc@giasbm01.vsnl.net.in

INDONESIA Franchise Association
Chairman (currently Mr. Anang Sukandar)
A 19 Darmawangsa X
Kebayoran Baru
Jakarta 12150, Indonesia
TEL: (62-21) 739-5577
FAX: (62-21) 723-4761
E-mail: sukandar@indo.net.id

IRELAND Franchise Association
Secretary and Legal Advisor (currently Mr. Bill Holohan)
88 Ranelagh Road
Dublin 6 - Ireland
TEL: (353-1) 497-8988
FAX: (353-1) 491-1916
E-mail: holohanb@indigo.ie

ITALY Franchise Association
General Secretary (currently Mr. Michele Scardi)
Corso di Porta Nuova, 3
Milan 20121, Italy
TEL: (39-02) 2900-3779
FAX: (39 02) 655-5919
Web site: http://www.assofranchising.it
E-mail: assofranchising@assofranchising.it

JAPAN Franchise Association
President (currently Mr. Isao Seo)
2nd Akiyama Building
Toranomon, 3-6-2 Minato-ku,
Tokyo 105-0001, Japan
TEL: (81-3) 03-5777-8704
FAX: (81-3) 03-5777-8711
E-mail: jfa@msh.biglobe.ne.jp

KOREA (SOUTH) Franchise Association
CEO (currently Kyoung Woo, Lee)
Zipcode 143-202, Hyosan B/D 3F
57-80, Gui-2Dong, Kwangjin-Gu
Seoul, South Korea
TEL: (82-2) 447-6094
FAX: (82-2) 3436-2162
E-mail: kfa01@netsgo.com

MALAYSIA Franchise Association
Secretary General (currently Awalan Abdul Aziz)
Suite 1045, Level 10, Block A2 / Leisure Complex
No. 9, Jalan PJS 8/9 - 46150 Petaling Jaya
Selangor Darul Ehsan - Malaysia
TEL: (60-3) 7877-1559
FAX: (60-3) 7877-1327
Web site: http://www.mfa.org.my
E-mail: secrtmfa@tm.net.my

MEXICO Franchise Association
General Manager (currently Mrs. Lorena Reynaud)
Insurgentes Sur 1783, #303
Col. Guadalupe Inn
Mexico 01020, D.F., Mexico
TEL: (52-5) 661-0655
FAX: (52-5) 663-2473
E-mail: amf1@prodigy.net.mx

NETHERLANDS Franchise Association
Managing Director (currently Mr. Andre W. M. Brouwer)
Boomberglaan 12,
Hilversum 1217, PR - The Netherlands
TEL: (31-35) 624-2300
FAX: (31-35) 624-9194
Web site: nfv.nl
E-mail : franchise@nfv.nl

NEW ZEALAND Franchise Association
Chairman (currently Mr. Winston Robinson)
1st Floor, 26 St. Heliers Bay Road
St.Heliers, Auckland - New Zealand
TEL: (64-9) 575-3804
FAX: (64-9) 575-3807
Web site: www.franchise.org.nz
E-mail: contact@franchise.org.nz

NORWAY Franchise Association
Managing Director (currently Mr. Torild Brende)
Drammensveien 30
0230 - Oslo, Norway
TEL: (47-2) 254-1700
FAX: (47-2) 256-1700
Web site: www.hsh-org.no
E-mail: franchise@hsh-org.no

PERU Franchise Association
President (currently Mr. Samuel Gleiser Katz)
Gregorio Escobedo 398
Lima 11, Peru
TEL: (51-1) 562-1000
FAX: (51-1) 562-1020
E-mail: cci-peru@camaralima.org.pe

PHILIPPINES Franchise Association
President (currently Mrs. Ma. Alegria S. Limjoco)
2/F Collins Building, 167 EDSA
Mandaluyong City, Philippines
TEL: (63-2) 532 5677
FAX: (63-2) 532-5644
E-mail: pfa@nwave.net

PORTUGAL Franchise Association
President (currently Mr. Raoul Neves)
Rua Viriato, 25 - 3
1050-234 Lisboa, Portugal
TEL: (351-21) 319-2938
FAX: (351-21) 319-2939

RUSSIA Franchise Association
President (currently Mr. Alexander Mailer)
2-nd Proezd Perova Polya, 9
Moscow 111141, Russia
TEL: (7-095) 305- 5877
FAX: (7-095) 305-5850
Web site: a-z.ru/raf
E-mail: franch@matrix.ru

SINGAPORE Franchise Association
Chairman (currently Mr. Rober Leong)
General Manager (currently Ms. Terry Wong)
Informatics Building
5 International Business Park
Singapore 609914
TEL: (65) 568-0802
FAX: (65) 568-0722
Web site: http://www.sifa.org.sg
E-mail: sifa@pacific.net.sg

SOUTH AFRICA Franchise Association
Executive Director (currently Mr. Nic Louw)
24 Wellington Road
2193 Houghton - South Africa
TEL: (27-11) 484-1285
FAX: (27-11) 484-1291
Web site: http://www.fasa.co.za
E-mail: fasa@fasa.co.za

SPAIN Franchise Association
President (currently Mr. Xavier Vallhonrat)
Avda. de las Ferias S/N
P.O. Box 476
46035 Valencia, SPAIN
TEL: (34-96) 386-1123
FAX: (34-96) 363-6111
Web site: www.franquiciadores.com
E-mail: aef@feriavalencia.com

SWEDEN Franchise Association
Executive Director (currently Ms. Karen Ericsson)
Massansg. 18 / Box 5243
40224 Goteborg, Sweden
TEL: (46-31) 836-943
FAX: (46-31) 811-072
E-mail: karin.franchiseforeningen@telia.com

SWITZERLAND Franchise Association
Managing Director (currently Christopher Wildhaber)
Lowenstrasse 11
Postfach CH-8023
Zurich, Switzerland
TEL: (41-1) 225-4757
FAX: (41-1) 225-4777
Web site: www.franchiseverband.ch
E-mail: info@franchiseverband.ch

TAIWAN Chainstore & Franchise Association
Chairman (currently Mr. Eric Lin)
7F, No. 197, Nanking E. Road, sec.4
Taipei, Taiwan
TEL: (886-2) 2712-1250
FAX: (886-2) 2717-7997
Web site: www.tcsa.org.tw
E-mail: tcsa@ms31.hinet.net

THAILAND Franchise Association
Managing Director (currently Somjit Likhitsathaporn)
20/25 Seri Village Onnui Sukhumvii 77
Pravate – BKK 10250 - Thailand
TEL: (662) 321-5129
FAX: (662) 721-2795
E-mail: fc_focus@bangkok.com

TURKEY Franchise Association
Chairman (currently Mr. Serdar Yanasan)
Ergenekon cad. Pangalti Ishani 89/15
Istanbul 80240, Turkey
Tel:(90-212) 296-6628
Fax:(90-212) 224-5130
Web site: www.ufrad.org.tr
E-mail: ufrad@ufrad.com.tr

URUGUAY Franchise Association
President (currently Mr. Rodolfo Montesdeoca)
Daniel Munoz 2240, CP 11.200
Montevideo, Uruguay
TEL. / FAX (598-2) 408-5189
E-mail: milbea@adinet.com.uy

VENEZUELA Chamber of Franchising
President (currently Mr. Rolando Seijas S.)
Oficentro Neur, 3 - Altamira, oficina N 5
Caracas, Venezuela 1060
TEL. (58-2) 261-8596 / 6855
FAX (58-2) 261-9620
E-mail : seibol@cantv.net

VENEZUELA Franchise Association
President (currently Mr. Arquimides Beliz)
Calle Orinoco con Perijá, Mini Centro Stela
Planta Alta, Oficina No. 5, Las Mercedes
Caracas, Venezuela
TEL. (58-2) 991-4078
FAX (58-2) 991-1401

YUGOSLAVIA Franchise Association
General Secretary (currently Dr. Zdravko Glusica)
Dr. Dorda Joanovica 6
21000 Novi Sad, Yugoslavia
TEL: (381-21) 432-205
FAX: (381-21) 469-496

ZIMBABWE Franchise Association
Fidelity Life Tower 98-Raleigh Street
P.O. Box 1934
Harare, Zimbabwe
TEL: (263-4) 753-444
FAX: (263-4) 753-450
E-mail : info@zncc.co.zw

Notes

The author wishes to acknowledge Bradley Steinbrecher, Shannon Haaf, and Maria Soto for their assistance in identifying and summarizing various materials for this chapter.

INDEX